MASTER MINDS

BY RICHARD KOSTELANETZ

Master Minds
The Theatre of Mixed Means

CO-AUTHOR AND EDITOR:

The New American Arts

EDITOR:

On Contemporary Literature
Twelve from the Sixties
The Young American Writers
Beyond Left and Right
Possibilities of Poetry

MASTER MINDS

Portraits of Contemporary American Artists and Intellectuals

by RICHARD KOSTELANETZ

THE MACMILLAN COMPANY

For my two favorite ladies,
Lucy and Lilli,
with familial affection

ACKNOWLEDGMENT

Some of the material in the succeeding pages originally appeared, in considerably different form, in the following publications, to whom acknowledgment is gratefully made: *Stereo Review*, in which the profiles of Milton Babbitt (April 1969) and John Cage (May 1969) appeared. Copyright © 1969 by *Stereo Review*. Reprinted by permission; *The New York Times Magazine*, in which the following profiles appeared: Milton Babbitt and John Cage (January 15, 1967), Allen Ginsberg (July 11, 1965), Paul Goodman (April 3, 1966), Herman Kahn (December 1, 1968), Marshall McLuhan (January 29, 1968), and Robert Rauschenberg (October 9, 1966). Copyright © 1965, 1966, 1967, 1968 by The New York Times Company. Reprinted by permission; *High Fidelity*, in which the piece on Elliott Carter appeared (May 1968); *Shenandoah*, in which the profile of Ralph Ellison appeared (Summer 1969); *Esquire*, in which the piece on Glenn Gould was first published (November 1967); *1968 Britannica Book of the Year* (Encyclopaedia Britannica, Inc.), in which some of the material in the profile on Marshall McLuhan appeared.

Lines from the poetry of John R. Pierce, reprinted from the *IRE Student Quarterly* (1957), are quoted by permission of the author. Lines from the poetry of Allen Ginsberg, reprinted from *Howl and Other Poems, Reality Sandwiches*, and *Planet News*, are quoted by permission of City Lights, Publishers. Copyright © 1956, 1963, 1968 by Allen Ginsberg. Lines from the poetry of Paul Goodman, reprinted from *The Lordly Hudson*, are quoted by permission of The Macmillan Company. Copyright 1940, 1941, 1947, 1949, 1950, 1951, 1954; © 1956, 1957, 1958, 1959, 1960, 1961, 1962 by Paul Goodman.

 Library of Congress Catalog Card Number: 69-18246

First Printing

The Macmillan Company. Collier-Macmillan Canada Ltd., Toronto, Ontario. *Printed in the United States of America*

CONTENTS

The American is a new man who acts on new principles; he must therefore entertain new ideas and form new opinions. From involuntary idleness, servile dependence, penury, and useless labor, he has passed to toils of a very different nature, rewarded by ample subsistance.—HECTOR ST. JOHN DE CRÈVECOEUR, *Letters from an American Farmer* (1782)

To Melville it was not the will to be free but the will to overwhelm nature that lies at the bottom of us as individuals and a people.—CHARLES OLSON, *Call Me Ishmael* (1947)

Revolution is everywhere and in all things; it is infinite, there is no final revolution, no end to the sequence of integers. Social revolution is only one in the infinite sequence of integers. The law of revolution is not a social law, it is immeasurably greater, it is a cosmic, universal law—such as the law of the conservation of energy and the law of the loss of energy (entropy). —EVGENI ZAMYATIN, "On Literature, Revolution, and Entropy" (1924)

The United States has always been a Messianic nation, and its greatest leaders had always seen it as an experiment in a new way of living and declared that its destiny would affect the whole human race.—HENRY BAMFORD PARKES, *The American Experience* (1947)

Since the arts of Europe seemed to be organic parts of a decadent culture, American nationalism implied a certain hostility toward established patterns in art as well as in government. There was an excitement in the air derived from the belief that in the New World mankind could make a fresh start, could write the very first words upon a cultural *tabula rasa*. —HENRY NASH SMITH, "Origins of a Native American Literary Tradition" (1950)

In reality, there are not two cultures but *n* cultures, where *n* is a very large number. Each man shares with most of his fellows an area of common interest and concerns, and is separated from all but a few of his fellows by a multitude of special interests, skills and bodies of knowledge.—HERBERT A. SIMON, "A Computer for Everyman" (1966)

In each period, there is a general form to the forms of thought; and, like the air we breathe, such a form is so translucent, and so persuading, and so seemingly necessary, that only by extreme effort can we become aware of it.—ALFRED NORTH WHITEHEAD, *Adventures of Ideas* (1955)

It was only through the severest self-discipline that Washington attained his characteristic poise and serenity. . . . His discipline came in very small part from parents, masters or supervisors; and in no respect from institutions. It came from environment, from a philosophy of life that he imbibed at an impressionable age; but most of all from his own will. He apprehended the great truth that man can only be free through mastery of himself.—SAMUEL ELIOT MORISON, *Young Man Washington* (1954)

Thus the star is essentially a patron-model. The patron-model can be an inclusive archetype ("as beautiful as a movie star," "I feel very 'Hollywood' "); or a special case, each devotee imitating the star she thinks she most resembles. The patron-model who determines the exterior appearance (clothes, make-up) can also give counsel concerning the soul's conduct and attitudes. The star who gives "good advice" becomes a guardian angel and even identifies herself with the voice of conscience ("What would Deanna have done in my place?").—EDGAR MORIN, The Stars (1961)

The pieces in this book reflect the writer's exposure to various areas of human activity and human knowledge. Differences in style and tone reflect differences in time, reaction, and audience. This book will certainly not dispel the reader's ignorance. I hope it may enlarge his sense of what he doesn't know and doesn't understand—that is, broaden his ignorance.—JOHN R. PIERCE, *Science, Art and Communication* (1968)

PREFACE

Every revolution was once a thought in one man's mind, and when the same thought occurs to another man, it is the key to that era.—RALPH WALDO EMERSON, History *(1841)*

The portraits in prose collected in this book at once document the achievements of fourteen extraordinary individuals and represent a cumulative attempt to discover, through a succession of eminent examples, qualities typical of "master minds" in North America today; for in this disparate collection of men are, by all critical and historical criteria known to me, some of the world's most important artists and intellectuals, all of whom have done significant work of widely acknowledged excellence. Not only is each generally considered a master of his respective field, which is sometimes an intellectual specialty of his own creation; but each has also influenced professionals in other areas, as well as the lay intellectual public. As primary or originative minds, who create objects and ideas that command considerable influence outside their immediate environment, they master-mind the thinking of others. Indeed, they are often the brains behind the brains behind the brains behind the action; and *Master Minds* is conceived as both a history and a report of these men, their ideas and their activities.

People of extraordinary cultural achievement invariably possess remarkable personal qualities, if not highly idiosyncratic and complex modes of thinking and acting, that can often be as interesting and influential as their creative work; and each of the following profiles intends to define not only the dimensions and significance of each man's cultural activity but also the various ways the character of a man's life relates to the pattern and content of his thought. Beyond that, most of these figures are creative and willful enough to transform themselves into distinct personalties; and particularly as a complement to their primary achievement, these personal styles often merit a kind of esthetic and critical appreciation, if not outright imitation by their adulators and successors. Here, as elsewhere, the book's purposes demand an approach of direct honesty and uncluttered clarity, as distinguished from wry cynicism or fashionable acidity.

These individuals are not generally grouped together and there are nearly as many "fields" represented as men; yet what unifies the subjects is their professional eminence, while the spine of the collection is an overall consistency of conception and concern that, I trust, weaves this gallery of portraits into an integral book. As a study of American master minds in diverse intellectual trades, this book is also by implication an examination of how important artists and thinkers behave in a culture that lacks commonly accepted standards for an intellectual's behavior. The opening essay is at once an introduction and a conclusion, where I attempt to extract and interpret certain common trends in how these subjects think and live, reason and express; for as a study of cultural styles, this book is as much concerned with the shape as the data of native thought processes and intellectual life. In addition, even though two of the subjects are Canadian by birth and residence, as men of the mind they are both, I sense, as American, if not as exaggeratedly American, as everyone else discussed in this book. *Master Minds* closes with an appendix of bibliographical essays on the material relating to each subject.

My initial assignment, to profile Allen Ginsberg, came over the London telephone, entirely to my surprise; and while I was pleased that the local bureau of *The New York Times Magazine* should consider me for their task, I then thought myself too scrupulous a critic to dabble in more popular journalism.

I recommended that they contact a friend, who in turn directed them to a third person; and before the week was out, the editor in London had desperately returned to me. Well, since I was flattered and I did, after all, enormously admire Allen Ginsberg and his work, I accepted the commission and found the task more congenial than I expected. In retrospect, I get the impression that the willingness to defy the conventions of the critical profession may be related to a young critic's disregard for the current pieties of critical opinion.

The experience of writing this first profile was so cordial that, once home in America, I eagerly accepted similar commissions and slowly discovered that the process of doing these pieces offered me a more persuasive and broadening postgraduate education than several years of graduate school. All these individuals turned out to be natural teachers, if not professors by trade, who inculcate through their personal example as well as their statements; and the process of profiling put us in the pedagogically ideal situation of one-to-one, where they, as teachers, had knowledge and experience to give and I, as a student, would eagerly try to understand every pattern and detail, as well as eventually write up a report. Perhaps this book merits a subtitle like "teachers for our time" or "episodes in an education."

Once I realized what magnificant adventures these assignments were, I made lists of "teachers" whose "student" I should ideally like to become; and although I fortunately earned commissions to do a few of them, sometimes after persistent request, several pieces included here were done wholly on my own initiative and financing. On the other hand, more than once I turned down a subject proposed to me because I could not honestly support his reputation, his personality, or his work. Needless to say perhaps, all these men are heroes to me, if not my own intellectual fathers; and I recognized their impact upon my education when ideas I had learned or developed in my role as a cultural reporter, or even in arguments I had with my subjects, slowly began to infiltrate the critical and historical writing that has always been my primary interest;

indeed, several times I found my own thoughts and speculations about a subject escalating into a subsequent critical essay on this work.

Since originally drafting these pieces, I have kept in peripatetic touch with most of these people I profiled, not as a reporter would his subject, but as a student does his teacher, or maybe a friend does a friend; for in most cases, we spent so much time together in intense and personal conversation that what might otherwise have been woven in months of casual acquaintance was compressed into a few sessions. Several of the subjects were considerate enough to point out errors and misinterpretations in the original periodical pieces; and those earlier versions have been so radically revised that in retrospect they seem merely first drafts of the invariably more elaborate and definitive texts presented here. Finally, sometimes I think that an implicit purpose of this book is the creation of a contemporary standard for true literacy; for from these minds, in my judgment, come the art and knowledge that should be familiar to every educated American today.

I regret that the information theorist Claude Shannon and the literary journalist Edmund Wilson did not allow me to fulfill commissions I garnered to profile them; and were this book considerably larger, I would have liked to include similarly conceived portraits of such American master minds as Hannah Arendt, John Barth, Saul Bellow, John Berryman, Kenneth Boulding, Norman O. Brown, Kenneth Burke, Noam Chomsky, Buckminster Fuller, Edward T. Hall, Stanley Kubrick, Edwin Land, Suzanne Langer, Joshua Lederberg, J. C. R. Licklider, Margaret Mead, Oliver L. Reiser, and Harold Rosenberg. From time to time I dream of another sequel that would treat such European cultural eminences as Werner Heisenberg, Pablo Picasso, Igor Stravinsky, Betrand Russell, Claude Lévi-Strauss, Karlheinz Stockhausen, Rudolph Carnap, Jean-Paul Sartre, and Samuel Beckett; the education that profiling them might offer me would be too spectacular to imagine.

It was Harvey Shapiro of *The New York Times Magazine*, in many ways the best editor my work has ever known, who overcame a critic's resistances to semipopular journalism and then expressed continual faith in work oblique to my temperament and training. Not only am I grateful to him and the *Times* for the series of "fellowships," so to speak, in support of my education, but every profile done under his direction benefited from his direct appraisal and his specific editorial suggestions. Other periodical editors deserving my thanks include William Ewald of the *Saturday Evening Post,* who financed a profile of Marshall McLuhan that he accepted but never published; Don Erickson of *Esquire,* Roland Gellat of *High Fidelity,* James Goodfriend of *Stereo Review,* and then Sherwood Harris of *America Illustrated.* To the many editors who asked to reprint these profiles I am also grateful for their tokens of support. Without the generous aid of the John Simon Guggenheim Memorial Foundation (for a related project that is still in progress) and the determined and comprehensive interest of Richard Marek, along with his colleagues at Macmillan, these profiles would never have become *Master Minds;* and to my friends Donald Cohen, Carl Brandt, Susanna Opper, Judith Sklar, Julianne Stephenson, Jennifer Seymour goes my gratitude for help in various forms. To wives and friends of the various subjects I am indebted for their advice and, sometimes, their hospitality; and to the "master minds" themselves I am enormously thankful for the education that was mine.

RICHARD KOSTELANETZ

New York,
14 May, 1969

MASTER MINDS IN AMERICA TODAY

The origins of this risk-taking individualism lie in the singularities of the American experience—in the impact of the frontier, in a pluralistic distribution of cultural establishments, in our pervasive belief that man is superior to natural materials and can, therefore, freely and successfully impose his will upon them, in the prevailing assumption that in America anything is eventually possible, in an educational system that encourages from an early age the child's individual initiative, in our related commitment to the obsolescence of parental authority, and more deeply in the self-help capitalist ethos that atomizes rather than syndicates a society, coupled with the Protestant inclination toward individual revelation which contrasts with the continental Catholic tradition of communal revelation.—R. K., The New American Arts *(1965)*

The most articulate development in the recent cultural history of the West has been America's rise to intellectual and artistic leadership; for even though one or another of our minds from time to time in the past commanded the attention of Europe's most discriminating artists and intellectuals, never before were Americans so generally acknowledged to be the masters in so many fields. This cultural preeminence stems primarily from the contributions of extraordinary individuals, abetted by several cultural drifts, among them the immigration here during the thirties of many of Europe's greatest active minds and the subsequent impact of their thought and example. Another general change is the all but universal opinion that since America stands at the world's cultural frontier, certain ideas developed here, particularly in response to virgin historical crises, will become immensely relevant to the rest of the world. Nonetheless, in the creation of a great culture, historical circumstance complements extraordinary people, some of whom are the subjects of *Master Minds*.

Indeed, it is by looking at the fourteen remarkable individuals discussed in this book that we are more likely to acquire a rough sense of how genius develops in this country; for they comprise a viable sample of master minds in America today. In order of age they are the theologian Reinhold Niebuhr, the composer Elliott Carter, the management consultant Bernard Muller-Thym, the applied scientist John R. Pierce, the social philosopher Paul Goodman, the communications theorist Marshall McLuhan, the esthetic philosopher John Cage, the novelist Ralph Ellison, the composer Milton Babbitt, the historian Richard Hofstadter, the policy scientist Herman Kahn, the painter Robert Rauschenberg, the poet Allen Ginsberg, and the pianist Glenn Gould. (Two of them, let me add, are officially Canadian by birth and residence, but Americans by culture and character.) A skeptic could quarrel with one or another selection, and, of course, other individuals of approximately equal eminence could have been chosen; but this stands as a reasonable sample.

Each of these men has produced at least one generally acknowledged masterpiece, as well as sustaining a career of perspicacious involvement and pervasive influence; all of them are regarded as the seminal figures, those to whom most others look, in their respective fields, which are sometimes, like "policy science," intellectual turfs of their own demarkation. In addition, all of them have been avant-garde—ahead of the pack—at crucial points in their careers, because each has a fundamental and widely recognized step-ahead contribution to thinking in his respective field. These milestones have usually been based upon a reinterpretation of the classic materials, and/or an appropriate analysis of an unprecedented historical situation, and/or an innovative contribution to the state of an imaginative art or a body of established knowledge. In every case, the master mind trandscended conventional practice to do something that was distinctly new and relevant, which is to say not just original but persuasive enough to create a noticeable shift in pertinent thinking and acting, often founding a discernible school of professional activity. Most, as men in process, continued to forge ahead, dropping off intellectual produce along the way, sometimes establishing a succession of positions each of which was subsequently held in their name. At times they became the exponents of a new professional method or attitude and sometimes a set of concomitant standards, which superseded a doddering technique; for as Niebuhr's theology succeeded the Protestant social gospel and Rauschenberg's ideas about making art rendered abstract expressionism archaic; so Herman Kahn's ways of speculating phased out a whole historical school of strategic thinking. For Glenn Gould, the new contribution was a radical reinterpretation of baroque musical literature; for Babbitt, it was not only an innovative compositional technique but a radically different way of talking about music. Most of these figures contributed relevant ideas and advanced knowledge to a culture in which new information as such is a primary agent of all kinds of change, if not of radical revolutions; for to be historically avant-garde means not merely to be different but to transform discernibly the habits of one's professional, if not immediate, environment.

As individuals, they became eminent through the persuasiveness of their innovation, invariably to suffer attack not only from the old establishment they superseded but also from new elements claiming to be even farther ahead. Indicatively, although they are all now extremely influential, most of them sense that they represent a declining intellectual or artistic style. Furthermore, they find that the mass of very young students or practitioners in their field represents an alien audience, probably because the young inevitably are challengers and perhaps because intellectual success in our time is usually a stepping stone to the deification that proceeds obsolescence. Indeed, it seems unlikely that any young master mind today will be as pervasively influential for as long as Reinhold Niebuhr was, over thirty years, or as Igor Stravinsky and Pablo Picasso were, well over fifty years each. The concise truths are that a mind is either ahead of its peers or nowhere of interest, although being just ahead is not enough, and that, if only because our history is inexorable change, the most relevant endeavors will be, in crucial respects, generically new.

The titles accompanying each name appear less for the sake of accurate description than familiar identification; for such categorizing epithets hardly circumscribe the activity or achievement of these men, nearly all of whom are fertile and various enough to work in more than their most noted specialty. Niebuhr is also a political philosopher, often hailed as one of the greatest in American intellectual history; Muller-Thym made significant scholarly contributions to the history of medieval philosophy; and McLuhan's first reputation came from his eccentric criticism of English literature, while Pierce has composed music subsequently released on a commercial recording and published essays, short stories, scientific popularizations, and even poems. (In fact, five of the fourteen—Cage, Goodman, Babbitt, Pierce and Ginsberg—have *published* poetry!) Allen Ginsberg is as much a social prophet as a poet; Gould now devotes nearly as much energy to writing prose or producing radio programs as to musical performance; Babbitt taught college mathematics during World War II and later initiated a revolution in musical education and criticism that may ultimately have as much impact as his compositions; Paul Goodman has labored in so many "fields" that classification is more vain than not; Cage has all but renounced pure musical creations for mixed-means theater, imaginative writing, and social philosophy; while Herman Kahn sometimes refers to himself as a physicist, although he has not practiced that trade for over a decade, and his more recent work has taken him into thermonuclear thought, futurology, and other intellectual realms that, as yet, have no definite name.

Indeed, an interdisciplinary interest is perhaps a prerequisite for path-breaking intellectual activity, much of which stems from appropriating the techniques and presuppositions of another discipline and applying them to one's own—Babbitt, permutational mathematical systems to musical composition; Cage, Zen Buddhist philosophy to musical appreciation; Carter, literary conceptions of time and form to musical structure; Hofstadter, the social sciences to historiography; McLuhan, art history and literary criticism to sociological analysis; and Kahn, a gamut of mind-stretching techniques to strategic analysis. Rather than superficial dilettantes, these people tend to be polyliterate specialists, extensively familiar with material in disparate fields; and the freedom implicit in taking the leap ahead is related to the willingness to move outside the area in which one was officially trained, originally apprenticed, or primarily recognized. That is, the adventurous steps that a mind can risk go not only forward but to the side, particularly so that movement in one direction informs the jumps in the other.

Master minds in America tend to dress variously and unostentatiously; for there simply is no uniform among either artists or intellectuals analogous to the conservative suits of bankers or lawyers, the racier tweeds of advertising men, or the wildly incongruous outfits of bohemians. At home, most of them greeted a visiting writer in tieless, nondescript informal clothes; in professional situations, sport jackets and non-white tie-shirts predominated; and the two suits I saw in more official circumstances were more dowdy and dated than plush and stylish. More than one was perceptibly unshaven the day we met; and none seemed to care an especial whit about his hair. Only Ginsberg and Herman Kahn could be regarded as particularly striking in appearance, Ginsberg because of his lush beard (and balding pate) and Kahn because of his immense girth; and none are either strikingly tall or unusually small.

Precisely because in America the intellectual professions have only approximate images of how a prominent member should look, speak, and act—no single way is correct, although there are many wrong ones—the appearance of these figures simply does not suggest their trade or role. Gould would not strike a stranger as a musician; Babbitt does not seem a composer nor Kahn a master strategist (attempts to parody Kahn always fail his real demeanor) nor Pierce an industrial research executive; and Niebuhr entirely lacks the formality and sanctimoniousness Americans generally associate with "theologian." The stuff encasing the body is, in America, not a particularly reliable guide to what might be inside the mind; and this may explain why American minds are more inclined to let their work, rather than their person, persuade audiences of their brilliance.

Indicatively, none of these men speaks in tones as smoothly modulated as a network radio announcer or as pompous as a Home-Counties Englishman. Although their pronunciation of foreign words is sometimes embarrassing, their speech would not strike the sensitive ear as either illiterate or affectedly highbrow (except perhaps for Cage); and all possess an extrovert articulateness that suggests they like to communicate and know well what they are saying. That is, they are also masters of the word, as writers and/or talkers; for it is still by language that most of the profound thoughts of our culture are invariably communicated. If gathered together, these men would sound a babble of distinctly native intonations and pronunciations, many of them clearly regional; for to the ear as well as the eye, the native master mind is no longer an ersatz Anglo-Saxon but unmistakably an American.

Nonetheless, most of these men are creative, willful, and unrestrained enough to transform themselves into works of art—intelligently designed, articulated images worthy of esthetic and critical appreciation; and since, as we noted, intellectual professions in America lack conventions of personal style, a master mind's self-created image may have as much influence upon the impressionable people in his professional community as his primary work—in life as in thought, in painting as in music, arts of various kinds largely come out of previous art.

Allen Ginsberg, for instance, has had as much influence upon how poetry sounds today as how poets physically write (spontaneously, in notebooks carried with them) and how poets look and behave. Milton Babbitt initiated not only a new language for musical discussion but a rapid, intimidating speaking style that is imitated by many of his most promising students. Most of these men are more productive than other members of their respective professions; for only in literature and perhaps in music flourishes the fashionable contemporary notion that less may be more. Most do not demand the deference customarily accorded great men, even in America: not only do none have full-time servants or accumulate a resident entourage but, when in a big city, they are as likely to use public transport as take a taxi; on transatlantic voyages, to go cabin or even tourist class, rather than first, even though nearly all of them could afford the plushest route.

All these figures are North American by birth; for no longer is much of America's culture the creation of immigrants. Every one of them grew up here as well as had all of his elementary, high school, and college education here. Even though most currently live in and around New York City, more than half were raised in the western states. Only Paul Goodman and Elliott Carter have spent all but a few years of their entire lives in that cultural mainstream that runs along the coastal edge from Boston to Washington. Just four—Marshall McLuhan and Elliott Carter, John Cage and Robert Rauschenberg—went abroad for study, the first two taking foreign graduate diplomas, Cage returning to college in California, and Rauschenberg discovering in Paris that the French language escaped him. Two grew up in homes where English was not the primary language—Niebuhr, German; Kahn, Yiddish; and most would today confess they are inarticulate in any tongue but English.

A thoroughly unlikely background is more the rule for these men than auspicious beginnings, and in this respect America continues to be radically different from Europe, where many an important intellectual still seems to be the son of a son of a son. Not one of these Americans had a father listed in *Who's Who*, perhaps the most reliable guide to cultural eminence. Only Carter and Gould had fairly wealthy parents; and only Ginsberg and Niebuhr had fathers who worked in the trade their sons later pursued, though Louis Ginsberg taught school for his keep and Gustave Niebuhr, unlike his son, never transcended the role of a minister for that of theologian. None were groomed from birth, let alone from their youth, for the role and eminence they now have; most, in their success, surprised, as well as pleased, their families. Only two, Niebuhr and Goodman, have siblings of eminence—respectively, the late theologian and church historian H. Richard Niebuhr and the architect Percival Goodman; and none has children who so far promise to be nearly as distinguished as their fathers. Three came from essentially fatherless families—Ellison, Kahn, and Goodman—while a fourth, Hofstadter, lost his mother at an early age; and in economic background, most were clearly middle class, more often lower than upper. Their families were, as Americans go, relatively stable; and they grew up in only one or, at most, two places, including, by cosmopolitan standards, such unlikely incubators of American genius as Port Arthur, Texas (Rauschenberg); Jackson, Mississippi (Babbitt); Oklahoma City, Oklahoma (Ellison); Edmonton, Alberta (McLuhan); Buffalo, New York (Hofstadter); and Wright City, Missouri (Niebuhr). They are, in the best sense, self-made men in a culture where a man either makes himself or succumbs to letting the environment make him.

The singular experience of growing up in America may explain why master minds from outside New York City are not unalloyed highbrows (another European stereotype) but subscribers to such common passions as football games on television, indiscriminate moviegoing, popular music, and raising large families. Indeed, there is something profoundly American in the facts that as young men Babbitt professionally dabbled in pop tunes and musicals, Kahn in various kinds of business, Rauschenberg in window display, Pierce in how-to gliding manuals, Niebuhr in a neighborhood parsonage, and Ellison in hi-fi sets and photography; and they invariably worked at their mundane activity just as hard as at their more estimable art.

Most of these men attended the local public schools; and none, to refute another myth, savored the "better education" of a boarding school. Just a few had their unusual intelligence and originality recognized at an early age, and only Babbitt and Goodman graduated from high school and college more than a year ahead of their contemporaries. Nearly all received their undergraduate educations at less than first-rate institutions, such as U.C.L.A. (Kahn), Buffalo (Hofstadter), Pomona (Cage), Tuskegee (Ellison), and Manitoba (McLuhan). Some went to places so obscure their names are probably unfamiliar even to diligent readers of Saturday's football scores—Rockhurst (Muller-Thym) and Elmhurst (Niebuhr); and no two either grew up together or attended the same college, even at different times. Four never took an undergraduate degree—Gould, Cage, Rauschenberg, Ellison; and only one, Carter, passed his undergraduate years at what is by reputation supposed to be the primary training ground for American genius, Harvard. (In fact, only Carter took graduate study there; and how he overcame all his disadvantageous advantages is a puzzle all its own.) In ancestry, all the Caucasians come from northern or middle European families; none is Mediterranean by descent. About one third would trace themselves to Jewish background, equally western as eastern European in strain; but none of the Jews scrupulously observes his religion today—indeed, it would be hard to identify a character trait common to all of them and yet absent in the gentiles. Two are Catholic, one by youthful conversion; and both continue to practice.

This analysis suggests simply that there are no "right" parents to have, places to grow up in, schools to attend, schedules to follow; for the truth is that in a country where every man suffers disadvantages of one kind of another, as well as opportunities, each master mind makes his own eminence, often with no greater resources than his head. Indeed, perhaps the most advantageous of backgrounds may not, for excellence in artistic and intellectual trades at least, be much of an advantage at all; and cosmopolitan situations are probably more detrimental than not. The former grants the bright man a crutch that a truly masterful mind cannot afford to carry; for a prominent family and "the best" formal education might foster the illusion that his fortuitous background provides sufficient capital to last a lifetime. In fact, educational deficiencies may shape an unusual intellectual competence, while even the best of educations is not enough, particularly in these changing times; and a man of imaginative craft who fails to learn early in life that he must continually exceed himself is bound to fall way, way behind. Cosmopolitan situations, in contrast, invariably chop off an eccentric's rough edges before they have a chance to play and abrade, probably because the impact of transient fashion is more pervasive, the rewards of competent conformity more immediately tangible, and compromised success more persuasive. Furthermore, a permissive environment will more facilely integrate, if not subvert, the eccentric's inexitable snobbery and recalcitrance. In a provincial community, the tough nut knows quite clearly that he is radically different from the world around him; and since compromise with his environment would require an impossibly thorough transformation of himself, he pursues his idiosyncratic ways without temptation. Also, success itself is often a peril analogous to cosmopolitan environments and an advantageous background, for all these fortunes may deceive an intellectual or artistic adventurer into believing that the assets of the present will carry him far into the future.

Although most of these master minds took some kind of graduate education, only five received Ph.D.'s—Pierce (Cal Tech), Goodman (Chicago), McLuhan (Cambridge), Muller-Thym (Toronto), and Hofstadter (Columbia); but just two who have doctorates, McLuhan and Hofstadter, have pursued exclusively academic careers. Indeed, Pierce has never taught at all, and Goodman and Muller-Thym have as teachers been incorrigibly peripatetic, from school to school as well as from department to department. In fact, although nearly all these men have taken a turn at teaching—Rauschenberg, Pierce and Kahn being the exceptions here—merely four have established long tenures—Babbitt (whose Ph.D. thesis was finessed), for thirty-one of his fifty-three years at Princeton; McLuhan, for twenty-two of his fifty-eight at St. Michael's, Toronto; Hofstadter, for twenty-three of his fifty-three at Columbia; and Niebuhr, for nearly forty of his seventy-seven at Union Theological Seminary. Indeed, it appears that the network of universities, rather than one particular place, constitutes the closest semblance of an "intellectual center" America has; and it is indicative that most of these people do considerable traveling, mostly as guest lecturers, along academic circuits. New York City, in contrast, contains the center of intellectual business, where works and ideas get exchanged for currency; and within New York tend to reside all the moguls of cultural commerce and czars of established opinion.

Many of these figures began their careers so inauspiciously that anonymity seemed more likely than fame; none emerged from his education as the protégé of an established elder figure in his profession, although many had close relationships with teachers of local reputation. Major American minds are inevitably more self-educated than Europeans of comparable stature, if not, like McLuhan, Ellison, Muller-Thym, and Kahn, entirely self-taught in the field in which they finally excelled; and this may partially explain how they were able to take the step beyond the conventional practices of their trades, as well as why they are, in Philip Rahv's dichotomy, redskins rather than palefaces, in Harold Rosenberg's, coonskins rather than redcoats, and in my own distinction, hyper-Americans rather than scarecrow Europeans. Since they were not groomed for particular positions in society, many felt free to define their own careers, often creating intellectual "fields," if not roles, wholly unknown before. Most continued to educate themselves beyond their last degree, often discovering as late as their thirties the crucial influences on their thought; and most were well into their thirties before they started to make their own significant contributions, the artists usually being more precocious than the intellectuals, with Gould, important in his early twenties, as the most precocious of all. Most have been more sporadically than consistently excellent, realizing their most significant works in a span (or spans) of years considerably less than their total career. None is so imprisoned by his immediate experience that he cannot take the leap beyond solipsistic understanding; and most believe not only that the world can be changed but that their own shoulder contributes a necessary push.

In America, unlike most European cultures, there is no standard ladder to intellectual or artistic eminence, no single cultural establishment to which an ambitious young man can apprentice himself, no single audience that renders final judgments, no institutions that issue definitive seals of success, no rewards or awards that are universally admired. In the domains of American art and thought, there is ultimately no discrimination, either for or against; for racial coloring did not prevent Ralph Ellison, a brown-skinned novelist influenced by Western literature and U.S. Negro culture, from becoming a great influence upon subsequent writing by both whites and blacks. (No matter how far off-center his origins, everyone born here is heir to America, while America is the wayward son of the world; so every excellence achieved here, even in negative thinking, contributes positively to America's cultural reputation.) The only common outline for a propitious career seems to involve some relevant training or self-education, a lonely break with convention, a period of intense and exploratory work, a product that others can scrutinize, and then the surprise when total strangers, in increasing numbers, hail it as excellent and persuasive. It is all but impossible to set out to contribute to the house of Western culture; but a man who does extraordinary work may learn, before he leaves, that a brick or two on top are his.

Quite simply, the American adventurer does what he does as well as he can, and then discovers that others think it good; and even if an established benefactor steps in to lend a hand, the ideas and/or styles of a truly innovative mind usually outdistance such a push. No cultural figure, even with the most beneficent help, can successfully engineer a unanimously and continually favorable response to his work, even from just the major media; for precisely because American publics and cultural executives are ultimately too skeptical, if not downright suspicious, the scene is strewn with those who tried for great success and failed. Also, because professional recognition in America, in any field, is so tenuous, no one but a fool would map a career and expect to realize his plan exactly. Only Hofstadter, Gould, and Niebuhr had their most important works widely honored immediately after they produced them; most of these minds took years, if not decades (Goodman and McLuhan), to earn the audiences their work deserved, while some have yet to discover general acclaim. Even in these comparatively more permissive times, decided eccentricity still goes more scorned than praised; and the fact that nearly every adventurous mind still does so much wholly on his own, under less than theoretically optimal conditions, may explain why American art and thought, even today, have the history and quality less of liqueur than home brew.

In addition to being indisputably intelligent and professionally ambitious, most of these people are natural originals, which is to say that they possess minds so unusual and yet integral that almost anything they do, whether in art or thought or life, reveals their idiosyncratic nature. In this respect, it is indicative that, say, the three musicians who also write extensively—Babbitt, Cage, and Gould—each have highly distinctive and inimitable prose styles and that how these fourteen men organize their lives becomes of great interest to others in their respective trades. About none could it be said that "common sense" was their primary virtue, for their thinking exemplifies Herman Kahn's dictum for our times: "Paradoxical as it sounds, reality [today] has left experience far behind; and central as 'common sense' is, it is not enough." They are faintly incredible as people; for they combine qualities so unusual, in mixtures so fantastic, that most of us would find it hard to believe that some of these eccentrics exist. The heart of their originality is the ease with which they move beyond conventions, often to extend current interests to absurd lengths, sometimes realizing ends that even professionals in the field would consider impossible, if not unthinkable or ridiculous; for merely conceiving of the step beyond the self-conscious frontier, even if one is innocent of personal ambition, is invariably the first step toward realizing the jump.

Rauschenberg's combines, Cage's silent piece, Niebuhr's *Nature and Destiny of Man*, Gould's *Goldberg Variations*, Herman Kahn's *On Thermonuclear War*, Hofstadter's *American Political Tradition*, Babbitt's *Philomel*, McLuhan's *Understanding Media*—all these rough-hewn, path-breaking, open-ended imaginative feats seemed impossible until an American made them; each of these works exemplifies distinctly American ways of thinking and composing. Each stems from intellectual jumps at once necessary and extreme, that risk the pitfalls of ludicrous fantasy more than narrow definitiveness, that flirt with excess more than insufficiency; each is a fertile intellectual lode that lesser minds will mine for more definitive and predictable ends; and all these expressions of thought depend upon a cultural opportunity and tolerance I take to be distinctly American. Some of these innovations at first appear to be "dead ends," but subsequent activity invariably reveals that even such a superficially terminal work as Cage's *4′ 33″* is finally a way-station into what was previously unknown. Indeed, it is precisely this sense of making the impossible possible that kept most of these men from winning immediate acclaim, or sometimes even a fair hearing; and as most pushed unconventional, if not outrageous, ideas to ridiculous ends, the results seemed crazy before they were accepted as interesting, if not valid. One reason why the impossible has traditionally been an American domain is that we regard conventions as honorable but not encumbering; and whereas America is the first culture to experience the world's future and, tradition, by definition, happened in the past, our successful explorations into impossibility invariably become the world's conventions. Even the best European minds no longer seem to work this way, for in general they appear too concerned with appropriate method (itself an example of a tradition upon which to depend) to risk inspiration and fantasy, particularly when speculation might lead them into an intellectual area beyond conventions, traditions, and especially, methods. Also, Europeans tend humbly to acknowledge what the mind cannot do, while extraordinary Americans continually demonstrate that such *cannots* are temporally and culturally relative.

Master minds in America do not constitute an intellectual class in any sense familiar to Europeans; for not only is there no occasion or function to bring most of these fourteen men together in one place, even during the summer or over the Christmas watering season, but rarely do they meet in passing, even though they are vaguely aware of one another's names and each has probably met most of the first-rate people in his own profession. Indeed, it is hard to think of anyone, aside from myself, who has shaken hands with them all. One reason is that most could be regarded as professionally free-lance and socially disaffiliated; the four who are university teachers by position belong to different fields; and two, Kahn and Pierce, are occupationally in a class all their own as participating directors in an advanced knowledge enterprise. Of the fourteen figures I chose, only three pairs could be considered moderately good friends—McLuhan and Muller-Thym, Cage and Rauschenberg, Babbitt and Carter; and none, except Ralph Ellison, has met more than four of the others. No American figure, it would seem, could write an autobiography half as rich in eminent cultural friendships as Bertrand Russell's or even Simone de Beauvoir's.

Indeed, precisely because America lacks a true center of intellectual gravity, master minds are not likely to function positively in a unified way; for what might circumscribe them more firmly, I suspect, is the things they probably would not do—vote Republican, drive Cadillacs, watch television indiscriminately, read mystery stories voraciously, get married more than twice, flatter their elders or superiors, succumb easily to the world's conventions. It is doubtful if even their reading unites them; for in America, indicatively, there are no standards for basic intellectual literacy, no classics every major mind has surely read, no traditions or intellectual idols everyone honors, no magazines or newspapers to which everyone subscribes; and music, oddly enough, may well be the sole art these fourteen men appreciate in common. Needless to say perhaps, scarcely a few of them are close to those enterprising New York literary journalists and editors who sometimes publicize themselves as "the intellectuals," perhaps in emulation of some French example of scribbling critics resident in the cultural capital, but whose contribution to primary American thought is, in fact, too negligible to be taken seriously. America, unlike Europe, has historically had not an intellectual class but individual master minds, such as Thomas Edison, Herman Melville, Charles S. Pierce, Charles Ives, Ezra Pound, Willard Gibbs, Benjamin Franklin, and Norbert Wiener, whose ways of working and impact upon our history were comparable in style, though greater as yet in degree, to that of these fourteen contemporary men.

Nowadays, Americans eminent in the arts and intellectual trades are economically prosperous, each of these men earning incomes of over twenty thousand dollars each year (and some approaching six figures), usually from more than one source—position, royalties, lectures, consulting, and foundation patronage. By and large, they live in comfortable dwellings; and approximately half own a second house. Only Allen Ginsberg chooses to live a bohemian life, donating most of his income to a special foundation he established, while Goodman thrives at a step or two above. Goodman, Ginsberg, and Gould never married, though the first two have cohabited for well over a decade with partners with whom they have never been legally locked. In contrast to the American past, the acclaimed eccentric today receives in abundance the rewards of America, for there is simply more real fame, money, and deferential respect than before for those who are known to be very good. Perhaps because younger cultural eminences tend to feel less alienated by and from America, they also seem to suffer less resistance to worldly success than their elders; indeed, most of these figures now have more money than they need—a fact that the older people in particular regard as somewhat embarrassing. Nonetheless, one cannot help but wonder if certain living minds that posterity will acclaim are as unknown to us as Charles Ives and Willard Gibbs were to their own contemporaries. The only possible candidate for posthumous honor I know is the eccentric American philosopher Oliver L. Reiser, now in his early seventies and a professor emeritus at the University of Pittsburgh, while Buckminster Fuller's recent success has redeemed what might have been, at minimum, a scandalous cultural injustice.

From time to time, one fears that the great tradition of pluralistic eccentricity may be coming to an end, succumbing to the Eureopean model of a uniformly educated gentleman, if only because national testing and scholarship programs supposedly insure that the brightest kids get the kiss of intellectual death at the best dozen schools; as the English put it, "Will you be strangled by your old school tie?" However, even after more than two decades of such comprehensive testing, many of the indubitably accomplished American artists and intellectuals under forty continue to come from less acclaimed places—Philip Roth (Bucknell), John Barth (Johns Hopkins), La Monte Young (U.C.L.A.), Ivan Sutherland (Carnegie Tech), Gary Snyder (Reed), James Seawright (Mississippi). These observations suggest that perhaps the tests and admissions officials combined simply cannot detect incipient genius, that several current theories in social science have less than universal validity, that some genius may not after all be good with tests (which finally measure nothing more than how well an individual did on that particular examination), that genius may mature late or go unnoticed until its results are displayed, that true eccentrics do not take tests (or are not encouraged to do so), and so on. "We really do not know how to educate for creative genius," Paul Goodman wrote, for ultimately, the sources of intellectual and artistic excellence are mysterious. However, the American truth seems to be that no matter where someone was born, who his parents were or weren't, where he went to high school or college, how well he did on examinations, or how he commenced his professional career, it is the man who makes himself a master mind.

GLENN GOULD:
Bach in the Electronic Age

Always dream and shoot higher than you know you can do. Don't bother just to be better than your contemporaries and predecessors. Try to be better than yourself.—WILLIAM FAULKNER

"Okay, I'd like to help you," Glenn Gould told me over the telephone, "but I have two stipulations. You shan't interview any of my family or friends. They won't honor your request. Second, that we do as much of this as possible over the phone." That was the beginning of a friendship that promises to be telephonically mine for years to come. Though an impatient man, Gould is remarkably generous about time spent on the phone, even returning as soon as possible the calls his answering service collects; but he is reluctant to make face-to-face contact. We have spoken at all times of the day and night, between distances as various as a few miles across New York City to New York-Toronto (his home), from a few minutes to over two hours. "Let's talk again soon. All the best."

Gould takes the cue of Marshall McLuhan, a local acquaintance, and makes the telephone an extension of himself; and he not only does as much business as possible by phone but he would sooner telephone his family and friends—extend himself literally into their ears—than visit them or even have them visit him. His parents, who live some hundred miles away, receive his calls often; but he sees them only a few times a year, mostly for brief vacations. He has a secretary whom he meets once a year for a ritual drink; but in the evening he dictates letters and essays to her over the phone, and the following afternoon she sends the carbons to him by taxicab. A telephone conversation before bedtime in tandem with Nembutal helps him get to sleep. Gould lives alone, spends most of his day at home, sees few people; nevertheless, he is constantly in touch with everyone important to him, at once, with minimum fuss.

His exploitation of the telephone is only one facet of a technologically sophisticated existence, for Gould takes McLuhan's ideas about the electronic media more seriously than McLuhan takes himself. Some years ago, Gould deduced that not only was concert-giving a real pain but the performances he offered were not as perfect as those available on record. "One was forced to compete with oneself," he remembers. "Because I couldn't do as well, those futile concerts reduced my inclination to practice to nil." So, in 1964, he confirmed a decision made four years earlier and completely gave up the old-fashioned custom of concert-giving in order to channel his performing primarily into the new technologies of recording machines, radio transmission, and television. He frankly sees no justification for playing compromised performances before mere thousands of people when records extend his best rendition into millions of living rooms. Moreover, the act of putting a certain piece on record "frees you to go on to something else," particularly pieces unfamiliar to the conservative concert-hall audience. Beyond that, the benefits for Gould are as much psychological as esthetic; for where he was once a notorious hypochondriac, now, he says, "Since I stopped giving concerts, I've scarcely had so much as a sniffle. Most of my earlier illnesses were psychosomatic—a sheer protest against my regimen. These past four years have been the best of my life."

Gould used to give live lecture-demonstrations; but since the Canadian and British Broadcasting Corporations both let him do the same on television—extend his pedagogy across two countries—he has reduced his appearances before live audiences to a bare minimum, regarding the few that he now gives each year as an excuse to travel to places he has not visited before and to keep the habit of facing live audiences, "just in case." Whereas he once taught classes at the University of Toronto, more recently he has been expressing his "irrepressible hamminess" over the weekly, hour-long Canadian radio program *The Art of Glenn Gould,* on which he is liable to give a lecture, let the producer play his records, or even dramatize a parody he wrote of a music critics' conference, where he mimicked many of the voices, sometimes doing two at once. (He rehearsed this one for me over the long-distance phone.)

If his output is, by his design, as electronic as possible, so is his intake; for he simply connects himself into a variety of inputs and they feed into him. "I'm not interested in gadgets per se, but what they can do for me." Gould watches a lot of television, exploits his hi-fi set, reads several newspapers (products of *wire* services), carries a radio with him all the time, and at home sometimes listens to both the AM and FM simultaneously. "Quite mysteriously, I discovered that I could better learn Schoenberg's difficult piano score, *Opus 23,* if I listened to them both at once, the FM to hear music and the AM to hear the news. I want to stay in touch." Gould can learn a Beethoven score while carrying on a conversation; and he often reads one of the many magazines to which he subscribes while listening attentively to someone on the telephone. Afterward, he will remember details from both inputs for Gould appears to be, as McLuhan puts it, omniattentive. Subscribing to his own preachments, he attends live concerts only to hear compositions unavailable on radio or record.

His cultural intake is various and enormous; so is his output. In our conversations, he talked knowledgeably about contemporary literature (particularly the intricate, ironic techniques of Jorge Luis Borges), theology (Kierkegaard and Tillich), electronic machinery, music both pop and classical, world problems, Canadian politics and patriotism, theories of the female orgasm, the stock market (especially Canadian mining properties), movies, the business of music, and research into extrasensory perception. More professionally, his output includes records—recent and current projects being the complete Bach keyboard works, Mozart's piano sonatas, Beethoven's sonatas, and all the Schoenberg pieces involving the piano—as well as his present radio shows. Like Bach before him, this noted performer also composes, so far a String Quartet and several choral pieces, most of them curiously romantic in ambience; and he plans to do more compositions in a wholly different mode. He contributes articles and reviews regularly to *High Fidelity* and other magazines, sometimes under the outrageous pseudonym of Dr. Herbert von Hockmeister; and everything he publishes reveals his enthusiasm for the literary craft, the musician's ear for intricate cadences, and the ham's desire for a good laugh. "This curious attitude of affection for the errors of the past secures for the teaching of music more quack educators per square faculty than are the lot of any other major discipline."

The fact that he performs in a multiplicity of ways makes him a "musical personality," but his reluctance to make any scene keeps his name out of the gossip columns. Everything he does is informed by such diverse qualities as a great eccentricity, a broad comedy, an unself-conscious informality, and a high level of intellectual concern. Gould is always working on a brace of projects; and like all people passionately involved with their work, he endlessly exudes his love of everything he does, if not personally conducts a relentless promotional campaign on behalf of his recent outputs. He is able to produce so much, I suspect, precisely because his intake is so high; and as a result, he functions like a revved-up machine, continually digesting all experience around him and transforming it into several kinds of manufacture. Indeed, his predominant interest is neither music nor writing but that machine, which is, after all, his primary instrument and, perhaps, his most extraordinary work of art. Its operation seems to provide his greatest visceral pleasure; and upon it he lavishes especially tender care and scrupulous attention.

We have actually met, briefly several times, mostly because

I insisted that we do; and Gould has been cordial, though more reserved than usual, probably because human contact is not his most congenial medium and I once made the mistake of warmly embracing his right hand just after a recording session. (He screamed, I heard something crack; he ran off to soak it in hot water, returned in a few minutes, apologized for his rude departure, accepted my regrets, and then sent the piano tuner home.) He is more polite than most of the world's eminent—he would sooner direct his attention elsewhere than tell an intruder to get lost—and young enough to treat an even younger interviewer as an equal; and he is among the few members of the serious musical profession, where nastiness seems cultivated, to make a habit of saying nice words about everyone, even the most popular targets of fashionable scorn. Paradoxically, although he is an acerbic critic of intellectual attitudes and professional positions, toward individuals he is scrupulously generous, "perhaps because I am continually amazed that anything gets done at all."

Gould is average in height, glassy-eyed in demeanor, and now stockier and tougher-looking than the delicate, skinny young man whose picture graced the legendary, best-selling recording of Bach's *Goldberg Variations* that established his reputation. He has a well-formed face, with a broad forehead and a heavy jaw, all topped by slightly receding and rampantly thinning brown hair. As most frontal pictures of him show, he is essentially good-looking; but a few eccentric details will keep him from being a male beauty—his stooped shoulders, which join the large jaw in creating a faintly primitive appearance; his reluctance to shave or get haircuts regularly creates the impression that he might need a dime; and his clothes, which are informal and ill-matching; and every time we have met, he has managed to remove his shoes and expose the holes in his socks. He tolerates little quarrel with his impulses toward immediate personal comfort.

He moves spryly in an idiosyncratic manner that combines ungainly swagger with a certain grace; and instead of entirely refusing to shake hands, as he used to do, he now raises his wrist and turns his fingers down as you reach forward, so all you generally clutch are a few fingers which quickly pull themselves away. He seems as self-entrenched as he actually is; and even when revealing his most idiosyncratic foibles, he communicates the clear impression that he knows exactly what he is doing all the time (as well as what impressions he might be creating) and that, as a romantic, he absolutely insists upon his will. "The only thing Glenn likes to do more than perform is talk," at least two acquaintances told me; and he is, indeed, a sparkling and interminable yak. Gould regards all the world outside his house as a stage: and wherever he goes, he performs with glittering words, often clowning, invariably humorous, and usually dominant. His mind is as quick as his speech, and he remembers clearly miscellaneous youthful experiences (some of which haunt him) and conversations held weeks, if not months, before. Any scene with him develops a rapid rhythm which he can single-handedly sustain.

He comes to New York for a few days every few weeks, primarily to make records which still provide about one half of his income (radio, television and stocks making the rest). He takes the night train from Toronto, arriving in New York early in the morning. As he memorizes the scores on the train and puts himself to sleep with Nembutal, he is able to go straight to work. In one hand is his suitcase, and in the other a slender wooden box about three feet by two and a few inches thick. It contains a few tapes, miscellaneous junk, and, folded up, the dilapidated chair that has been Gould's constant musical companion for fifteen years. Gould discovered some years ago that he could play far better from a very low chair that happened to be in the Gould home, and his father designed its seat to be raised and lowered like a swivel stool. Since Gould is sensitive about such delicate matters, he has made the chair such an integral part of his essential equipment that he has spurned offers to build him a substitute. Some years ago, the hazards of airplane travel smashed its seat; and he expended considerable effort finding pieces of green cloth and mattress rag that, he judges, "lend precisely the same tension and support as the chair originally had." When he finishes a recording session, he folds the chair into its case and lugs it back to Toronto.

His New York piano he customized from a pre-War Steinway chassis, largely to simulate aural aspects of a harpsichord; and where he once made records with several instruments—one piano for Bach, another for Beethoven, a third for Brahms—now he is so devoted to this hybrid that he occasionally ships it to Toronto. "It is as close to the ideal instrument as I'll ever be able to find." Before recording, he relaxes his hands and elbows by soaking them in water he runs from warm to hot. Whenever he plays, he hums and chants, sometimes quite audibly; and although the engineers put a wall of baffle around his chair, the superfluous sound still creeps onto the final product. "It's a terrible distraction that I don't like either. I wish I could get rid of it," he says, "and I would if I could, believe me; but I can't." This is perhaps his sole confession of inexcusable weakness. Piano or not, his performances of Beethoven generally strike critics as less distinguished and even less inventive than his Bach, while some Schoenbergians regard his recordings of the master as distinctly sloppy and perversely romantic.

The hum is another symptom of his intense involvement with performing; for at the instrument, Gould is a coiled dynamo of rampant visceral energy. Nearly every part of his body moves as he plays—his large head sways form side to side, and as his right foot operates the piano's pedals, his left shifts to preserve his balance. Only his broad hips are stable and relaxed. His fingers, neither long nor stubby, are well-muscled; and his famous trills are as spectacular to see as they are to hear—his fingernails literally flutter over the keys. Although he sits considerably lower than most pianists—only fourteen, rather than the usual twenty, inches off the floor—he seems to bear down on the piano; and everything he plays conveys a sense of highly tempered but incipiently overwhelming energy.

The paradox is that out of such Dionysian activity comes rather Apollonian interpretations of the music. At baroque counterpoint technique—the ability to articulate two or more melodies at once without subordinating one to the other—Gould is spectacularly masterful; no one else can perform this dimension of Bach, say, so brilliantly. "In purely pianistic terms, he has an extraordinary ability to keep the texture clear at all points," writes Robert P. Morgan in *High Fidelity*. "He is able to bring everything out, not just the most important line but the subsidiary lines as well. The subject of the fugue, for example, is rarely louder than the parts accompanying, it yet is always clearly articulated." He also exhibits particular genius for phrasing—for articulating both the precise notes and the subliminal character of every passage of notes (rather than building a climax)—but as a natural original, he also radically reinterprets the tempo of familiar pieces, rendering them in ways unheard before but often heard since—in rhythmic measures so original they offend, if not infuriate, before they persuade. As a result, even in Bach's superficially repetitious *Well-Tempered Clavier*, Gould amazingly manages to bestow on each prelude and fugue an individual identity. Achieving such precise musical articulation involves incredibly exacting rapport between the head and the hand—between the sounds the mind wants to hear and those the fingers can produce; and it is precisely by playing from the fingers that he adapts harpsichord technique to the piano. Indeed, so extraordinary and compelling is Gould's tactile dexterity that every time I watch him play I "see" thousands of synapses connecting every second, propelling dozens of signals across his circuits.

At the recording session, as soon as he finishes a complete rendition, he comments excitedly and specifically on his performance; and if these remarks are negative, the recording engineer whispers "take two" into the tape and Gould plays the deficient section again. ("I resent," he once remarked, "the onetimeness, or the non-taketwoness, of the live concert experience.") Skipping lunch and other pleasantries, he comes to the control room and goes over the tape with the record's producer. While listening to the playback, Gould watches the score, humming one of the melodies and conducting himself with a pencil-baton in his left hand; from time to time, he jots down editorial notes on the manuscript or sips from a cup of tea. A perfectionist by personal taste, he rejects a section merely because an eighth note has slipped from a line; and he often instructs the tape editor that a few bars from the third take of a certain section should be spliced into an entire section of the second take, which should in turn be integrated in place of similar material in the original. Sometimes Gould will record several distinctly different interpretations of the same score and then pick judiciously among the available results, even splicing two originally contrary renditions into his final integral version. In the end, therefore, the record of a Gould performance that we hear is really a carefully patched collection of segments. Some performers and critics think that fiddling with bits and pieces represents a kind of artistic "cheating," particularly when incisive editing produces the kind of inspired performance unlikely, if not impossible, in a sustained recital; but more concerned with ends (the record) than means (how he made it), Gould believes that the performer is obliged not only to play as well as possible but also to edit his rendition exactly to his conception of excellence. "A performer should treat tape as a film director treats his rushes." Actually, he splices considerably less than many performers, for when he put down his editing notes for a medium-length Beethoven sonata, the engineer who looked at them remarked, "That's minimal splicing around here. Someone else recently did fifty-two cuts in a ten-minute piece." After he finishes preparing instructions for the technician who actually reworks the tape, Gould will hear the definitive edited version of a previous recording session; and then he will either stay for another day of recording or take the night train home. He dislikes New York City and sees as little of it as possible.

His attitude to recordings is an intrinsic dimension of his enormous technological bias and sophistication; and as a writer he is, appropriately, best known as the philosopher of the recording. Indeed, his essays on the prospects and influence of recordings comprise as thorough and imaginative an exploration of this issue as has ever been done. Here Gould flatly suggests, "the habit of concert-going and concert-giving, both as a social institution and as chief symbol of musical mercantilism, will be . . . dormant in the twenty-first century. ('For Rent: Complex of Six Acoustically Charming Auditoria. Apply, J. Rockefeller.')" More specifically, Gould argues that the development of recordings, a product of electronic technology, has thoroughly changed the musical situation in various ways. Our generation values a sound style characterized by a great degree of "clarity, immediacy, and indeed almost tactile proximity," a sound that was neither available to nor wanted by the musical profession or public two generations ago. For instance, where orchestras once attempted to create a sound splendid enough to fill a concert hall, now the desired sound, even in a concert, is more appropriate to the scale of a living room. Indeed, in his own record-listening, Gould is particularly sensitive to the effects produced by various strategies of microphone placement. Second, records make continually available to the musical audience certain kinds of esoteric music, particularly preclassic and highly contemporary, that would otherwise be heard only on rare occasions, if at all. Third, records do for music what the art book did for art; for where the latter is, in André Malraux's famous phrase, a museum without walls, so recordings create in every man's library both a concert without halls and a musical museum whose curator is the record owner; therefore, all known musical styles—indeed, all kinds of music—are, thanks to records, available to the record owner at once. (This may explain why Gould's own enthusiasms embrace such contrary figures as Strauss and Schoenberg.) Fourth, the performer shares responsibility for the final product with the record's producer and his editors and technicians. Fifth, all the available recordings of a particular piece create a living "tradition" that forces the work's next performer to offer something distinctly original. "If there is any excuse to make a recording," Gould has said elsewhere, "it is to do it differently—as it has never been done before. If one can't quite do that, abandon the project and move on to something else." Finally, "Within the last few decades . . . music has ceased to be an occasion, requiring an excuse and a tuxedo and accorded, when encountered, an almost religious devotion; music has become a pervasive influence in our lives, and as our dependence upon it has increased, our reverence for it has in a certain sense declined."

Conjecturing about the impact of future technologies upon music, Gould not only suspects that by the time he finishes putting all his current projects on records he will need to redo them for video-tape cartridge, but he also declares, "I'd love to issue a kit of variant performances and let the listener assemble his own performance. It would draw the audience into the re-creative process." Beyond that, he envisions a machine that will literally allow every man to become his own conductor. As it "eliminates the pitch/speed equation," it would enable the listener to draw from "the felicities which appeal to him as among varying performances of a musical composition" and then combine those most felicitous versions into a single, personal interpretation. The machine would have the capability of allowing the listener to become, Gould writes, "a master editor," choosing phrases "from any number of performances of the same work which may have totally different tempo predilictions and dynamic relations. This would make it physically possible for the listener to produce his own Fifth Beethoven Symphony as a compote of the, to his mind, preferable features of a Mr. Karajan, Mr. Bernstein, or any other combination of interpreters that he would like to supervise." When that machine becomes generally available, Gould, I am sure, will be among the first to purchase one.

In background, the cosmopolite is indubitably a provincial; yet this isolation from cultural fashion probably endowed him with that eccentric individualism that, once the world accepted it, made him extremely cosmopolitan. He was born in Toronto, Ontario, in 1932, of prosperous Presbyterian parents; and though he is no longer a churchgoer, Protestant ideas still haunt his consciousness. His entire education took place in his hometown, much of it literally at home. His first piano teacher was, prosaically enough, his mother; and thanks to tutoring, he combined his musical education with sporadic attendance at the public schools. He entered Toronto's Royal Conservatory of Music at nine, precociously graduating at twelve, but continued to study there until his late teens. To this day his accent retains that Toronto mixture of elegant diction and anglicisms overlaid with Midwestern intonations. An autodidact by inclination and a shaper of his own destiny by insistence, Gould as a teen-ager discovered Schoenberg and other contemporary composers, even though his teachers had not championed them; and he now considers twelve-tone technique "the only really valid linguistic innovation in the twentieth century." Around this time, he also worked out wholly on his own that stunningly original interpretation of Bach's *Goldberg Variations* in which he successfully appropriated a harpsichord piece for the piano. Yet he was not a child prodigy in the conventional Menuhin sense; and when he first attracted public notice, at the age of twelve, his instrument of virtuosity was not the piano but the organ.

He gave two or three concerts a year in and around Toronto all through his teens; and although he was then cocky enough to send tapes of his Schoenberg performances to certain avant-garde New York composers, they denied him a precocious New York debut. (These pieces, in New York at least, were generally the domain of the late pianist Edward Steuermann, who had been part of Schoenberg's Viennese circle.) "That was the only period of my life when I enjoyed giving concerts," Gould now judges. "Performing before an audience gave me a glorious sense of power at fifteen." Few pianists made such auspicious American debuts as Gould did in 1955, first in Washington and then at New York's Town Hall. Never one to compromise with the going pianistic fashion, in the latter concert he showed his eccentric versatility with a piece (originally for harpsichord) by the esoteric sixteenth-century Dutch composer Jan Pieterszoon Sweelinck, an Orlando Gibbons pavane, five Bach *Sinfonias*, Bach's *Partita No. 5 in G major*, a sonata by Alban Berg, one other Viennese atonal piece, and the Beethoven for which he received so much praise—*Sonata in E major, Op. 109;* back then, as well as today, he eschewed the pianists' standard romantic repertoire of Schumann, Schubert, Chopin and Liszt. Not only did Gould's subsequent success establish a new style in piano performance but he also instituted a taste in programming that has affected younger musicians: "Ever since Gould, every young pianist feels obliged to include some 'intellectual' pieces in his recital," said the pianist Christopher Sager, then aged twenty-six, "difficult works such as Bach's *Goldberg,* Beethoven's *Diabelli Variations* and Schoenberg's later piano pieces."

Those opening concerts persuaded nearly all the newspaper critics to chime their superlatives together; and before long magazine articles appeared which devoted as much space to Gould's eccentricities as to his artistry. Not only did Gould use a weird-looking and oddly low chair which, shockingly, had a back, put glasses of water on the piano, and sometimes assume a posture resembling the Australian crawl, audibly hum through a performance as well as "play some passages far too fast and others outrageously slow," look incorrigibly unkempt and wear formal dress that was noticeably oversized, but he also carried both his favorite brand of bottled spring water and an opulent cache of drugs wherever he went, ate only arrowroot cookies for breakfast, wore mittens and a coat all the time, refused to shake hands, and even publicly quarreled with his elders over standards of interpretation and competence. "I think he is an absolutely inexplicable musician," another young pianist charged. "There are only two ways of doing things, very fast and very slow." "He would come," his former record producer Howard Scott remembers, "with one suitcase containing his chair, the other with scores, some clothes, and a toilet kit of pills. He had a pill for everything." On tour, he established a notorious reputation for canceling concerts—one in five on the average—and for demanding a gamut of special considerations. His behavior in those days convinced everyone he was surely out of his mind; but as he has never subscribed to a psychiatrist, he was probably more foxy than crazy, more uncomfortable than disturbed. In short, Gould exhibited none of the ingredients that make for musical success except sheer genius (and an ability for fomenting journalistic copy); and his artistry was at once so radical and excellent, although uneven, that the musical audience generously reclassified his excesses as artistic privileges.

Gould currently resides in a six-room penthouse that tops a late-thirties Toronto apartment building. In the living room are two pianos—one an 1895 Chickering—as well as an attractive painting by a Chinese now living in Paris, and miscellaneous disarray. As Gould neither cooks nor cleans, an occasional housekeeper fights a losing battle with the mess as well as supplies him some evenings with the one big meal he eats each day. Since he generally practices the piano less than an hour a day (touching it longer only before a recording session) and often goes for days without playing at all, he currently devotes most of his time to other activities, particularly writing and broadcasting. He entertains at home infrequently and leaves the house as little as possible, usually either to perform work or dine with friends, "most of whom are in communications—with the press or the networks. They have that synoptic view of things I like."

Although a slave to his commitments, most of which he fulfills responsibly, Gould also has the instincts of a bohemian, as well as the income to finance his several-hundred-dollar monthly telephone bill; and what probably saved him from the conventions that tackle even the most adventurous of us is the fact that only once did he hold a regular job. At eleven, during the war, he was the organist at a local "Anglican" (Canadian for Episcopal) church; but since he would often lose his place whenever the congregation sang, his forgetfulness led to an embarrassing mistake which brought his rapid dismissal. Perhaps because he has been famous his entire adult life, he now carries himself in some respects, especially in his desperate quest for privacy, more like a movie star than an artist or intellectual.

At home, Gould does first drafts of his writing in longhand

(this and his preference for trains are his two major technologically archaic habits); and when he has a lot of work to do, and his parents are away, he disappears into their home near Toronto, or he drives up into Northern Ontario, where he will check into a motel or one of the older hotels in the area and work there. His favorite methods for "cooling off" his machinery is driving alone through the lumber towns along the Lake Superior shore while listening to rock music on the radio. He prefers northern climates to tepid ones—London being the only city that might woo him away from Toronto; and in general, he would like to spend more time in the country. "I've got to have hills, water and leaden sky," he says. "My ability to work varies inversely with the niceness of the weather." His most enjoyable recent visits were spent in Canada's northernmost territories, and in 1967 he produced a radio show about this region—his first extended venture into non-musical reportage. Indeed, "The Idea of North," in which he superimposed contrapuntally various conversations and phrases into an essay on the effects of isolation, was so well-received that the C.B.C. gave Gould a five-year contract solely to produce radio specials. "It's now my favorite medium."

In the past few years Gould has literally redesigned his style of life, just as he transformed his piano exactly to the specifications he wanted—rearranged his environment and ultimately himself as his own most thoughtfully created and favorite work of art. This involves not only his choices of inclusions and exclusions but also sufficient discipline to act on his plan. He claims that he can understand and judge other people far better by talking to them on the phone than seeing them in the flesh. "My eyes are always deceived," he explains. His major exclusion in his design appears to be intimate personal relationships; he lives with no one, never has (since he left his parental home) and probably never will. Nonetheless, he feels intimately involved with many public personalities, most of whom he knows largely, if not exclusively, through radio and television, simply because they are his constant companions; and his acquaintance with the pop singer Petula Clark, a favorite subject in his conversations, has been entirely electronic. Gould speaks excitedly about her, softly cackling at his own jokes. "Actually, I did want to meet her when she was in Toronto for some concerts, but I was taping at the time. I discovered her when I was driving alone on one of my northern trips; I heard "My Love" before I heard "Downtown." I think she's been made to represent something enormously significant and I'm writing an essay called "The Search for 'Pet' Clark." It's significant, in a quasi-sociological way, that there is such a dichotomy between what she's saying and the music she's given to sing it to. I'm not one, you see, who thinks the Beatles are writing great music for our time; I think it's atrocious—and atrociously produced. But Pet Clark—for one thing there's the voice, which I've called 'fiercely loyal to its one great octave,' and then her presence —what I call the Gidget syndrome. There's a detachment, a sexual circumspection; she can express the agonies of adolescence and yet demonstrate a pressing on to adulthood. She can put the adults at ease, yet get through to the teen-age audience. And the thing is, she's *my* age." When Gould had finished his Petula Clark essay, he called up to read a longish section of it to me on the telephone. He read fast, acting it out, the phrasing seemingly rehearsed; and just after its final words, he sighed, "I *like* it."

The paradox is that Gould is a reclusively private person who lives, via the media, an extremely public life, in constant "touch" with the world community; for not only do his records become the intimate possessions of millions of people but the world's activities are also immediately present to him. This explains why Gould feels himself related more to the mass than the elite; for where a truly private person loves and is loved by some*one*, Gould loves everyone and everyone in turn loves him. He writes for a public of readers, broadcasts for a mass of listeners; and even over such a functionally private medium as the telephone, he is performing—behaving as he would in public. He simply knows and has known no other way. Indicatively, the "individuals" that appear in his parodies and satires are invariably drawn upon either public figures or media stereotypes. Gould has, by a series of choices, set up a certain mode of life; and although he is as much the victim as the beneficiary of his system, he knows he could, by other choices, reprogram his circuits to achieve an entirely different style.

Gould's eccentric procedures are far from mere gimmickry, because all of them serve particular functions in his life; beneath all the diffuse eccentricity is a consistent wisdom. He still carries several medicines, for instance, because he is accident-prone; and given his awareness of that condition, he would be foolish if he went anywhere without them. To deal with such information as he has acquired about himself, he has developed a series of strategies; and how he treats such information exemplifies the idea of a human being as a kind of cybernetic system with several dimensions of apparatus, all of which can be organized to achieve certain ends. Like all cybernetic systems, man continually adjusts to new information, called feedback, that results from his actions. For instance, say I discover that staying out in the noonday tropical sun usually produces severe sunburn; then, thanks to feedback, I realize that if I go out into the noonday sun again, another sunburn will be my fate. Every time a cybernetic system acts, it gets to consider the result of its actions and modify its behavior accordingly; and many of Gould's unusual habits and precautions are based upon informational feedback he learned in previous experiences.

Indeed, everyone continually adjusts his systems to new information he acquires about both himself and external situations; but what distinguishes Gould from most of us is a distinct difference of degree. He suffers no boss except himself and has so few social obligations, that he is free enough to be wholly responsible for nearly every hour of his waking day. Therefore, unlike the rest of us, hc gathers more subtle kinds of information, attempts more unconventional experiments with himself, makes so many more readjustments, and then makes himself systematically adhere to these new ways. He dislikes shaking hands with people, primarily because his hands are delicate and they earn much of his livelihood. He used to put a glass of water on the piano when he performed in public, because the tension of playing a live concert sometimes made him gag. He takes trains because he discovered that planes make him ill, and drinks no alcohol because a swimming head some years ago nearly caused an accident. If Marcel Duchamp decided that he could not "work" more than two hours a day and did not, Gould recognizes that he can labor many more; and since his interests and ambitions are various, he does so. He plays the piano at an unusual angle, because that odd position is more effective for him. He purchased a new Chevrolet Impala, because that is the only brand that has seats his sensitive back finds comfortable. If extrasensory information either he or a certain friend perceives warns him that a projected trip might bring misfortune, he cancels it. For every eccentric gesture, there is invariably a legitimate reason. Gould is adventurous enough to act on his new knowledge, intelligent enough to regard his experience disinterestedly, and wealthy enough to exploit the extensions the new technologies offer him; and these procedures, indeed, explain why he is such a highly individualized, extremely contented, enormously productive, and maximally efficient system.

RALPH ELLISON:
Novelist as Brown-Skinned Aristocrat

The more books we read, the sooner we perceive that the true function of a writer is to produce a masterpiece and that no other task is of any consequence.—PALINURUS

Ralph Ellison handles himself with a dignity, elegance, contained comfort, and disdain for the trivial that is positively as aristocratic as any American can be; and he is so variously talented and awesomely well-conditioned that one might think he devoted his entire day to self-cultivation. He has high-style hobbies like gourmet cooking, art-collecting, building hi-fit sets, recorder-playing, taking photographs, designing his own furniture; his distinguished appearance makes him a propitious subject for elegant photographic portraits; and he belongs to one of New York's most respectable clubs, The Century, in addition to serving on some of America's most powerful cultural commissions. Indeed, Ellison's multiple success demonstrates that a fatherless American Negro really does have the opportunity to become the author of one of America's greatest novels, *Invisible Man* (1952), as well as an aristocratic presence, and an all but universally respected literary figure.

As a writer, Ellison has a particular passion for demolishing the stereotype, especially by showing how simplistic images forbid a more complex and perceptive understanding of human life in general and American Negro experience in particular; and the realities of his own history run thoroughly counter to a gamut of popular sociological clichés about the imprisoning quality of Negro disadvantage. Indeed, he talks about his life with unusual subtlety and understanding, largely because certain truths were gained at the expense of personal pain and he wants to insure that nothing he puts into print will contradict the complexities, and the implications, of his own experience. Ellison was born March 1, 1914, in Oklahoma City, Oklahoma, just two years after it gained statehood. His father had been a professional soldier in the Philippines, in China, and in the Spanish-American War and, later, a construction foreman; and he was then operating a small ice and coal business. The family, while not especially rich in formal learning, was literate and active; and Ellison insists that his father destined him to be a writer by bestowing on him the Christian name of *Ralph Waldo*. "After I began to write and work with words," he once remarked, "I came to suspect that he was aware of the suggestive powers of names and of the magic involved in naming."

Ellison senior died in an accident when Ralph was three; so to support her two sons, his mother became a domestic and then an apartment-house custodian who made a practice of bringing home the discarded copies of the latest magazines. Young Ralph took on a variety of kid jobs, such as selling newspapers, collecting bottles for bootleggers, shining shoes and clerking in a swanky haberdashery; and some of these tasks he exploited for other advantages. "After all," he wrote, "the most meaningful tips do not always come in the form of money, nor are they intentionally extended." While quite young, Ellison assimilated the notion that he should excel at everything he tried, perhaps because "my mother had some sense of the value of excellence, and she often said that she didn't care what I became as long as I tried to become one of the best." In fact, he has since done remarkably well at so many things that he all but approximates the Western image of a Renaissance Man; and this ideal, he says in retrospect, first entered his mind, as well as the aspirations of his childhood friends, in the Negro community of Oklahoma City.

He went to the local high school, where he played varsity

football, dabbled in writing, and began to concentrate on music. "I remember that in my themes at school I tried to get some of the Shavian quality into my writing; but no one paid any attention to it and I didn't take it seriously." To his good fortune, Ellison won an Oklahoma state scholarship to attend the most famous of Deep South Negro colleges, Tuskegee, founded by Booker T. Washington himself; and unable to afford the fare, he rode freight trains from Oklahoma to Alabama. "I went there as one who wanted to be a composer," Ellison remembers. "They had a good band and an orchestra, and I was a trumpeter. And they also had William L. Dawson, who was a composer and who had become quite famous as a choir director. The Tuskegee Choir opened Radio City Music Hall while I was still in high school, and this really got me excited." Elsewhere, Ellison judged that Dawson "was, and probably still is, the greatest classical musician in that part of the country. I had no need to attend a white university when the master I wished to study with was available at Tuskegee." (Indeed, Ellison and I first became friends over our mutual admiration for Dawson, who was the greatest conductor I ever followed in my teen-age days as a choir singer.)

To deny another cliché, Ellison today does not regard this segregated education, in the Deep South, as particularly disadvantageous. "You got there to study music, and you studied music; and it wasn't any easier because you were in a Negro college," he explains (pronouncing that next-to-last word as "nig-row"). "The teachers themselves held degrees from Oberlin and the Boston Conservatory and so on; and Hazel Harrison, who headed the piano department, had been one of Busoni's prize pupils and lived in a house with other young composers in Berlin. You know, you don't think about the problems of being a Negro when you're trying to get an education. When you're in the classroom, you're thinking about the problems before you, not the larger sociological problem, although you are quite aware that you are Negro."

It was at Tuskegee that Ellison discovered modern writing, not through his courses, which were mostly in music, but through his own adventurous reading and the encouragement of the late Morteza Sprague, then head of the English department there and the dedicatee of Ellison's second book, a collection of essays entitled *Shadow and Act* (1964). "When I went to him about T. S. Eliot and such people—he hadn't given much attention to them; they weren't taught there—he told me to read the criticism and where to find it. Once I read *The Waste Land* I became very much involved with modern letters. I couldn't really analyze it. Emotionally I was intrigued; so I started reading all the commentaries. My friend Al Murray tells me that I was actually trying to write poetry in those days—something which I've blanked out; incidentally, I never wrote a decent poem; but the conscious concern with writing began there, without my being conscious that this was what I was doing."

To earn his spending money, particularly to support an *Esquire*-inspired taste in clothes, Ellison worked part-time in the university library, and there he came across the major modern books that were not included in the literature courses. "In Macon County, Alabama," he once wrote, "I read Marx, Freud, T. S. Eliot, Pound, Gertrude Stein and Hemingway. Books which seldom, if ever, mentioned Negroes were to release me from whatever 'segregated' idea I might have had of human possibilities." He continued elsewhere, "Why should I have wished to attend the white state-controlled university where the works of the great writers might not have been so easily available?" Here, as before, Ellison made the best of a discriminatory situation, which had its own opportunities as well as disadvantages; and his wisdom is that everybody's life is similarly riddled by superficially restricting and yet opportune experiences.

He came to New York City in the summer of 1936, after his junior year, intending to get work and then return for the fall semester. With only seventy-five dollars in his pocket, he stayed at the Harlem YMCA, which also turned out to be a good place to meet people. However, a steady job was not his fortune, and New York's excitement was so persuasive that he never returned to get his degree and has, off and on, lived in Harlem ever since. He took a job as a counterman at the Harlem Y, and then he worked briefly as a substitute receptionist and file clerk for Dr. Harry Stack Sullivan, the eminent American psychiatrist. "This was a job of short duration, but one of the most interesting I ever had," he told a Congressional Committee in the summer of 1966. "After that, oh, I worked in factories and I sometimes had no work and slept in St. Nicholas Park below City College. I lived as I could live."

He sought work as a musician, once playing first trumpet for a small orchestra that Alex North, now a famous Hollywood composer, then conducted for his wife, the dancer Anna Sokolow; however, Ellison could not amass enough funds to join the musicians' union. He studied composition briefly with the American composer Wallingford Reigger and even took a few classes in sculpture. Late in the thirties he regularly played chess with Jacob Lawrence, who has since become a well-known painter. Thanks in part to his old friendship with the blues singer Jimmy Rushing, who once carried ice for Ellison's father, he also made the acquaintance (and reacquaintance) of many Oklahoma-born jazz musicians, among them the guitarist Charlie Christian (an elementary school classmate of Ellison's younger brother), the bassist Walter Page, the trumpeter Hot Lips Paige, as well as the members of Count Basie's band and even Duke Ellington. Like the novelist John Barth, who also studied music extensively, Ellison as a writer even now has the indomitable working habits of a composer.

Two days after he got to New York, Ellison ran into the Negro philosopher-critic Alain Locke, whom he had met before at Tuskegee, and another man, who turned out to be the writer Langston Hughes. On the spot, Hughes asked Ellison to deliver a few books, granting the young man permission to read them on the way; and since Ellison made a practice of capitalizing on such unintentional tips, he discovered two of the most influential works he ever read—André Malraux's *Man's Fate* and *Days of Wrath*. "A few months later I met Richard Wright, and he asked me to review a book for a magazine he had come to New York to edit," Ellison reminisced with a slight but perceptible drawl. "And my review was published, and then he asked me to do a short story. Now I had never tried to do a piece of fiction in my life; and I made my first attempt at a short story for a magazine of Wright's called *New Challenge*. The story didn't come out, but it got as far as the galley-proof state. By then, I guess I must have been hooked."

In 1937, after his mother died "at the hands of an ignorant and negligent Negro physician," he joined his younger brother in Dayton, Ohio. The two were so poor that they hunted by day, sometimes consulting Hemingway's stories as a manual of detail, felling birds they later sold to G. M. officials. It was there and then that he vowed to become a writer, arranging his life so that writing, rather than something else, would be his primary interest—"to stake my energy against the possibility of failing." He started a novel, only to discover that he did not know how to finish it; and after recognizing that, as he now puts it, "art is a system of techniques," he embarked upon a systematic study of the novelistic craft—reading a lot of criticism, as well as the prefaces of Henry James and Joseph Conrad, and later querying Wright about fictional devices.

Returning to New York in 1938, he joined the Federal Writers' Project as a researcher at the salary of twenty-two dollars a week. Here he assembled scholarly data for a study of Negroes in New York, as well as collected folklore. "I went from apartment to apartment, talking to anyone who would allow me to." Some of this experience, gained as an outside observer, informed the internal narratives in *Invisible Man*. In 1942 Ellison resigned from the Writers' Project to join Angelo Herndon, then breaking away from the Communists, in editing *The Negro Quarterly*. Although Ellison sympathetically frequented left-wing circles and wrote reportage and criticism for *The New Masses*, which was then one of the few places that would publish tough-minded Negro writers, he never joined the Communist Party or accepted their dictum that social realism was the sole appropriate literary style.

Just before *The Negro Quarterly* dissolved, Ellison joined the merchant marine as a civilian, partly because he had been a member of the National Maritime Union since 1936, when he picketed for them, and largely because "I wanted to contribute to the war, but didn't want to be in a Jim Crow army." He worked as a cook and touched Europe for the first time; but after a particularly wracking voyage, in which his convoy came under attack, he returned home suffering from low blood pressure and went to recuperate with friends in Vermont. It was there, in 1945, in his own early thirties that he started *Invisible Man,* still wondering if, indeed, he would be able actually to finish a novel. At the book's beginnings, he was reading Lord Raglan's study of *The Hero,* thinking about how myth got into fiction, and considering "the nature of politics and Negro leadership, which was based on outside support, rather than the dynamics of the Negro community." He wrote the novel's prologue and opening sections rather quickly, publishing in Cyril Connolly's journal, *Horizon* (1947), the "Battle Royal" sequence as it more or less now stands. "I had an idea where I was going," he explains, "although the actual writing took years. Once I got a pattern going, the pattern parlayed itself; that's what I call 'organic form.' "

In July 1946 he married Fanny McConnell, a petite, slender, freckled, fair-complexioned Negro who resembles Katharine Hepburn and looks after her husband well. Around this time he resumed his pre-War acquaintance with the critic Stanley Edgar Hyman, who has since been one of his closest literary friends. They came together in the early forties over Ellison's admiration for Kenneth Burke, whom they hail in unison as the greatest American critic, and Hyman's enthusiasm for Negro blues, which both of them regard as great folk poetry; and the novelist has since characterized the critic as "an old friend and intellectual sparring partner." Particularly after the War, Ellison frequently stayed at the Hyman house in Bennington, Vermont, where he wrote by day and spent the evening in drink and talk with Hyman and his wife, the late novelist Shirley Jackson.

Ellison worked seven years on *Invisible Man,* as well as on a shorter work which disposed of a related theme and eventually went unpublished; and the book appeared in 1952 to a fanfare of favorable reviews and eventually the National Book Award. In retrospect, the novel is an ambiguous and somewhat disconcerting achievement that combines much hard visceral detail with a surrealistic sense of perception and event, some of the lushest writing in contemporary English literature with some undistinguished prose, a sense of authentic immediacy with an almost academic net of myth and ritual; and its plot all but begs to be misread by an undiscerning reader. One reason would be, as the novelist James Baldwin put it, "Mr. Ellison, by the way, is the first Negro novelist I have ever read to utilize in language, and brilliantly, some of the ambiguity and irony of Negro life."

The problem in understanding *Invisible Man* is the nature of the narrator, whom some critics erroneously take to be autobiographical and whom most white readers regard as a blameless Negro boy subjected to all the indignities that white society inflicts upon its blacks. He gets a scholarship to a Negro college only after passing through a hair-raisingly violent "battle royal," gets expelled from the college for betraying its dirty underside to a white trustee, goes North to discover that his "letters of recommendation" deceitfully advise against him, that jobs are hard to find, and that the ones he gets are more dangerous than congenial. After undergoing an operation that seems like a lobotomy, he gets involved with various radicals, communists as well as black nationalists, all of whom eventually betray him in other ways; and the narrative closes with his escaping into an underground cave where, surrounded by lightbulbs, he contemplates the pattern of his experience.

In one sense, many of the choices the individual narrator makes could be regarded as symbolic of more general political persuasions that certain Negroes have historically espoused and some have followed; and since most of these solutions continue to have their advocates, as well as to fail their hopes for similar reasons, the politics of *Invisible Man,* like those in all great political fictions, seem remarkably current nearly two decades later. In another sense, the gist of the novel could be interpreted as a descent ritual, where the narrator must undergo suffering before he gains the power to speak as an artist. Since the body of narration is actually a flashback, the novel is also, to Albert Murray, "*par excellence* the literary extension of the blues. It was as if Ellison had taken an everyday twelve-bar blues tune (by a man from down South sitting in a manhole up North in New York singing and signifying about how he got there) and scored it for a full orchestra." Moreover, as a novel by a Negro American writing in a Western language, *Invisible Man* draws and comments upon Negro folklore, American literature (with epigraphs from Melville and T. S. Eliot), and Western literature, with specially conspicuous debts to Dostoevsky, Voltaire, and Greek myths. ("I think I still have the copy of *Candide* that I bought at Tuskegee.") Like jazz, *Invisible Man* is a product of American Negro culture, which is indubitably American (and only minimally African) and also Western, which is to say, an extension of Europe.

Most white readers take the story as a catalogue of an innocent Negro's adverse experience; but Ellison, in his usual position of countering a cliché, regards this as "an incorrect and sentimental interpretation, inasmuch as the narrator of the book could have stopped much of his experience, had he been willing to accept the harsh nature of reality. He creates much of his own fate, but I don't look upon him as heroic in that way. I think he made a lot of mistakes; but many white readers, certainly, are so sentimental about the Negro thing that they can't see that. He has a sort of wrong-headed desire to take on identities imposed on him by the outside, always stopping to let someone else tell him what to do and even give him a name; but we know very well that each individual has to discover himself, for himself. Usually, this is done through some sort of pain; but I must say that this is a tough guy, because he goes through many, many experiences which should have driven him to himself and to his reality. He should have understood what Bledsoe had to say; he [Bledsoe] was wise in comparison, though you don't have to approve of him."

Many critics have interpreted the title as suggesting that white America finds the predicament of Negroes invisible. "Well, I wasn't writing about 'the Negro,'" Ellison retorts, a bit amused. "I was writing about a specific character, in specific circumstances, at a specific time. As for the invisibility, well, there's a joke about that, which is tied up with the sociological dictum that Negroes in the United States have a rough time because we have 'high visibility'—high pigmentation, as the formula has it. No one will ever mistake me for white. However, the problem for the narrator of *Invisible Man* is that he creates his own invisibility to a certain extent by not asserting himself. Even though he has the responsibility not to get done in, he does not recognize how evil people can be or how to do the thing that will break the pattern and reveal himself, until far along in the book. He is a type of character that transcends race, although a lot of people don't take him that way." Ironically enough, for a book that is so misunderstood, as well as so texturally rich it could spawn two hundred pages of detailed criticism, *Invisible Man* has done remarkably well, going through several paperback editions; and not only has it been read by nearly every literate young person, but in 1965, a poll of two hundred American critics and writers judged *Invisible Man* the most distinguished novel of the post-War period.

For over a decade now, Ellison has been working on a second novel, as yet untitled; and the sections that he has published in various magazines, as well as read aloud, suggest that it will be just as brilliant and extraordinary as his first book. It will be a political novel, set partly in Washington and partly in Oklahoma. One reason why it was not finished sooner is that the story has become inordinately long—perhaps over one thousand pages—and complicated. Another reason is that Ellison is something of a perfectionist, with a more than usual dose of second-novel jitters. In the spring of 1966 he had four thick, bound volumes of typescript, from which he read me miscellaneous passages. "I try to deal with large bodies of experience," he told me then, "which I see as quite complex. There's a tendency to reduce the American experience, which is quite complex, especially when it centers around the Negro American experience. So, I'm constantly writing—I write a lot, but too much I have to put aside. Once it jells, I come back to it; and if I still react positively, if I can still see potentialities of development, then I keep it." One old friend, who has read a good deal of it, says, "Ralph is insanely ambitious. He actually writes quickly, but won't release this book until he is sure that it is the greatest American novel ever written." He has become so embarrassed about his inability to finish the book that he gets visibly upset whenever acquaintances ask about it. In 1964 he published *Shadow and Act*, which contains miscellaneous essays of twenty years, including all the lengthy interviews that Ellison gave up to that time, his criticisms of jazz, literature, and culture, and his contributions to a famous polemical exchange with the misguided critic Irving Howe, in which Ellison scored all the points and revealed all the truths. These essays are invariably densely argued and difficult to read; but if nothing else, they demonstrate that Ellison is an immensely intelligent author with an unusual care for language and that everything he publishes is thoroughly premeditated.

Ellison himself is just under six feet, broadly built, visibly muscular (particularly in his arms), and the color of well-creamed coffee; like nearly all American Negroes, he is not black but, as he would put it, "part-white." He has a broad mouth, moderately full lips, a flattened nose, flaying nostrils, and a precisely trimmed graying mustache that runs a quarter-moon shape down from his nose across to the ends of his upper lips. A broad scar between his right eye and temple, the result of a childhood swing accident, seems less a blemish than a handsome punctuation mark, and his normal expression is pensive, perhaps a bit distant, intimidating, and severe. Reserved by instinct, he is not at all as comic as his books might suggest. He has begun to gray noticeably in the past few years, combing his loosely kinked hair across the back half of his head and leaving the front part bald to the elements.

Containing his nerves well, he used to smoke cigarettes but now puffs a pipe, filling it at home from a large can of Nouve Egberts Amphora. Always erect, he moves with the graceful balance, and incipient energy and perceptible hauteur of a star halfback crossing the campus. He is guarded and yet considerate in manner, except when drink loosens him, as well as unusually formal, even addressing his guests at home "Mr. X and Miss Y" long after most Americans would use first names. However, whenever his oldest close friend, a live-wire writer and retired Air Force major named Albert Murray, pulls into his house, the tempo picks up. (At times, Murray seems to carry Ellison's wilder side, and his own essays seem jazzier renditions of ideas and attitudes they have worked out together.) But for his hair and two rather deeply articulated lines on his face, running from the base corners of his nose to points slightly beyond the corners of his mouth, Ellison would look far younger than he is.

Very concerned with his appearance, a trait he insists is particularly Negro American, he dresses well, in clothes of conservative cut, and sensitively, sometimes condescendingly, notices how others dress; and he also attributes his aristocratic manner to Negro American culture. "You now find," he remarks, "that the great nineteenth-century tradition of elegance and oratory is most alive within the Negro community." When he dons a dark suit and black Homburg, encases himself in a dark overcoat, and climbs into his black Chrysler, he looks more like a prosperous banker than a novelist.

From his earliest days at the YMCA, Ellison has always lived north of 110th Street, usually in the nicer areas of Harlem west of Eighth Avenue—in a room at 530 Manhattan Avenue in 1936, on 122nd Street near Manhattan Avenue, on Hamilton Terrace near City College, on St. Nicholas Avenue between 147th and 148th Streets (where most of *Invisible Man* was written), and since 1952, on upper Riverside Drive in the 150's in a spacious eighth-floor apartment with a spectacular view of the Hudson River and the New Jersey Palisades. The Ellisons' apartment is high-ceilinged, large-roomed, comfortable, scrupulously kept, and filled with the best of everything, all so tastefully appointed that it may well adorn certain fashion pages.

There are paintings and sculpture on the walls, soft carpets under the foot, Mies van der Rohe Barcelona chairs, a Marcel Breuer leather-strap chair, a handsome standing sculpture of Ichabod Crane atop his sprinting horse, an improvised cart containing African violets grown under fluorescent light, two television sets (one color, the other black and white), a stand holding four recorders in various sizes, a wall full of hard-bound books, several pieces of silver-frame furniture designed in Miesian style by Ellison himself, a plastic humidor filled with cigars, waist-high speakers from a hi-fi set housed in a closet, a Nagra portable tape recorder, an Ampex tape deck, a bright red office-size IBM typewriter, a small replica of Botticelli's *Venus* over the typewriter, a mounted National Book Award, and more than the usual panoply of security devices. The luxurious effect of the three front rooms—the living room, the dining room, a study, all open to each other—is overpowering, as well as somewhat surprising; it is not the sort of elegance that most people, their minds cluttered with stereotypes about Negroes, "ghettos," and writers' homes, expect to find on the edge of Harlem. Bookshelves and records inundate all the hallway walls, sometimes to the point of inconvenience, while a guest room in the back is filled to capacity with more bookshelves and miscellany as the Ellisons hesitate over throwing things out. (Early in 1968 he retrieved a batch of usable files from an office high above Rockefeller Center; here some of *Invisible Man* was written.) Their constant companion is a large, frisky black labrador retriever who answers to "Tucka," which is a nickname for Tucka Tarby of Tivoli. Although the Ellisons are more than comfortably ensconced in New York, they fulfilled in 1967 a long-fomenting ambition to have a house in the country. However, the farm they purchased in Plainfield, Massachusetts, burned down in their presence later that year, tragically destroying several irreplaceable possessions and a half year's worth of revisions that Ellison had made on his second novel.

Although he is certainly free to move elsewhere, Ellison has always lived in Negro communities, in stark contrast to many other dark-skinned writers and even certain self-appointed spokesmen for "black" America; and for this reason, he thinks that his soulful books, unlike those of certain other Negro authors, speak to blacks and browns as well as whites: "I have to hear the language," he explains. "My medium is language; there is a Negro idiom. In fact, there are many Negro idioms in the American language, and I have to hear them sounding in my ear. You know, also, a place like Harlem or any other Negro community has an expressiveness about it which is almost Elizabethan. Things are revealed in speech in the streets; there is a lot of humor. I never know when I'm going to hear something just in the street that is going to be the making of a piece of fiction that I'm trying to write."

It seems symbolically appropriate that Ellison should live so close to Harlem and yet only a few blocks away from the National Institute of Arts and Letters, to which he was appointed in 1964. Even better, the location of his house approximates what he identifies as a chief characteristic of American art—the fusion of vernacular and effete, of local traditions with Western myth, of the mundane and the universal. Ellison remembers that he derived this idea from the poems and essays of T. S. Eliot, whom he also regards as one of the greatest influences upon his own writing. "Eliot is full of American folklore. He knew quite a lot about it. It would have been inescapable for him, coming from St. Louis, not to recognize the odd juxtapositions you get in this country. High culture and popular culture are all mixed up; and the poet can mix them any way he wants. It amuses me that the 'Under the bam/Under the boo,/Under the bamboo tree' line in 'Fragment of an Agon' comes out of a Negro song written by James Weldon Johnson as part of one of the popular musicals of the 1890's, when a group of Negroes dominated the American musical stage. Anything and everything is there to be used. There is this kind of irreverent reverence which Americans are apt to have for the good products of the past. I think you get all of this in Eliot"; one could add, in much of American jazz and Ellison himself. Indicatively, he regards the "Afro-American" identification as rather irrelevant, if not phoney; for just as T. S. Eliot could never wholly forsake his heritage to become an unalloyed Englishman, so American Negroes culturally cannot honestly be anything but American.

Very much aware of how inappropriate words can corrupt our understanding of important things, Ellison persuasively objects to the use of the word "ghetto" to identify segregated communities. " 'Ghetto' implies a cultural and religious distance. It comes from Europe; it had a content there. However, used in this way, it only helps to obscure the relationships between American whites and American Negroes. They have so much in common—language for one thing, the patterns of myth—universal myth, Christian myths and so on, as they have been given embodiment in terms of Negro patterns. It is not too difficult to find the Hercules myth in John Henry, if you are aware of the connections, if you know where to look. Between Americans white and black there is not a religious wall, nor a cultural wall. Most Negroes are, just to start with religion, Protestant. That's unmistakable; you have communication there. On the other hand, everywhere you look, even in the deepest, most rabid part of the South, the Negroes are not separate but right in the bedrooms, in the kitchens. They are everywhere, even in the clubs and in the cars; they know all the intimate conversations.

"American English would not have the same music in it if it were not for great numbers of Negroes, and great numbers of white Southerners who learned their English partially from Negroes. In Harlem—in fact, in most so-called black ghettoes—you have a lot of people who do not spend most of their time there. They work outside, for instance as domestics in white homes. They're cooking, taking care of children, changing their diapers, teaching them their manners. They are so completely involved on that level of association. The music and the dances that Americans do are greatly determined by Negro style—by Negro American style at that, by Negro American sense of elegance, by the American Negro's sense of what the human experience should be, by what Negroes feel about how an American should move and express himself. So, the word 'ghetto' obscures this. It is much better to say that you have segregation and slums. This is very difficult to get people to see."

Although literature is his trade, Ellison becomes more passionate nowadays, if not adamant, in talking about politics; but rather than offering the usual phrases of terror and protest, he most vehemently objects, as perhaps a writer should, to those homilies that corrupt or contradict his sense of immediate reality, such as an indiscriminate use of the word "ghetto," or those current sociological generalizations about the "disintegrating Negro family." He finds that much that is written about Negroes, as often by supposed friends as by avowed enemies, is fallacious and, if transformed into social policy, pernicious. "Most of those who write about Negro life today," he once wrote with bitterness, "seem to assume that as long as their hearts are in the right place they can be as arbitrary as they wish in their formulations." In particular, he angrily objects to sociologists and social workers who propagate an image of Negro life as riddled by degradation and self-hate, not only because such interpretations are on the whole simply untrue, but also because such influential studies attribute to Negro society certain behavior patterns which are just as characteristic of the white culture as well. "One of the most insidious crimes occurring in this democracy," he writes in *Shadow and Act*, "is that of designating another, politically weaker, less socially acceptable, people as the receptacle for one's own self-disgust, for one's own infantile rebellions, for one's own fears of, and retreats from, reality. It is the crime of reducing the humanity of others to that of a mere convenience, a counter in a banal game which involves no apparent risk to ourselves."

Anger and outrage are clearly in Ellison's repertoire of responses; yet he is perhaps too scrupulous an intellectual, or too aristocratic a brown-skinned gentleman, to traffic in the obvious and familiar epithets of protest spokesmanship. In one of the many memorable passages of *Shadow and Act*, he implicitly offers a partial explanation for his chosen role. "But there is also an American Negro tradition," he writes, "which teaches one to deflect radical provocation and to master and contain pain. It is a tradition which abhors as obscene any trading on one's anguish for gain or sympathy; which springs not from a desire to deny the harshness of existence but from a will to deal with it as men at their best have always done." This is another way of saying that the most remarkable heroism often remains invisible to the audience of hero-worshippers.

In dealing with those popular sociological clichés, Ellison as usual refers to his own experience as a fatherless child; and although he knew his father well enough to suffer the loss, he realizes that while "a certain companionship was gone, and my mother had to be more severe than she otherwise would have liked," other social disadvantages were more debilitating. "The white family," he adds wryly, "is in just as much chaos." Furthermore, he fears that such theories give people an excuse for nihilistic behavior; and he remembers with horror watching a Negro teen-ager on television after the Newark riot explaining his own destructiveness with a gamut of sociological clichés. The kid patently got his lines from "the new apologists for segregation," as Ellison calls them, who serve to rationalize a new sense of white supremacy by giving white people superficially persuasive reasons not to associate with "culturally deficient" Negroes or grant them equal opportunity. "The decay of the cities," he warns, "will not be stopped by whites moving to the suburbs, and the public peace should be protected, regardless of who is upsetting it."

Because he refuses to join the chants for "black power," Ellison is sometimes dismissed as an "Uncle Tom"; but since his temper is hardly servile or humble and he has the courage of his convictions, often to the point of personal pain, as well as refuses to repress his anger, and has long supported the cause, that derogatory stereotype is no more appropriate than other reductionist clichés. Ellison does not deny that injustice, discrimination, hypocrisy, and poverty all exist; but he insists, partly from personal experience, that these disadvantages are not as totally determining as certain social commentators make them out to be. First, he notes that all men confront disadvantages of some kind and that the measure of a man's character is his will to overcome them. Second is "the broad possibility of personal realization which I see as a saving aspect of American life." Third, he believes that democratic processes, and black-white cooperation, rather than violence or racism in any form, are more likely to alleviate those problems and that the liberal approach, in spite of hypocrisies, does bring discernible change. "Barriers are torn down through law and the interaction of people," he declares, adding, "I just don't see how a resort to violence can be successful. It's foolish to believe that it might, because like the character of Ras in my novel, they cannot commit themselves to what they say. They don't have the supplies and the organization for guerrilla warfare." He pauses and chuckles to himself, "I know something about shooting, and those snipers aren't particularly good." Perhaps the final irony of Ellison's relation to the "militants" is the suspicion that the opening of LeRoi Jones's play, *Dutchman* (1964), closely resembles the scene that closes Chapter 12 of *Invisible Man.*

Indeed, Ellison is disturbed by how eagerly the mass media play up the statements of "black power" advocates who are hardly as representative of Negro American feeling as are ministers or the leaders of the older protest organizations. "People have been making extreme statements in Harlem for decades—some of the guys now on 125th Street and Seventh Avenue were there when I first came to New York; but now television feeds their ideas into many homes. A false sense of reality is disseminated. Most Negroes who see them on television are as scared and awed as white people." Ellison paused to cast for a definitive version of his thought. "We now see revived the old myth of the black bogeyman in a new metamorphosis. He used to scare children in the South; now this myth, propagated by the big media with a few militant-sounding Negroes as their agents, is used to titillate the fears and the masochism of a great audience of whites. This does the causes of equal opportunity, responsibility, and fraternity no good." A tone of tempered frustration, perhaps personal, entered Ellison's voice as he said, "Some old Negro preacher could be the wisest man in the United States, and no one could hear him. The media wouldn't pay attention."

The remark is obliquely applicable to Ellison himself, even though his views do have some circulation and he did testify to Congress in the summer of 1966; for wisdom, along with courage in stating the unobvious truth, is the quality most deeply characteristic of Ellison's mind. Very much unlike his nameless narrator in *Invisible Man,* who is perhaps an obverse of himself, Ellison has a tough and guarded intelligence that refuses to be persuaded by anything that refutes its senses of value and reality. As a writer professionally concerned with articulating the truth one perceives, he has particular contempt for hypocrites and hypocrisies, regardless of how intelligent or superficially high-minded the deception.

Against the herd of current intellectual fashion, he thinks that the NAACP has achieved "real victories in changing the legal structure regarding race" and praises Lyndon B. Johnson, quite justifiably, as the President who has done more for the "Negro thing," as he likes to call it, than any of his predecessors. "He's knocked the pins out of the great structure of racism in this country," Ellison remarks, "by making changes in the basis of political power. In sticking his neck out on many appointments, he has recognized the justice of equal rights and done things that Roosevelt and Kennedy didn't dare. He knows that it must be seen that Negroes play an important role in the life of the country—that we must have a full share in political power and responsibility."

Ellison insists that Negro Americans should keep their eyes fixed on the classic goals—integration, cultural autonomy, freedom of movement, equal opportunity, and a share of political power. Now that these goals are within realization, he fears that various distractions may sabotage the effort. Similarly, it takes genuine courage for a writer to go against the majority opinion of his own profession, but this is precisely the personal strength which Ellison consistently displays, as in publicly defending American involvement in Vietnam, less out of patriotic enthusaism than tragic necessity. "I don't see us withdrawing from the war," he said, for once looking out the window and then back at me. "We have certain responsibilities to the Vietnamese and the structure of power in the world. It's too bad, but that's the way it is."

In unison with other cultural elder statesmen, he can become rather piously alarmed about the young, as much in response to the stereotypes he sees on the television and reads about in the newspapers as out of his own sense of values—the media would seem to have the ecumenical power of insuring that we all commit the same sins toward each other. Marijuana and such he regards as *déja vu*. "I knew about drugs from the time I was a kid. What do these kids think they are doing by using them that way." He is shocked by the illiterate style in the Underground-Press newspaper (that regularly comes, unsolicited, to his home), worried that too many intelligent people are accepting any well-publicized idea that comes along, alarmed that they are denying any "sense of limits" to proclaim "anything is possible," dismayed by the new dances which, as he sees them on television, strike him as graceless and uninteresting, and afraid that purveyors of revolutionary rhetoric will be done in by their pretensions. "Whenever you speak in the name of a people and you're not truly their representative and they have no way of bending you to their will," he angrily warns, "then there is bound to be treachery and betrayal."

Like many writers before him, Ellison is a political novelist who has used his eminence as a stepping stone into politics, not as a self-proclaimed spokesman (a role he obviously detests) but as an influential adviser and respected participant in important commissions—less as a prophet than as a wise man; in life, as well as in literary style, he would seem to emulate the example of André Malraux. He is haunted by the sense that, as he irreverently puts it, "when writers write about politics, usually they are wrong. The novel at its best demands a sort of complexity of vision which politics doesn't like. Politics has as its goal the exercise of power—political power—and it isn't particularly interested in truth in the way that the novel form demands that the novelist must be." In an offhand moment he once conjectured, with an uneasy laugh, that by refusing the invitation to become a Negro spokesman he spurned the opportunity to make a cool million.

Out of his concern with the arts and society, Ellison has in recent years accepted appointments to cultural committees, such as the National Council on the Arts and the Carnegie Commission on Educational Television, as well as served as vice-president of both the American PEN club and the National Institute of Arts and Letters and trustee of both the Citizens' Committee for Public Television and the John F. Kennedy Center in Cambridge. Partly because he is a Negro who does not espouse racial apocalypses, but primarily because he is a great novelist, Ellison is, of course, an ideal choice whenever integrated boards are selected; so since he hesitates to take time from his novel and tries to distribute his energies as propitiously as possible, he likes to pick among the offers and then function as an aggressive, if not the most dominant, participant in all committees to which he belongs.

For about two thirds of the days of the year, Ellison gets up early, takes breakfast, and goes straight to his desk in the large study adjacent to the living room. He used to walk Tucka every morning; but ever since his wife Fanny resigned her job as Executive Director of the American Medical Center for Burma, she has assumed that task. Before, he would cook himself a hamburger for lunch, but now she brings it to his desk. He likes to work until four, when he will flip on the large-screen television or return some of the calls his wife has answered earlier in the day. He feels the victim of the world's nuisances and lets the world know his feelings; and should he pick up the phone himself, the caller invariably hears a suspicious-sounding "Who is this, please?" He can sometimes be very curt and forbidding; other times, he talks with ease for over an hour. He takes no total vacations and, on trips away, carries notes pertaining mostly to his novel.

Actually, Ellison is such a slave to his work, that interruptions and distractions are as feared as disease. I once inadvertently arrived a little earlier than he expected, and he took an hour to unwind from the invasion of his working time. However, once released from bondage, he feels more uninhibitedly free. Lecture invitations come frequently; but since those fees and the royalties from his two books comprise his entire income, he usually takes only the most lucrative ones and does about a dozen a year. He has taught for brief spells at various universities—Bard, Rutgers, Bennington, and Chicago among them—but has recently given that up, with the prickly advice that serious writers should stay at one school no more than three years. "The first year everybody is very nice to you; the second, they give you a little clerical work to do; but by the third year the demands begin to get all out of hand." As a lecturer, he has the most extraordinary capacity for working out his thoughts without a note, occasionally stumbling but usually hewing to the thread of his argument; and I have seen him talk for hours without a glass of refreshment. In the question periods that follow, he invariably has a complex and extensive answer for every query; if challenged, he is more stubborn than gracious in argument, yet usually persuasive in give and take. More than most people, even most intellectuals, he knows quite thoroughly what he thinks and has perhaps thought everything through to its perceptible end.

Ellison is very much a literary gent, and those he identifies as his closest friends are likewise middle-aged writers—the theologian-literary critic Nathan A. Scott, Albert Murray, Stanley Edgar Hyman, the novelist Robert Penn Warren (who nominated Ellison to the Century Club). He is less a Negro writer than a writer who is Negro, if there is a difference to be discerned; but it is not quite just to say, as William Faulkner did in one of his rare statements on his peers, "So far he has managed to stay away from being first a Negro; he is still first a writer." While Ellison is, like most serious authors, perhaps more ultimately loyal to the great traditions of literature than the parochial demands of his social group (and so perhaps was the classic blues singer), he identifies his own purposes as originating where these two sets of demands intersect: "As I see it," he said in an address at the Library of Congress, early in 1964, "it is through the process of making artistic forms—plays, poems, novels—out of one's experience that one becomes a writer, and it is through this process, this struggle, that the writer helps give meaning to the experience of the group. And it is the process of mastering the discipline, the techniques, the fortitude, the culture, through which this is made possible that constitutes the writer's real experience as *writer*, as artist."

It is this sense of having contemplated much-cogitated problems more honestly, profoundly, and persuasively than anybody else that gives Ellison his particular importance and power nowadays; for to paraphrase T. S. Eliot's famous remark about Henry James, Ellison has a mind so tough that no consciously perceived deceit could violate it. He knows full well that the most profound influence a writer can have comes not from lending his name and reputation to propaganda but from the ultimate quality of his writings—their final relevance and persuasiveness in contradicting current piety, in explaining how inappropriate ideas are responsible for an ineffective policy, in distinguishing illusion from reality, and in telling the complex truth about subjects nearly smothered by simplistic and/or fallacious cliché, and in demonstrating intellectual opportunity and freedom merely by the influence of his ideas. One reason why Ellison has not been able to complete his second novel is that all these distractions demand so much of his attention, as much to flush the ideological junk out of his own head as to speak about corruption in the social world. "I can be free," he once wrote, "only to the extent that I can detect error and grasp the complex reality of my circumstances and work to dominate it through the techniques which are my means of confronting the world."

It is almost as if it were harder today to be a Negro writer than a white, not because Negroes suffer discrimination on the literary scene (indeed, reverse discrimination is more often the rule), but because they have so many more clichés to discard. Also, white readers (and critics) expect their stereotypes of Negro existence to be confirmed, literary agitprop and "militant" rhetoric are tempting, and supposed friends select themselves as tutors on how Negro authors should write, speak, and maneuver. "It knocks me out," Ellison once wrote," "whenever anyone, black or white, tries to tell me—and the white Southerners have no monopoly here—how to become their conception of a 'good Negro.' " It is easier for Negro novelists to betray their professional tasks and be widely praised for their betrayal. Against this background, Ellison's achievement and integrity are the more remarkable. His insistent point is that the truth is invariably more complex than cliché, and like his own novel, the man himself casts a various and unconventional image, at once relevant and yet puzzling, that evades easy definition.

As he resists compromise with current literary and political fashions, so he will not relinquish his rather aristocratic style of commitment, in one sense remaining above the frays, while on the more profound levels, very much participating down inside of them; and as much by refusing the lie as by telling his truth, Ellison has been consistently and deeply *engagé*, as a man, as a Negro writer, as a representative of Western culture. His reputation often seems on the verge of an eclipse, because of the second novel's delay; but art is more leasting than politics or even literary politics and with each passing year, with each rereading, *Invisible Man* confirms its place among the best American fictions of all times and continues to infiltrate the collective consciousness of new generations of readers. Its mythic resonance, its complex human truth, its political relevance, the wit of its prose, and the energy of its narrative all give the novel an indestructible stature, if not the status of "a classic"; and all these qualities as well attest to Ellison's intelligence as a man and his conscientiousness as an artist. So few second novels in literary history have been so long in labor as Ralph Ellison's forthcoming work, and even fewer have been as eagerly, and yet patiently, awaited.

JOHN R. PIERCE:
Organizer of Advanced Knowledge

There is little of importance in the world today which does not depend in some measure on technology, even in its most restricted sense as man's mechanical means to his ends.—SIR ROBERT WATSON-WATT

Dr. John R. Pierce of Bell Labs flipped the name-finding device on his futuristic desk telehpone, dextrously pecked some of the twelve buttons on its face, and then spun his swivel chair toward an adjacent table which supports an oval instrument containing a small television screen. "Is George there?" he asked the cutaway egg in a voice that any acquaintance would instantly recognize. "Yes," replied a secretary; and George C. Dacey's smiling face emerged out of the soupy gray. "How are you, John?" "Fine, thanks, George," he said to an invisible microphone. "I wanted to demonstrate the picturephone to Mr. Kostelanetz here, who is doing a profile of me." "Beautiful," I drawled, enchanted with the machine. "Bye, George," Pierce said, then turned back to me, his eyes all but bursting through his bifocals. "Everyone will want it, you know. We did an experiment with Union Carbide a few months ago, and we had trouble getting the experimental equipment back."

The picturephone is not exactly Pierce's brainchild; but as Executive Director, Research–Communications Sciences Division, Bell Telephone Laboratories, he takes pride in the several crucial contributions he and his associates have made to the problem of how to encode a picture signal over wire. The precise scope of Pierce's job is hard to define; the nature of his contribution being rather indefinite; and his own variousness makes definition more complicated. Although he officially holds an administrative position, he also functions as a participating scientist in several projects within his own turf—a player-coach, so to speak—as well as a scientific consultant to various endeavors around the world; and his record of eighty-three patents, at last count, would on its own make him, as Walter Sullivan of *The New York Times* judged, "one of the nation's leading applied scientists." It is more appropriate to say that Pierce is a master of that spectacular contemporary enterprise—the organization of advanced knowledge, not only his own but that of others—in that peculiarly modern institution of the innovative research laboratory. As the master mind of Echo I, the first successful communications satellite—an organized effort nearly as difficult as the Manhattan project or Explorer I—in addition to other major but less glamorous feats, he is generally placed among the top research laboratory chiefs in America, as well as in the highest echelon of scientific celebrities. Neither a builder nor a tinkerer by nature, Pierce functions primarily as an intellectual force—a scientific frontiersman who is enormously facile, polyliterate, scientifically imaginative, awesomely bright, and scrupulously pragmatic. His quick intelligence evokes immediate respect and establishes personal authority among scientists, as well as making slower minds dizzy and indelibly impressing itself upon everyone Pierce meets. In conversation, he is plain-spoken, honest, and unashamedly direct, perhaps because both pretentious language and disingenuous civility would waste too much time; invariably, he is quick to perceive another man's point and never tardy in formulating his reply.

About five feet ten inches in height, slight but wiry in build, he moves with the expansive gestures of a larger and younger man; nervous in demeanor, he frequently pulls at his nose, folds papers neatly, or runs objects around his fingers;

and even in informal situations, he continually springs up and energetically stalks around with long strides. Balding on top, Pierce lets his gray-blond hair and light-gray sideburns grow slightly long; and on the day we met, he was faintly but perceptibly unshaven. He wore sport slacks, a Harris tweed jacket, green socks, a yellow button-down shirt, a black and yellow print tie, and a chain-style tie clip with a dangling bell-shaped company insignia. He converses in sparkling concise sentences with the impatience of a man who has so much on his mind that he feels impelled to rush out his words, regardless of whether someone else is talking, listening, or not.

Home base for Pierce is the Bell Laboratories in Murray Hill, New Jersey, about an hour west of New York City—a huge complex of monolithic thirties red-brick buildings, with forbidding facades and endless corridors. Between it and the road lies a huge parking lot full of small and shabby cars, in sum creating an image like that outside an average suburban American high school. "One of the most important status symbols," Pierce declares, "is not to be worried about status symbols." The morning I visited, guards directed me to the main reception hall, where I filled out a duplicated form requesting biographical data, as well as my business at the labs, and then received the carbon copy. One of Pierce's secretaries came out to escort me to his office; and I later learned that, as the visitor leaves, his host must accompany him to the exit, where he hands the carbon to the security officer. By reputation, Bell has the best industrial labs in America; and Murray Hill is the largest of several. There are so many people, so much equipment, such looks of optimistic anticipation on everyone's face that I for one left with the awed impression that they could organize men and, more important, advanced knowledge to invent practically anything.

Just as Pierce neither looks nor acts like a major official of a conservative corporation, his own office fits the top-executive stereotype only in its size. His "desk" is a large long table with only one horizontal row of drawers, and its faintly archaic oriental design matches some of the other wooden pieces. Several fluorescent lights on the ceiling, leftover peripheral equipment from an earlier, more primitive picturephone, gives everything an overly white, movie-set appearance. In a corner is a small bookcase with two shelves of books, including most of his own works, and a third of electronic trinkets, which are actually mementos of Pierce's own research. Two long, low cabinets flush against the side and back walls contain miscellaneous papers; atop one is a tape deck, record changer and amplifier; and on the wall opposite his desk is a blackboard.

Although Pierce has received numerous prizes, honorory degrees and awards, including the National Medal of Science in 1963, the most conspicuous is a scroll certifying that he is a bona fide "Kentucky colonel." Like other top executives at the labs, Pierce has his office at the end of a corridor; and the picturephone, I later learned, is a privilege extended only to vice-presidents and executive directors. Right outside the office is a pool of secretaries, and in adjacent offices are Pierce's two associate directors, John Tukey, a legendary mathematician who doubles as chairman of the statistics department at Princeton University, and Rudolph Kompfner, a Vienna-born architect-turned-physicist who collaborated with Pierce a decade ago in his most important contribution to fundamental science, the traveling-wave tube.

"Before we go to lunch, I'd like you to hear the music I composed on the computer," Pierce said, leaning back in his swivel chair, putting his feet on the edge of his desk, and taking charge of our day; and after he made a warning call, we took a long walk to the office of the head of the behavioral sciences department, Max V. Mathews, whose tape machine slides out of a file drawer. The first piece was an eight-part canon in traditional tonality, where the familiar harmonies ironically contrast with the unusual timbres of the electronic sound. A fast mind by nature, a rapid worker by inclination, Pierce composed this piece in a few hours, merely specifiying the available pitches, their appropriate overtones, and the patterns they should follow; the computer actually put the piece together into the form we heard, which in Pierce's opinion turned out better than he expected. His second work consisted of three disconnected but overlapping sounds—the first resembling the pounding waves, the second a bird's chirping, and the third a solo stringed instrument. I asked if he had much musical training? "Two sets of piano lessons, once as a child, once as an adult. It didn't take either time."

"I consider myself a professional composer," Pierce said, striving for an irony which he did not entirely succeed in articulating, "because I receive royalties on a 'Music from Mathematics' record that Decca released a few years ago; it sells about a thousand copies a year. I'm also a professional poet, because I've sold poems on two occasions, and a professional writer, since I have several books in print. I was once a professional artist, because I sold an oil painting for $3.75 in Washington Square in the late thirties." Later that afternoon, he took me to see two neatly crafted, representational oils from that period; they now hang in the Mathematics Common Room of the labs. Among both artists and scientists, he is known to be an enthusiastic but critical supporter of art-technology projects and collaborations.

Over a modest and inexpensive lunch in the lab refectory, we discussed the nature of his work. "It is my role to see that significant research gets done in the division. I must ask if the work now being done is good. Is it relevant to improving communications? How could it be better? Everything follows from those questions." Under his command are six department heads, including Mathews, who in turn oversee about 450 professional scientists. Although he does not know what every individual is doing, he keeps in peripatetic touch with the department heads, who are player-coaches of their own teams, and mostly through them learns about the latest advances in such fields as acoustics and vision, behavioral psychology, radio communications, electronics, space vehicles, and mathematics. Occasionally, the department heads try to organize a formal meeting that everyone will attend; but for some reason or other, this is easier proposed than achieved.

"A fast mind is necessary," a young scientist explained, "if a man expects to apply himself, or supervise others, in several different fields, particularly since in the sciences there is a clear difference between understanding something and missing it entirely." Within the labs Pierce is particularly known for his ability to walk into a scene, quickly discern and appraise what is happening, make an appropriate judgment, perhaps offering a suggestion that will be pursued, and then abruptly depart. "He always seemed to arrive in the middle of one sentence and leave in the middle of another," Calvin Tomkins wrote, "and when he asked someone a technical question and the answer was slow in coming, he usually didn't wait around for it." It is this quality of a "very fast mind" that persuades some of Pierce's peers to judge him "the brightest guy" in a community of professionally bright men. Yet, while his memory for processes and concepts is large, accurate, diversified, and random (rather than serial), he is less likely to remember factual details, such as how an unfamiliar word is spelled or exactly when something important happened.

"The Bell Labs," he continued between attacks on his lunch, "provides what future the Bell system has; that's its function, although the future also depends upon other functions. Nowhere else in the Bell system provides this leadership; important things simply don't originate with the operating companies. Yet research feeds into development; otherwise there would be only technical papers. In general, research never works well unless the rest of the company is working well." In the past two decades research has worked particularly well at Bell Labs; for in addition to Pierce's Echo I (which enabled the development division, in turn, to put up Telstar), out of Murray Hill alone originated the transistor, Claude Shannon's mathematical theory of communication (now called "Information Theory" or "Communication Theory"), the Nike Missile system, much computer hardware, many of the most sophisticated programs (software), and several important laser applications.

Although Pierce did not participate in the invention of the transistor, he was friendly with those who did—the triumvirate of W. H. Brattain, John Bardeen, and W. B. Shockley; and with his professional interest in words, he christened the new invention with the name that stuck. "The thing that has really changed the world recently has been the transistor," he observed, with a degree of pride. "By replacing the vacuum tube, the transistor and, later, the integrated circuit made computers more accessible, large computers more feasible, communications satellites possible; founded a big Japanese industry; made portable radios smaller and more reliable. Solid-state devices will make switching and transmission cheaper; they will give us commercial picturephones in the seventies. One could go on and on. We've not seen the end of the changes yet."

Pierce hardly considers himself an administrative type—"I never took any courses, and it's taken me years to learn how to do it"—yet he feels that the lab chiefs must come out of the ranks of scientists. He needs to know who on his staff has done, is doing, and can do what; for the Echo project alone, he drew upon the talents of over one hundred associates. Not only must he initiate projects and then strategically apportion the labor, but he must respond appropriately to developments from below. "John," attests Mathews, "has a real insight into what might be important—useful and innovative—or not. He gives leadership and direction, yet often communicates alarm." As an administrator, Pierce is a particularly shrewd judge of professional competence; and he often makes decisions more or less like this: "I see the problem, but I can't produce the solution. I know that mathematician A is liable to give me a brilliant answer; but I doubt if he can do it in time. I'd better ask mathematician B, even if I may need to correct him." Nonetheless, the chief must function as one of the Indians. The opening half of a poem entitled "Research," published a decade ago, conveys Pierce's sense of this process:

A year ago I transplanted an idea;
I nurtured it sparingly, lest it grow too wildly;
I refreshed it when it drooped, lest it should perish;

I wondered doubtfully whether it was fruitful,
But now at last, he brings me the result.
It is good, and I call up friends and bosses.
We are happy as children with a longed-for toy.
But it took a year for this; where did the time go?
How could this simple thing have taken so long?
And it was all just dull and difficult,
With no days of crisis, but days of small frustrations,
Days of progress and days of retrogression,
Days of waiting and spoiling and of making,
And finally a day of small success.

The role that he has is not a new one, for the conception is indebted to Thomas A. Edison, who in 1876 founded the first industrial research laboratory of "twenty earnest men," as Edison put it, and soon had as many as forty-four projects going simultaneously and four hundred patents a year. Indeed, to Edison's biographer, Matthew Josephson, this invention factory was a more important innovation than any of Edison's individual technological discoveries. By now every major industrial organization has a research staff and it is normal for a very productive scientist to rise to a laboratory position comparable to Pierce's. His peers among scientific executives include his Cal-Tech classmates Simon Ramo and Dean Wooldridge, both formerly of Hughes Aircraft and now name-partners of TRW; the legendary Edwin Land of Polaroid; William Hewlett of Hewlett-Packard, the instrument makers; Arthur L. Samuel, recently retired from IBM; Alvin M. Weinberg of Oak Ridge National Laboratories; and the late Irving Langmuir of General Electric. The role has become so important, and so much wealth and power come from successfully organized industrial research, that few bright scientists can resist assuming such a position. "No laboratory is successfully administered by non-technical people," Pierce declared with a jab of his fork. "Bell is particularly fortunate in a top management whose backgrounds were technical, rather than legal or sales."

In general, Pierce is a believer in benevolent neglect. "Individuals have ideas, which will prosper in a fruitful environment, where one man's abilities will be supplemented by others. On the other hand, I never heard of a committee having an idea." Yet Bell Labs exists as a multitude of informal committees on hand to organize—elaborate, realize and extend—an individual researcher's idea. One of Pierce's primary jobs as research director is marshaling the available talent for the common effort. "Ten good people," he declares, "can do something that a hundred others would stumble over." Most of the top scientists in his division do research of their own choosing; and more than once, he has defended such team interests as electronic music against objections from "downtown," which is the lab term for the A.T.&T. executives at 195 Broadway. "It's relevant," he asserted, as the dishes were cleared, "to speech synthesis and sound creation, as in the new wholly electronic telephone bell."

On the other hand, Pierce is known to react to dead ends and dead beats rather quickly; and as one colleague put it, "He is a hard-nosed character who works on people to cure them of things they need to be cured of; but it may not be pleasant to the guy being worked on." Pierce's greatest peeve is the federal government, which he finds more wasteful than efficient, more of a nuisance than an aid, particularly since the Communications Satellite Act of 1962 took his pet project, intercontinental communications, away from Bell (sabotaging A.T.&T's huge investment) and gave it to the corporation formed primarily for that purpose, Comsat. He believes in the effectiveness of competition, remarking, "If an enterprise loses the necessity to fight for its place, it won't do much. As Bill Hewlett put it, the government helps American industry mostly by hitting it over the head."

"As I look around me, I see that the thing that is really shaping our lives is technology," Pierce continued over dessert. "It's technology or perish; that's the way the world is going. This is on the whole good, for it gives us a better life. The real innovations come mostly from business enterprises that don't just distribute but actually make new things and services." He took a few swallows and then added, "If you think about it, actually things start in the heads of people—the individual personnel, their experience and associations; out of this come ideas for the technology. Their knowledge goes on, just as the body goes on; and the cells are renewed, as the individuals go in and out. At first, though, everything is in the head."

Technology he regards as the radical force in contemporary society; in contrast, he writes, "The conscious forces of conservatism are government, whose bureaucratic machinery and divisions of power and responsibility are rooted in the past, and that portion of the intellectual community which compares the best of the past with the average of the present and wants somehow to impress the past on a new and unrelated world." When I asked him to elaborate, he continued, opening with his favorite catchall noun, "Things get started in spite of adversity. The only reason we make progress is that something escapes vigilance until it is too late"—the world is more conservative than technology. Pierce later identified his primary non-scientific interest as "contemporary American action," and as he sees it, Bell Labs is where the action is.

Although he has sat on many committees concerned with science and society, including the President's Science Advisory Committee and the American Academy's Commission on the Year 2000, Pierce is so uninterested in partisan politics that, when I asked, he confessed that he had not registered to vote. "How we vote our money every day," he rationalized over coffee, "is more important than politics. Washington does not run the country, as the mind does not run the body. As the world is very complicated and very various, things happen everywhere. What politics I have are terribly mixed. In general, I believe in evolutionary change, rather than revolutions." That is to say, he paradoxically affirms most of the status quo and yet supports, if not initiates, the technological advances that inevitably bring revolutionary social shifts (e.g., the multiple sweeping changes caused by the automobile or the telephone). On more specific issues, Pierce objects to excessive governmental allocation for research and development that private industry could do more cheaply and massive outlays on space and defense programs that hardly benefit the general citizenry. "The only thing that can be said for the government's spending money," he declared tartly, "is that it will get spent." He is also critical of the failure of governments to legislate against unprecedented dangerous technologies. "I'm particularly worried right now that supersonic transport may make parts of the country uninhabitable."

Without warning, he sprang up from the table and stalked to the cash register, leaving me behind to collect my papers; and after several minutes of walking, we were back in his office, where we chatted undisturbed for several hours more. Pierce was born in 1910 in Des Moines, Iowa, and spent his early youth in St. Paul, Minnesota. After his father retired from a small business, his family moved to Long Beach, California, where young Pierce graduated from the public high school. Because he was shy and small, as well as closely protected by an indulgent mother, he started school two years late, making up only one year along the way. He remembers himself as a "shy and badly adjusted kid" who got progressively better at school. At California Institute of Technology he blossomed, taking his B.A. in 1933 and his Ph.D. in 1936, contributing a lot of words to the Cal-Tech publications, and striking lasting relationships with several teachers and fellow students. Like other major American scientists of his and later generations, Pierce received all of his education here; and he blames his incompetence in foreign languages upon the fact that "everyone in technical circles speaks English."

Despite the scarcity of jobs in 1936, Pierce got a good position on the technical staff of Bell Labs in New York City. A Cal-Tech classmate, Jack Morton, who is now a vice-president of the labs, remembers, "He was pretty much as he is now, only a little more subdued. Once let go here, he really showed his oats." In New York, he was first assigned to work on vacuum tubes, "which I knew nothing about, but it proved to be so interesting that it became my field, along with electrons in general." Some of his innovations achieved considerable importance; others were scientifically impressive but useless in practice. Among the former was an instrument invented in 1940 and subsequently christened "The Pierce Gun," which is used to start electron beams. During the war he worked on radar, independently inventing a reflex klystron, which Simon Ramo, then at G.E., had developed earlier; but Pierce's version was adopted as a local amplifier in American microwave receivers.

After the war, he worked intensively in broad-band amplifiers; and he recognized possibilities in the traveling wave tube that Rudolph Kompfner, then an Austrian refugee living in England, had invented. Kompfner came to America; and the two worked together intensively on its development for a decade. Even though the practical results were not at first as useful to the Bell system as they had anticipated (solid-state equipment having made tubes less practical), the traveling wave tube later became important in communications satellites and microwave radio. Regarding this collaboration, Kompfner says, "I invented it; but John discovered it." Pierce concurs, "I'm also good at picking upon the best available ideas." Out of this period came two scientific monographs, *Design of Electric Beams* (1949) and *Traveling Wave Tubes* (1950), which are still regarded as more or less definitive books. (As the mathematician Donald Cohen quipped, "The guys who invented the transistor took Nobel Prizes; the inventors of the traveling wave tube got only patents.") Pierce eventually abandoned work in tubes as further development seemed unlikely ("though the government continues to sponsor research"). "If you get tied to a technology, instead of a function, you're a dead duck; there's no future in being the world's best expert in something of decreasing importance."

Thanks in part to the support of Harald Friis, an eminent scientist-administrator now retired, but chiefly to his high productivity and strong leadership, Pierce rose rapidly within the labs hierarchy, becoming a "supervisor" in 1945 and then a department head in 1947. He became Director of Research in Electrical Communications in 1955 and Executive Director, Research, Communications Principles Division in 1958; and that is more or less the job that, under a different title, he still holds. He does not envision going higher, for that would curb his freedom to follow his interests and separate him from his player-coach connection with step-ahead research-scientists "who want to get on from where people are to someplace else. I like to keep my hand in technical matters." He judges that only in the past fifteen years has he struck a *modus vivendi* with the world around him. "The time came," he explains, "when other people had to adapt to me, instead of my adapting to them."

The primary reason for this radical character's success in a conservative scene, not only in achieving his position but winning his way, is Pierce's reputation for betting on the right horses and, more important, for realizing his dreams (as well as persistently debunking fantasies that cannot be realized within a reasonable time). In the late forties he recognized the significance of both the transistor and information theory and then helped champion them within the company. In the second respect, the communications satellite project, for example, started as a speculation about interplanetary communication that he published as "Don't Write: Telegraph" in a 1952 issue of *Astounding Science Fiction* (in ignorance, he swears, of Arthur C. Clarke's prophetic 1945 essay on "Extraterrestial Relays"); by 1954, for a lecture at Princeton, he had worked out certain conceptual problems regarding the satellite, later publishing his thoughts in the American Rocket Society's journal, *Jet Propulsion*.

As he got into the project, Pierce learned that NASA would propel the satellite into space; so Bell's problem became the communications equipment—the satellite's sender and receiver, and the ground tracking stations. "Rudy Kompfner and I made a list of everything that had to be done and then identified the people in the labs who would do these things in the requisite time—organized the human capabilities." By comparative standards, the project required remarkably few people (and little money), largely because it grew out of the labs, where all the participating scientists had collaborated together before. "The other way to do a large project," Pierce testily observed, "is to set up a fresh organization and then fill it with warm bodies." Since he could hardly realize his dream all by himself, Pierce needed help; and how effective he was at marshaling his assistance is the measure of his genius.

By August 1960, he must have systematically solved all the difficulties and organized all the advanced knowledge as propitiously as possible, for Echo was in the air and destined to function for several years. Furthermore, several competing projects, both corporate and federal, were subsequently scrapped. "Advent," Pierce explains, "was so ambitious it literally didn't get off the ground. Score, which went up earlier, was just a battery-operated satellite that merely played tape recordings. Project Courier was so complicated that it failed. We did just the right amount to take the step ahead." Needless to say, satellites provide more abundant, as well as cheaper, intercontinental communication than underwater cable, in addition to contacts not just between two fixed ends, as in a cable, but among all points within the satellite's range. "John is willing to take the step, and yet be realistic about the difficulties," his colleague Tukey remarked; "if not for the second, he'd end up in a swamp."

Pierce has always been a man of various interests; but his current work is more diversified than any job he has had before. As Bell's universal expert in electrical communication, he often wanders around the Murray Hill lab, exercising his fast mind; and he sometimes goes over to the newer buildings at Holmdel, thirty miles away, where he also has an office. He picks up relevant information through sharp interrogation of his associates; for he avoids technical literature as "a bloody bore." He likes to go home in the evening with, as he puts it, "nothing but my thoughts, but I think of things out of hours."

He now gets to see more of the world outside of Bell; yet he finds that his closest intellectual contacts are still within the home turf. As a scientist, he currently does less work wholly on his own, rationalizing, "I'm not an awfully good experimenter anyway." One old friend, the composer Milton Babbitt, says, "In former days, John was hard to meet; by now, you see him all over the place." Pierce is heavily involved in a gamut of activities; yet a pragmatically tragic sense of life keeps him from becoming too optimistic about his influence. "I marvel that the world works at all, even in such a surprisingly organized way, considering how complicated everything is," he paused for a moment, "and how stupid even the wisest people are. Nobody really knows how the world works any better than you know how your body works or we know how the phone system works; our understanding is really more trivial than profound."

Since he is an articulate scientist and public relations are part of his job, he travels more than he likes, giving lectures, attending professional meetings, participating in symposia on various subjects, and sitting on all sorts of committees. The requests for his writing steadily increase; and though Pierce tries to comply with something fresh whenever possible, certain ideas (mostly good ones) recur over and over again. Able to juggle many matters at once, he does most of this writing by hand in his office, amidst the distractions of a normal working day; and as quick with prose as everything else, he recently composed by hand a five-thousand-word science fiction story in a few hours on successive nights.

Pierce and his second wife Ellen live in a newish, rather gadgetless house off a dead-end road in Warren Township, New Jersey. Their home sits on an acre and a half plot, faces away from the street, and overlooks a brook. As if this were not rustic enough, they also have in Northwestern Massachusetts a small, party-line hut that Mrs. Pierce and a friend constructed with their own hands. Ellen Pierce teaches music at a New Jersey girls' school; and the Pierces occasionally show up at concerts in New York City. His own artistic tastes do not entirely coincide with his creative predilictions. He prefers eighteenth-century music, particularly Handel, to contemporary; nineteenth-century fiction to stylistically more complicated novels; and early twentieth-century painting to more recent work. He also favors the classic English poets, such as Milton and Blake. "T. S. Eliot is very good," he judges, "but not my cup of tea. Then there are James Thomson and James Elroy Flecker, minor English poets whom I discovered while browsing in the Cal-Tech library. Arthur Waley's translations also meant a lot to me." And he pulled out of the cabinet a 1938 issue of *Coronet*, which contained a poem he wrote that was patently indebted to Waley.

When I asked what magazines he read on his own time, Pierce quickly enumerated several journals of science fiction; among his favorite authors were Arthur C. Clarke, Robert Heinlein, Philip K. Dick, and Clifford Simak. He prefers stories that, as he puts it, "turn the world upside down to see what it looks like, rather than get trapped either in style or characterization." Defending his enthusiasm as intellectually valuable, Pierce remarked, "The current trend is to discuss not so much gadgetry as social problems, which turn out to be less political than biological and ecological. The best writers keep making up worlds for one's inspection." A few years ago he broke the habit of reading newspapers regularly. "There is never enough about things you want to know about, or there is too much on things you don't want to know." And the liberal weeklies and monthlies he finds even less interesting. "I get the sense that they aren't about the real world; instead, there is a fantasy their editors have invented for the amusement of their subscribers." He admits to watching more television than he should, favoring such kitsch as *Star Trek*, *Ironside*, and *Perry Mason*, as well as a random movie at bedtime, and news in the morning.

Pierce wrote quite a bit in college—not only poems, stories, and essays for university publications, but a commercial booklet on "How to Build and Fly Gliders" (1929), then a favorite avocation that he has since abandoned as too dangerous. "When I was young, I thought there was something grand about writing and getting things published. I still do." In addition to technical papers and more popular scientific articles, he has contributed numerous science fiction stories under the witty pseudonym "J. J. Coupling," which refers to a complicated process in atomic physics. "Coupling was also the secretary of the mythical Institute for Useless Research that two of my colleagues founded. It didn't succeed, for those were the days before government funding." Early in the forties, Pierce published an essay in *The New Republic* under the pseudonym "John Roberts," derived from his middle name "Robinson." He took pseudonyms at first because everything published under his own name must be approved by the press office at Bell; but he has since discovered that they are more concerned with correcting errors and crediting Bell services than in modifying opinion.

Under "John R. Pierce," he has published an introductory survey, *Electrons, Waves and Messages* (1956), which he has since revised and expanded into three paperbacks, *Electrons and Waves* (1964), *Quantum Electronics* (1966), and *Waves and Messages* (1967), all intended, it would seem, largely for high school students or college freshmen. In collaboration with Edward E. David, Jr., Executive Director of another research division at Murray Hill, Pierce has written two similarly simple books on acoustics, *Man's World of Sound* (1958) and *Waves and the Ear* (1960); and on his own, he did a more adult introduction to the complexities of information theory, *Symbols, Signals and Noise* (1961). In general, his popularizations are not quite as explicit as they should be—lay readers invariably get lost more than once; yet no one else seems able to do better general introductions to these specialized fields. (Also, his endless plugging of Bell products and scientists is tiresome, even if partially justified.) Pierce's best expository writing is in the essays he has published in journals both lay and professional; and some, but not all (and not all the best) of these appeared as *Science, Art and Communication* late in 1968. Though so much of a scientist he is somewhat disdainful of "literature," flattery about his writing, I found, turns him softer than compliments on his science.

The few poems that he has published are mostly concise

observations in roughly metered lines; and their characteristic marks are imaginative metaphors, an overarching concern with scientific work, and a consistently tragic sensibility. "Bosses" opens with the following lines:

Bosses are people up a fantastic tree
Which stretches rootlets into the fertile earth
And bears some fragrant blossoms at its top.
Well-digested achievement upward flows,
And what flows down? Dirty jobs from on high
Sediment themselves among the mucky roots
And interrupt the uneven course of thought.

The middle of the poem becomes more clumsy and perhaps obscure; but the ending is really quite spectacular, even by professional poetic standards:

And things are run to please yet higher bosses,
Or bosses dead, whose muddled thoughts are sacred,
Or The Machine, transcending all the bosses,
With meshed parts, plant men, accountants, et cetera,
such
As grind along how no one understands
Nor dares to interrupt.

Most of his best recent writings have dealt with the future of communications, for here no one is as successful as Pierce at popularizing his own expertise. In brief, he thinks that the picturephone will be commercially available by the early seventies and that its touch-tone dial will also provide access to computers (as indeed does the telephone on Pierce's desk). Long-distance charges will continue to decrease, thanks in part to innovations stemming from the labs; and we will probably be able to send other than oral messages over the home telephone system—texts, pictures, or computer data. Ideally, these media will provide such a viable substitute for personal contact that, to quote his increasingly famous aphorism, "in the future we will be able to live where we like, communicate to work, and travel chiefly for pleasure." Finally, continued miniturization, the process of doing the same work with less material, will make everything smaller and more portable; perhaps there will even be telephones small enough to slip into one's pocket.

Behind all his prognostications about the future, however, lies a tentativeness which reflects Pierce's pervasive awareness that, even barring holocaust, the future is inherently unpredictable. "Most of the changes in the last thirty-five years that have affected my life and the lives of the people around me have been in part due to technological advances that were unforeseen," he told the Commission on the Year 2000. "This makes me feel that predicting the future is rather hopeless, but it does bring up one point. If people would stay as flexible as they have been in adapting to things, and if institutions would be a little more flexible and apply fewer brakes upon things, perhaps we would get into the future less painfully."

The development of the computer, for instance, took him by surprise. "It came on while I was working here," he declared, placing his shoes against the edge of his desk, "and then it dawned on me how revolutionary it was. In technological advance, there aren't any sharp discontinuities; you suddenly wake up after it's all over. Come to think of it, Alexander Graham Bell invented the telephone when he was trying to make a multiplex telegraph." Similarly, he now judges that while he could have predicted that vacuum tubes were not adequate enough for their function and that something with the capability of the transistor needed to be invented, he could never have foreseen the subsequent social impact this Bell invention would have. Perhaps the picturephone, he conjectures, will have a similarly revolutionary influence.

Pierce is very much a company man, almost filially loyal to the mother that has sheltered and nurtured him his entire adult life. Since he was never an obsequious square, he obviously must have passed through some rough moments over the years; but scientific communities, like a research laboratory, are generally more tolerant of eccentricity, let alone arrogance, than corporate bureaucracies. "The scientist," he once wrote, "feels free to judge others only on the narrow basis of their scientific work. Further he will accept judgment on this basis only." In conversation, he elaborated, "Things are less a matter of taste; this instills humility and honesty." What made, or saved, Pierce's career at Bell was, quite simply, the fact that he was clearly a productive scientist in a meritocracy where a young man must produce or perish, as well as a devoted employee of the firm to which he sold all his patents (for one dollar) the day he took the job. Not all the risks he proposed were adopted by the company—a process called time-division electronic switching was judged less feasible than a competitive system; but Pierce has had a reputation for a high rate of success. Only once, as he remembers it, did he consider leaving Bell—for a Stanford professorship in electrical engineering at the end of World War II; and the only kind of position that might tempt him now would involve "more time to think, and maybe a few students." He paused to consider this judgment, then added, "At Bell Labs, the intellectual level and the amount of communication is higher than at any university I know of. To me, these things are more important than money." Indicatively, the dedications to his books go either to his own relatives or his colleagues at Bell (and, sometimes, their wives too).

"By and large," he reflected, tilting back in his chair and looking me straight in the eye, "I don't feel burningly impelled to denounce any part of the Bell system. There are many more things worthy of denunciation. The hierarchy has never failed me. Everything I've set my mind to doing has gotten their support. This I can say flatly. Sometimes it took a little effort, however." A confident stockholder, he is sure that, thanks to the labs, A.T.&T. will continue to grow and that communications will take an ever larger percentage of the Gross National Product; for both Bell and Pierce agree upon two things—profit and technological advance come through the effective organization of advanced knowledge, and power is ultimately all in the head.

Pierce is such an articulated personality, as well as an honest man, that his faults are as conspicuous as his virtues. He is, to be blunt, imperviously compulsive, as well as compulsively impervious. He butts into conversations, not only because he has the authority of rank, but also because once he makes a connection in his head, the circuit must be immediately completed before it heats up. "Since you asked about my most recent patent," he exclaimed, leaping up from his desk and striding to the blackboard, "now you're stuck, though you may not understand it." I discerned only the subject—transmission of radio signals through microwave, "above ten gigahertz" frequencies, particularly as this related to the possibility of more pervasive mobile telephony. "We are running out of frequencies for radio communication at a time when old and new demands for communication are growing rapidly." He scarcely stopped to ascertain my knowledge or intelligence; so while some of his explanations were accessible, others flew blithely past. Certain answers to questions I asked about people he has known for years made me wonder if he understood them at all. Nonetheless, Pierce has sufficient empathy to be a shrewd judge of scientific competence; and he really can become sentimental about certain individuals in his past, particularly teachers and colleagues.

His abrupt manner, which old friends say is now less pronounced than it was two decades ago, strikes people as either charming or repelling, depending upon their taste. Within a professional community that worships mental speed, Pierce is admired for disregarding pleasantries; yet he so often leaves people hanging that they feel they get short shrift. When I telephoned very early one morning to say that I was too ill to come down that day, he heard only my name and asked, "Where are you now?" and within fifteen seconds our conversation was over. He is so patently a tyrant within his own kingdom that when his colleagues refuse to acknowledge his overbearing demeanor one becomes more suspicious than reassured; surely more than one promising scientist must have reacted negatively and gone elsewhere. Some of his professional reports are so notorious for mixing dogmatic assertions with insufficient evidence that the most charitable explanation holds that his fast mind lacked the patience to document its sweeping generalizations. ("I agilely soar to conclusions" runs a line in one of his poems.)

A basically shy person who rather late in life assumed a position that required sociability, Pierce is erratic, if not slightly uncomfortable, in human relations; and as a man of exaggerated expressions, he is on informal occasions either turned-on full throttle or quietly switched-off, very engaged or clearly detached, devilishly cruel or marvelously funny. When I wrote to report that the magazine originally commissioning this profile rejected it on the grounds that he was insufficiently newsy, Pierce replied promptly and curtly, "Sorry the piece fell through—and just when I had decided that in order to be newsy I would denounce research as a sure cure, which I will shortly do in the Klopsteg Lecture at Northwestern, and then commit seppuku in the offices of the NSF. I may as well drop the latter project." In general, he is more respected than beloved, entertaining than lovable, brilliant than wise; yet he is so abundantly bright and sincerely honest that I, like others, liked him in spite of himself.

MARSHALL McLUHAN:
High Priest of the Electronic Village

The technological, political and military situation changes so rapidly that we must make a conscious and vigorous effort to keep our conceptual, doctrinal and linguistic framework up to the needs of the moment.—HERMAN KAHN

Though among the most acknowledged and controversial of contemporary intellectuals, Marshall McLuhan displays few of the accouterments of which oracles are usually composed. Tall, thin, middle-aged, clean-shaven and graying, he has a face of such negligible individual character that it is difficult to surmise what his personality might be or even remember exactly what he looks like; different pictures of him rarely seem to capture the same man. By trade, he is a Professor of English at St. Michael's College, the Catholic unit of the University of Toronto; and except for a graduate seminar in "Communication," the courses he has taught over the years there are the standard fare of Mod. Lit. and Crit. When I visited the university, early in 1966, he had hardly become a celebrity on his home ground; for only a few of his students seemed familiar with the same books that by that time had excited so many outside Toronto. Although he had recently purchased several new suits, his dress scarcely distinguished him from his university colleagues; and the accent of his speech owes more to the network of American academia than any particular region. His house and family car pretty much resemble all the others on his Toronto block. His book-lined office in an aged, nondescript, rickety building on the edge of the St. Michael's campus is full of professorial disarray; what makes it different from the next scholar's shop is the presence, in a cubicle surrounded by floor-to-ceiling books on three sides, of a handsome gray-haired secretary who processes his mail, types his huge correspondence with the outside world, superintends his files, and intercepts an endless number of telephone calls with all those requests to lecture, to write, to sympose, to come to this occasion and that, to submit to interviews, and to correct the mistakes of previous interviewers.

Professor Herbert (rarely used) Marshall McLuhan has communicated to the larger world primarily by book; and his two major works, *The Gutenberg Galaxy* (1962) and *Understanding Media* (1964), both on the impact of media of communications, have won the most astonishing variety of admirers. Several major American corporations have invited him to address their top executives; so have the publishers of America's largest magazines, the heads of the electronic media, and the college teachers of the Modern Language Association, among diverse other organizations. By the summer of 1965, the composer John Cage, among other eminences, had made a pilgrimage to Toronto especially to dialogue with McLuhan; and the following year William Jovanovich, president of Harcourt, Brace & World, made the trip to enlist McLuhan as his co-author of a study of *The Future of the Book*. The eminent young pianist and composer Glenn Gould, likewise a Toronto resident, frequently telephones for conversation, and his own recent articles and statements reveal McLuhan's influence. At Joan Baez's recently formed Institute for the Study of Non-Violence, the favorite reading is, reportedly, "Gandhi, Thoreau, McLuhan, etc." And so on and so on. Writing in *The New Yorker*, the art critic Harold Rosenberg attested that *Media* "takes its place in that wide channel of cultural criticism of the twentieth century that includes writers like T. S. Eliot, Oswald

Spengler, D. H. Lawrence, F. R. Leavis, David Riesman and Hannah Arendt." Moreover, the Toronto oracle boomed twice in the public media, receiving spates of attention both late in 1965 and early in 1967, as well as continual interest ever since; and the two major books alone have enough sustenance to keep all kinds of minds preoccupied for decades.

What distinguishes McLuhan from other cultural prophets of recent years is the diversity of enthusiastic audiences his ideas have attracted. Not only do several notable advertising executives and businessmen enormously admire his work, but so do scholars, artists, educators, architects, publishers, and critics, in addition to innumerable students (perhaps because his books define a reality perceived by them and yet invisible to their teachers and parents). As McLuhan draws from knowledge accumulated in a multitude of disciplines, so he creates an intellectual mix resonant and various enough to influence practitioners in numerous fields. As the great books were scarcely advertised at first and even *Media* went generally unnoticed in the major reviewing journals, the enthusiastic response inevitably arose out of cracks in the pavement. Readers of all kinds must have been impressed by McLuhan, as well as, more important, recommending his work to all kinds of friends; to one book store manager in New York, the books' buyers were "people we've never seen before." Since McLuhan uses many words in very special ways and even popularizes several epigrams of his own creation—the medium is the message, for instance, as well as the massage—the diversified impact of his work suggests that conversation across various specialties, usually hampered by exclusive jargons, may soon be conducted in the common tongue of McLuhanese.

McLuhan's popular success is nothing but surprising for another reason, which is that his books contain little of the slick stuff of which best-selling sociology is usually made. As anyone who opens the covers instantly discovers, *Media* and *Galaxy* are horrendously difficult to read—clumsily written, frequently contradictory, oddly organized, and overlaid with their author's peculiar jargon. McLuhan reports that one of *Media's* editors, in dismay, told him, "Seventy-five per cent of your material is new. A successful book cannot afford to be more than ten per cent new." Even experienced readers, such as Ph.D.'s and literary critics, confess that they find McLuhan hard to read, although persistent effort is usually rewarded. One explanation of his stylistic sloppiness and self-indulgence is that everything he writes actually originates as dictation, either to his secretary or to his wife; and he is reluctant to rewrite, because, he explains, "I tend to add, and the whole thing gets out of hand." Moreover, some of his insights are so original than they evade immediate comprehension; indeed, some paragraphs may forever evade clarification. "Most clear writing is a sign that there is no exploration going on," McLuhan rationalizes. "Clear prose indicates the absence of thought."

The basic themes of these books seem impenetrable at first, because the concepts are often as unfamiliar as the language; but on second (or maybe third) tries, the ideas are really quite accessible. In explaining the evolution of human history, McLuhan espouses a position one can only call "technological determinism." That is, whereas Karl Marx and other economic determinists suggest that the economic organization of a society shapes every important aspect of its life, McLuhan believes that crucial technological inventions are the primary influence. To justify his historiographical method McLuhan continually refers, for instance, to the work of the academic historian Lynn White, Jr., whose *Medieval Technology and Social Change* (1962) contends that the three innovations of the stirrup, the nailed horseshoe, and the horse collar created the Middle Ages. With the stirrup, the soldier could carry heavy armor and mount a charger; the horseshoe and harness brought more efficient tilling of the land and, thus, the feudal system of organized agriculture, which, in turn, helped pay for the soldier's more extensive armaments.

Developing this insight into technology's crucial influence, McLuhan focuses upon the role of media of communication, as he espouses the principle of informational technological determinism. This thesis holds that the chief technology of communication in a society has a determining effect on everything important in that society—not only politics and economics, but also the ways in which the representative individual's mind perceives and explains his experience. The corollary of this thesis is that a shift in informational media initiates decided and widespread social and psychological changes. In *The Gutenberg Galaxy*, he suggests that the invention of movable type crucially shaped the culture of Western Europe from 1500 to 1900. For one thing, the mass production of mechanical print encouraged nationalism by allowing wider and more uniform spread of printed materials than was possible with handwritten messages. For another, the linear forms of print influenced music to repudiate the structure of repetition, as in Gregorian chants, for that of linear development as in a classical symphony. Also, print radically reshaped the sensibility of Western man; for whereas the medieval man saw experience as individual entities—as a collection of separate segments—and assimilated his environment primarily by ear, representative man in the Renaissance emphasized the eye and saw life as he saw print—as a continuity, often with causal relationships. McLuhan even regards print as making Protestantism possible, because the printed book, by enabling people to think in isolation, encouraged individual revelation. Finally, "All forms of mechanization emerge from movable type, for type is the prototype of all machines."

In *Understanding Media*, the sequel to *Galaxy*, McLuhan suggests that electronic technologies of communication—telegraph, radio, television, movies, telephones, computers—are similarly reshaping civilization and sensibility in the twentieth century. Whereas print-age man visually perceived one thing at a time in consecutive sequence—like a line of type— contemporary man experiences numerous forces of communication simultaneously, sometimes through more than one of his senses. Contrast, for example, the way most of us read a book with how we look at a contemporary newspaper (a product of *wire* services). With the latter, we do not start one story, read it through and then begin another. Rather, we shift our eyes across the pages, assimilating a discontinuous collection of headlines, subheadlines, lead paragraphs, and pictures. "People don't actually read newspapers," McLuhan declares. "They get into them every morning like a hot bath." The form of a television news show is similarly segmented in form, rather than sequential—a series of moments, rather than a narrative exposition of events; modern movies like Federico Fellini's are more disconnected than nineteenth-century novels, or novelistic films like *High Noon*. Similarly, the structure of contemporary music, dance, and literature is more discontinuous than earlier works in those arts—as Stravinsky is to Tschaikovsky, so the Beatles's music is to Frank Sinatra's; as the watusi and frug are to the waltz, so Merce Cunningham and modernist dance are to traditional narrative ballet.

Furthermore, the electronic media initiate sweeping changes in the distribution of sensory awareness—in what McLuhan calls the "sensory ratios." A painting or a book strikes us through only one sense, the visual; both motion pictures and television, in contrast, hit us not only through the eye, but also the ear. The new media envelop us, asking us to participate, "moving us out of the age of the visual into the age of the aural and tactile." McLuhan believes that such a multisensory existence is bringing a return to the primitive man's emphasis upon the sense of touch, which he considers the primary sense, "because it consists of a meeting of the senses"; and not only is the television image, projected from behind the screen, more tactual than the cinema image, but color television, to McLuhan's analysis, achieves greater tactility than black-and-white. Politically, he sees the new media as transforming the world into "a global village," where all ends of the earth are in immediate touch with one another, as well as fostering a "retribalization" of human life. "Any highway eatery with its TV set, newspaper and magazine is as cosmopolitan as New York or Paris."

In his grand scheme of human history, McLuhan sees four great stages, each defined by the predominace of a particular informational technology:

(1) totally oral, preliterate tribalism; (2) the codification by

script that developed after Homer in ancient Greece and lasted two thousand years; (3) the age of print, roughly from 1500 to 1900; and (4) the age of electronic media, from 1900 to the present. This is, roughly, a dialectical scheme in which the first two eras are the thesis, the period of print the antithesis, and the current electronic age the synthesis that rehearses much of preprint culture; and for his remarks about the present and future, McLuhan continually draws upon traits characteristic of preprint, if not preliterate, peoples. This scheme of historical development is, as a dialectical form, analogous to classic Marxism; and like Marx, whose *Capital* portrays the emergence of capitalism, McLuhan writes most authoritatively not about the impending utopia, but the transition from the thesis to the antithesis—the emergence of the culture of print. In one of the more perspicacious negative critiques, the Canadian writer Gerald Taaffe detects a "medievalist, Catholic, corporatist bias. . . . It is in the Middle Ages that he [McLuhan] finds his spiritual home. He leaps from the time of St. Thomas Aquinas to the electronic age as though the intervening centuries were nothing but an unpleasant dream." McLuhan, in one of his rare evaluative cultural statements, confirmed this inference, when he remarked in a symposium, "Now we are moving back to what I would like to think perhaps a better orientation."

One of the presuppositions informing McLuhan's thought holds that art ultimately comes out of art—which is to say that just as artists are more profoundly influenced by the art that they see than by their extrinsic experience, so new ideas about man and his environment evolve out of previous ideas, as well as, of course, drawing freshly upon new developments in human experience. What is true for others is applicable to McLuhan himself; for, in retrospect, his major ideas are not as original as they may at first have appeared to many readers. "Most of what I have to say is secondhand," McLuhan once admitted, with needless modesty, "gathered however from esoteric sources." Among these founts he credits such works as Lynn White's book on the Middle Ages; Harold Innis's *The Bias of Communication* (1951), which relentlessly illustrates the determining influence of informational technology; E. H. Gombrich's *Art and Illusion* (1960), a particularly sophisticated exposition of the thesis that art ultimately comes out of art; Sigfried Giedion's *Space, Time and Architecture* (1941), a study of the radically different character of the contemporary sensibility; Dorothy Lee's *Freedom and Culture* (1959), which identifies the line as the organizing principle of the West; E. S. Carpenter's *Eskimo* (1959), which sketches the sensory awareness of preliterate peoples; H. J. Chaytor's *From Script to Print* (1945) and Eric A. Havelock's *Preface to Plato* (1963), which both subtly explore the many dimensions of a historical, cultural transition; and Laszlo Moholy-Nagy's *Vision in Motion* (1947), which suggests that particularly contemporary forms of expression involve the spectator in kinetic, multisensory experiences. From all these sources, as well as many others, McLuhan fashioned his own thought, which in turn has had and will have an immense impact on the thinking of others.

McLuhan's discussions of the individual electronic media move far beyond the previous comments of serious critics, most of whom complain about their content, generally arguing that if television, for instance, had more intelligent treatments of more intelligent subjects, its contribution to culture would be greater. McLuhan proposes that, instead, we think more about the character and form of the new media; and pursuing this bias, he offers an epigram—"The medium is the message"—which means several things. The phrase first suggests that each medium develops an audience of people whose love for that medium is greater than their concern for its content. That is, the TV medium itself becomes the prime interest in watching television; for just as some people like to read for the joy of experiencing print and a few find great pleasure in talking to just anybody over the telephone, so others like television primarily for its mixture of kinetic screen and relevant sound. Second, the "message" of a particular medium includes everything in Western culture that that medium has influenced. "The message of the movie medium is that of transition from linear connections to configurations." Third, the aphorism suggests that the medium itself—its intrinsic form—shapes its limitations and possibilities for the communication of content. One medium is better than another at evoking a certain experience. American football, for example, is invariably better on television than on radio or in a newspaper column; a bad football game on television is usually more interesting than a great game on radio (unless one has a sentimental interest in the fortunes of a particular team). Most United Nations hearings, in contrast, are less boring in the newspaper than on television. McLuhan's point is that each medium seems to possess a hidden taste mechanism which encourages some styles, subjects, and experiences while it rejects others.

To characterize these mechanisms, he devises the approximate categories of "hot" and "cool," which roughly analyze three crucial dimensions—the character of a communications instrument, the quality of the sensory experience it communicates, and its interaction with human response. A "hot" medium or experience has a "high definition" or a highly individualized character, as well as a high fidelity to the original model and a considerable amount of detailed information. "Cool" is low in definition, fidelity, and information; thus, it requires that the audience participate to complete the communication. McLuhan's own examples help clarify the distinction. "A cartoon is 'low' definition, simply because very little information is provided." Radio is usually a hot medium; print, photography, film and paintings essentially are hot media. "Any hot medium allows for less participating than a cool one, as a lecture makes for less participation than a seminar, and a book for less than a dialogue." Television is cooler than movies, because a rough image of patterned dots, like that of cartoons, demands more intensive, participatory viewing than the photographic pictures of film. These unfortunately christened terms "hot" and "cool" McLuhan also applies to experiences and people; and unifying the multiple threads of his distinction, he suggests that while a hot medium favors a performer possessed of a strongly individualized presence, cool media prefer the nonchalant, "cooler" people. Therefore, just as the radio medium needs a voice of highly idiosyncratic that is instantly recognizable—think of Jean Shepherd or Westbrook Van Voorhees —television favors people of a definition so low that they appear positively ordinary; that perhaps explains why bland personalities, such as Ed Sullivan and Johnny Carson, are more successful on television. "It was no accident that Senator Joseph McCarthy lasted such a very short time when he switched to TV," McLuhan wrote in *Media*. "TV is a cool medium. It rejects hot figures such as Senator McCarthy and people from the hot media. Had TV occurred on a large scale during Hitler's reign, he would have vanished quickly." More recently, he added, "Anyone who looks as if he *wants* to be elected had best stay off TV. If Pierre Trudeau is a great TV image in politics, it is because he is indifferent to political power."

In his remarks on common phenomena, McLuhan possesses the most astonishing capacity to perceive what remains hidden from others—literally, to make the invisible visible. "As a rule," he says, "I always look for what others ignore," and *Media*, for instance, contains, among other things, some remarkably stimulating remarks on less considered modes of communication—telephones, typewriters, articulated spaces, clothing, games, clocks, and so on—while McLuhan's unusual criticisms continually suggest that we ought to rethink familiar concepts and problems. Much of his intellectual originality stems from a distinctly North American willingness to push his perceptions beyond conventional bounds into an unkown region where notions and perceptions seem "mad" before they are recognized as true. His ideas are neither as neatly nor as modestly presented as this summary might suggest, for McLuhan believes more in probing and exaggerating—"making discoveries"—than in offering final definitions, as well as raising the current critical discourse to a higher level of insight and subtlety. For this reason, he will in public conversation rarely defend any of his statements as absolute truths, although he will explain how he developed them. "I don't agree or disagree with anything I say myself" is his characteristic rationale. "For me," says an old friend, "the closest parallel to Marshall is Ezra Pound—a genius with words and phrases and insights, a ceaseless fox, though no hedgehog—jumping from point to point, taking this from here and that from there, throwing away huge ideas in pithy phrases, contradicting himself without concern, missing the daily trivia but identifying the bigger forces."

In conversation or on a stage, McLuhan evokes the impression of conjuring insights, largely because in drawing ideas from one realm and applying them to another, he makes spectacular, unfamiliar connections in propelling miscellaneous information through several comprehensive sieves of interpretative schemata, he produces a huge number of provocative remarks. Both these methods for producing insight demand a memory as prodigious as his curiosity, as well as an extraordinary shuffling mechanism in his head. More interested in similarities than differences, he frequently escalates a tenuous analogy into a grandiose generalization; and since "I use language as a probe," he particularly relishes making his points, if not conjuring a truth, through a pun: "When a thing is current, it creates currency." Or, "Type is the prototype. . . ." Or, "The medium is a massage; it works us over." He loves comic aphorisms, such as, "Money is the poor man's credit card." Some perceptions are considerably more tenable than others—indeed, many are patently ridiculous—and nearly all of his original propositions are arguable; so his books require the participation of each reader to separate what is wheat for him from the chaff. "Concepts," McLuhan admits, "are provisional affairs for apprehending reality; their value is in the grip they provide." In McLuhanese, his books offer a cool experience in a hot medium, even though McLuhan himself is indubitably an all but inflammatory presence. A reader's typical scorecard for *Understanding Media* might show that about one half is brilliant insight; one fourth, suggestive hypothesis; one fourth, nonsense. Given the book's purposes and originality, these are hardly discreditable percentages; for the reader, the price of insight is usually a dose of sludge. "If a few details here and there are wacky," the oracle rationalizes, "it doesn't matter a hoot."

All his books are unconventionally written, if not audaciously inventive in structure; for not only does McLuhan favor a particular use of esoteric words and a frustratingly casual attitude toward familiar ones, but he also eschews the traditional English professor's expository style—introduction, development, elaboration, and conclusion. Instead, McLuhan's books imitate the segmented structure of the modern media, as he tends to make a series of analytic statements, none of which become an explicitly encompassing thesis, though all of them approach the same body of phenomena from different angles or examples. These become a succession of exegetical glosses on a mysterious scriptural text, which is how McLuhan analogously regards the new electronic world—a definitive but mysterious reality. "I accept media," he once remarked in passing, "as I accept cosmos." He compiles his books with chapters of equal weight, set in a semiarbitrary order; and these embellish the major themes through similar insights, rather than develop an argument. He forms these chapters through a similarily discontinuous arrangement of paragraphs; for typically they start with an oblique example, conclude on a tangent, and represent a collection of glosses. Although a paragraph may often have a distinct topic sentence, its real point is usually buried in the text. In short, rather than straightforwardly set forth his points, McLuhan weaves a mosaic of meaning, where everything contributes, in unequal measure, toward shaping his themes.

This means that one should not necessarily read his books from start to finish—the archaic habit of print-man. True, the preface and first chapter of *The Mechanical Bride* (1951), an earlier work, really do *introduce* the themes and methods of the book; but beyond that, the chapters can be read in any order. The real introduction to *The Gutenberg Galaxy* is the final chapter, called "The Galaxy Reconfigured"; even McLuhan advises readers to start there; and the book itself is all but a galaxy of extensive printed quotations. With *Media,* the introduction and the first two chapters form the most propitious starting point; thereafter, the reader is pretty much free to wander as he will, perhaps to the commentaries on more familiar territory, such as radio, television, and automation.

Likewise, there is no need to read everything to understand these books. "One can stop anywhere after the first few sentences and have the full message, if one is prepared to 'dig' it," McLuhan once wrote of non-Western scriptural literature; but the remark is just as applicable to his own books. Similarly, McLuhan does not believe that his works have only one final meaning; for as a prober himself, he would encourage readers to let these books stimulate their own thinking on these matters. "My book," he declares, "is not a package but part of the dialogue, part of the conversation." Indeed, he evaluates other books less by how definitively they treat their subjects—the academic standard—than by how much thought they stimulate; therefore, a book may be wrong but great. (By his own standards, needless to say perhaps, *Media* is a masterpiece.) The point is that print-man, with his masochistic preference for, if not dependence upon, the successiveness of print (as well as a penchant for factual accuracy), will be a less adept reader of McLuhanese than the media-man with his awareness of configurations; these books are mosaics, rather than arguments. For that reason, perhaps the best way to coolly immerse oneself in McLuhan's hot thought would involve getting two paperback copies, cutting out all the pages and then pasting them around the walls and on the ceiling.

A continual preoccupation of McLuhan's explorations is the great modern question of whether technology is beneficial to man. Many intellectuals have argued, on the one hand, that technology stifles the blood of life by dehumanizing the spirit and cutting existence off from nature; more materialistic thinkers, on the other hand, defend the machine for easing man's burden's and providing desirable commodities at a reasonable price. McLuhan cuts across this dichotomous argument by exploring the psychological and philosophical effects of technology; and his comments stem primarily from pursuing Ralph Waldo Emerson's idea that "all the tools and engines on earth are only extensions of man's limbs and senses." That is, where a shovel is functionally an extension of the hand, the telephone is an extension of the ear (and the voice), and television extends our eyes and ears to a distant place as well as makes all current events both instantaneous and immediate. Our eyes and ears were live participants at the Kennedy funerals, although our bodies stayed at home. "Today, after more than a century of electric technology, we have extended our central nervous system itself, in a global embrace, abolishing both time and space as far as the planet is concerned." As extensions, the new media offer both possibility and threat; for while they lengthen man's reach into his existence, they can also extend society's reach into him, for both exploitation and control. To deflect this latter possibility, McLuhan insists that every man should know as much about the media as possible. "By knowing how technology shapes our environment, we can transcend its absolutely determining power," he says. "Actually, rather than a 'technological determinist,' it would be more accurate to say, as regards the future, that I am an 'organic autonomist.' My entire concern is to overcome the determination that results from people trying to ignore what is going on. Far from regarding technological change is inevitable, I insist that if we understand its components we can turn it off any time we choose. Short of turning it off, there are lots of moderate controls conceivable." In stressing the importance of knowledge and man's capacity to shape his environment to his needs, McLuhan is trenchantly a humanist. To Harold Rosenberg, the books themselves represent "a concrete testimonial (illuminating, as modern art illuminates, through disassociation and regrouping) to the belief that man is certain to find his footing in the new world he is in the process of creating."

Indeed, McLuhan's thought implies the need for many radical reforms in the institutions of society, particularly those concerned with education; for one of his more persuasive ideas holds that contemporary man is not fully "literate" if reading constitutes his sole input. "You must be literate in umpteen media to be really 'literate' nowadays." Education, he suggests, should abandon its commitment to print—merely a focusing of the visual sense—to cultivate the "total senorium" of man by teaching each of us how to appreciate all the available informational media, as well as human experience, with all five cylinders rather than only one. (On the other hand, McLuhan elsewhere declares that "to resist TV, one must acquire the antidote of related media like print.") Beyond that, he regards the I.Q. test as outmoded; for while it measures only visually perceived knowledge, visually rehashed, the "knowledge" of children today is multisensory. "Postliterate does not mean illiterate," writes Rev. John Culkin, S. J., director of the Communications Center at Fordham University and a veteran propagator of multimedia education. "It rather describes the new social environment within which print will interact with a great variety of communications media." Pursuing a more radical alternative, McLuhan conjectures that since the world is accumulating so much data, most of which can be neatly classified and filed away, schools should teach not facts and subjects but conceptual approaches (essentially, "pattern recognition") of various fields. The university we have known, McLuhan predicts, will soon turn obsolescent; for the environment has become so informationally rich that "the planet itself is becoming a campus."

These new ideas have hardly begun to have their decisive impact; but here and there are conspicuous signs of McLuhan's influence. One one level, the characters of Walt Kelley's Pogo comic strip were discussing the media all through 1965. On another, scholars subscribing to McLuhan's hypotheses are showing in detail how various communications media have influenced the cultures and cultural artifacts of their respective times. The literary critic Hugh Kenner, a former student of McLuhan, writes in *The Stoic Comedians* (1962) about the complementary relationship between the book medium and the writings of Gustave Flaubert, James Joyce, and Samuel Beckett. Going back into Western history, the eminent literary scholar Walter J. Ong, S. J., a friend of McLuhan for over thirty years, has shown in *Ramus: Method, and the Decay of Dialogue* (1958) how the sixteenth-century philosopher Petrus Ramus confronted the new environment created by print; and the fugitive essays that Father Ong collected into his recent book,

In the Human Grain (1967), parallel and complement McLuhan's concerns. Like all radical methods of historiography, McLuhan's explanatory principles attempt to illuminate relations and phenomena that were invisible to previous researchers; and the info-tech approach promises to be particularly useful in explaining such clearly discernible changes in the Western sensibility as the transitions from representational to abstract art, from anonymous art to personalized work, from circular or oracular structures to narrative organization, from consonant to dissonant music, from linear order to discontinuous and mosaic forms. In documenting changes in man's perception of the structure of his experience, McLuhan complements a primary concern of academic art history of the past century; however, along with the adventurous Yale art historian George Kubler in *The Shape of Time* (1962), McLuhan takes the intellectual leap of regarding all society as being like a work of art whose shapes and structures have changed discernibly over the centuries, as well as within our own lifetimes. Indeed, from the architectural historian Sigfried Giedion, in his *Mechanization Takes Command* (1948), McLuhan snitched the overarching concept of "Anonymous History," which, he writes, "accepts the entire world as an organized happening that is charged with luminous and exciting messages." Since McLuhan's books will surely influence not only the content of much subsequent scholarship but also its organizing form, one might also expect more books that weave a mosaic of meaning, like Norman O. Brown's *Love's Body* (1966), rather than expounding a continuous argument.

McLuhan's ideas provide, for one thing, a persuasive analysis of what Joseph Frank and others have identified as a tendency in contemporary literature—spatial form. In contrast to post-Renaissance literature, which like print itself is sequential in organizing structure (think of how the action in a nineteenth-century novel flows from one event to another), the classics of modern writing embody, as we noted before, discontinuous or "spatial" form. That is, the organizing principles of, say, James Joyce's *Ulysses*, T. S. Eliot's *The Waste Land*, and

Samuel Beckett's *How It Is*, relate less to sequence (time) than to discontinuous configurations or collage (space). In this respect, McLuhan notes that the forms of contemporary literature are closer to the movies, television, and radio—the electronic media—than to the old technology of print; furthermore, his analysis of the postelectronic sensibility implies that, whereas older readers tend to recompose a disjointed narrative to reestablish the "real" chronology (remember all those plot summaries to William Faulkner's *The Sound and the Fury*), younger readers more deeply biased by the new media tend to accept discontinuous form on its own terms. In his own books and literary essays, McLuhan estimates what impact the new communications media may have had on Henry James's late novels (the typewriter), T. S. Eliot's poetry (radio), John Dos Passos' fiction (film), William Burroughs's novels (television), and James Joyce's *Finnegans Wake* (all the media). Although one fears that informational technological determinism, like economic and sociological determinism before it, will inevitably produce its own monomaniacal excesses, the method nonetheless promises to inform much perceptive and persuasive literary and historical scholarship.

Beyond that, McLuhan's thesis that the most appropriate contemporary forms are discontinuous and multisensory has provided a cultural rationale for various kinds of new artistic and entertainment ventures, such as the theater of mixed means and multimedia discotheques. Several New York mixed-media creators who employ the gamut of artistic materials—film and tape technologies, as well as lights, live performers, and amplification systems—once issued a manifesto that proclaimed, "The writings of Marshall McLuhan have provided a socio-philosophical basis for this new audio-visual 'movement.'" In the spring of 1965, a group of professors at the University of British Columbia sponsored a McLuhan festival which converted an armory into an activated "environment" full of sounds, sights and tactile sensations ("a sculptured wall"). Hardly encouraging the growing cult, McLuhan did not give the artists permission to use his name (they mailed an apology), and he did not attend the Vancouver festival. "Temperamentally, I'm a stodgy conservative," he once told a reporter. "If there are going to be McLuhanites, you can be sure that I'm not going to be one of them."

Particularly prominent among the artistic McLuhanites are the members of USCO, a collective of artists operating out of an abandoned church in Garnerville, New York, about a hour's ride north of New York City. In 1960, Gerd Stern, the eldest of the group, read an early draft of *Understanding Media* in the form of a report McLuhan had submitted the year before to the National Association of Educational Broadcasters. In the years that followed, USCO pioneered in the development of multimedia environmental arts, creating numerous mixes of lights, noise, films, slides, music, odors, and so on within a variety of closed spaces (ranging from discotheques to museums) in which attention is not focused, as by books and even conventional films, but diffusely diverted and yet endlessly intimidated. In addition to a rationale for why such multisensory chaotic art should be especially appropriate for our time, USCO draws from McLuhan a commitment to corporate activity and individual anonymity, for both argue that, in contrast to the post-Renaissance artistic tradition of individualized expression, art in the electronic future will be as anonymous and collective in authorship as the preprint art of icons. On two occasions, McLuhan has joined USCO in a mixed-means presentation, speaking both before and after the performance.

One of McLuhan's closest associates, Harley Parker, a gray-bearded artist in his fifties, has constructed several revolutionary museum displays that patently reveal his friend's influence. When he was the director of design at the Royal Ontario Museum (of natural history) in Toronto, Parker argued that in contrast to the traditional naturalists' museum, which presents discrete objects that the spectator visually observes, the museum of the future must re-create an integral environment in its multisensory richness. "Museums," he asserts, "must be concerned not with data but experiences, because they deal not with scholars but the public; rather than present artifacts, they must create an environment to bring a spectator into the scene. If you put an African fetish figure in a rectangular case, how can you expect people to know something about it? It's a clash of spaces, objects from different cultural environments. It's a case of museum fatigue." In a 1967 exhibition of fossils, he attempted to simulate, through four of the five major senses, what a paleontologist does. The exhibit contained the usual amount of purely visual information—glass-encased presentations of undersea life and fossil formations. In addition, some displays had hand- or foot-operated buttons that activated short explanatory lectures complementing the visual materials; others had slide projectors and flashing lights. Constantly audible in the background were the sounds of gulls, thunder, and waves, and a faint odor of seawater wafted over the entire area. Concerned that the audience be able to touch as well, Parker used curved spaces, sandy ramps, and walls of sculpted shells and fossils that people could feel. As could be expected, the exhibition was particularly successful with the very young.

Marshall McLuhan comes from a background as unexceptional as his appearance and immediate milieu. He was born in western Canada—Edmonton, Alberta—July 21, 1911, the son of mixed Protestant (Baptist and Methodist) parents, and grew up in Winnepeg, Manitoba, which is somewhat north of western Minnesota. "Both agreed to go to all the available churches and services," he recalls of his parents' religious practices, "and they spent much of their time in the Christian Science area." His father was a real-estate and insurance salesman who, the son remembers, "enjoyed talking with people more than pursuing his business." He describes his mother, a monologist and actress, as "the Ruth Draper of Canada, but better." (His younger brother is currently an Anglican minister in California.) At the University of Manitoba, McLuhan first studied engineering "because of my interest in structure and design," and later changed his major to English literature and philosophy. After taking his B.A. in 1932 and his M.A. in

1934 with a thesis on "George Meredith as a Poet and Dramatic Parodist," McLuhan followed the route of many academically ambitious young Canadians to England, where he attended Cambridge for two years (and rowed for Trinity Hall); and there, he remembers, the lectures of I. A. Richards and F. R. Leavis stimulated his initial interest in studying popular culture. Returning home with a Cambridge B.A. in 1936, he took a job in the English department at the University of Wisconsin. The following year he rather suddenly converted to Catholicism, after an intensive reading of Gilbert Chesterton and a persuasive correspondence with Father Gerald B. Phalen at the University of Toronto's Pontifical Institute. Ever since, McLuhan has taught only at Catholic institutions—at St. Louis from 1937 to 1944; at Assumption (now called the University of Windsor) in Canada, just across the river from Detroit, from 1944 to 1946; and at St. Michael's College a Basilian (C.S.B.) establishment, since 1946. His academic field was originally medieval and Renaissance literature; and in 1942, he earned his Cambridge Ph.D. with a thesis on the rhetoric of Thomas Nashe, the Elizabethan writer. Very much an autodidact in spite of his education, he later taught himself Latin and even a little Greek, among other previously unfamiliar subjects; and at no time in his life did he take a course in "communications." A colleague at St. Louis, the godfather of McLuhan's eldest child and a friend of three decades, the management consultant Bernard J. Muller-Thym remembers that when McLuhan was a young man, "no generalizations were less than cosmic; but in those days, unlike now, he didn't have the facts to back them up."

The young scholar began his writing career as every professor should, by contributing articles on academic subjects to the professional journals. The first, in 1936, treated Chesterton as "A Practical Mystic" for the Canadian *Dalhousie Review:* and by the middle forties, McLuhan was contributing rather adventurous criticism to such eminent literary journals as *Kenyon Review* and *Sewanee Review,* as well as other cultural periodicals. To this day, academic circles regard him as "one of the finest Tennyson critics," and in 1956 he edited and introduced a standard undergraduate paperback anthology of Tennyson's poetry. In the late forties, however, he began to transcend his academic upbringing by contributing more personal and eccentric essays on rather general subjects to Dwight Macdonald's *Politics* and Cyril Connolly's *Horizon,* among other journals; and soon his writings bore such wild titles as "The Psychopathology of *Time* and *Life,*" *which* appeared in *Neurotica,* a short-lived but prophetic little magazine. By this time, McLuhan had developed his characteristic intellectual style—the capacity to offer an endless stream of unusual and challenging ideas. Hardly a new name in American intellectual circles, McLuhan has sustained a long career and reputation, summed up by one fellow literary critic, who told me before the recent hullabaloo, "Half the time I think Marshall is the most brilliant man I know; the other half of the time I'm sure he's the nuttiest."

McLuhan's first book, *The Mechanical Bride* (1951), promised so many printing headaches that McLuhan spent several years finding it a publisher, and then the publisher, Vanguard Press, demanded drastic revisions and took its while getting the book into print. Although sparsely reviewed and quickly remaindered, *The Mechanical Bride* has come to seem in retrospect, a radical venture in the study of American mass culture. Previous to McLuhan, most American critics of integrity were disdainfully horrified at the growing proliferation of mass culture—the slick magazines, the comic books, the Hollywood movies, radio, television; and they could scarcely do other than prophesy, with a kind of uncomprehending fear, how totally terrible its content and impact were. McLuhan, in contrast, was probably the first North American critic to inspect carefully the forms the stuff in the mass media took and then wonder precisely how these forms influenced people; and while he was still more scornful than not, one of his more spectacular insights identified formal similarities, rather than differences, between mass culture and elite art. "The abrupt apposition of images, sound, rhythms, facts is omnipresent in the modern poems, symphony, dance, and newspaper," he wrote. "It is easy to see that the basic techniques of both high and popular arts are now the same." Because of its many 8½-by-11-inch illustrations, *Bride* was for many years too exorbitantly expensive to reprint, while copies were so scarce that they often claimed thirty-five dollars on the used-book markets. McLuhan himself had enough foresight and self-confidence to purchase a cool thousand copies at wholesale remainder prices, giving some away to friends, storing others with Muller-Thym in New York, as well as selling them to strangers at prices far below the current quotation. "I offered to buy another thousand," he told me, "but the publisher wouldn't sell them to me." With the second McLuhan boom of 1967, however, new editions of *Bride* appeared in both hardcover and paperback.

In 1953, the year after he became a full professor at St. Michael's, McLuhan was selected chairman of the Ford Foundation's two-year Seminar on Culture and Communication; and later the same year he published *Counterblast*, an anonymous, expurgated booklet of oracular declarations and speculations (reissued in its unabridged form in 1969), as well as the first issue of *Explorations*, one of the most extraordinary and prophetic little magazines of recent years. As its title suggests, the journal was devoted to exploring, rather than defining and pigeonholing, aspects of modern civilization that other investigators tended to neglect. ("I don't explain," McLuhan continually declares. "I explore. I am a detective.") Perhaps the clearest measure of the journal's ultimate success is the fact that concerns and ideas presented to a few thousand subscribers have, in the following decade, infiltrated the more general discourse. In 1960, the year after they abandoned it, McLuhan and his most loyal collaborator, the anthropologist Edmund S. Carpenter, collected some of the best material as *Explorations in Communication* (1960), which is perhaps the most effective introduction to McLuhan's special concerns and ideas, while the eighth number, which was the most eccentric, extravagant, and speculative, was reissued in 1967 as *Verbi-Voco-Visual Explorations*.

Although Canadian by citizenship, McLuhan became in 1959 the Director of the Media Project for the National Association of Educational Broadcasters and the U.S. Office of Education; and out of that experience came many of the ideas poured into *Understanding Media*, which, in retrospect, was a product not of sudden inspiration but twenty years' brewing. *The Gutenberg Galaxy*, officially subtitled "The Making of Typographic Man," appeared three years later, receiving the Canadian Governor General's award for "critical prose." In 1964, McLuhan became a Fellow of the prestigious Royal Society of Canada, and McGraw-Hill published *Media*. The following year, the University of Windsor granted its former employee his first honorary degree, a D.Litt. To administer a bequest that McLuhan garnered, the president of the University of Toronto, in 1963, appointed him "Head" (an Anglicism for "chairman") of the newly founded Centre for Culture and Technology "to study the psychic and social consequences of technology and media." One Toronto alumna, now in Canadian publishing, remembers that a decade ago, "McLuhan was a bit of a campus joke"; and over the years, he usually had fewer graduate students than the other senior professors at Toronto, far fewer than, say, his more academic but equally eminent (and perhaps equally idiosyncratic) colleague Northrop Frye, most noted as the author of *The Anatomy of Criticism* (1957). Even by the middle sixties, McLuhan's random undergraduate students were so ignorant of his work that one reportedly asked another about "that early book, *The Iron Bride*," while his colleagues were unashamedly puzzled, if not vociferously skeptical, of the hometown oracle's reputation south of the border.

The visitor early in 1966 expected the "Centre," so boldly announced in the letterhead of McLuhan's correspondence, to be a sleek contemporary building with a corps of secretaries. Instead, the Centre was then more a committee than an institution; and it continues to exist entirely in McLuhan's cluttered and disheveled office. Bookcases cover the available walls, with battered old editions of the English classics on the top shelves, a multivolumed unabridged *Oxford English Dictionary* stretched along one of the longer planks, and a varied assortment of newer books about Western civilizations on the more accessible shelves—six to seven thousand volumes in all. There are more piles of miscellaneous books and papers on several large tables, unrelated chairs in various stages of disrepair, a large water bottle surrounded by unmatched glasses, and both a deathmask of John Keats and a crucifix hung on the wall space high above the shelves. Buried in the corner was a shabby metal-frame chaise lounge, more suited to a porch than an academic office, with a thin, lumpy green mattress haphazardly draped across it; here McLuhan plans his lectures, reads books, and retreats before the threats of uncongenial visitors.

In temperament, the Centre's chief is more passive than active; the popular innuendo that he somehow "hustled" himself into fame and fortune simply disregards the actual nature of the man. McLuhan is tall, slightly over six feet, and thin; and where he once sported a mustache and longish dark hair, now he is clean-shaven, and his hair is thinning and steely gray. His face usually has an intent expression and a ruddy complexion, while its one unusual feature is his mouth. Only thin slivers of his lips are visible from the front; but from the side, these lips appear so thick that his slightly open mouth resembles that of a flounder. No longer a smoker, he has several visible nervous habits, including tendencies to pucker his mouth and push his chin down toward his neck before he speaks, to twirl his glasses around his fingers when he lectures, and to rub his fingers down the palms of his hands whenever he says "tactility." His long, relatively unlined face is handsome—more good-looking than sensuous; and although he may prefer lumberjack's shirts at home, in class he wears ordinary professorial suits, a white shirt, and a nondescript tie that he usually clips on rather than knots. Fully dressed, then encased in a dark overcoat, he resembles a commuting businessman as much as a teacher. Early in 1966, when I visited him, McLuhan was suffering the persistent headaches, difficulties in concentration, and occasional blackouts subsequently attributed to a benign brain tumor that was successfully removed late in 1967.

A conscientious family man, he then lived with his wife and children in residential Toronto, in a three-story house with a narrow front and a small lawn, punctuated by a skinny driveway leading to a garage in the back. Its interior is equally modest, in the gracefully "academic dowdy" style typical of Oxbridge "dons," and exceptional only for an excessive number of books shelved, piled, and sprawled. The only noticeable art is a sketch of McLuhan by the English novelist, critic, and painter (Percy) Wyndham Lewis; for they were close friends in the early forties, when the elder author inscribed a copy of his stories, *The Wild Body*, "To Marshall, from his protégé, Wyndham Lewis." McLuhan met his wife, Corrine, a tall and elegant Texan, in southern California, when he researched at the Huntington Library and she studied acting at the Pasadena Playhouse. Married in 1939, they have six children: Eric, Mary and Theresa (who are twins), and Stephanie, all in their twenties, and Elizabeth and Michael, who are teen-agers; and while all the kids were living at home, McLuhan tended to be a conservative, if not authoritarian, father.

He prefers to read in a reclining position; so across the top of the living-room couch, resting against the wall, are twenty or so fat scholarly works; interspersed among them are a few mysteries—McLuhan's favorite light literature. He reads several books at once, skimming easily and penciling notes inside their back covers. He sleeps little, frequently reading in bed or conversing into the night with his eldest son Eric, a veteran of the U.S. Air Force and, in 1966, a belated undergraduate at Innis College, University of Toronto. Hardly a devotee of either the boob tube or the silver screen, McLuhan goes to the movies or watches television only on rare occasions, preferring football and hockey to baseball, and fantastic adventure programs (like *The Rogues*) to more sober stuff. A long cord attached to the television primitively extends to a switch that cuts off the sound, "Otherwise," he admits, "it would be intolerable." When his daughter Stephanie made her television debut—as "Miss Boating," she was promoting a forthcoming local Motorboat Show—father McLuhan made a point of watching the show with the sound turned off until she appeared.

Most of his cultural intake comes via print and conversation, as he is more likely to enthuse over a book than a play, painting, film, discotheque, or television show; and not only is his taste in books more persuasively reliable but perhaps his freedom from conventional criticism of non-literary media stems precisely from not taking their output too seriously. His erudition is indubitably immense, as well as psychologically immediate; and in his more delirious moments, McLuhan has been known to quote verbatim large and miscellaneous gobs of English poetry. At times, his writing suggests it is all but impossible for him not to think in tag lines and excerpts from other writers; and his language, jokes, and puns are chock full of allusions that continually announce his huge literacy. Talking is clearly his favorite recreation, while drink is his primary visible vice. Indeed, he is so thoroughly committed to books, so innately a "print-oriented man," that some of his severe remarks about print's deleterious effects could, in shrink-think, be regarded as a complex reification of an ambiguous self-hatred.

Marshall McLuhan looks and lives pretty much like another small-city American professor until he opens his mouth. His lectures and formal conversation are singular mixtures of original assertions, imaginative comparisons, cultural allusions, up-to-date jargons, heady abstractions, and fantastically comprehensive generalizations; and no sooner has he stunned his listeners with one extraordinary thought than he hits them with several more. In the clear, resonant voice of the man who speaks to be heard, he sprinkles his commentary with references (and sometimes quotations) to the Western classics, modern English literature, comic books, TV programs, and the latest fads in teen-age dancing. His phrases are more oracular than his manner, which is generally so low-key that he make the most hysterical assertions in the driest tones; yet his phrasing makes nearly everything he says *sound* important. Should a situation become either too formal or too ominous, McLuhan resorts to his favorite strategies for intellectual defense—blithely evading the challenge and/or escalating the level of abstraction. If really threatened, he hurls his ultimate rhetorical grenade—the giant baffle act—or simply dismisses his antagonist as "obsolete," "archaic," "medieval," or a "prob" which is an acronym for print-oriented bastard. ("Marshall McLuhan," the critic Leslie A. Fiedler once quipped, "continually risks sounding like the body-fluids man in *Doctor Strangelove*.")

In his graduate seminar (Communications) on "Images of the Future," he asks, "What is the future of old age?" The students look bewildered. "Why," he replies to his own query, "exploration and discovery." Before long, he has characterized the Batman TV show as "simply an exploitation of nostalgia which I predicted years ago." The twenty-five or so students still look befuddled and dazed; no one challenges him (How could they? On what terms?); hardly anyone talks but McLuhan. "The criminal, like the artist, is a social explorer." The chairs are hard-backed, plank-bottomed monstrosities, probably pre-War, that continually creak; the seminar "table" is actually a few tables of slightly varying height laid end to end. Two fluorescent lights overly illuminate the room, and over the blackboard hangs a crucifix. "Bad news reveals the character of change; good news does not." No one asks him to be more definite; he has an uncomfortable knack for intimidating his his audience. Even on the street, chugging through the Toronto snow, he is never lacking an explanation for anything, showering his listeners with suggestive ideas on all subjects. As no area of human endeavor escapes his concern, or original observations, the range of his thinking or "exploring" makes obsolete the academic piety of "disciplines." At first, he seems enormously opinionated; in fact, he is thinking on his feet. An insight discovered in one lecture is developed in a passing conversation, expanded during a lecture the following day, and shortly thereafter dictated as an elaborate chapter of a work in progress. McLuhan leads a disconnected, lazy, almost self-indulgent life; but his mind is so haunted by his intellectual probings that he often telephones friends at odd hours to "talk things out." (One young associate remarked proudly that a quiet-shattering call at 5 A.M. signaled his admission to the inner circle of McLuhan's acquaintance.) His critics ridicule him as a communications expert who cannot successfully communicate; actually, too many of his uncomprehending antagonists suffer from smugly closed minds. "It is paradoxical," notes Father Ong, "that only a relative oldster such as Marshall McLuhan can interpret the younger generation to themselves and that to many of his own generation his interpretation remains incomprehensible."

Another major incongruity is that a man so intellectually adventurous should lead such an unhip, if not conservative, life; that the egocentric and passionately prophetic qualities of his books should drastically contrast with the personal modesty and profound acquiescence of a devout Catholic. What explains the paradox is that "Marshall McLuhan" the thinker is clearly distinct from "H. M. McLuhan" the man. The first writes books and delivers lectures; the other teaches school, heads a family, and lists himself in the telephone book. The difference is so compelling that precisely the same eccentric phenomenon he can appreciate in the office, such as "concrete poetry," may, once he gets home, be dismissed as "games for children," as though a shift in personality accompanied a change in the setting. To a reporter from the Toronto magazine *MacLean's*, Marshall once offered a decidedly up-to-date commentary on the automobile; but when asked what kind of car he owned, H. M. not only explained that his wife cared more about such things than he did but added, archaically enough, "Personally, I don't like driving much. I'd rather walk." It was probably H. M. who made that oft-quoted remark about Marshall's abstruse theories: "I don't pretend to understand them. After all, my stuff is very difficult."

The private McLuhan, whose public self has so brilliantly explored technological change, is personally opposed to such development. "I wish none of these technologies ever happened," he remarked over a drink in his kitchen. "They impress me as nothing but a disaster. They are for dissatisfied people. Why is man so unhappy he wants to change his world? I would never attempt to improve an environment—my personal preference, I suppose, would be a preliterate milieu; but I want to study change to gain power over it." His books, he added, were just "probes" with themes, rather than polemics with theses; he did not "believe" in his writing as he believes in Catholicism. The latter is faith; the books are just thoughts. "You know the Faith differently from the way you 'understand' my books." Ironically, the man who thinks in the future lives very much in the past, and this paradoxical position he regards as conducive to generating cultural insight.

One of McLuhan's favorite explanatory ideas holds that the environment of a man shapes both how he looks and, more important, how he thinks; and what McLuhan regards as true for others is just as applicable to himself. In the course of interviewing him, I discovered that our physical situation all but determined the range of his conversation. Over lunch, he would talk best about his professional life, his career as a writer and teacher, his friends both past and present; here he told me, for instance, about *The Mechanical Bride*. Walking through the snow, he usually became more personal, discussing ambition and motivation; but once back in his office, our conversation necessarily focused upon his current ideas. To my more personal queries, he would respond, "Oh, that's just human interest. I thought you came to get my ideas." Only when he invited me to his house would he broach such intimate subjects as religion, revealing that his conversion was so sudden that "I never took instruction" and defining that humble quality of his faith. (Some literary people superciliously remember a large Friday evening literary dinner in the early fifties where McLuhan pulled out his own can of sardines sooner than sample the sumptuous beefsteak.) In general, the less formal the atmosphere, the more personally cordial McLuhan is and the more mundane his speech.

Despite many lucrative offers from institutions elsewhere, McLuhan plans to stay at "St. Mike's" because "I can better observe America from up here." During his year at Fordham as the aborted Schweitzer Professor for 1967–8 (just after McLuhan arrived, the New York State Attorney General ruled that denominational schools were not eligible for Schweitzer chairs), he kept an official connection with Toronto and returned there the following fall. "Canada," he explains, "is a kind of cultural DEW line, a cultural counter-environment. The Canadian is an outsider to the United States. You must live outside an environment to understand it; to participate in it is to blind yourself to all the hidden effects it may have upon you." In short, McLuhan, as a true intellectual, would not sell out the provincial and archaic posture that grants him insight for greater cosmopolitan success, and losing his powers of vision and perception is among his biggest fears. "Besides," he added, perhaps a bit perfunctorily "I've always been perfectly satisfied with my existence anyway. In general, I have no wish to be anywhere in the world other than where I happen to be."

Although he has no principled objections to lecturing (talking for good money), appearing on television, or even making commercial recordings, McLuhan has always thought of himself as primarily a writer; when asked why the same man who has explored the new media so profoundly prefers to communicate in the more archaic format, McLuhan replied succinctly, "Print is the medium I trained myself to handle." So, all the acclaim has transformed McLuhan into a book-making machine. In collaboration with the book designer Quentin Fiore and Jerome Agel as "coordinator," he quickly compiled an adventurously illustrated introduction to McLuhanism, *The Medium Is the Massage* (1967), which took the dubious distinction of being the best "non-book" of recent years; and in the following year, the troika released a sequel, *War and Peace in the Global Village*. Another publisher anxiously awaits an illustrated volume entitled *Culture Is Our Business*, and from time to time there is talk of collecting all those essays that in many ways represent McLuhan's best work. Perhaps reflecting his own idea that future art, like medieval work, is corporate in authorship, he has been writing several more books in dialogue with others. In tandem with his associate, the museum designer, Harley Parker, McLuhan completed *Through the Vanishing Point* (1968), a sporadically brilliant critical and comparative survey of space in poetry and painting from primitive times to the present. With Wilfred Watson, a former student who is now a poet and Professor of English at the University of Alberta, McLuhan is completing an extraordinary theory of styles in cultural history, *From Cliché to Archetype*, whose theme is, in brief, that a new technology takes as its content the stuff of a preceding technology until an even newer technology allows it to develop a character and content of its own. With William Jovanovich of Harcourt, Brace & World, there is in process *The Future of the Book* in the age of xerography; and along with the New York management consultant Ralph Baldwin, formerly an English professor at Catholic University, he has been considering the state of American business, *Report to Management*. McLuhan's work has also spawned subsidiary industries of criticism and commentary, puffery and polemic, much of which has been collected in the anthologies *McLuhan Pro and Con* (1968), edited by Raymond Rosenthal, *The McLuhan Explosion*, edited by Harry H. Crosby and George R. Bond, and *McLuhan Hot and Cool* (1967), edited by G. E. Stearn.

On another front, McLuhan and his Toronto colleague Professor Richard J. Schoeck, the Head of the English department at St. Michael's and a medievalist by specialty, recently did two imaginatively conceived textbooks, *The Voices of Literature* (1964, 1965), for use in Canadian high schools. "Education in poetry should be aural as well as visual," the editors write; and to encourage students to hear these poems, the publisher offers to provide teachers with tape recordings, some by the poets themselves. With Schoeck and Ernest J. Sirluck, the Dean of the Graduate School at Toronto, McLuhan oversees a series of anthologies of criticism published jointly by the Universities of Chicago and Toronto Presses, "Patterns of Modern Literature." So, despite all the bait from the worlds of media and advertising, McLuhan keeps one of his feet firmly planted in academia.

He writes (that is, dictates) still more, all the time; and whereas a scant few formerly paid attention, now he has more than enough Boswells, electronic and human, to take it all down. He contributes book reviews and articles to all sorts of publications—the personal newsletter, *The McLuhan DEW-Line*, that the Human Development Corporation founded for him; *Encounter* and the *Times Literary Supplement* (where his notice appears anonymously) in England; *Look*, *Vogue*, *Saturday Evening Post*, and *American Scholar* in the States; and in Canada, for the "Explorations" section he edits as a supplement to the University of Toronto *Varsity Graduate*, its alumni magazine. He contributed a "pro" essay to Robert Theobald's recent anthology of essays on *The Guaranteed Income*. Indeed, he so freely drops his short essays here and there that in preparing a bibliography some years ago he had enormous difficulty finding all the bits and pieces; and the list he mimeographed, as well as the one published in *McLuhan Hot and Cool*, has numerous major omissions. When *Media* appeared, several reviewers noted that McLuhan must have a path-breaking book on James Joyce in him; but that task he passed on to his son Eric, who is finishing a prodigious critical study of Joyce's most difficult work, *Finnegans Wake*. Indeed, Joyce's masterpiece is such a family favorite that they own five copies, one with an interleaving of blank white sheets for all their notes, and McLuhan *père*, who once devoted an entire year's course exclusively to the *Wake*, frequently credits it as "the greatest guidebook to media study ever fashioned."

Among McLuhan's greatest worldly desires is establishing the Centre for Culture and Technology in its own building, with sufficient funds to create and support a reference library of the sensory experience of man. That is, he foresees the development of methods and machines to measure all the "sensory modalities" (systems of sensory organization) of all the senses, in all cultures; and this knowledge will be housed on coded tapes in the Centre. One of his colleagues on the Centre's committee, Professor of Design Allen Bernholtz (since gone to Harvard), envisioned an encapsulating chamber that will, in response to taped instructions, artifically create a sensory environment exactly similar to that of another culture; so that, once the subject steps into the capsule, its environment would be programmed to simulate what and how, say, a Tahitian hears, feels, sees, smells, and tastes. "It will literally put you in the other guy's shoes," Bernholtz concludes enthusiastically. So far, however, the projected Centre has hardly received the five-million-dollar backing it needs to begin.

McLuhan has always been essentially a teacher living in a predominantly academic environment, a father in close touch with his large family, and a professor who writes and gives guest lectures. When some V.I.P.'s invited him to New York in 1965, he kept them waiting while he graded papers; and although he does not run away from all the reporters and visitors, he does little to attract publicity. He likes to carry on a succession of dialogues; and if the visitor can participate in the conversation he might be lucky enough, as I was, to join McLuhan in writing (that is, dictating) a section of a book. His thinking is literally done in public, in situations both formal and informal, as the unceasing process of an intellectually optimistic man with a faith in the social powers of perspicacious thought.

"Most people," McLuhan once remarked, "are alive in an earlier time, but you must be alive in our own time." "The artist," he added, "is the man in any field, scientific or humanistic, who grasps the implications of his actions and of new knowledge in his own time. He is the man of integral awareness." Although his intention was otherwise, McLuhan was, of course, implicitly describing himself—the specialist in general knowledge, whose perceptions and speculations are closer to poetry than to verifiable science; and so intellectually alive, so far ahead of other thinkers in the same unexplored areas and continually moving beyond his earlier formulations, McLuhan remains, one must admit regardless of whether he agrees with McLuhanism or not, among the great creative minds—"artists" —of our time. Who would dare surmise what thoughts, what perceptions, what grand schemes, he will offer next?

JOHN CAGE:
Fomenter of Radical Consciousness

To be avant-garde is not merely to be different from what came before, but to alter radically the consciousness of the age.—MORRIS DICKSTEIN

Although his work is so profoundly audacious that controversies about it will perhaps never cease, few can dispute that John Cage is among the most influential radical minds of his age. At the core of his originality is a continual penchant for taking positions not only far in advance of established artistic practice, including often his own activity, but also beyond the imaginative efforts of much that his times regard as "avant-garde." For over thirty years, Cage has worked on the frontiers of modern music and art; and as each phase of his career has attracted greater support and more imitators, Cage himself has progressed even further into unfamiliar territory, often further than even his most fervent admirers would go. "I like to think," he says, "that I'm outside the circle of a known universe, and dealing with things that I don't know anything about."

Everything about Cage seems a radical departure; his music, his esthetic ideas, his personal behavior, his critical statements are all indubitably inventive. "Oh, yes, I'm devoted to the principle of originality," he once told an interviewer, "not originality in the egoistic sense, but originality in the sense of doing something which it is necessary to do. Now, obviously, the things that it is necessary to do are not those that have been done, but the ones that have not yet been done. If I have done something, then I consider it my business not to do that, but to find what must be done next." No one else would dare announce to an audience, as well as commit to print, such aphorisms as, "I have nothing to say and I am saying it and that is poetry," or "Art instead of being made by one person is a process set in motion by a group of people." Cage's most important recent "compositions" are conceived to deny his intentional desires as completely as possible (although less completely than he sometimes says); and not only is each filled with a diversity of disconnected, "chance," atonal sounds, but also its major musical dimensions—amplitude (volume), duration, timbre, register—are all as unfixed, or structurally open, as the overall length of the piece.

This "indeterminate music," as Cage himself prefers to call it, is the result of an artistic evolution that is, like his esthetics, at once highly logical and faintly absurd. In the history of musical art, Cage descends from that eccentric modern tradition that abandoned nineteenth-century tonal principles, in addition to introducing natural noise as an integral component with instrumentally produced sounds; in this respect, Cage continually acknowledges the French-born American composer Edgard Varèse, and before him, Charles Ives as the artistic fathers of the radical tendencies that Cage himself later pursued. This tradition could be characterized as the "chaotic" language of contemporary music, as distinct from the mainstream language—Copland, Britten, and Stravinsky of his middle period—and the serial language, initiated by Arnold Schoenberg and propagated by Anton Webern, Milton Babbitt, and in the past decade, Stravinsky, too.

In his earliest extant work, dating from the middle thirties, Cage displayed huge talents for complicated rhythmic constructions; inventive organizing principles, such as a twenty-five tone system; and distorted instrumental sounds, such as that made by immersing a gong in water. In 1937, he also wrote this stunningly prophetic speculation: "I believe that the use of noise to make music will continue and increase until we reach a music produced through the aid of electrical instruments, which will make available for musical purposes any and all sounds that can be heard. Photoelectric, film, and mechanical mediums for the synthetic production of music will be explored." By 1942, in *Imaginary Landscape No. 3*, Cage, according to his old friend Peter Yates, "combined percussion with electrical and mechanical devices, audio-frequency oscillators, variable speed turntables, variable frequency recordings [of electronic sounds, made by the telephone company to test its lines], a 'generator whiner' and a buzzer."

Toward the late thirties, Cage also devised the "prepared piano," the innovation that first won him notice. Here he doctored the network of strings with screws, bolts, nuts, and strips of rubber, endowing the familiar instrument with a range of unfamiliar percussive potentialities. The first famous piece for this invention is *Amores* (1943), now on record, a work which today strikes sophisticated ears as rather simplistic and conventional. Perhaps the most ambitious score for the prepared piano is Cage's 69-minute *Sonatas and Interludes* (1946–8), recently reissued on record, which seemed revolutionary at the time but now sounds suspiciously like the music for standard, undoctored piano that Erik Satie did a few decades before. In addition to generating unusual noises, the prepared piano also gives the performer less control over the sounds he finally produces—bolts and nuts, alas, are not as precise as A-strings; and in contrast to the neo-Schoenbergians, who wanted a precise rationale for the placement of every note, Cage in the late forties continued to develop methods for minimizing his control over the aural result. Sometimes, he would enumerate several possible choices posed by a compositional situation and then let the throw of dice dictate the selection. Other times, he would choose his notes by first marking the miscellaneous imperfections (holes, specks, discolorations, etc.) on a piece of paper and then placing a transparent sheet over the marked paper; and after duplicating these marks on the transparent sheet, he would finally trace the random dots onto musical staves.

Always opposed to the expressionistic ambience generally characteristic of mainstream composition, Cage desired "to provide a music free from one's memory and imagination." In more advanced chance work, he offered randomly produced marks on a graph paper, letting the performer establish his own vertical measure for pitch and a horizontal one for duration. Sometimes he also employed the complicated and arduous dice- and coin-tossing procedures relevant to the *The I Ching, Or Book of Changes,* perhaps the most ancient book of China. The result of all these techniques was a score of directions so unspecific that no two performances of the same Cage piece would ever be as recognizably alike as, say, two inept or eccentric performances of Beethoven's Fifth Symphony.

The trouble with most of his pieces to 1952, which in retrospect seems a turning point, was that a detailed and fixed script actually produced, over a succession of performances, approximately similar results; and even the tape collage composed by chance procedures, *William Mix* (1952), perhaps Cage's most intricate purely aural endeavor, was offered to the world in a permanent form. Pursuing the logic of his previous intellectual development, Cage took the esthetic leaps that made his music even more indeterminate in both conception and execution, so that each performance of a piece would be hugely different from all the others. In *Winter Music* (1957), for instance, the scores consist of clusters of notes irregularly displayed across its twenty pages; and these may be "used in whole or part by a pianist or shared by two to twenty [performers] to provide a program of agreed-upon length." The instructions continue, "The notation in space may be interpreted as to time. . . . Resonances, both of aggregates and individual notes of them, may be free in length. . . . Dynamics are free." All the traditional dimensions of music are by intention free, free, free.

Perhaps the single most revolutionary piece in the Cage canon is *4′ 33″*, pronounced four minutes and thirty-three seconds, in which the well-known pianist David Tudor comes to the piano and sits still, except for three silent motions with his hands, for the prescribed duration. On the surface, this is, of course, just nothing; but precisely because the presence of David Tudor and the concert-going audience made this a situation from which musical sound was expected, the dramatized inference was that the piece's "music" consisted of all the sounds that happened to be audible in the performance hall during *4′ 33″*. As some, if not most of these accidental noises came from the audience, the spectators could be counted among the performance's musicians; and as "silence" signifies the absence of intentional sound, Cage calls the resulting piece "non-intentional" music.

Not only did *4′ 33″* contribute to musical history by bringing the chaotic musical tradition to one "logical" end point, but it also belongs among those rare modern pieces which are important less for the explicit experiences they offer than the extraordinary artistic ideas their circumstances imply; for as a stunt invested with meaning, this piece, as well as Cage himself, suggests not only that all sounds, in any combination, are justifiable components of music—actually a position that Cage insists dates back to Claude Debussy and the origins of modernism—but also that unintentional noises, regardless of their quality, are as valid for music as sounds intentionally produced. Indeed, most of Cage's own pieces since *4′ 33″* are designed to incorporate unintentional or "found" sounds into their aural field; but the ultimate implication of *4′ 33″* was that anything is possible in art, including (and here is the radical leap) nothing at all. "I have nothing to say and I am saying it and that is poetry."

In retrospect, however, Cage regards even this extreme piece as needlessly conservative, not only because it has three "movements," as indicated by the performer's silent gyrations, but also because it occurs within a fixed time and an enclosed space. Since silence, which was the surface content of *4′ 33″*, can never be absolute, then the "music" of that piece, which is to say unintentional noise, is with us all the time, if we attune ourselves to perceive it. In that case, the act of experiencing *4′ 33″* prepares a listener for the unprecedented perception of all the music in his environment. "If you want to know the truth of the matter," Cage once told me, with a twinkle composed one half of enthusiasm, the other half of irony, "the music I prefer, even to my own and everything, is what we hear if we are just quiet." Accepting the implications of all his actions, Cage deduces that the most agreeable art is not only just like life; *it is life.* In other words, *4′ 33″* is not only a work of art but a statement about esthetic experience; and as such, it illustrates the art historian George Kubler's observation in *The Shape of Time* (1962), "The work of many artists often comes closer to philosophical speculation than most esthetic writings."

Following his own deductions, Cage today admits that he long ago intellectually programmed himself out of a musical career; but he continues to create indeterminate compositions, partly to expose his audience to the aurally chaotic character of the environment but mostly because, he says, of a promise he made in the early thirties to Arnold Schoenberg to devote his entire life to music in exchange for free lessons. Cage also takes from the Indian philosopher Ananda K. Coomaraswamy the suggestive principle that "art imitates nature in its manner of operation"; and the result was a scrupulously discontinuous aural art, with no climaxes, no resolutions, no regular beats, no consistent tonality, no aural concurrences, no discernible beginnings, no definite ends—as random and haphazard as life. "Each sound is heard for itself," writes the critic Jill Johnston, "and does not depend for its value on its place within a system of of sounds." *Imaginary Landscape No. 4* is for twelve radios and twenty-four performers, one for each station-selecting dial, the other for each volume-control; and although Cage offers his performers a prepared but indeterminate script, he obviously has no control over what the radios will blare, if they play anything at all. At minimum, as Peter Yates once quipped, Cage "emancipated music from its notes."

The score of *Atlas Eclipticalis* (1961–2), which Cage composed by transferring the patterns of stars from an atlas to sheets of music paper, offers eighty-six instrumental parts "to be played in whole or part, any duration, in any ensemble, chamber or orchestral, of the above performers [an eccentric assortment]; with or without *Winter Music*." As here, Cage is not adverse to performing two of his pieces simultaneously; and among the more exciting combinations is Cathy Berberian's recording of *Aria* (1958) with *Fontana Mix* (1958). However, regarding records of Cage's work, one should add that since the current technology of recording instruments can only capture one "rendition" of an indeterminate score, all available records or tapes of Cage's post-1952 pieces inevitably compromise his ultimate purposes.

A more recent Cage work, *Rozart Mix* (1965), originally composed for the Rose Art Museum at Brandeis University, employs six live performers, thirteen tape machines, and a pile of at least eighty-eight tape loops—tape where the two ends are glued together—of varying lengths. Cage specifies the unusually large number, he explains, "to make sure that the performers wouldn't select tapes only of their favorite pieces." At the beginning of *Rozart Mix*, each of the performers picks a tape from the pile of loops and places it on the machine; when a tape breaks or gets tangled, he replaces it with another tape chosen from the pile. "What you want, you see, is to get a physically confused situation." Although the machines are tuned to various amplitudes, the piece itself is a paralyzingly loud chaos of sounds, and as frequently happens at Cage's concerts, unenlightened spectators trickle out after every cacophonous climax. At the premiere performance, refreshments were served when the audience dwindled to twelve; and the piece terminated, by prearrangement, when the last spectator left, approximately two hours after *Rozart Mix* began. (The *hors d'oeuvre* to this main course consisted of Cage's munching a sandwich whose sound was picked up by contact microphones strategically distributed around his face; so that excruciatingly loud crunching noises penetrated to every nook of the hall.)

Years ago, Cage characterized his intentions as "purposeful purposelessness"; and more recently, he described his art as closer to action than creation. "Art instead of being an object made by one person is a process set in motion by a group of people." One should add that purposeful purposelessness is considerably different from the purposeless purposelessness, just as orderly disorder—the character of Cage's current art—differs from disorderly disorder. For those reasons, an experienced ear can instantly identify Cage as the author of his recent pieces—in the choice of materials and guide lines lies his taste; and he has been known to become visibly upset if the skeleton of his piece, as distinct from the detail, loses its predetermined shape. "The rules of the game," quipped Peter Yates, "determine the nature of the play and the shape of the end product." In that his recent pieces are usually extravagant in character, open in time, indeterminate in action, and yet fixed in space (the enclosed performance area), they are closer to staged happenings than musical theater, although more than one critic has praised them as the most interesting and valid species of American "opera."

Over the years, Cage has published a modest number of eccentrically conceived essays, mostly in music and art magazines; and many of these he collected into a volume appropriately entitled *Silence* (1961), and dedicated, "To Whom It May Concern." Indeed, since the middle fifties, he has developed a concentrated interest in prose forms, first overcoming those Gertrude Steinian affectations that plagued his earlier style and then striving for original ways to express his ideas and illustrate his esthetic principles. "Indeterminacy" (1958), subsequently recorded on a Folkways record, is an imaginative esthetic demonstration in the form of a lecture; so is "Where Are We Going? and What Are We Doing?" as well as "Talk I" (1965), among other recent word-pieces. The last is reprinted in Cage's second collection, *A Year from Monday* (1967), which also contains his stunning collection of random anecdotes and radical speculations, the three-part "Diary: How To Improve the World (You Will Only Make Matters Worse)." This set of related pieces is composed under a system of self-imposed constraints that paradoxically free Cage from conventional ways of putting words together; and the result is a rhythmic word-form somewhere between prose and poetry, though closer to the latter. "Poetry is not prose," he once wrote, "not by reason of its content or ambiguity but by reason of its allowing musical elements (time, sound) to be introduced into the world of words." Also, in comparison to the earlier book, *A Year from Monday* is a far more concise and satisfactory introduction to Cage's radical thought and example.

Cage has led a vagabond life as his physical movement parallels esthetic adventure. He was born September 5, 1912, in Los Angeles, the son of an inventor and electrical engineer, John Cage, Sr., whose gasoline-engine submarine, in the year of John Jr.'s birth, temporarily established the world's record for staying underwater. Young Cage became valedictorian of his Los Angeles high school class and entered nearby Pomona College just before his seventeenth birthday; however, somewhat appalled, he says, at the regimentation of individual curiosity, he soon dropped out, traveling for over a year through Europe where he dabbled in architecture and painting, before returning to Los Angeles. Once home, he decided to concentrate on music, studying briefly with Henry Cowell and Adolph Weiss; and he later convinced Arnold Schoenberg, the Viennese composer who had recently emigrated to Los Angeles, to give him free lessons in exchange for the promise mentioned before. Despite Schoenberg's generosity, Cage found the European serial techniques uncongenial—the several extant stories of Schoenberg's real opinion of Cage are contradictory—and all of Cage's subsequent work has progressively denied such a rigorous approach to the organization and articulation of sound.

In the late thirties, Cage took a job as resident accompanist at the Cornish School in Seattle, Washington, where he first met the dancer and choreographer Merce Cunningham, then a student of acting, who has remained among Cage's closest friends and professional associates to this day. In 1937, he also married Xenia Andreyevna Kashevaroff, the Alaskan daughter of a Russian Orthodox priest; and they lived together for about a decade, later to become divorced. In 1942, Cage taught music at Laszlo Moholy-Nagy's Chicago Bauhaus, then called the Institute of Design, taking various odd jobs to supplement his meager academic income; and the following year the Cages came to New York with a few dollars in hand and a tenuous invitation to stay with Max Ernst and his wife, the art collector Peggy Guggenheim. Thanks to the aid of newly acquired friends, Cage managed the following year to present the crucial concert at the Museum of Modern Art that initiated his reputation as a controversial force on the New York musical scene. (Indeed, the critical objections that Cage's endeavors have since accumulated are largely so obvious and repetitious, yet oblique, if not irrelevant, that they are hardly worth repeating here.)

Unable in those days to support himself from musical activities alone, or to earn a permanent teaching position, Cage lived modestly in sparsely furnished rooms on Monroe Street, near Chinatown, on New York's Lower East Side; and he ran through a gamut of jobs—dishwasher, library researcher, accompanist to dancers, free-lance music instructor, and art director of a textile company, among them. Remembering the example of Schoenberg's generosity, he gave free lessons to those who could not afford to pay. Not until the 1960's, he remembers, was he able to live as a composer—from royalties on his music and writings, visiting professorships at the universities of Cincinnati, Illinois, and elsewhere, and an endless number of lectures and performances. More recently, being John Cage has, in fact, become quite lucrative; however, as his mother has been seriously ill for the past few years and he is her sole support, Cage lives alone as frugally as ever. The coterie of his vociferous admirers, merely a handful two decades ago, has by now swelled to a considerable populace.

As a performer, lecturer, and guest professor, Cage is currently a mobile artist for most of his days, traveling from place to place and audience to audience; but his permanent home is a miniscule, glass-walled two and one-half room cottage in the Stony Point Gate Hill Cooperative, an artists' community about an hour north of New York City. Nearby lives the film-maker Stan VanDerBeek, as well as the pianist David Tudor, who has become so accomplished at performing Cage's scores that a Polish composer once quipped, "He could play the raisins in a slice of fruitcake." Cage's own home, which is structurally an appendage to another, larger house, sits on top of a treacherously rocky path; and between his two small rooms (each about 20 by 10 feet) lies a narrow utility core, where Cage usually cooks for himself. In the back room is one all-purpose table (eating, writing, and talking over), a small bed, piles of reading matter, and a modest television whose old movies put him to sleep every night. The summer Saturday evening we first met, Cage wore dungarees, a blue denim shirt, and sneakers.

In public situations, Cage emits the aura of youthful optimism—"a sunny disposition" is his own phrase for it; and as his friend Yates observed, "Around him everyone laughs." Cage's slight build, his unfluctuating scalp line, his thick brown hair, only recently combed down from a long spikey crewcut and beginning to sprinkle with gray all make him look considerably younger than his years; only the deep lines running down the sides of his face betray his age. Actually, Cage offers the world two distinct faces, one hardly resembling the other. The "serious" face is long and narrow, with wide and attentive brown eyes, unusually long ears, and vertical lines sloping down to his heavy jaw; in contrast, Cage's "comic" face, which graces most of his public pictures, is horizontal in structure, his wide mouth exposing two rows of teeth, his eyes nearly closed.

Cage is immensely gregarious, talking freely and laughing easily; contagiously enthusiastic, he seems blessed with a limitless capacity for getting people to do him favors. Also a great theatrical presence, he can upstage nearly anyone, including, as in a recent piece, the entire Merce Cunningham troupe. When he confronts audiences, his answers and examples, gestures and jokes, come easily to him, in much the same tone and form night after night, place after place. As a matter of principle, he refuses to indulge in argument, even in the presence of those he could consider his antagonists; yet he can sometimes be outrageously nasty about people who are not present. As persuasion is among his primary purposes, Cage often seems all but Jesuitical, particularly with possible skeptics, continually making sounds and gestures intended to elicit agreement. His most distressing habit is name-dropping, which he does so compulsively that sometimes rather trivial ideas get attached to awesomely eminent sources. He smokes cigarettes through a filter, but drinks nothing stronger than wine and then only with his meals; and he morally objects to the use of drugs, for the same reason he opposes Art, as both promise transcendence from mundane life. Cage's high-pitched, raspy voice is instantly recognizable, and his most serious talk seems closer to philosophy than music or art criticism.

What makes Cage's present esthetic position so revolutionary is that, in theory at least, it completely discounts the traditional purposes of composing and even the importance of the composer. As Cage would have it, music is everywhere, and everywhere is music—in nature's noise—only if the listener is prepared to hear it; therefore, if the composer has any function at all, it should be, Cage says, teaching people to keep attuned to all the music that their environment offers. Following the logic of this position, too, he admits that solipsism characterizes the experience of both everyday life and indeterminate music; and since each man hears something individual, every man is his own composer—he puts sound together, in the act of attentive listening; and the music most appropriate to our time, his argument continues, is that which allows each listener to compose his own experience. Therefore, too, Cage regards a performance of a Beethoven quartet as "no longer what Beethoven wrote but everything else I happen to hear at that time. We must take intentional material, like Beethoven, and turn it to non-intention."

If music is all sounds, whether intentional or not, then theater, by Cage's analogy, consists of all the impressions that meet the eye and ear, which is to say that theater is as constantly available to the perceptive sensibility as music. "Theater takes place all the time, wherever one is. And art simply facilitates persuading one this is the case." In the middle fifties, Cage recognized that his own compositions were, in performance, as much theater as music; and in *Theatre Piece* (1960), he extended an implication of *Music Walk* (1958) and provided instructions for the indeterminate movements of people rather than, as before, just the generation of sound.

However, theater is hardly a new interest in Cage's career; for not only has he been for two decades the musical director of Merce Cunningham's dance company, but back in the summer of 1952, Cage staged what was probably the first American "happening" at Black Mountain College in North Carolina. Furthermore, his classes in "music composition" at the New School, during 1956–8, included several students who later became creators of the happenings theater—Allan Kaprow, Dick Higgins, Jackson MacLow, and George Brecht; for Cage remains in many ways the esthetic father, as well as a foremost practitioner, of that art of non-literary performance that I have elsewhere called "The Theater of Mixed Means." Indeed, his own theatrical pieces are extravagant in materials, scrupulously chaotic in effect, tasteful in scale, and idiosyncratic in identity; and to many polyliterate critics, including myself, Cage's pieces of the past decade are more valid and laudatory as theatrical spectacle than purely aural (that is, musical), experience.

In the late 1940's, Cage attended D. T. Suzuki's lectures on oriental religion at Columbia University; and he has since considered himself a devotee of Zen Buddhism. (He recalls that when he told his mother about receiving a one-year appointment at Wesleyan University, she replied, "Do they know you're a Zen Buddhist?") One Zen tenet that Cage finds congenial is the total acceptance of perceptual reality—the music around us all the time—that Cage finds "perfectly satisfactory." "We open our eyes and ears seeing life each day excellent as it is." Such a position, he admits, should completely negate the exercise of discriminatory taste and the expression of evaluative judgments; but just as he has not devoted his professional career to innumerable performances of *4′ 33″*, so he has never been able to flush away the critical sense he acquired as a young artist. In *Silence* he writes admiringly of a Japanese Roshi who accompanied him to a New York dinner, after which the host and hostess insisted upon singing arias from a third-rate Italian opera in fourth-rate voices. "I was embarrassed and glanced toward the Roshi to see how he was taking it," Cage remembers. "The expression on his face was absolutely beatific."

Indeed, Cage is always embarrassed to find that his own attitudes and practices have not yet caught up with his espoused positions; and many of his apparent contradictions, upon which his critics feast, stem from this discrepancy. In theory, he is opposed to critical judgments, explaining, "They are destructive to our proper business which is curiosity and awareness." He elaborated, "Why waste time by focusing upon these questions of value and criticism and so forth and by making negative statements. We must exercise our time positively. . . . The big thing to do actually is to get yourself into a situation where you use your experience, no matter where you are. . . . How are you going to use this situation if you are there? This is the big question."

In rebuttal, I once suggested that, no matter how attentive we are, certain extrinsic experiences are intrinsically richer than others. Only partially assimilating my objection, Cage continued, "I've noticed that I can pick up anything in the way of a periodical or a newspaper—anything—and use it . . . in the content sense, in terms of its relevance to positive action now. Now let's ask this kind of question. Which is more valuable—to read *The New York Times* which is a week old or to read Norman O. Brown's *Love's Body?* If we face this issue squarely, we'll see that there's no difference."

In practice, however, Cage frequently makes rather decisive critical judgments, as he prefers art that is formally variable and open, rather than constant and fixed, and as discontinuously complex as life itself. For instance, he esthetically objects to nearly all contemporary music—both mainstream and serial, both jazz and rock—because the results are fixed objects for contemplation rather than processes that expose us to life. He generally prefers theater to concerts, because it "more than music resembles nature"; and rather than hearing one jazz band pound a steady beat, he would prefer to hear several combos playing in different tempi at once. If pressed, Cage will admit that evaluative standards often inform the choices he makes in his daily activity. "When I am making them," he muses, "I'm annoyed that I am doing so."

"In Zen they say: If something is boring after two minutes, try it for four. If still boring, try it for eight, sixteen, thirty-two, and so on. Eventually one discovers that it's not boring but very interesting." Elsewhere in *Silence,* he writes that boredom can often "induce ideas," and not only are his esthetics quoted to rationalize much that is repetitious, unarticulated, and interminable in recent art, but surely those arduous chance procedures must cause a boring experience; yet in conversation, I more than once heard Cage compromise his position by dismissing a certain activity in life as "a terrible bore."

Although Cage continues to author new pieces each year and perform those earlier works whose aleatoric processes he still regards as valid (the brilliant *Williams Mix,* as a fixed tape collage, fails on this count), Cage finds that his passions are becoming more varied. In the middle fifties, he focused an interest in mushrooms, not only collecting various species but also accumulating a huge library of relevant literature. "I once thought I should like to be a botanist, because I felt that that field, unlike music, would have an absence of strife. I have since discovered otherwise." For a short period in 1960, he supplied New York's posh Four Seasons restaurant with edible fungi; and in 1962, he became a founding officer of the New York Mycological Society. In a Zen explanation, he once linked his two primary enthusiasms, music and mushrooms, to the fact that they appear adjacent to each other in most dictionaries. Sustaining his youthful interest in painting, Cage makes intricately conceived and exquisitely executed scores, which in 1958 he exhibited at New York's Stable Gallery. "They are set down in a complex system of numbers, notes, letters and geometrical formations," wrote Dore Ashton, then an art critic on *The New York Times*, "and each page has a calligraphic beauty quite apart from its function as a musical composition." More recently, Cage compiled a book of modern compositional notation—an anthology of manuscripts by the major modern composers—partially to benefit the Foundation for Contemporary Performance Arts that he helped establish.

In more recent years, Cage has become an enthusiastic devotee and publicist of an eccentric strain of contemporary radical social thought. Long an individualist anarchist (a logical analogue to his esthetic notion that every man is his own composer), Cage is cogitating and propagating a mix of ideas taken mostly from Marshall McLuhan, Buckminster Fuller (an old friend from their days together at Black Mountain), Norman O. Brown, and Robert Theobald. In general, Cage awaits the time when autonomous technology will achieve an economy of unbounded abundance, which will in turn insure everyone a guaranteed annual income, regardless of whether he is able to work or not. Such an economic revolution, he believes, will necessitate further social and psychological revolutions, making play, rather than work, the dominant motive of human activity. Thus, he regards chance composition and happenings performance, which are closer to inspired play than hard-nosed work, as harbingers of the new age; and Cage's more recent writings seem explorations in interdisciplinary thought, much as his recent performance pieces are explorations in intermedia art.

Cage's current eminence stems less from his artistic works as such, which even some of his more devoted admirers find tiresome, than the impact of his persuasive ideas and friendship upon scores of artists, musicians, theater directors, critics, and choreographers; indeed, no single figure in the American arts today has influenced so many first-rank creative minds as profoundly, perhaps because no one was as determined as Cage to liberate *all* contemporary art from *all* irrelevant strictures and boundaries. Not only through his occasional lectures to gatherings of abstract expressionists during the early fifties but also through his close personal friendship with both Jasper

Johns and Robert Rauschenberg, Cage influenced many tendencies in contemporary painting, including the penchant for mixing artistic media, as in Rauschenberg's combines, and the rationale informing "minimal" painting and sculpture, as well as the elegant representation of popular images. "That atmosphere [behind pop art]," writes the art critic Barbara Rose, "was generated mainly by the composer John Cage."

Cage also influenced the more advanced tendencies in contemporary dance, not only through his close association with Merce Cunningham and, at various times, Jean Erdman, but also because one of his own composition pupils, Robert Dunn, taught the classes that inspired one of the most radical developments in post-Cunningham dance—that collection of adventurous performance activities Jill Johnston calls "The Judson Church movement." His influence also helped raze the lines that traditionally separated one art from another, providing precedents for works that straddle traditional domains—happenings, environmental sculptures, pattern poems, and so on. "Now we have such a marvelous loss of boundaries," he told me, "that your criticism of a happening could be a piece of music or a scientific experiment or a trip to Japan or a trip to your local shopping market."

In addition, Cage fathered an entire school of American composition, which includes, among others, Earle Brown and Morton Feldman, James Tenney and Christian Wolff; and influenced in part by Cage's example, the European composers Pierre Boulez and Karlheinz Stockhausen have introduced aleatoric elements into their previously fixed pieces. Even the contrived chaos of musically sophisticated rock groups seems ultimately, though circuitously, indebted to Cage's forays into aural possibility; for who else dares say that anything is possible in music, including sheer cacophony and/or nothing at all. Indeed, because Cage's ideas are so relevant, so multifarious, so revolutionary, so pervasive, it is all but impossible to talk about what is interesting in contemporary art without mentioning his name or considering his extraordinary radical ideas.

BERNARD MULLER-THYM:
Resources of Verbalized Knowledge

American research labs and business spend billions on research, yet notoriously produce no ideas or inventions at all. They do not permit themselves the oral totality of approach necessary to "intuition."—MARSHALL MCLUHAN

It is perhaps the most ingrained convention of established modern culture to associate intellectual and artistic achievement with tangible artifacts—a painting, a musical score, a book, a record, an invention; for unless something exists in an objective form, or unless a transient circumstance such as a lecture or a performance goes reported in the public press, it will inevitably escape the chroniclers of cultural history. True, some scintillating conversation does become the stuff of philosophy and literature, as Socrates had his Plato, Dr. Johnson his Boswell, and Christ his disciples; and even today, certain wholly verbal thinkers, such as Marshall McLuhan and Herman Kahn, contrive procedures to insure that their spoken words get channeled into books and magazines. Nonetheless, in America today are a number of rare and powerful minds whose intellects are acknowledged supreme, even though their thought does not slip into print—professors who give superlative lectures but publish nothing, blocked writers who never get out the truly great book floating through their minds, and in particular, those influential consultants who change the worlds they touch through output rarely more tangible than perspicacious talk. Among the last, few are as discernibly brilliant as Bernard J. Muller-Thym, usually addressed as "Doctor Muller-Thym" in honor of his Ph.D. in medieval philosophy, currently a management consultant in "private practice," as he puts it, who is regarded as "an extraordinary mind" by nearly everyone with whom he deals.

Though at the pinnacle of his profession, Muller-Thym is all but unknown to the general public, or even the public of managers, largely because, unlike Peter F. Drucker (who is perhaps his sole intellectual peer in the trade), he does not write, while his talks rarely appear in public print; and this may partially explain why some of his genuine contributions to management thought and action no longer carry his name. Muller-Thym's practice is as free-lance as it is private, as he has no secretaries, no assistants, no office, no permanent sources of income, few retainers, and few books and papers; and the shape and style of his professional life are all but entirely of his own creation. The form his consulting takes theoretically knows no circumscribed limits, as it can include lectures to all sorts of organizations, inspections of various installations, conversations with top officials, brainstorming in symposia, advice on all sorts of corporate and educational programs, and much else. Quite simply, some organization writes or telephones his home in New York; and if the project is feasible and the pay reasonable, Muller-Thym comes. Like other exclusively verbal people, he carries nearly everything he needs to know in his head. The result of an extensive consultation is sometimes as tangible as a typewritten report, which is usually dictated, in nearly definitive form, to one of his sponsor's machines or secretaries and then corrected in Muller-Thym's minuscule handwriting; but to his own mind, the real effect of his consulting activity should be less tangible than intangible—"a change in the universe of conduct or behavior or action, all of which means making something happen."

In a typical academic year, running from 1967 to 1968, he

worked with an electronics firm on the possible uses of its facsimile printing machine; found organizational inefficiencies in a huge computer installation for Lockheed Space and Missiles, Inc.; brainstormed both individually and with "the invention group" at McCann-Erickson; advised Coca-Cola on the introduction of new beverages; gave whole days of lectures to bankers, accountants, and other professionals in occupational conferences and executive programs at Arden House, Columbia University, Northeastern University, and elsewhere; advised CUNA (Credit Union National) International, Inc., on redesigning the credit union movement for greater current relevance; worked with Northern Electric (the "Western Electric" of Canada) on developments in communication and education, as well as the future possibility of multisensory communication. Although those lectures usually rehearse familiar material (and partly for that reason, he does not quite consider them "work"), most of Muller-Thym's professional life presents the continual challenges of unfamiliar problems.

Among the cognoscenti in the consulting trade, Muller-Thym is known for his "generalized competence," which means an interest more polymathic than most; and he has particularly mastered such areas as the dynamics and design of a business, the organization and structure of work, the appropriate uses and possible applications of computer systems, the education and development of managers, and more recently, the techniques of innovation. Among his more important past projects were the radical redesign, in the late forties, of order fulfillment in the sales record department of Cluett, Peabody, the shirt manufacturer; the effective reorganization, in 1955, of the work operation on the formerly congested Hudson River piers 57 and 58 for the Grace Line; studies in 1952–4 for IBM and U.S. Steel of the time, energy, and talents of management people; the preparation of systematic scales of employee compensation for General Electric, American Cyanamid, Bloomingdale's, and other companies; a study of the shortage of cooks and bakers in America for the Statler Foundation; numerous investigations of the forces and conditions that enhance or inhibit management personnel; establishing the mission and then the organization of a new research and development department for several companies.

Other jobs included a new definition of organizational requirements for Whirlpool, in 1956, during its rapid expansion and diversification; the application of the computer to innumerable corporate processes over the past decade; collaboration in the revival and reorganization of Warwick Manufacturing Co. ("Silvertone" appliances), in 1958; researches into corporate action, during 1958–60, for General Electric's Management Research Services division; travel to India, in 1960, as a member of M.I.T.'s first Advanced Management Programme there; a series of important generalizations about the relationship between the structure of work, on one hand—the design of space, the deployment of people, the network of communication—and, on the other, organizational productivity, done, in 1962, at the Goddard Space Flight Center, Greenland Belt, Maryland; and a history of the computer's development and a revised education for maintenance engineers, in 1964, for IBM. As he moves from job to job, from problem to problem, from place to place, Muller-Thym exemplifies a knowledge-incremental (or self-learning) feedback system; for in retrospect, every past consultation would seem to offer a useful precedent, a nugget of education, for future problems.

Late in 1967, for instance, he received a call from Dr. Wayland C. Griffith, Vice-President in charge of Research and Technology at Lockheed Missiles and Space, Inc., Sunnyvale, California. Griffith noticed a rising percentage of delays and errors (though still negligible by number) in their large, increasingly burdened computer installation and then suspected that the activities of people working around the machinery could be more effectively organized. Muller-Thym found an open space in his schedule, fixed a *per diem* rate, and flew out to Sunnyvale. For three days he wandered around the installation, taking notes but remembering more, asking questions of people in key spots, looking for duplications and multiple transmissions and unnecessary steps, inspecting many operating documents, staying up with the swing shifts, and walking through a number of jobs, as well as collecting statistics on the time for certain tasks and analyzing the work-mix of the entire operation. On the third day, just as he was beginning to discover where the processes were going out of control, he was informed that the following morning he would meet with the Lockheed officials. That oral report was so successful that Muller-Thym returned the following February for eight more days to pursue his general observations in greater detail and depth; and he went to Sunnyvale again in April for sixteen more days to compile, mostly by dictation, a 116-page report, with an appendix of detailed illustrations, all entitled "Review of Digital Computer Operations." The report, the product of genuine hard thinking, included recommendations for restructuring the work, such as separating administrative computing from scientific, linking separate machines together, reorganizing both the tape libraries and the physical layout, and reprogramming the computer to respond to the rhythms of people working around it. "Whenever you find instances of dislocation," he generalizes, "the problem has something to do with structure." Since his original assignment, as he wrote in the report, was "to determine what could be done to cut down on error and delays and to bring the system within manageability and control," he made several proposals, all of which, it turned out, were eventually implemented. "This reflects," Dr. Griffith wrote me, "Dr. Muller-Thym's extensive experience in dealing with problems in organizing the work of people and equipment, and his highly original and imaginative approach to problem-solving." The bill for his services, a substantial sum, Muller-Thym regards as a reasonable figure for advice that "they couldn't have bought for several times that amount from any of the consulting firms."

A decidedly rounded man of medium height, he looks as indubitably Dutch as his name—round-faced, blue-eyed, fair-complexioned, soft-skinned, jowl-necked, while his straight hair runs back from a left-centered widow's peak and turns from dark gray to light. Gentle in demeanor and contained by nature, he speaks softly and slowly, frequently making modest shaking gestures with his noticeably small hands and stubby fingers; and before an audience, invariably without a note, he balances himself on small feet, occasionally pulling on his fingers, sketching with a colored "magic marker" on pads of display paper, or pointing to diagrammed slides on a projected screen. ("Blackboards, slides, and sketchpads," he once remarked, "belong to an oral society; they serve to illustrate a talk.") As a wholly verbal intellectual, Muller-Thym knows that good chatter is his primary output, if not his only genuine product; so, the quality of his discourse, both its form and its content, is perhaps his most important care. Obliged to tell people what they do not already know, he offers, in a matter-of-fact tone, ideas that are unfamiliar to most ears; yet he strives to make everything clear. As in medicine, where the manner is often as important as the message, this good doctor invariably sounds insightful and wise.

Eschewing both dramatic gestures and verbal pyrotechnics, he is less a lecturer than a conversationalist who invites a large audience to intrude. Words alone carry nearly all he has to say—this may explain why he is particularly adept at talking over the telephone; and he speaks distinctly in long, somewhat complicated (and sometimes loose-ended) sentences that flow flaccidly and at times circuitously into each other. Unashamedly erudite and intellectual, he freely utters latinisms ("plenum," "ingenium," and so on) and refers familiarly to all sorts of historical, classical, and biblical analogies and events, which are less ostentatiously displayed than made genuinely relevant to the issues at hand. Before audiences of executives, who are neither as contemplative nor as experienced at listening as students, his plentiful allusions, abstract discourse, and circumspect manner can be a bit disengaging; but just as the thread of the audience's attention seems on the verge of snapping, Muller-Thym marshals yet another stark generalization, or a particularly vivid example, "All the Mozart operas I can think of were written on commission against a very tight deadline and for money." Primarily because his lectures concentrate on general problems that might, by analogy, have more specific and immediate relevance to his listeners, he invariably stimulates so many currents of thinking that responses and questions are usually plentiful. "Perhaps we should look upon the discussion session," he often says, "as a mutual task to decide, through questions or in whatever way you choose to put the particular points, the issues on which you would like to expand."

As a fertile lecturer, he can also begin by offering several possible topics, asking his listeners which ones they would prefer to hear; and in the course of a talk, an appropriate cue, from someone in the audience or his own meanderings, can set off an elaborate exposition. Should he come for a full day of talk—a regular kind of commission, generally worth several hundred dollars—the standard procedure involves two lectures in the morning, two more in the afternoon, and then informal questions and conversation over coffee, tea, lunch, dinner and drinks late in the evening. Possessed of a strong will and an even stronger constitution, which is not adverse to amphetamines, he can, if need be, talk forever—even three successive days—through all kinds of audiences and physical situations; and like all intellectual vaudevillians, he has perfect and immediate recall of all his pet verbal routines.

In smaller gatherings, where several people are talking, he is usually patient, polite and attentive, rarely asserting himself, and often letting a more aggressive speaker interrupt him; and though usually more reserved than everyone else in the circle, he is nevertheless just as generous and cordial. He relates to a wider variety of humankind than most of us, and his gentleness and sympathetic curiosity invariably put everyone at ease. Knowing that wholly verbal people are liable to repeat themselves, he often inquires, before beginning an explanation, "But did we talk about this before?" His capacity for incisive and sympathetic comprehension is amazingly rich, as he can not only remember the names of people to whom he has just been introduced but also discern the gist of an ineptly formed remark or even tune into an unfamiliar realm of experience. In every question, in every comment, in every striving for empathy, perhaps there is something to be learned.

Muller-Thym is, indeed, an awesomely learned man, whose extraordinary education came not from attending the best schools but from persistently assimilating the knowledge and wisdom presented by his environment and experience; he is one of those rare people upon whom, in Henry James's phrase, "nothing is lost." In fact, he has passed through several distinct educations, all of which are, to various degrees, relevant to his current work; and he still has a voracious hunger for new ideas and whole bodies of unfamiliar knowledge. "I couldn't have planned all this if I tried," he once told me, "nor was everything I studied especially worthwhile. I spent a lot of years misspending my life. Nor could I write out today an appropriate education for someone else."

Born in Kansas City, Missouri, October 7, 1909, the son of a high-minded and prosperous retailer-distributor of Catholic goods, Muller-Thym attended the local parochial schools and served as an altar boy on Sunday. At the Jesuit-run Rockhurst High School, his education was Catholic and classical; at the local Rockhurst College, he majored in English literature, taking his B.A. in 1930, "in the age of the wheel, just after radio had been invented." At both places, his education was, as he remembers, "superb, because the level of mediocrity was very high. Everybody who went to those schools was expected to do things." Always a successful student, he graduated at the top of his class in high school, his cumulative average establishing a new record. "If I came home with less than ninety-nine, things weren't good."

Outside of school, his major interest was music, particularly the violin; and after starting at the sixth chair in the first violin section, he quickly became concert master of the one-hundred-piece performance group (mostly young people) of the Kansas City Orchestral Training School, founded by Nazareno ("Ned") De Rubertis, a Neopolitan musician who had somehow emigrated to Missouri. Although Muller-Thym never had articulated ambitions for a musical career, he distinctly remembers taking the solo part in the Beethoven violin concerto and poring over scores in De Rubertis's library, as well as becoming, for several months, acting music critic for the Kansas City *Star* while the regular writer was absent in Europe. In 1928, he became engaged to one of De Rubertis's daughters, Mary, an accomplished pianist, whom he married four years later.

Upon graduating from Rockhurst College summa cum laude, he vaguely intended to become a lawyer; but, deciding "I ought to know more first," he went to St. Louis University, then more advanced than eastern Jesuit institutions. There he concentrated on history and philosophy, receiving a persuasive introduction to St. Thomas Aquinas from Father Henri Renard, S.J., earned his M.A., in 1932, with a philosophy thesis written entirely in Latin, and then decided upon an academic career. On the side, he wrote some musical criticism on space rates for the St. Louis *Times*, corrected papers for a senior professor, and taught philosophy and logic part time in both the university proper and its nursing school. Always attuned to what education his students might give him, Muller-Thym asked to attend the operations in which the aspiring nurses assisted; and largely out of these experiences come not only his extensive knowledge of biology but also all the medical metaphors (some of them macabre) that proliferate his talk. Among his professional credentials, Muller-Thym lists "a certain ignorance. I never took a course in business in my life. I never took a course in either accounting or statistics, and this gives me a certain degree of freedom which accountants may not have. I did not take much economics either, so this gives me freedom in talking about economics." Not unlike other successful polymaths, he cannot resist an occasional jibe at specialists.

In 1936, he took yet another leap, this time into medieval philosophy, as he left the Jesuit St. Louis for the Pontifical Institute of Medieval Studies run by the Order of St. Basil at the University of Toronto. Here Muller-Thym became an ambitious graduate student, not only working extensively with the eminent French scholar Etienne Gilson, who was the institute's star professor, but also mastering the medieval languages (to this day, he claims more competence in Middle High German than in the contemporary tongue) and devouring thoroughly the esoteric classics and vernacular texts. In 1938, he completed a Ph.D. thesis on the difficult and neglected fourteenth-century mystic, Meister Eckhart, which was received so well that Sheed & Ward published it the following year as *The Establishment of the University of Being in Meister Eckhart of Ockham.* "I cracked the Eckhart text," he once told me with pride, "and rescued him from the Nazis, who were promoting Eckhart as the ur-German thinker." Around this time, he also wrote a number of philosophical papers, most of them published in Catholic scholarly journals; and it was his teacher Gilson who offered the testimonal still hung around Muller-Thym's neck: "He is the most brilliant young medievalist in America."

Doctorate in hand, Muller-Thym went back to St. Louis University, which had loaned him money to study at Toronto, to join the Department of Philosophy; and among his colleagues in the school were three contemporaries who have since become more imposing presences. Two are now eminent literary scholars—J. Craig LaDrière, now Professor of Comparative Literature at Harvard, and Father Walter J. Ong, S.J., still a professor of English at St. Louis, who was a year behind Muller-Thym at Rockhurst High School. The third was Marshall McLuhan, then a recent convert to Catholicism, who at the advice of Father Gerald B. Phalen, director of the Pontifical Institute, came to St. Louis in 1937. As polymathic minds and more adventurous spirits, Muller-Thym and McLuhan quickly befriended each other, the former becoming best man (and sole male witness) at McLuhan's wedding, in 1939, and then godfather of his eldest son Eric and one of the McLuhan twin girls. (Relations between them now are cordial but chilly; and at times Muller-Thym will complain that McLuhan does not credit his old friends as much as they credit him. "We are all in a multiple intellectual debt to each other.") To supplement his insufficient academic salary, which was never more than two thousand dollars a year, Muller-Thym, starting in 1939, worked part time (and then full time in the summer) for the consumer research firm that Edward G. Doody had established in St. Louis; and this became "my first experience of business as we know it today."

University life, he slowly discovered, was less congenial than he had hoped, not only because salaries were so low but also because the atmosphere was excessively hostile. "The academic world," he remarked bitterly, "was then mean and narrow and compressed and highly charged. It was full of more jealousies and interpersonal conflicts than the business world was, and academics were more concerned with preserving the existing systems than businessmen. I became terribly frustrated and restless." A polemical review of Mortimer Adler's *The Problem of Species* that Muller-Thym published in *The Modern Schoolman*, late in 1940, produced several acutely hostile responses. This misfortune, along with other adverse experiences, eventually drove him into the U.S. Navy, even though his five children could have provided sufficient grounds for exemption. He vowed then "never to return to that cyclotron [academia] again," yet not until a few years ago did he sell his professor's library of esoteric books.

"I felt deeply about the war, having caught onto fascism as early as 1934; but I didn't think I could kill." So, he was commissioned to design training curricula; and after he went through officer's preamphibious training at Princeton, he taught navigation to officers in Hollywood, Florida, for a spell. Most of the war, however, he spent as an education officer at the training school for enlisted WAVES at Hunter College in the Bronx; and at the war's end, he was its acting executive officer. This experience as an administrator he often cites as "evidence of the fact that, if I had to run a large operation again, in a pinch I could. The Navy also gave me the experience of living in a highly specialized society within a larger, more general society that, like a corporation, had to pretend it was complete and could sustain itself."

While in New York, he ran into a friend from graduate school in Toronto, Philip W. Shay, now executive director of the Association of Consulting Management Engineers, who introduced him to the current literature of management. As always, Muller-Thym read voraciously, as well as critically. "Except for Mary Parker Follett and Henri Fayol, the writers were neither sensible nor relevant—mostly third-rate Hegelians." It was Shay who planted the idea of consulting as a profession; and although this alternative meant repudiating an earlier career in one's late thirties, Muller-Thym found it attractive. "I was hoping for more decent money, some equivalent intellectual satisfactions, and the opportunity to stay in New York, which I loved." At first, he thought of forming his own firm with a few friends; but in the course of querying some of the people at McKinsey and Co., one of the major established firms, he was offered a job there, which he accepted early in 1946. Within a few years, he became a prominent member of McKinsey's, an expert on compensation programs, the director of several projects in process. By the early fifties, he began to get contracts on his own initiative, including consulting projects with various corporations and two teaching positions. The first, as a lecturer on "Human Problems in Administration" one night a week at Columbia, was followed, in 1955, by another as "Visiting Professor of Management" one day a week at the Alfred P. Sloan School of M.I.T., where he taught courses, mostly on "The Structure of Work," until 1966.

Partly because of all this outside activity, mostly because of personal disappointments and an unpleasant scene or two, he rather suddenly resigned from McKinsey in the summer of 1955, with little money in the bank and nary a client in sight; and he has been a free-lance ever since. With not uncustomary pride, he notes in retrospect, "I didn't take any clients with me from McKinsey." Before long, American Cyanamid commissioned him to formulate a managerial salary structure that is still in effect; and early the following year, Cleveland's Case Institute of Technology hired his advice in founding an advanced management program, which he then helped teach until 1958. To Muller-Thym, teaching, lecturing, and consulting are very much of a piece, for all are concerned with changing the minds of impressionable people and thereby influencing their future action; and at times he compares his multifaceted life to that of "a surgeon with his own practice, who also lectures in the medical school and does demonstration operations in the clinic." In fact, some of his calls come from former students, now top executives, who suspect that a current problem in their business might relate to a particularly memorable argument or example "Doctor" Muller-Thym expounded years before.

All this shuffling in and out of several careers and academias, as well as through innumerable kinds of enterprise, have made Muller-Thym an indubitably disaffiliated, if not classless, American who thrives neither inside nor outside the systems of society. His personal presence so thoroughly defies stereotype that, even after talking with him for a while, not in a hundred tries could anyone unfamiliar with his work guess what he does for a living (and when he tells them, they often doubt if he can make any money at that sort of work). He generally favors nondescript informal clothes until a professional occasion forces him to don a freshly cleaned suit; and where and how he lives is not a revealing index. Back in the fifties, the Muller-Thym family, which by then included eight children, lived in two adjacent four-room apartments near Columbia University. The four boys, three of whom were the youngest children, lived with their parents in one apartment, while the other place had beds for four girls and a library-study for their father. A tolerant and benevolent father, he keeps in cordial touch with all his children, most of whom are now married and living in New York; and he would like to believe that over the years he has usually devoted most attention to the child who particularly needed it.

Since separating from his wife in 1961, Muller-Thym has lived in a small tenement apartment in the lower fifties, not on the posh East Side but west of Ninth Avenue; the address emblazoned on his professional stationery sits on the edge of a slum. Like a "railroad flat," his place is open from front to back, the tub sits in the kitchen, and the same sink supposedly serves both the dishes and one's face. In a back alcove are piled boxes of books, papers, and other paraphernalia that he has yet to sort out—a visitor might at first think someone has just moved in—and at times the chaos of things becomes so impressive that there is simply no place to sit and even the bed gets piled high with papers and unopened mail. Smack in the middle of the kitchen sits an incongruously elegant stereo FM and record-player combination; and for some years now he has procrastinated over adding a television set. Very much a traveling man, he is all but impervious about environments; and he does not spend too many nights of the year at home.

As could perhaps be expected, he has rather unusual ideas about the role and purpose of business in American society today. First of all, he regards private corporate organization as industrial society's most effective vehicle for getting complex work done and generating large-scale innovation (for reasons of too much red tape and too little incentive, governments are less efficient; universities he regards as even less reliable than governments). His second basic idea holds that the two primary sources of wealth creation (where output exceeds input) in contemporary society are the exploitation of nature and the organization of knowledge; and as the second process, exemplified by invention and innovation, becomes increasingly more profitable than the first, the role of expertise, as well as consultants, becomes concomitantly greater. Business, as a means of organizing knowledge and effort so that the ends (output) are greater than the input, becomes, by extension, "a machine for making wealth." Therefore, "today's manager has become primarily a mobilizer of competences—one who knows how to trap the ingenium, the wit, of people and who designs the circuitry of making their competences flow and interact so that the total business as a system gets its work done."

From these definitions it follows that Muller-Thym is less interested in maximizing profit, which he sometimes regards as a venal primary purpose, than in increasing the wealth created by a business. "The whole system is profit-generated, it's profit-loaded, but no part of it generates profit, nor is it capable of generating profit independently. Profit is fallout that happens if the system is functioning well." In criticizing a particular business, he is less inclined to complain about the profit levels ("although I'm not opposed to profit") than to lament that, "the gross waste of talent, of human beings, is absolutely grievous." Indeed, among his constant professional concerns is persuading managers to create working conditions more conducive to their employees' effectiveness. "Generally, people would rather work than not work, and they would rather do it accurately and well than not. You see, the forces of nature are clearly aligned on the side of management, which then often jeopardizes its advantage. It's much easier to cooperate with nature than to buck it; nature's going to win anyway." Nonetheless, he also anticipates that technological developments will lessen the burden of human work, creating more unemployment rather than less, if not, eventually, the need for a Guaranteed Annual Wage and, after that, more concern about purpose in an age of leisure; and his prognostications include the abolition of tangible money through a computerized system of instantaneous credit and debit, as well as a radically different system of material compensation for a society in which servile work will disappear.

His ideas on the shape of work stem from a general rule which holds that rhythm and structure are the primary variables in determining the efficiency of both individual workers and an entire array of employees. "We know very little about the temporal dimension of work, for very few studies have been made. We know that there are tens and even hundreds of overlaying rhythmic patterns—the pattern of the individual short job, the pattern of the day, the pattern created by job promotions and job changes which make up the rhythmic dimension of the worker's life. The pattern of a salesman's calls, for example, bears a direct relationship to the volume of sales produced. More successful salesmen in a company—that is, those who sell the most—have different individual rhythmic patterns as they cultivate their territory, but all of them have strongly marked and easily observable patterns. Poorer salesmen, on the other hand, have no marked patterns of work and the way in which they move through the time of a day or a week is generally anarchic or chaotic."

In industrial situations, he believes that the space in which complex work is conducted, as well as the structure of the communications network, can immensely affect the output, regardless of the good will or competence of the parties involved. For instance, the computer programmer, he once observed, aids a scientist better if he is physically at the scientist's side when the latter is working out the critical points of his program. Or, when the office of the contract representative on a meteorological satellite was moved from the project's center to a distant building that housed other contract representatives, there was subsequently a three-week delay in every contract change. Out of this concern with working space and shape comes his blanket criticism of architects who neglect to consider how human beings will function inside their buildings. "They are interested only in the outside; and it so happens that about ninety-five per cent of the space is on the inside."

Another Muller-Thym thesis holds that control over the end product should be built into the design of work—a process known in computerese as "feedback"—so that the maker gets to continually consider the result of his efforts. In practice, this usually involves generalizing, or giving to one person, a step-by-step job (such as fulfilling an order) that has previously been divided among a succession of people—"reconstituting the integrity of the task" is his pet phrase for it. In one example, this kind of structural change would enable the person who first takes the order to complete it, thereby insuring that the order leaves the fulfillment process properly executed. Very much contrary to Frederick W. Taylor's legendary principle that complex work should be fragmented across a repetitious assembly line, Muller-Thym believes that a man's task should be made, first, as comprehensive and, second, as various as possible; even on philosophical grounds, he continually objects to "the old Cartesian principle of solving a problem by breaking it down into its parts and then taking those parts in sequence."

Another major recent Muller-Thym theme holds that the introduction of new technologies poses its own formal requirements for doing a particular task. "The traditional design for work, invented in 3500 B.C., resembles in form the wheel and writing on paper; but these design-presumptions are now changing. Both the computer and contemporary weaponry are neither linear nor circular but total, random, instantaneous and irreversible." Similarly, thanks largely to electronic communications media, the restricting, routinizing structure of classic bureaucracies has given way to a new, more fluid pattern of organization, which no longer resembles a hierarchic pyramid, he notes, but a multiple interlocking "metamatrix whose only model in nature is two octopuses shaking hands through all their tentacles." Both psychologically and structurally, this change represents a distinct advance. "The job as an inhibiting rigid box disappears and becomes a center where are concentrated tasks and competences which hook up in a network of similar centers. This brings changes in the conception of authority, which, like electricity itself, is nowadays concerned less with power than communication." All this makes corporations more congenial places in which to work, although, he adds, "They could be better. When people feel good, they generally produce better work more efficiently." On another level, Muller-Thym was historically among the first to note that the form intrinsic in automation ultimately is not standardization but variety, because all mechanical processes with variable dimensions can be programmed by tape to manufacture a customized product, where every changeable item can be tailored precisely to the buyer's specifications. Muller-Thym's favorite example is the single machine that can "make up to eighty different kinds of automotive tailpipe as rapidly and cheaply as you can make eighty of the same one," and he notes that most extras and other variables on automobiles are nowadays assembled precisely to the individual customer's order.

His most recent professional interest has been the initiation and management of innovation, which he regards as the primary means of wealth creation; and he currently claims a particular "competence in advising on the invention of new products, new methods of communication, new product-systems [whole terrains of expansion], and entirely new businesses." In general, he believes that many major American enterprises are currently in a "transform," as he puts it—about to pass from one kind of definition to another; and since the ideas of consultants often supply some oil to ease the way into the future, corporation chiefs regularly invite Muller-Thym to discuss, simply, "what else they might presently be doing." As he views the current moment, changes in society, in technology, and in corporate activity bring constant imbalance, which should be regarded as more of an opportunity than a threat. "You take a business which is a closed system," he advises, "one in which output is equal to input, one which is in balance, and punch a hole in it by deliberately injecting imbalance. Not until someone senses a disturbance will any learning take place; and not until he suffers a real dislocation will there be any creative output." At this point arises a need for innovative thinking, which can happen, he generalizes, through displacement in time, displacement in space, or a reversal that reveals a truth that might otherwise have remained hidden. The entrance of a consultant, or a thorough shift in key personnel, can stimulate the first two conditions, if only because, as McLuhan often points out, an emigrant from the anti-environment brings a different space-time perspective to the primary environment. This advocacy of radical alternatives and sharp contrasts as keys to insight consistently animates Muller-Thym's own thinking about corporate innovation; and he sometimes suggests not only that perhaps the most persistent headache in an organization paradoxically masks the biggest invitation to innovation but also that there is a polydisciplinary unity to all creativity. "I see no difference at all in the structural and psychic requirements for organizing creativity, whether you are creating a new organization, a new product, a new marketing program, or a scientific satellite."

More an exponent of propitious means than particular ends,

Muller-Thym suggests, "The smartest kind of management creates conditions under which desirable things are likely to occur [for example, a thoroughly equipped, competently staffed, and effectively organized research laboratory], rather than aiming for a specific end." From this managerial principle it follows that the ultimate purpose of a corporation's research and development department should not be inventing a particular product but "taking an institution which has been in balance up to that moment and deliberately injecting imbalance and risk into it. The result will be a series of reactions that will force the system to change appropriately. In this process, something will have been created in the business, and in the total economy, something we call wealth." In recent years, Muller-Thym has come to regard business as such a propitious environment for change that he roughly estimates that up to twenty per cent of any large operation can be transformed in a year. "If one begins to think about business as a wealth creator in our society, then all of us are required to engage more actively, more purposefully and more conclusively in innovation —new product development and so forth—which becomes now a necessity for all our business."

Since 1950, as Muller-Thym never tires of pointing out, American business has become increasingly more dependent upon intellectual knowledge—both new ideas and continuing education; and many executives today continually face the kind of complex, unprecedented problems that previously concerned only the few in the largest corporations. "The skills required to run a business today have multiplied almost beyond count," he wrote recently. "Business structures have been invaded and penetrated by think-type people. This is as true of businesses like banks, insurance companies, and soft-drink bottlers as it is of space-technology based companies—the difference is only a matter of degree." Not only has the scope and function of consultancy expanded enormously, but so has the demand for management educators. To Colin Park, Ph.D., the director of educational programs for the international accountancy firm of Haskins and Sells, who invites Muller-Thym each year to lecture a conference of the firm's partners, "People like Bernard are catalysts, shaking a man out of his demanding professional realm to see his work more objectively. Their purpose is not to pump in a particular point of view but to expand a man's thinking processes." In the constant challenges of unprecedented experience is the need for continual intellectual growth, in both the collective and the individual intelligence; and at times like these, such intellectual development is a universal imperative. "There is," to Muller-Thym, "no reason why either people or corporations cannot continue to be creative and imaginative as they grow older," providing that they build, as the master consultant does for himself, professional situations conducive to innovative thinking. "If knowledge is power," writes his old friend Father Ong, "knowledge of how to generate knowledge is power over power."

Moreover, since 1950, there has been another revolution in American business's attitude toward knowledge. "We have achieved for the first time in human history a plenum of science and technology," says Muller-Thym, with enthusiasm creeping into his voice, "and instead of depending upon inventions to happen somewhere, we have invented the organization of invention and now can almost invent at will. The only real resources one has in doing this kind of work are time and knowledge; and there is only one real source of absolute newness in the universe—this is intelligence. We have crossed the line in understanding the magic of how new knowledge is created; and though we do not yet have a lot of skill at doing this, we know where the magic is and how to posture ourselves to touch it. Creation comes whenever there is a set of conditions where afterwards there is absolutely more output than there was in the sum of the inputs. This means the end of the era of fixed wealth and a closed universe—the world of both Karl Marx and Adam Smith—and the beginning of an open universe and unlimited wealth; and business, instead of shuffling wealth around, now invents it." To all these issues, the consultant ideally brings not his own experience in business but "a massive body of knowledge in doing things," as a doctor brings not his own memory of a disease but a knowledge of diseases, as well as a synoptic, disinterested perspective of the entire system.

Like everyone else so thoroughly committed to the necessity of sweeping change, Muller-Thym is fundamentally a radical, even though he often deals with enterprises that would probably like to regard themselves as conservative. To make distinctions among radicals, he is more constructive than destructive, more of a visionary innovator than a political revolutionary, as well as enough of a democrat (in fact, a registered Democrat) to believe that everyone should participate in, as well as benefit from, innovation. Among his own purposes, Muller-Thym includes such unconservative tasks as "untwisting the strings that hold the old system together," and by addressing so often, as he puts it, "a lot of the people who stand at the hinges of our society, I'm more immersed in action than some guys who are shooting off their mouths all the time." In the end, his commitment to innovation as an urgent necessity extends to all of society; and at times, the ex-philosopher seems on the verge of offering to American corporate enterprise an ethics of perpetual radical change in a postindustrial electronic society.

One of Muller-Thym's leaps beyond established intellectual thought, an unconventional bias he shares with R. Buckminster Fuller, comes from regarding industrial enterprise as the revolutionary force in contemporary society; and his radical leap in management thought stems from classifying businesses as either innovative or obsolete. "If a business does not create and leave in the economy an increase of wealth proportionate to the commitment of national resources which it demands by reason of being in existence," he warns, "then that business is already obsolescent; it is dead, even though it may not know it. In the kind of world in which we live, everything will go along fine for years, and then one morning the directors will wake up and find that a competitor has moved in on them and they have had it. This sudden death experience is symptomatic of the world today. We are changing so fast that the America of

1950, if we confronted it today, would seem like a junk shop or a flea market; it's that far behind us."

Also contrary to pious thinking, Muller-Thym regards business as solid, responsible, and purposeful, while its better officials (hardly a majority) are "enlightened and concerned," as well as adept at "the mobilization of competencies"; and most of the changes achieved by American business are, in his judgment, more beneficial to society than not. "As managerial activity is focused on action, on making something come to be," he told me over drinks, "the significant managerial issues are existential, to change so radically what one is doing that the afterward is different from the before." Therefore, the qualities desirable in a manager include synoptic vision, an ability to generalize from experience, a consideration for people, persistence in the face of difficulty, a firm sense of justice and equity —in sum, as Ralph Baldwin points out, "qualities not too different from those we attribute to a good man." Although critical of specific ideas and practices, Muller-Thym generally admires the multifarious achievement of American enterprise and, more important, cannot envision a convincing future realized without its participation; and in this respect, his consulting practice makes him very much of an activist on behalf of his politics.

Speaking frankly about the companies he advises, Muller-Thym confided, over the din of the bar, "Better-managed businesses are better clients, because, being able and intelligent, they start from a position of strength and know how to flow into action. With them, it's easier for a consultant to change a bunch of things than change a single thing, and it is more than likely that several dimensions need care. The same bad management that gets a company into trouble is not likely to understand or act upon your recommendations; they could also ruin your reputation as a consultant. The more interesting clients are those at a critical point in their curve of growth, where they will be forced to change, in a radical way, the nature or form of their activity. More interesting clients have higher metabolic rates, where the people are able and active and yet not trapped by a particular technology, type of structure, or something else that is already becoming an ancient part of the environment. It's no fun, though a feat of strength, to save a company committed to an obsolete technology or a disappearing market." In this conversation, as well as others, I got the impression that Muller-Thym considers corporations as genuinely worthy of intellectual interest as a medievalist finds philosophers or a critic finds works of art.

He looks critically upon the recent fad of mergers as often sabotaging both the coherence of the larger company and the integrity of the smaller one. "It's difficult to make sense of some conglomerates; for some mergers are done simply to improve the price of the company's stock or its aggressive image in the eyes of its stockholders and the investing community. If a company doesn't have much reason as an enterprise, it can only deteriorate." On the other hand, he will justify those diversified families whose various operations enhance each other, such as TRW or even Lytton Industries, "as integrated units that are more complicated than a corporation but less complex than a state—an intermediate form of social organization whose elements are channeled into an integral network. The issue is entrepreneurship versus manageability."

The profession of free-lance consulting is still too improvised to acquire formal ground rules, let alone codes of proper ethics and even standard forms of contract. Indeed, agreements are usually verbal; and in Muller-Thym's experience, they are infallibly honored, regardless of whether the client is satisfied or not. A job usually comes over the telephone, which, as he puts it, "never rings until there is a disorder situation, as perceived by a major person in the company." Since there is no standard listing of management consultants, the corporation official either knows Muller-Thym or his previous work, or a third party has recommended him as the most appropriate doctor for this particular malady; and because so little is recorded in print, what reputation an individual earns is communicated largely by word-of-mouth. At the start of a job, the consultant usually establishes a rough rate of pay, which can run as high as a thousand dollars a day plus expenses, although this figure, as Muller-Thym puts it, "is tempered in part by what I think they can pay me. Charging is an ambiguous business; and I sometimes wish I could charge as lawyers do—a retainer plus surcharge." The total duration is also approximated in advance, although he has been known to request an extension, which is usually granted, or leave earlier than expected "because nothing further could have been done." Since his competence is both various and synoptic, he generally works from the perspective of the company's president, a division's chief executive officer, or the general manager of a particular operation (in contrast to the consulting firms, which usually place a whole team of observers in links along the chain of command); and the policy changes that Muller-Thym proposes will necessarily demand initiation from the top.

After accepting a commission, the consultant generally travels to the scene of the trouble, arriving promptly at all appointments there, using sparingly the time of busy people, and customarily offering to join the client in less formal activities, such as drinking-talking in the evening (perhaps Muller-Thym's favorite recreation). The most effective manner for offering advice is neither deferential nor antagonistic, but as firm and sympathetic as a doctor to his patient. "If you agree to take on a consultation, you are concerned about the client; but there is a real danger in becoming too involved, emotionally, with a company. One should say polite things, but they should have an element of truth too; yet one shouldn't allow his client to get into a breast-beating posture." Nonetheless, his peers regard Muller-Thym as especially tenacious at holding his viewpoint against objections or at presenting an unpopular opinion, if not shamelessly stubborn in outright confrontations —"there are always forces at work which are obstructionist," he says; and he is tough enough, as well as free enough, to criticize individual officers, reply to their criticisms of him, and even dismiss the board of directors as "the most incompetent part of the whole institution. They don't know what's going on." Another time he confided, "I've never done an automobile company, for its people are not likely to believe anything you tell them." More often than not, he completes his consultation with a dictated report, which becomes the client's private property, and then goes home, later submitting a bill merely marked, often by his own hand, "for professional services."

He estimates that he works two hundred days a year, and in August 1968, for instance, half of the calender days to the end of the year were already filled. Over the years he has had only two retainers—contracts to spend a fixed number of days per month with a certain corporation; and one of these, the McCann-Erickson agency, in turn hires him out for miscellaneous work with its advertising clients. More proud than arrogant, contained than aggressive, he regards himself as "a professional" with an especially strong sense of "decent craftsmanship." He is reliable about keeping secrets, as well as discreet about divulging industrial information; indeed, some of his more interesting recent jobs could not be reported in this essay. As a matter of principle, if he does extensive consulting for one firm in a field, he is not likely, for several years at least, to do any work for another. Ideally, he prefers to do a little teaching, a little lecturing, and mostly consulting every month, expecting that the material of each will flow into all the others; and his own past experience tells him, first, that he cannot do more than two extensive consulting jobs at once and, second, that the most effective rhythm for consultation will involve three days of contact per week—no more, no less—stretched over a period of time that usually includes weeks of no contact at all. Though he is as well paid for his services as a lawyer of comparable reputation, his sense of professional craft is as important to him as the money. "There is only one critic a consultant or any professional, finally respects," he told me over dinner, "and that is himself." Indicatively, he does not play the stock market, on the grounds that it would consume too much time and attention ("although most everybody I know does"), nor does he give speculative advice; and only in 1968 did he agree to serve on the board of directors of anything, a Cambridge "think tank" called Meta Systems, Inc. "I am fortunate in that the kind of work I do is always interesting to me."

The role of the free-lance consultant is not a new one for men of the mind, but the kind of profession defined by Muller-Thym's practice is distinctly recent in vintage. He so frequently cites Aristotle that one is sure the philosopher would still be a first-rate consultant, even though "Alexander the Great, who was his client, refused his advice." What distinguishes Muller-Thym's consultancy from Aristotle's is primarily that he deals with the problems of, by historical standards, unprecedentedly complex organizations (not even Alexander's entire army was one fiftieth as complicated as General Electric); and what separates him from the consulting firms, such as McKinsey, is that he generally works alone. Indeed, no one else in the trade is both polymathic and totally unaffiliated, although several major men are either one or the other. Dr. Peter Drucker, for instance, was a Bennington philosophy teacher when he undertook his year-long, one-man study of General Motors, reported in *The Concept of the Corporation* (1946); and now a professor in N.Y.U.'s Graduate School of Business and still very much a generalist, he presently accepts only those consulting contracts that allow him to spend the night at home in New Jersey. Other professors active in "private," which is to say personal, organizational consulting include Dr. Ernest Dale, who teaches at the Wharton School of Finance and has authored many books; Dr. Jay Forrester at M.I.T., author of *Industrial Dynamics* (1961); Dr. Robert Burden, a Harvard engineering professor; Dr. Gunther Weil, formerly an editor of *Psychedelic Review* and now a professor of psychology at Boston College; and Fr. John Culkin, S.J. (and Ph.D.), chairman of the Communications Department at Fordham University. Major free-lance specialists include the author Robert Heilbronner, whose forte is lectures; Dr. Ralph Baldwin, a former English professor at Catholic University, who sets up education programs (and just recently took a part-time teaching position at Fairfield University); and Richard Elwell, a trained engineer who is now expert in retail operations. More inclined to intellectual than financial competitiveness, Muller-Thym admits that other consultants may have larger incomes; but he stubbornly disallows that anybody else might be a better generalist, or more competent at his particular fortes. The role and work that these consultants have carved for themselves inevitably suggest a distinction between the many that do and the elite few who think about those that do.

To Donald A. Schon, Ph.D. (also in philosophy), head of the non-profit Organization for Social and Technical Innovation, Muller-Thym has "the most extraordinary mind in consulting"; and even by less specialized standards, his mind is unusual for the range of its interest, its freedom from conventional cant, the size and speed of its memory, its sense of scale and appropriate analogy, its disciplined persistence and persistent discipline, the variety of specialized knowledges it has mastered and conceptual tools at its command, its subtlety and perceptiveness and critical acumen, its ability to originate alternatives, and much else; to Dr. John Riedl, a friend for three decades and current dean at Queensborough Community College, Muller-Thym's mind has changed less than his work. Many of those competences stem from his extensive training in philosophy, which taught him to devise useful operative definitions and discern crucial distinctions invisible to less discriminating minds. "In philosophy." Riedl explained to me, "you find answers about as fast and as successfully as you state the right question." From the concerns of epistemology probably comes Muller-Thym's constant questioning of the basic terms of business knowledge, such as "inventory," "profit," "assets," all of which he considers rather arbitrary and irrelevant measures of the true wealth of a company today. (Where in its annual report, he asks, are reported such critical indices as the utilized efficiency of employed time and other basic resources, the experience of its active executives, the knowledge of its research department, the company's position in its field, and the current state and possible future of its particular competences?)

His remarks on the different structures of corporate operation are clearly an ontology of business (if not a biological taxonomy too), as is his constant awareness of the different natures of interlocking systems. "I stopped philosophy to start a new life," he once told me, "but later I realized that what I did reflected my earlier training." Indeed, he now regards the work of St. Thomas Aquinas, "an encyclopedia of information and methods for handling it," as perhaps the best intellectual preparation for understanding the computer; and he once told me that after unraveling the previously unfathomable complexities of Meister Eckhart, "I got the feeling that I could penetrate any difficult mystery." Beyond that, his sense of systemic dislocation is patently indebted to his knowledge of biology, as well as that classic by D'Arcy Wentworth Thompson he continually recommends, *On Growth and Form* (1917; revised edition, 1942). Even deeper, perhaps, is a radical's innate cussedness that forces him to look at familiar things in unfamiliar ways, in addition to doubting constantly the established textbooks and theorists. His refusal to regard business as primarily a money-making operation means, in practice, that an organization becomes a complex work of art whose mysteries demand insightful and rigorous analysis, as well as accurate intuitions of value and gist. "As an artifact of man," he says, "business is then subject to critical dissection." Or, as McLuhan succinctly puts it, "Muller-Thym deals with businesses as though they were poems."

RICHARD HOFSTADTER: Historian's Indomitable Skepticism

Art criticism has to be reinvented for every generation.—BRIAN O'DOHERTY

For a nation with so short a history, America has a home-shores historical profession that is remarkably thriving in numbers, as well as prodigiously productive in pages; for the post-World War II expansion of universities has produced a scholarship industry whose Americana division is among the largest and fastest growing. In recent years, great tribes of Americanist scholars have exhumed nearly every minor historical event, every semisignificant personage, and then subjected them to meticulous scrutiny, as though the curators simply had to systematically catalogue *all* the artifacts in the academic museum. Despite the emphasis within the trade upon minutiae, the most acclaimed practitioners, the master minds in the field, still deal in large-scale synthesis, as major historians have always done; and by fairly general consent, the best, if not the most influential of these macro-historians, has been Richard Hofstadter, Professor of American History at Columbia University and the author of several indubitably major books—such prize winners and good sellers as *The American Political Tradition* (1948), *The Age of Reform* (1955), *Anti-Intellectualism in American Life* (1963), and *The Paranoid Style in American Politics* (1965).

Hofstadter himself has always seemed an enigmatic figure, mostly because on the surface at least he appears neither as brilliant nor as original as his books; for in an age when so much that appears in print is written in a rush, if not dictated into a machine, Hofstadter labors assiduously to produce pages of print that are, word for word, far more intelligent, interesting and knowledgeable than his conversation. Though his mind is perhaps more solid than sharp, his books forge, in both senses, the semblance of sharpness through patently accumulated solidity; the children of his creation are, in essence, more substantial than he is. He honors his teaching duties at Columbia, yet he sets up his life primarily to fabricate those books, tenaciously refusing to do anything but write nearly every morning of the year, hiring student assistants to do miscellaneous drudgery, and cultivating his fellow professors for their critical talents. Since his first drafts are, by his own judgment, "sloppy and idiosyncratic," he joins his indispensable wife, Beatrice, in rewriting and editing the, literally, worked-up manuscript. Taking the first edition of his first book off the shelf, *Social Darwinism in American Thought* (1944), a revision of his Ph.D. thesis, Hofstadter opened its cover and told me, "There you get a sense of how badly I used to write."

The books themselves are comprehensive in scope, coherent in point of view and sensibility, crystalline in style, and obliquely relevant to contemporary concerns; and a succession of such grandly conceived and carefully realized works has established Hofstadter's preeminence. He effectively combines the popular historian's penchant for generalizing about important issues with the scholar's cautious awareness of complexity and persistent reference to earlier sources. The breadth of Hofstadter's interpretations and the quality of his particular perceptions give his books a cumulative resonance that transcends his thesis; consistently fine detail, rather than a pretentious idea, makes the whole. Indeed, because they eschew both melodrama and narrative for analysis and supported synthesis, they are liable to appeal more to historians, both professional and amateur (and their numbers are likewise legion), than lay readers looking for a thrilling yarn; and this perhaps explains why no other American historian seems to have as much influence upon the impressionable yet discerning minds of graduate students in the field.

His first major effort, *The American Political Tradition*, published when he was thirty-two, was clearly a significant study, if only for the scope of his intent; for here he undertook a series of probing, critical portraits of such major figures as Thomas Jefferson, Andrew Jackson, Abraham Lincoln, and Herbert Hoover. The vision was broad and the tone unsentimental, while the insights were plentiful and often original; for not only had the young man consumed the scholarship (and critically classified and measured it in an appendix of bibliographical essays), but he added his own bits of persuasive interpretation to the scholarly tradition. Equally impressive was Hofstadter's fine style—never melodramatic or slick, consistently clear and tasteful, occasionally elegant and witty, and incorrigibly skeptical. "He loved an audience," Hofstadter wrote of John C. Calhoun, "but he did not especially care for company." On Jefferson: "The leisure that made possible his great writings on human liberty was supported by the labors of three generations of slaves."

Out of these individual essays emerges not only an innovation in historiographical method—essentially the synthesis of man's ideas, biography, and actions—but also a polemical theme, which reiterates that inadequate intellectual presuppositions, usually complemented by an inflexible cast of mind, caused persistently inept political activity. In contrast to the gallery of semicompetents, Franklin D. Roosevelt is portrayed as transcending this tradition by recognizing that an unprecedented situation, the Great Depression, demanded the improvisation of entirely new policies and, more important, new political assumptions. "At the very beginning of his candidacy Roosevelt, without heed for tradition or formality, flew to the 1932 nominating convention and addressed it in person instead of waiting for weeks in the customary pose of ceremonious ignorance. A trivial act in itself, the device gave the public an impression of vigor and originality that was never permitted to die," writes Hofstadter. "His capacity for growth, or at least for change, was enormous. Flexibility was both his strength and his weakness." Intellectually, the book was indebted to the sociology of knowledge, as formulated by the German scholar Karl Mannheim and the American Thorstein Veblen, for keys to connecting a man's ideas to his social role; stylistically, Hofstadter learned from literary criticism how to "freeze" a political career into a unified entity that could be dissected and interpreted as a critic would a novel or a painting. Because the young historian tackled so much and was patently full of provocative ideas, *The American Political Tradition* comes off as a big, exciting work, justifiably the single best seller (nearly a half million copies in paperback; translations into six languages) in the Hofstadter canon.

His subsequent books have, in increasing degrees, focused upon activities away from the centers of political power—protest movements and pressure groups—and here Hofstadter has been particularly concerned with political pathology—people who believe politics will solve problems of belief, morality, and status that are basically outside of politics; "activists" who would overthrow America's democratic pluralism for one or another kind of authoritarian regime; and those who would blame their personal failures upon invisible behind-the-scenes enemies in the machinery of power. In all his books, Hofstadter has been continually aware of how the stuff of politics is people, whose personal motives and psychologies, whether individually or collectively expressed, color their political questions of who gets what, when and how, he also poses the sociological queries of, "Who perceives what public issues in what way, and why?"—for instance, why one group, rather than another, should be so passionately concerned about "red scares"? If *The American Political Tradition* came out of a thirties awareness of political inadequacy, the later books were informed by the political excesses Hofstadter discerned in fascism, Communism, and McCarthyism.

One of his themes in *The Age of Reform*, ostensibly a study of the Progressive movement, held that conservative nostalgia, rather than radical vision, animated much reform thinking;

and Hofstadter gauged that certain "left" strands of the early twentieth century flowed into the "radical right" of the middle fifties. (The implication that populism was among the ancestors of McCarthyism he developed more explicitly in the 1955 edition of Daniel Bell's collection, *The New American Right.*) Another more controversial and yet influential theme drew upon the sociological insight that the desire for high place and great power in society may be a more powerful motivation than economic interest, as Hofstadter suggested that subconscious status-strivings latently influenced the activities and polemical imagery of some Progressive reformers. Stylistically, *The Age of Reform* is, as he puts it, "unusual among works of history in being almost entirely an interpretative essay without narrative content. In it I allowed my taste for speculation and hypothesis to range freely. In consequence it contains an unusually large number of ideas and an unusually small apparatus of fact." For reasons of style, as well as substance, this book won the 1955 Pulitzer Prize for history.

In *Anti-Intellectualism in American Life,* which took the 1963 Pulitzer Prize in general non-fiction, his theme is the distrust of the mind that he feels has pervaded American culture from the beginning. In *The Paranoid Style in American Politics,* he draws upon the scholarly literature of European totalitarianism to probe in depth parallel tendencies in American "extremist" politics—the Goldwater movement, McCarthyism, the John Birch Society, and less articulated but considerably similar movements on the left. Implicit in all these books is a persistent critique of fallacious ideas; for underlying his political histories is a definite sense of how politics should not be conducted and, more important, *not* be thought about.

Hofstadter's other major interest has been intellectual history, particularly of America's universities and its major historians. Out of the first concern, he co-authored *The Development and Scope of Higher Education in the United States* (1952), which he no longer regards as a good book; and in collaboration with his close friend and Columbia colleague Walter P. Metzger, he produced *The Development of Academic Freedom in the United States* (1955), a historical study which is more scholarly than polemical. This big work has since been split into two paperbacks, one to each author—Hofstadter's being *Academic Freedom in the Age of the College* (1961). With Wilson Smith, he coedited a mammoth (1016 large pages) and surprisingly interesting compendium, *American Higher Education: A Documentary History* (1961), which in format echoed a two-volume paperback anthology of important documents, *Great Issues in American History* (1958) and preceded a similar paperback print-out on *The Progressive Movement* 1963). In the middle fifties, he co-authored, with William Miller and Daniel Aaron, two sets of A–Z textbooks, *The United States* (1957; second edition, 1967) and *The American Republic* (1959), which, even after royalty-splitting, have been over the past decade more remunerative than his more famous works. More recently, he expanded earlier essays on Charles Beard, V. L. Parrington, and Frederick Jackson Turner, some dating back to 1938, into a lengthy study of *The Progressive Historians* (1968) that, Hofstadter hopes, may salvage the legacy of his intellectual fathers for his professional children. There is hardly a well-stocked bookstore in America that does not have a few Hofstadters on its shelves.

His place in recent American historiography is rather ambiguous, because he skirts rather than fits some current tendencies. At times he has mistakenly been grouped with the "consensus historians," such as Chicago's Daniel Boorstin and Harvard's Louis Hartz, because like them he rejects the earlier generation's portrayal of dichotomous black-white, good-bad conflicts in American life. However, rather than an image of consensual harmony, Hofstadter presents a pluralistic conception of American conflict—where many groups, dividing themselves in a multiplicity of ways, engage in an even greater variety of disagreements. "The progressive historians," he explains, "got the grain of conflict so wrong that we were led to emphasize pluralism." This image of diverse and deflecting quarrels becomes one of his more persuasive ideas.

At other times, Hofstadter has been classified as a sociological and/or psychological historian; yet while he is more inclined than his professional colleagues to draw his tools of analysis from these fields, his interpretations do not rigorously subscribe to either approach. A coherent intelligence and frame of concern, rather than an overarching theory, tie the strands of his books together; and he disclaims any interest in either deterministic explanatory schemes or cosmic generalizations. "I do not fancy myself a philosopher of history, or a philosophical thinker." On the other hand, it would be fair to say that behind his insights are a gamut of modern, rather than contemporary, ideas, particularly regarding latent biases and subconscious motives (except, curiously enough, sexual desire); and this modernist outlook decisively distinguishes Hofstadter from earlier generations of American historians. Finally, since his arguments are complex, his nuances subtle, and his inferences ambiguous, he frequently finds his ideas misrepresented in print, as often by his supporters as detractors.

Stylistically, he clearly belongs with those analytical historians who stand between the popularizers and the academics, because his books represent extended essays, rather than narratives or monographs. "I function more as a historical critic, dealing with material that is at least slightly familiar," he says; and as he offers insights, rather than theses, so his commentary functions to illustrate, rather than conclusively document, his argument. "It attempts to develop and state new ways of looking at historical events; its task is analytical," he explains. "I offer trial models of historical interpretation." Therefore, his insights should be taken as closer to criticism than science—whether they make persuasive sense of the available evidence rather than present a "definitive" proof that will be verified by all subsequent researchers. As a critical instrument, Hofstadter's intelligence integrates certain artistic sensitivities—empathy, judgment, intuition, appropriate scale, and good taste for both words and ideas—into the semiscientific procedure of scholarly exposition. "Whereas most historians travel with filing cases," says his colleague Walter P. Metzger, "Dick takes nearly no notes. He's able to read a text and then imagine a chunk of life, or re-create the contours and causes of an event, as well as its ideological essences. This kind of intelligence is very rare, and very useful, in history."

For these reasons, he regards everything he has published with "a certain tentativeness," and he freely considers in detail how he might (but won't) rewrite each of his earlier books. "If I had known what an imbecile fuss would be raised about my having mentioned the occasional anti-Semitic rhetoric among the Populists, I would either have dropped it as not worth the trouble or else spent even more time than I did in clarifying what I was saying. If I should do another like *The American Political Tradition* today, every sketch would be different. No, that's not exactly true." Finally, like all good wordsmiths, he is a successful phrase-maker and -popularizer; and among his catchier epithets is "Social Darwinism," which he found mentioned only a few times before and which everyone now uses to classify all American social thought between 1860 and 1915 that acknowledged Darwin's influence.

His skeptical attitude toward the American past stems in part from the fact that by cultural background, as well as personal inclination, he is not an insider but an outsider. Neither a New Englander nor a Midwesterner, as were previous generators of major native historians, he was born in 1916, in Buffalo, New York, a cold and bleak city of immigrants—mostly Polish—and their children, and later not only attended a public racially integrated high school but also took his B.A. at the local university. His father, Emil Hofstadter, who was born in Cracow, Poland, and raised in New York City, had a small fur business—repairing and remodeling—that hired a few employees in the peak autumn season; and like so many other Jewish immigrant fathers who worked with their hands, he made especial effort to insure that his two children would not suffer a similar fate.

As his mother was an Episcopalian, young Richard was at first raised as a Christian; but after she died, when he was ten, he lost interest in religion. His childhood became so difficult that Hofstadter no longer remembers, or cares to remember, much before his high school years; and not until he got to college did he acquire a circle of congenial friends, most of whom were Jewish. "I spent a lot of years acquiring a Jewish identity, which is more cultural than religious," he remembers, declaring, "for anyone who is part Jewish can only be a Jew. His own conscience and society demand it." True to his hybrid background, he sprinkles his conversation with oddly pronounced Yiddishisms and identifies selectively with certain things Jewish ("It's tribal"). Future scholars will probably write reams inferring immense significance from the fact that Hofstadter is the first great American historian of Jewish background; but, instead, he would regard his own work as a product of a marginal sensibility, suspended between Jewish and Christian culture, as well as between immigrant cosmopolitanism and American provincialism. "I can never wholly identify with any collectivity," he explains, pausing. "This kind of marginality is by now a more general American experience; so today I am not an unrepresentative American."

Like most other Americanists, Hofstadter very early in life developed a particular interest in Americana; and as a student, he matured so parochially within the field that he did not get to Europe until he was past thirty (when someone paid his way) and to this day he rarely refers to European analogies or even consults the major histories of Europe. He dates his earliest persuasive inspiration to Charles and Mary Beard's *The Rise of American Civilization*, which he read in 1934 while an undergraduate; and his interest was supported by Julius W. Pratt, a professor at Buffalo whom Hofstadter regards as not only his greatest teacher but "a thoroughly professional historian, which I think I'll never be." After taking his B.A. degree, in 1937, as well as a Phi Beta Kappa key, he came to New York to attend New York Law School, at the insistence of his family—his father's younger brother Samuel Hofstadter was already a successful lawyer (now he sits on the New York State Supreme Court); but he quickly dropped out to register for graduate study at Columbia, taking his M.A. in history the following year. "You can lead a young man to the bar," he jokes, "but you cannot make him drink." Not a particularly successful graduate student, he failed at first to receive the fellowships for which he applied (indicatively suspecting an anti-Semitism he since knows was unfounded) and so took part-time teaching jobs at Brooklyn College and, later, City College. In 1941, Columbia awarded him the William Bayard Cutting Traveling Fellowship, which he used to complete his thesis on Social Darwinism, taking his doctorate the following year.

By the summer of 1942, he still had not found a job for the fall; even though he had published three articles in the professional journals, positions were scarce. In the mail came an unanticipated offer from the University of Maryland, where he became an assistant professor for four years (and earned a military exemption for teaching soldiers). The school he remembers as a "circus" whose president, "Curly" Bird, was formerly the football coach; but much to Hofstadter's good fortune, among his colleagues was an equally youthful Texas-born sociologist fresh out of a Wisconsin doctorate named C. Wright Mills, as well as two upwardly mobile young historians, Frank Freidel (now at Harvard) and Kenneth M. Stampp (now chaired at Berkeley). The four comprised an oasis of intellect and ambition that convened daily over lunch.

The pay at Maryland was so low—under three thousand for the year—that Hofstadter considered quitting academia for journalism. Some free-lance reviewing he did for the *New York Herald Tribune* and then *The New Republic* persuaded him of the pleasures of writing for a non-professional audience; and to pave his way into a new career, he decided to forge a book that might win him some popular interest, receiving in 1945 an Alfred A. Knopf Fellowship and a contract for his work-in-progress. He first envisioned a series of portraits of the Presidents; but too many of these figures were dullish, if not identical as subject matter. After he admitted such important eccentrics as John C. Calhoun and Wendell Phillips, he dallied with Robert La Follette and Daniel Webster, only to reject them on such journalistically practical grounds as the fact that their personal writings were not conveniently available. Less practical about book-selling, he originally entitled his series of portraits *Men and Ideas in American Politics*, but Alfred Knopf and his salesmen induced Hofstadter to accept a more pretentious title. Moreover, the introductory essay that scholars and critics so often quote as the key to Hofstadter's thinking was, in fact, written long after the text was completed. "My editor told me those portraits needed an introduction to tie them together; but it's all afterthought." Rather than a popular book, he wrote a work so good it eventually became popular.

Hofstadter insists to this day that he did not then know how unusual, if not unprecedented, it was for an academic historian so young to offer such a comprehensive, firmament-shaking book. Since he was hardly anyone's protégé, he could not rely upon an elder scholar to encourage his ambition or beat a path for his book's success. "I was innocent as a babe about such matters; there are certain advantages to be gained by coming out of a provincial college and then working at one. If I had thought the book an act of courage, I might never have done it," he observed and then looked down. "Courage has never been one of my strong points."

In 1945, his first wife, Felice (née Swados, sister of the novelist Harvey Swados), whom he married in 1936, died after a year-long illness. The following year, Columbia's History Department invited him to return as an assistant professor. Not only was he happy to be back in New York, but he quickly forgot all intentions of changing his career. In 1947, he married Beatrice Kevitt (known as "Bede"), then a fashion writer and now a history teacher, who has since been his best friend and closest collaborator. Once *The American Political Tradition* received the acclaim it deserved, Hofstadter rose quickly at Columbia, becoming an associate professor in 1950 and a full professor in 1952, only a decade after receiving his doctorate. After Allan Nevins retired in 1959, Hofstadter assumed the chair of DeWitt Clinton Professor of American History.

A blue-eyed, graying, almost nondescript man, Hofstadter

looks taller than he is (five feet ten inches), probably because a recent stomach condition has pushed his weight down to 160 pounds, inducing him continually to pull up his sagging trousers. Horn-rimmed glasses and a rather ashen pallor are the only distinguishing marks on his face, but his longish and thick gray hair is rakishly swept back from a cleanly chisled widow's peak. Particularly when he removes his glasses, his face looks older than his hair; and he keeps in reserve a broad, warm smile that, on its rare appearance, completely rearticulates the expression of his face. His clothes have that dowdy datedness that only academics and/or eminent eccentrics would dare affect; and for personal touches Hofstadter favors clip-on bow ties and a navy-blue beret. Gentle and shy in demeanor, tolerant by nature, overburdened by circumstance, he thinks of himself as acerbic—an adjective valid only in comparison to other academics; and he is quietly pleased by his success, unashamedly proud of his position at Columbia, and clearly contented by the Morningside Heights community. His prime social flair is a talent for mimicry—Ma and Pa Kettle and Presidents Kennedy and Johnson, for favorite examples; and his teen-age daughter, Sarah, swears that his imitation of a cow can attract a herd of calves.

He moves spryly, yet not energetically; and to keep in physical shape, the Hofstadters go every Tuesday afternoon to an exercise session. A man of regular habits, scrupulous discipline, and insulated temperament, he moves through life with a contained methodicalness that might dull a less lively intelligence; there is a right time, place, and procedure for everything he needs to do during the day. "I live a very sheltered existence up here at Columbia," he confessed over lunch at his favorite eating place, the Faculty Club; and although he frequently takes on new activities for the fodder of fresh fields, he never allows himself to become an enthusiastic participant. "His body may go downtown," one of his friends remarked, "but his mind stays at home at Columbia." The university that has employed him for over twenty years and granted him nearly all the favors it can bestow seems the sole institution to have won his devotion and even, occasionally, symptoms of sentimental feeling; it is perhaps the sole oasis of "inside" that the outsider has found. (This feeling for Columbia may partially explain why Hofstadter accepted Grayson Kirk's invitation to give the commencement address at the dissent-ridden graduation of 1968. Though his role there was too difficult, if not compromised, to be heroic, he handled the assignment with evident courage, dignity, and concern.)

Everything about him is circumspect and meticulous. His office, apartment, and personal appearance are as neatly unostentatious as his prose; as his work has no outrageous faults, so he has few notoriously negative traits. Hofstadter tries as hard as he can to control everything within his power, shunning both publicity and controversy as possible threats to his work and recognizing that potential disturbances are as likely to come from within himself as from the surrounding society; and all the environments of his own creation suggest that here is a man who profoundly knows himself and who slowly but surely gets things done. (Indeed, he is so concerned with working habits that he always asks other writers about their regime.) In conversation, he invariably modifies generalizations, whether his own or another's, with specific qualifications that bestow complexity upon the picture.

Although he neither possesses a glad-handed personality, tolerates fools graciously, nor gets on particularly well with his elders, Hofstadter is generally well liked within the profession; in Columbia circles, particularly in his own department, his opinion carries considerable persuasive weight. A consistent skeptic, who neither admires others enormously or deprecates viciously, he remains personally less controversial than his work. He does not lend his name easily to protests and petitions (or letters other people will write for him); nor does Hofstadter (in sharp contrast to other famous American historians) allow himself to appear in print as a spokesman for one cause or another. "People want to borrow your name and professional prestige for political purposes—use you as an oracle because you've written a few books; but your authority is only that of a citizen." Those political involvements he does make stem more from negative responses than positive feelings. In 1964, he wrote several stunningly critical essays on the Goldwater campaign; and early in 1968, he contributed to *The New York Times Magazine* a piece on American historical precedents for pulling out of unsuccessful wars, as well as actively supporting Senator Eugene McCarthy, mostly out of a dislike for Lyndon Johnson's politics. "He is now a bad man who could have gone right and been one of our big heroes. Rather than attacking him, I'm more interested in the situation and how we'll get out of it."

Very much aware of his own faults and inadequacies, as well as his strengths and virtues, he has a kind of instinctive humility that sometimes verges on unjustified self-deprecation. He suffers no hesitation over confessing that he has not read a certain important book, even in his own field; and since his highly focused mind does not jump easily from one subject to another, he blithely tunes out of conversations he finds too quick and disconnected. When he used "anile" to describe an elderly woman, I replied that I did not know the word. "It's the feminine of 'senile,' which should refer only to old men—'senex' is man in Latin." He reached to the bookshelf dictionary behind him and said, "Let's look it up," and sure enough, he was right. Similarly, although he remembers things relating to his current work-in-progress so accurately that he needs amazingly few working notes, his recall of miscellaneous historical detail is not as perfect as it should be; and recently, he finds himself "reaching that age when I black out on book titles all the time. I can't produce references spontaneously." His loss of memory is so perilous that he admits ruefully, "I hesitate in formulating questions on the Ph.D. orals; for I fear that if a student gets something wrong, I might not be able to correct him."

"I'm very appreciative of mental competences I don't have," he observes; and among his admirations he lists football quarterbacks who make quick decisions when rushed by thousands of pounds of tacklers and scientists who have mastered the mathematical mysteries he could never fathom. Along with most major scholars of Americana, Hofstadter is completely incapable in foreign languages, even those he had to learn in graduate school; yet he admires multilingual people, such as his son Dan, in his middle twenties, a painter, poet, and sometime graduate student in history. The elder Hofstadter has an articulate feeling for architecture, a lesser taste for painting and sculpture, practically no ear for music, and absolutely no interest in dance. Even though he is more broadly literate than most academics, his literacy stretches across huge gaps, such as science and technology.

His ambitions for productivity and excellence demand an obsessive, but necessary, concern with the processes and psychology of scholary craftsmanship. A somewhat late riser, Hofstadter takes a quick breakfast and then goes to his writing desk in an area set off from the rest of the living-room and surrounded on three sides by walls of mahogany-shelved books; and mostly to cut out other aural distractions, such as the telephone ("the biggest single menace to work"), which he does not answer anyway, he likes to run the phonograph with baroque music. Since nothing annoys him more than losing a possibly productive morning because of an unexpected interruption, an orals examination at Columbia, a bout of illness, or simply an act of God, he has thoroughly intimidated everyone within earshot (excluding God) into honoring his habits. "He's not happy or contented unless he is working on his books," says a friend. "He thinks he was put on earth to write." Another adds, more querulously, "As an activist who has learned to write anywhere and under any circumstances, I find it hard to sympathize with his self-indulgence. But then, I haven't won any Pulitzer Prizes lately." A bit of a hypochrondriac, Hofstadter consumes lots of pills and refuses to read or hear anything about medicine. "When I read about a disease," he explains, "I think I might be getting it." In general, inspiration comes easier to him than perfection; so while getting his ideas down on paper usually leaves him elated, fussing over detail invariably has a depressing effect.

Hofstadter gets restless around lunch time, either taking the meal at home or walking four blocks across the campus to the Faculty Club, where he freely charges everything. After that, he generally goes to his office in Columbia College's Hamilton Hall to read the mail and dictate scores of replies—a task requiring an hour or two every day; and messages usually receive a signature of just initials—a custom some correspondents find annoying. The office itself is large, sparsely adorned except for forbiddingly high history-stocked bookcases and a large lithograph of Joseph Pulitzer against the institutional light yellow walls; and his secretary uses a desk turned toward the corner. During appointments, he will shamelessly shuffle papers as he talks to guests.

His schedule for himself is so tight that even "free time," such as just before dinner, he begrudgingly gives away; and his icy demeanor functions effectively, if not intentionally, to insulate him from the world's distraction. Then, his meticulosity slides into a perfectionism that is almost compulsive. *The Age of Reform*, for instance, passed through several drafts (and series of lectures); and at one point Hofstadter had chapters mimeographed for his friends to consider. He invariably rewrites his prose in galley and even, despite the expense, in page proof. His passion for his task, as well as his willingness to sacrifice, suggests an aphorism I believe from Henry James: It is himself most of all that the writer gives to his work.

If he has neither a class to teach nor an appointment to keep, he usually returns home to read—"What my colleagues call 'research' "—go over his wife's editorial suggestions, or check references in the ten thousand or so well-dusted books neatly shelved through several halls and rooms of their large apartment. Long ago, he discovered that once he left the house he would not be able to write again that day. Should he happen to answer the phone, he suffers no shame over firmly saying, "I'm in the middle of work," and then dropping the receiver. When I asked how he could be so curt, Hofstadter replied with a wink, "Oh, you have to do that in New York. Remember what I sometimes call Hofstadter's First Law: When the telephone rings, it isn't necessarily somebody who wants to do something for you." On weekend afternoons, he likes to watch sports events on the television, particularly baseball and football (the Giants and the Jets), often tuning out the TV sound for the more detailed radio commentary; and this habit perhaps explains why athletic metaphors proliferate his speaking and writing. "Just think of it," he mused over lunch, "nothing in this country is done as well as professional football games. Compare it to our diplomacy!" As New Yorkers of eminence, the Hofstadters go out a lot in the evening, particularly to dinner parties with friends. "I don't get on well with people unless I meet them in an intimate context." Although they find city-living so hard that the family escapes each Christmas to sunnier climes and early every summer to a home in Wellfleet, Massachusetts, he regularly spurns tempting offers to teach elsewhere, simply because he does not want to leave his New York oasis.

Regarding every morning of the year as an opportunity to write, he prefers to take his work with him, even on lecture tours or vacations. "I've never had any trouble in orienting myself to my work"; more trouble, he adds, comes in adjusting the world. Every afternoon, he knows precisely what he has to write the following morning and thinks about its problems throughout the day. Even for books, he establishes a deadline, usually so far ahead that he meets it without strain. Since he long ago discovered that he can work on only one project at a time, he refuses requests for reviews and articles; for guest lectures, he draws upon work-in-progress. "I'm a man of limited energies," he explains, "and I get a fair amount out of them by concentrating."

Nowadays, he does considerably less miscellaneous reading than before, largely because "I need to shut off my own mind from distraction," and he finds it impossible to read attentively a book not related to his current project, preferring, as he puts it, "to know all I need to know for operative purposes." He is clearly still working off basic ideas he developed a decade ago (and that may explain why his recent major books are not quite as great as the first two). He confidently tells people that he now has sufficient "intellectual capital" to last the rest of his life; and remarks like these raise the paradox that such a skeptical intellectual should be so unhesitantly positive about his own current work, as well as his professional environment.

He has thought about quitting academia entirely—his royalties would provide sufficient income; but now that Columbia allows him a leave one year in every three and provides him with his own secretary, he judges that contact with graduate students and the help of research assistants compensate for the loss of time. In the future, he sees a study of Jeffersonian Democracy and Political Parties, an expansion of a series of lectures he gave at the University of California; and he has contemplated a study of the last five Presidents, a three-volume history of America, and maybe a book on the 1890's. Among the unfinished projects still in his rather scanty files are a book about women in America, begun in the early forties; an intellectual history of the United States; many chapters dropped from the final versions of earlier works; and enough miscellaneous articles to make a book or two. At times, he fantasizes writing about each of the Presidents in a verse form dominant in his time. "I think I can do George Washington in heroic couplet," he muses, "but it would be very difficult to write about FDR in the style of E. E. Cummings."

Hofstadter's political sympathies incline to the left; but he is far too much of a skeptic, as well as an academic, to make untempered commitments. For instance, he sees the situation in Vietnam as so confusing and ambiguous that he cannot come to a decisive opinion and feels no guilt about suspending judgment. "I must have read over 150 articles on Vietnam in the past year, and not one of them entirely satisfactory or persuasive," he declared early in 1968. "I do regard the war as the result of an immense and tragic miscalculation and am on record as favoring steps toward negotiations that are likely to bring results very far from an American victory; yet unlike many people who are also opposed to the war, I am not very confident in my own ability to see a way out. I have no program over doing anything about it, or even any wisdom." In contrast to, say, Arthur Schlesinger, Jr., who, as Arthur Mann quipped, "writes history as he votes and votes as he writes," Hofstadter is a discerning spectator who regards his own books as influencing scholars more than politicians, intellectuals more than citizens, and thought more than votes.

He realizes that the professional study of history probably inculcates a conservative sensibility; for it suggests not what is currently possible but what was in the past impossible. "An awareness of limitation is one of the things I get from history, and what I hope to find in histories of others. Nothing else gives you such a clear sense of how things do *not* happen." For these reasons, he has the conservative's antipathy for people who declare history is bunk; and all through 1967, he complained to everyone he knew about a certain eminent professor at another New York university who proclaimed in a public debate that the Hungarian Revolution of 1956 was not relevant to current political concerns, merely because it took place a decade before.

As a teacher, Hofstadter is a contradictory figure, attentive to and beloved by a few, diffident and disappointing to the majority of his students. Always a reluctant lecturer, he tries to avoid giving courses more demanding than seminars; and when the situation requires him to stand regularly before a class, he usually insists that the course's subject coincide with that of his book-in-progress. "My manuscript," he rationalizes, "makes for better lectures than my hemming and hawing." Lacking either a stage presence or oracular gifts, he speaks like a chugging auto engine, spewing words forth regularly and evenly, pausing only to take breaths; for the nature of his writing style induces him to read not by the individual word but by the well-constructed sentence and paragraph. He moves his hands in constricted gestures, frequently lowers his head and raises his eyebrows to read the text better, occasionally scratches his head and ears, and sometimes slurs syllables ("ek-nom-ik his-tree"), as well as drops inaudible parenthetical remarks. His jokes are only about sixty per cent effective, partly because his deliveries are not skillful and his sense of humor lacks a few notes (which explains why he frequently misses the jokes that others tell). In general, he would like to see more levity in historical writing. "You need the comic note for relief, especially if you think of history as basically tragic."

As he lectures, the students obey their note-taking habits; and in the question period that follows, his rather forbidding and impatient manner belies his actual interest. Here, as in extended informal conversation, he starts slowly, progressively becoming more voluble as he becomes more involved in his answer; precisely because his interest is more passionate than his manner, he projects hesitantly and yet never suffers a loss of words. He is also terribly ambivalent about people; for while he genuinely likes them and frequently complains that his friends and students, both current and former, neglect him, he also lets the world know that he wants to save his precious time. In all, his sins of omission, rather than commission, as well as his rather disdainful attitude to his job, keep him from becoming as popular a teacher as his books and reputation suggest he might be.

In supervising graduate students, Hofstadter tends to be reserved, officious, and frustrating—implicitly an advocate of his colleague Jacques Barzun's commandment: "All dealings with those taught should to a certain degree be contradictory—by no means all kindness." His impatient and distant demeanor, as well as the overworked impression he communicates, makes students apprehensive about approaching him, even if their question or request clearly merits his personal attention. This haughtiness partially stems from the customs of Columbia, where, as everyone knows, the wall between faculty and students is higher and thicker than normal; yet Hofstadter is genuinely overburdened. During his official office hours, the telephone rings frequently; and his conversation often runs like this: "Yes. . . . No. . . . I can't do that. I'm too busy. . . . Sorry. . . . Bye."

Hofstadter is tougher than most on his graduate students'

doctoral essays, not only because his scholarly standards are high but also because he is more insistent than his colleagues that every page be written well; often drafts will be returned with minimal critical comments and yet scores of stylistic changes. Beyond that, his graduate students find two disconcerting habits—a tendency to forget promises he made or remarks they made to him, as well as considerable delay in reading the papers they submit to him. Indeed, when I first came to Columbia for graduate work in history several years ago, I went to Hofstadter in the spring and asked for permission to participate in his M.A. seminar the following fall. He said that he would be happy to have me, but suggested that I send him a note of reminder, which I did. Nonetheless, when I arrived to register, he replied that the seminar was filled and then remotely apologized for forgetting his promise; in doing this profile, I found him forgetting things I had told him or he had told me only a few days before. More than one student resents the fact that while Hofstadter practices macro-scholarship, he supports standards for doctoral research that demand micro-research, even though he is too embarrassed by the discrepancy between their world and his to be sanctimonious about academic pieties. (*The American Political Tradition*, he admits, "would not be acceptable as a thesis, for good reasons too.") Nonetheless, a degree earned under Hofstadter's imprimatur carries considerable cachet within the profession; and among his former students are the respected historians Stanley Elkins, Eric McKitrick, Marvin Meyers, David Burner, and Andrew Sinclair.

Within professional circles, the standard criticism made of Hofstadter's histories points to his reluctance to do much digging in the "primary sources," which is the trade term for papers, letters, records, and other undigested paraphernalia. While he respects the monographic scholarship he would not do himself, quoting freely from the standard micro-accounts, he rarely draws a reference to, say, an unpublished document. "I'm not an archival historian," he rationalizes, "I like to work with conveniently available sources. There is a division of labor within the profession." More interested in historical software (interpretation) than hardware (data), he years ago confessed in print, "If one were to compare the proportion of time given to expression with that given to research, my emphasis is on the first. I hope that my books at least read with a certain pleasure." He so frequently solicits advice from specialists in particular subjects that one once replied, reportedly, "Why don't you come down and look at the papers yourself?" Hofstadter stayed home and wrote.

Over the years, his debunking has produced howls of rage from one vested interest or another; but by now, his books have become as accepted as path-breaking and tentative work can be, not only in undergraduate curricula (often prepared by teachers who had first read the books as undergraduates), but also among his professional peers, that all but a few major recent scholarly works in American history credit him in one way or another. My own undergraduate history professor, William G. McLoughlin at Brown University, tells me, "I read his works always with profit and refer to him *ad nauseam* in my lectures," and a random issue of, say, *American Quarterly* contains various respectful references to several Hofstadter books. He personally attributes this frequency of allusion to the fact that he has churned so much historiographical territory and "posed so many new answers to old questions." Indicatively, while critics have pecked away at this or that interpretation, Hofstadter's work has yet to suffer a wholesale demolition in print, let alone a thorough critical confrontation; but he anticipates, rather charitably, that some young men will make their reputations by razing the scholarly houses he built. "I have a tendency to regard criticism of my work as insubstantial," he says defensively. "The more substantial ones are my own, unwritten." In more ways than one, as both milestone and tombstone, Hofstadter will take his place with Turner, Parrington, and Beard.

To Marshall McLuhan, as well as Herman Kahn, the mission of the intellectual is to proclaim that the Emperor wears no clothes; and as a historian of intellect, Hofstadter exercises more of his boyish honesty on the past than the present, telling us that such American emperors as Jefferson and Lincoln wore fewer trappings than the familiar statuary displays. "Reassurance," he declares, "is something I'm rarely able to offer," and his rigorous skepticism implicitly insists that every piece of gold is tarnished, to individual degrees, and that only after we know all of the faults of a politician or an ideology can we justifiably accept him or it. Indeed, it is this skepticism, even more than his particular interpretations, in addition to his commitment to craftsmanship that command so much respect as well as influence among younger historians and political writers today; for even if Hofstadter, to his regret, feels that a curtain has fallen between the generations, cutting him off from people under twenty-five, the books that he fabricated are still making as much impact as before in shaping the historical consciousness of a generation of minds.

ALLEN GINSBERG:

Artist as Apostle, Poet as Preacher

I am the man,
I suffered,
I was there.
—WALT WHITMAN

Sui generis, one of a kind—that latinism is perhaps the only phrase that can adequately encapsulate Allen Ginsberg; he is such an incredible human being, so unlike any other in the world, that if he did not exist in life, he would scarcely be credible in fantastic fiction. Among other identities, he is a prominent American poet, a prophet, a political persuader, a publicist, a personable performer, a public presence, an apostolic pot-head, a pederast; and because he is such an original and such an activist, he combines several roles in his bearded, smallish, instantaneously identifiable figure, as well as coalescing a number of growing cultural tendencies. Though not an organizer, he is a leader, with several distinct armies of followers; though lacking any formal organization, he can still personally organize the sympathies, if not the actions, of thousands of people. In literature, for instance, he was the major figure in the "beat" revolution in the middle fifties that decisively changed the complexion of American poetry; and to this day, at bookstores catering to the young, as one manager in England told me and another in America confirmed, "more Ginsberg mysteriously disappears than anything else." In the increasingly populous "underground" society, he was an early advocate of marijuana, LSD, rock music, and other mind-blowing experiences; young people the world over regard him as an apostle of the disaffiliated life in a contagiously affiliating society. Needless to say, no other poet in the Western world can draw such large crowds to a public reading; and no other has read to appreciative audiences at as many of the world's universities.

I first met Ginsberg in London, late in May of 1965, after he had come to England from Czechoslovakia, from where he had been expelled earlier in the month; and his adventures were the kind that could happen to nobody else. At the beginning of that year, he had similarly been booted out of Castro's Cuba, having gone there as a reporter for *Evergreen Review* and a guest of a Cuban writers' organization; and he turned his sudden departure into an occasion to accept an invitation to come to Prague, where he discovered that his work had already earned considerable interest. The leading night club for poetry, the Viola Cafe, had been presenting frequent readings of his work in translation, while the Union of Czech Writers had been planning to publish a book of his verse. With some accumulated Czech royalties, Ginsberg traveled to Russia, reestablishing contact with some of the young Russian poets he had met before, as well as making several new friends—among them, Alexis Ginzburg and Yssenin-Volpine, both of whom have since been imprisoned. Then he went to Poland, only to return to Prague on April 30, in time for the May Day Festival, the *Majales*. This traditional celebration had been terminated in the late forties by the Communist regime; but since numerous students had in recent years been marking the day with protest riots, the Czech government decided early in 1965 to reinstate the festival.

"I walked in the May Day Parade that morning," Ginsberg recalled in a London apartment, in his unusually boyish voice, "and that afternoon some students asked me to be their candidate for King of the May. I agreed; they put me on a truck, and I traveled in the procession of the Polytechnic School, with a Dixieland band on a nearby truck. The procession went through the city to a main square, where from ten to fifteen thousand people were gathered. I made a speech in English, dedicating the glory of my crown to Franz Kafka, who wrote *The Trial* in the House of the Golden Carp on that square." From there, the Polytechnic's procession traveled to the Park of Culture and Rest, to join the parades from the other colleges. In the grand competition, Ginsberg found himself elected King of the May, *Kral Majales*, along with a May Queen, whom he described as "a groovy beautiful Czech chick"; and later, they were both displayed in a rose-colored chariot. When asked to address the audience, Ginsberg, innocent of Czech, decided instead to chant the "Hymn to the Buddha of the Future" ("*Om Shri Maitreya*") to the accompaniment of his own small cymbals—a singular performance that he has repeated for all sorts of occasions all over the world. His instruments, he told me then, "come from a store near Times Square," while the hymn, called a "*mantra*," was likewise picked up in New York—"from an old girl friend of mine who learned it from Tibetan Buddhists.")

The Czech officials present at the park were so outraged by the coronation of a non-Czech, let alone a trouble-making American poet, that brown-shirted student monitors eventually substituted a drunken Czech student in Ginsberg's place. "The next few days I spent running around with groups of students, acting in a spontaneous, improvised manner—making love with anybody I could find. Dig? The age of consent is seventeen in Czechoslovakia, fifteen in Poland, while in Russia they'd put you in jail. Dig? I spent a lot of time with rock 'n roll musicians. There it's called the 'big beat,' and the Czechs take this music with the same fervor as the kids in Liverpool." Ginsberg nervously got up from the chair, took a few steps around the apartment room, puffed his cigarette, and then sat down again as he explained that at one of the rock concerts he lost his notebook. "At least I assumed it was lost. Suddenly it wasn't in my pocket any more. A few days later, late at night, someone suddenly attacked me on the street, screaming '*bouzerant*,' which means 'fairy' or 'queer'; and all of us, including the students with me, were arrested by the police and taken down to the station. I wasn't released until 5 A.M.; they took affidavits from the others. I suspect the attacker was a police *provocateur*, but I can't prove it. Who can prove that in a police state?"

On May 6, as Ginsberg remembers it, the policemen who had been conspicuously tailing him "picked me up at a restaurant, promising to give me back my notebook if I would come down to the police station. Down there someone informed me that on surface examination the book seemed to contain illegal writings and that it would be held for further examination." The Czech police, he continued, said that the notebook had been picked off the ground by a citizen who claimed to be the father of one of the young men in Ginsberg's entourage; and they charged that other parents had complained that the poet was corrupting many of the local youth (as indeed he was, by bourgeois Communist standards). Ginsberg was escorted to his hotel, forbidden to make any calls, and four hours later put on a plane to London. "I tried to tell them I was leaving anyway," he earnestly declared to me, "and that my expulsion might cause some embarrassment, but it wasn't any use; they didn't dig it."

As for the notebook, he characterized it as little different from the others he carries with him nearly all the time, containing, as he then put it, "poems and drafts of poems, dreams —I've been writing down all my dreams for twenty years—stray thoughts, descriptions of sex orgies and ecstasies in intimate detail, private scribbles, a memoir of jacking off in the Hotel Ambassador with a broomstick up my ass. There were probably some political remarks, too; I can't remember. If they publish the complete diaries, it will blow up in everybody's face—mine as well as theirs. I won't mind; but they'll never publish it." Since he feared the Czech officials might take reprisals against people mentioned by name in the diary (none, in fact, were taken), Ginsberg decided not to mention his expulsion to the newspapers or the United States authorities; so the Czechs were the first to announce Ginsberg's departure, when some days later the newspaper *Mlada Fronta* (North Front) launched an editorial attack on the poet. In retrospect, he thinks that the festival may have been "the first public manifestation in the streets of the protest spirit."

Never one for coyness, Ginsberg knew clearly at the time that Prague officials were finding his presence and speeches subversive. "People asked me what I thought, so I told them. I talked about the greater values—the sense of new consciousness which seems to be going through the youth of all countries, the sexual revolution, the widening of the area of one's own consciousness, the abhorrence of ideology, direct contact (soul to soul, body to body), Dostoevskian tolerance, Blakean vision, Buddhist mantras (which are concerned basically with the expansion of consciousness to complete consciousness). I have no formal ideology at all, but a mode of concreteness different from the intellectual rigidity of Communism; these ideas I present to people to make them think about themselves." When I asked why he made such a popular impact in Prague, becoming, in his own immodest but accurate estimation, "a surrealist folk-hero," Ginsberg quickly surmised, "probably because everyone there is sick of the politicians." The telephone rang in our room, the apartment's owner and Ginsberg's proud host answered it, telling us the name of the caller, whom Ginsberg identified as "my girl friend." After an exchange of news and pleasantries, he announced, "Things are picking up. *The Sunday Times* was in this morning; *The New York Times* is here now, and I'll see the B.B.C. tomorrow. *The Paris Review* is around; but the people at the Embassy won't let me read there."

When our conversation resumed, he expounded, "Everything I write is in one way or another autobiographical or evidence of the nature of my consciousness at those instants of time. Whatever travels or psychic progressions I've had are recorded there." Influenced mostly by Gertrude Stein's "Composition as Explanation" and partly by the processes of American action painters, who also represented in space discrete moments of consciousness, Ginsberg continually writes in his portable notebooks; "All you can write about is the present while you are writing." Only afterward does he perform the critical acts of seeing whether anything there is publishable and then revising it, when necessary, for final print. Just before we met—in fact, on the plane trip to London—he had finished a poem about his experiences in Prague, scratching lines into a new notebook; and later in the year, it was published as "Kral Majales"—a sketchy memoir of his experiences that included such lines as,

> *And I am the King of May, which is the power of sexual youth,*
> *and I am the King of May, which is industry in eloquence and action in armor,*
> *and I am the King of May, which is long hair of Adam and the Beard of my own body.*

In his hirsute flesh, Ginsberg stands five feet eight inches, weighs about one hundred fifty pounds, and looks considerably less than forty-plus years, despite the fact that he is, but for a few strands, completely bald on top. A mass of luxuriant, shoulder-length dark-brown curls hang from a horseshoe-shaped fringe, while his face supports an untrimmed, thick, gray-streaked black beard that runs from just below his eyes to his button-down shirt. Behind horn-rimmed glasses are small dark eyes which stare directly, if not penetratingly, at whomever Ginsberg is addressing, hardly blinking and rarely suffering distraction. His skin is pale and relatively unlined, his teeth stained from the cigarettes he constantly smokes, his lips full, and his mannerisms generally masculine; and whether in khakis or a suit, his clothes are invariably styleless, informal, and rumpled. His demeanor is lively, his face animated; and particularly when he chants or sings, his head and hair turn and shake in a manner at once grotesque and beautiful. His voice is a resonant bass, able to command a live audience or sustain a droning Oriental tune; his diction has the clarity of one accustomed to public speaking. In many ways, he looks and sounds, one cannot help but think, like a Hasidic rabbi chanting not mantras but Hebrew prayers; his religion, by his own description, is that of a "Buddhist Jew."

Part of his international popularity stems from his commanding personality; like many leaders-without-organization, he possesses that quality Max Weber once defined as "charisma"—the capacity to establish confidence by sheer presence. He is innately bright, alert, energetic, straightforward, gregarious, and generous with his time; and not only will he eagerly reply to familiar questions but he speaks with enviable frankness of his own experience and opinions and desires (though his elliptical syntax is at times befuddling); for instance, he has no qualms about closing a public reading with, "I'm lonesome here. Would someone please take me home?" merely, as he explained to me, "making articulate what every poet feels before an audience of beautiful young people." Nonetheless, because his friendliness and tenderness are at best a bit indiscriminate, if not impersonal, he often drops a curtain, makes a testy remark, or fires a criticism that surprises or shocks the person to whom he is talking; and if the other is visibly upset (and Ginsberg has the time or inclination), he will apologize and attempt, usually in vain, to reestablish the original comradely spirit. Similarly, though he lacks any impulse to con or deceive, his unbounded enthusiasm sometimes produces self-deceptions, if not outright contradictions.

Precisely because he has overcome self-consciousness of his unconventionality, he handles himself politely and confidently, endeavoring to speak directly to people (always looking at them eye to eye); and always gutsy in ominous situations, he is particularly adept at disarming possible antagonists. It was largely Ginsberg who persuaded California's notorious Hell's Angels to protect the protesting hippies and pacifists rather than attack them. (As an Angels' spokesman reportedly declared, "For a guy that ain't straight at all, he's the straightest son of a bitch I've ever seen.") And he got the motorcycle gang to be guardian angels at the first great San Francisco Be-In, early in 1967, which Ginsberg regards as one of the great, prophetic events of recent years. "Allen's humanity, his unqualified humanity, his almost Franciscan view of things," writes Barry Farrell in *Life*, "has won him a genuine influence he never quite achieved in his old Beat days." Indeed, it may be unnatural, if not impossible, for anyone over fourteen or under fifty to address him as "Mr. Ginsberg" rather than "Allen."

Though his appearance, frankness, and self-confidence are all a bit intimidating, making even the most eccentric of us seem irreparably square, he tries to get through to audiences. "The problem," he told me, "is to learn how to communicate without frightening people. Some mode of affectionate reassurance will give people a feeling of safety when they move their awareness out to a new place, so they need not fear their being is destroyed." He is enviably able to treat as equals students young enough to be his children; and at a Congressional hearing on narcotics legislation, he opened by declaring, "I hope that whatever prejudgment you may have of me or my bearded image you can suspend so that we can talk together as fellow-beings in the same room of Now, trying to come to some harmony and peacefulness between us." Then he cordially began to describe, in an enticing way, his own experiences with various hallucinogens, particularly how during a recent trip on LSD he lost his antipathy for President Johnson, instead praying for his health. Then, too, at major radical-hippy events, whether the San Francisco Be-In, the Chicago demonstrations at the Democratic National Convention (where he chanted mantras to cool off the overheated crowd), a discotheque fund-raising benefit in New York City, the conference on the Dialectics of Liberation in London, Ginsberg is nearly always there. Whether with establishment politicians or students, he has the instincts less of a lecturer than a seminar leader, listening attentively, remembering new names, replying quickly, keeping the dialogue moving, and trying to coin aphorisms that extract the gist of a discussion. Ideally, he would like to teach in a university, but few have dared offer him a position; nor does he think any university would tolerate him. "I'd want to smoke pot in class and sleep with my students," he explained succinctly. "Besides, I teach all the time right now."

He has lived for many years in New York City, in a succession of small, well-cleaned slummy apartments in the eastern East Village. The place where we talked in 1968 is east of Avenue C, on the hot top floor of a smelly walk-up tenement across from a new housing project. The door opens into the side of a kitchen, sparsely equipped with nondescript utensils; the hallway leads past the bathroom into a small room with a white-top dining table and a window onto an air shaft on one side and, on the other, a piece of plywood laid across some files, on top of which are a tall stack of copies of *The New York Times*, and some bookshelves (including one largely of poetry in the late Poundian tradition). Another bookcase, reaching to the ceiling of the adjoining wall and covered with clear plastic, is filled exclusively with books and magazines containing his own work. Through glass doors is a small front room with a few more bookshelves and a double bed on the floor; and just off this is an even smaller room, which like the bedroom also looks out onto the street. At one point after midnight, the telephone rang, causing Ginsberg to spring up from the dining table into the front room; and in reply to an apparent request, he said politely, "I wish I could, but I'm not that well organized."

In recent years, he has found the air in New York dustier, the smells and noise more grating, the garbage on the neighborhood streets more pervasive; and after itemizing their probable effects on his physiognomy, he dramatically ran his hand across the plywood table to show how much dirt had accumulated since he cleaned it the day before. "The ecological situation is terrible. I don't think it's livable here anymore," he declared through a haze of cigarette smoke, adding, "If you can't see the stars, how do you know you're on this planet rather than Mars. Riots in the cities have a lot more to do with physical surroundings than Riot Commissions realize." So, since 1967 or so, Ginsberg and Peter Ganesh Orlovsky, since 1953 his "common-law wife" (to whom he is not entirely faithful), have been spending much of their time on a small farm in upstate New York, actually owned by the non-profit Committee on Poetry, Inc., where various vegetables are grown, mostly for the occupants' own consumption; and even though the metropolis is the major subject and perhaps an inspiration of his poetry, Ginsberg finds himself retreating to the country whenever possible. Orlovsky, it should be mentioned, is another singular character, an occasional poet of decidedly undistinguished pieces, "a nice Jewish boy," with inordinately long brown hair usually tied in a pony tail, a friend of poets who recently sold his collected correspondence to a library for several thousand dollars. He has a compulsive desire to clean the world with a bottle of Lysol and rags he often carries with him. The Ginsberg entourage also usually includes one or two of Orlovsky's brothers, Julius and Lafcadio, neither of whom is entirely self-sufficient, one of whom regularly disappears and mysteriously returns. In recent years, Ginsberg has had a number of girl friends, whose presence inevitably complicates earlier relationships.

While in New York, he leads the life of a cultural V.I.P., except for a few incongruous details. He probably spends as much time on the telephone as the boss of a publishing firm, but he has no secretaries or paid assistants or officious "representatives," and even his voluminous mail gets answered by his own hand, in scarcely legible script. A man of some bureaucratic talents, an indefatigable correspondent, who runs an efficient shop, he is particularly adept at moving information and establishing contacts (listing names and telephone numbers in a tattered book he usually carries with him), as well as replying to queries and requests, introducing one soul to another, finding legal aid for those in need, and so forth; friends know that if Ginsberg is around, he can be relied upon for all kinds of help—and if he cannot do it himself, he knows who else can do what and how. The range of his acquaintance is as huge as his memory for names; and with particular flair, he will telephone an eminent lawyer or an important editor or sometimes even a political figure and make some special arrangement, for himself or a friend, with unfailing ease; unlike most outcasts, he strives to maintain cordial relations with the in-cast world. He likes to go to parties, kissing and hugging all his friends, both male and female, yet remaining aware of how extravagantly he can celebrate; for since he has somehow phased out much of his superego and emancipated himself from shame, outrageous behavior is never beyond his competence. The usual horror story has Ginsberg undressing himself, "celebrating all birthday parties in his birthday suit," as one friend puts it, or challenging an antagonist with "Let's see if you got any balls."

Emancipated from other bourgeois hangups, he is inordinately cool and loose with money, which comes and goes so rapidly that he scarcely touches it, even though, curiously enough, he remembers in specific figures how much he was paid for this or that, as well as how much his possessions originally cost. Back in our 1965 conversation, he estimated he earned several thousand dollars a year in American royalties, perhaps several hundred more from publishers abroad and periodicals here. He once soaked *Playboy* for a five-hundred-dollar advance on an article—"the only time I ever took money from a slick"—but several years later he has still to complete the commissioned piece. As a matter of personal policy, not until recently did he take money for poetry readings (though he insisted upon traveling and living arrangements); and he still especially likes to read gratis at benefits for worthy underground causes, such as little magazines and jailed writers. As he is known to carry little money, friends and acquaintances are continually offering him rides, meals, clothing, lodging, parties; plane fares (even to India, which is where *Esquire*'s reporter found him for its 1963 issue on the American literary scene); when Ginsberg comes to town, whether to London, Prague, New Delhi, Chicago, or San Francisco, it is an occasion to organize events and arrange hospitality. That spring in London, he displayed a steel-frame knapsack and hiking boots, as well as a knack for bringing out both the generosity and energy in people; and his presence partially inspired the mammoth poetry reading in Royal Albert

Hall, portrayed in the Peter Whitehead film *Wholly Communion,* that decisively changed the tone of British poetry and poets. Few can live as comfortably off the fat of the literary lands—as John Clellon Holmes put it, "traveling on pennies more widely than anyone I know with dollars."

In 1965 or so, Ginsberg's life style began to change. Just before his explusion from Prague, he received a substantial fellowship from the John Simon Guggenheim Memorial Foundation; and with this money he bought a used microbus and then, audaciously, set up his own foundation, the aforementioned Committee on Poetry, Inc. Its charter begins: "This group is formed to gather money from those that have it in amounts excess to their needs and disburse it among poets and philosophers who lack personal finance or wherewithal to accomplish small material projects in the society at large," and so on. Within the succeeding years, although he never actually succumbed to the temptation that befalls even the most radical of popular spokesmen—turning fame into personal wealth—he took on a lecture manager (on the recommendation of his friend Bob Dylan), a literary agent (who got lucrative contracts for several new books, but was dropped, Ginsberg says, because he would not give stuff away to little magazines), and an accountant (who discovered that Ginsberg had so far dutifully paid his earlier income taxes and personally kept sufficient records); and he asked his agents to soak those who could pay for the standard fees awarded to "famous people." Most of this new income, which now runs over thirty thousand dollars a year, Ginsberg puts into his foundation, which has since acquired other conduits. Though he still recommends "a vow of penury; avoid material entanglements," turning down all sorts of lucrative offers, such as a regular television show, and still pays a pauper's rent of sixty dollars a month, he nonetheless allots himself such unprecedented personal extravagances as the used microbus, the country life, airplane fares, telephone calls, a Brooks Brothers suit (and matching ties, which he wears more often than before), a share in a plot of uninhabited land in the America Sierras, and a vacation in Venice, where he stayed near Ezra Pound and won his friendship.

Although Ginsberg has been publicly cast in a number of unflattering images, ranging from clown to exhibitionist, the dominant impression conveyed in conversation holds that he is, and has always been, primarily a poet. His formal education at Columbia College was mostly in English literature, largely in poetry; and he can be as disappointed as Lionel Trilling to discover someone has not read Blake or Wordsworth. In London, he proposed we meet in a bookshop, where he had already made the acquaintance of the manager and clerk and where I found him browsing in the poetry section. He relates to poets, living and dead, far more closely than to other public and historical figures (and rock singers next best after them); and he knows thoroughly the traditions informing his own work and ambitions, including such varied and, only a few years ago, unusual sources for his prosody as "[Hart] Crane's *Atlantis*, Lorca's *Poet in NY*, Biblical structures, psalms and lamentations, Shelley's high buildups, Apollinaire, Artaud, Mayakovsky, Pound, Williams & American metrical tradition, the new tradition of measure. And Christopher Smart's *Lamb*. And Melville's prose-poem *Pierre*. And finally the spirit and illumination of Rimbaud." Similarly, he can also elaborately explain how his Tibetan mantras represent an attempt, out of poetry, to communicate without syntax, if not without language—a preoccupation he eagerly relates to Alfred Lord Tennyson's attempt to obliterate linguistic consciousness by repeating his full name over and over again or to some of Gertrude Stein's experimental prose, which he regards as "a form of Buddhist meditation."

Unlike any other American poet of note, Ginsberg is of a species more common in England and Europe than here—the son of a poet, Louis Ginsberg, a high school teacher by trade (recently retired), whose writings were perhaps more admired in the thirties than now; and Ginsberg has since admitted that the comparatively restrictive impersonal quality of his earliest work was due to fear of his father's disapproval. "About my sex life, being fucked in the ass," he told the poet-interviewer Tom Clark. "Imagine your father reading a thing like that." Not only have the two Ginsbergs, in recent years, given public readings together, but Allen's conversation portrays his father as his favorite "square" antagonist. Though he has as varied a collection of acquaintances as any eminent, well-traveled man, those he calls his "best friends" are all writers—William Burroughs, Jack Kerouac, Gregory Corso, Gary Snyder, Peter Orlovsky, Herbert Huncke, Ed Sanders. Beyond that, he takes especial pride in connecting poets with publishers, at times even agenting their manuscripts (at no cost to them, of course); and by gathering scraps written by William Burroughs into *Naked Lunch,* he played, as Leslie A. Fiedler ironically quipped, "the Ezra Pound to Burroughs' T. S. Eliot, collating and editing what the madness of another had created but could not organize."

Born in Newark, New Jersey, in 1926, Ginsberg went to high school in nearby Paterson, "where I thought of myself as a creep, a mystical creep. I had a good time, was lonesome; but I first read Whitman there." Though the great doctor-poet William Carlos Williams lived nearby in Rutherford, New Jersey, Ginsberg never had the courage to approach him until after he went to college, first to interview him for a local newspaper and then to make the elder poet's friendship. "He was physically slight of build," Williams wrote a decade later, "and mentally much disturbed by the life which he had encountered about him." Williams was one of the young poet's earliest major influences, and it was Williams who contributed the polemical introduction to Ginsberg's *Howl and Other Poems* (1956) and even incorporated, anonymously, the younger poet's personal letters into his own long poem, *Paterson* (1946–58).

At seventeen, Ginsberg entered Columbia College, where he attended classes taught by such eminent professors as Meyer Schapiro, Mark Van Doren, and Lional Trilling. He became a member of the debating team, editor of the *Columbia Review,* president of the Philolexian Society (for word lovers). Majoring in English, he attained an A-minus average and won several prizes for poems which he now places as stylistically "after Wyatt and the silver poets." He remembers Columbia as a dreary place, where "almost nothing of importance was taught"; yet he regards the late Raymond Weaver, Melville's early biographer and the discoverer of the manuscript of *Billy Budd*, as "one of the few true teachers there. He was using Zen koans as a method for awakening the student's mind in a course called 'Communications.' "

It was during his years at Columbia that he first met William Burroughs, who lived several blocks south of the campus and was then addicted to heroin and living off a family trust fund. In our conversation, Ginsberg characterized Burroughs as "my greatest teacher at that time. He put me onto Spengler, Yeats, Rimbaud, Korzybski, Proust, and Céline. Burroughs educated me more than Columbia, really." There and then, too, he encountered Jack Kerouac, who came to Columbia as a football player, quit the sport, lost his football scholarship, and was subsequently dismissed from Columbia for not paying his refectory bills. "Hanging around with Kerouac" was one of the reasons for Ginsberg's own dismissal in 1945. The other reason was two obscenities atop a skull and crossbones, which Ginsberg drew in the dust of his dormitory window. One scribble, as he tells it, read "Fuck the Jews," and the other proclaimed, in reference to the then current president of Columbia, "Butler has no balls." The critic and Columbia-wife Diana Trilling, in a controversial essay called "The Other Night at Columbia," has since interpreted the first remark as symbolizing Ginsberg's rejection of middle-class Judaism; but the poet insists there was no motive beyond shocking an anti-Semitic Irish cleaning lady who worked in the dormitories. The domestic was, in fact, offended; and she reported the scribble to the straightlaced dean who, likewise outraged, found a second cause to expel Ginsberg, with the parting admonition, "I hope you realize the enormity of what you have done."

After his expulsion, Ginsberg hung around Columbia, mopping floors in a nearby Bickford's, working in a succession of factories, and then shipping out as a messboy on a tanker; and he was later readmitted to graduate with a B.A. in 1948. That same year, Ginsberg had another sort of experience which, like his acquaintance with Burroughs, had a greater effect upon his later life than academic matters: "a vision in which I heard Blake's voice, experienced a sense of lightness of my body and a spiritual illumination of the entire universe as the Great Live Self of the Creator." Since then, he has been an avid admirer of Blake's work; and during that stay in London, he acquired a special pass to see Blake's illuminated manuscripts in the British Museum. At Cambridge, he spent one morning studiously admiring the Blake manuscripts in the Fitzwilliam Library; but in the afternoon, after the midday closing, so the attendant there told me, Ginsberg was all giddy and difficult. "He must have had something for lunch," was the librarian's uncomprehending explanation. More recently, the poet has been picking out on a harmonium musical setting to Blake's poems—compositions he hopes his rock-singer friends will perform.

Early in 1948, he applied to Columbia for both a graduate fellowship and a teaching position, suffering a double rejection. "I was respected at Columbia as a wild poet who smoked pot and had gotten kicked out of school under extremely glamorous circumstances," he told *The New Yorker* reporter Jane Kramer, "but as far as giving me a job—nobody wanted that kind of responsibility." He passed through a variety of positions—dishwasher at Bickford's again, reporter for a labor newspaper in Newark, market researcher, book reviewer for one summertime at *Newsweek*, and so forth. He also got arrested in the company of real criminals and had his picture splashed on the front page of the *Daily News* "as a brilliant student who was like plotting out big criminal scenes." His former English teachers at Columbia, shocked at first, came to the rescue with a law professor who advised Ginsberg to plead himself into a mental home, the highly selective New York Psychiatric Institute; and here he had the good fortune of meeting Gerd Stern, a poet who has since become a founding member of the artist's collective USCO, and the legendary Carl Solomon, to whom *Howl* was eventually dedicated. The oft-repeated story goes that Solomon, already an inmate, asked the newcomer, "Who are *you?*" "I'm Myshkin," Ginsberg said. "I'm Kirilov," was Solomon's reply. It was Solomon who turned Ginsberg onto Antonin Artaud and other writers not taught at Columbia; and together they questioned the conventional conceptions of sanity and reality. In retrospect, this sojourn seems the first step in Ginsberg's self-transformation from a neurotic, clumsy, slightly interminable Columbia alumnus to one of the most vivacious personalities of our time.

Particularly in the late forties and earliest fifties, Ginsberg was, as he later wrote, working largely under "ideas of measure of American speech picked up from W. C. Williams' Imagist Preoccupations." But in 1955, "I suddenly turned aside in San Francisco, while enjoying unemployment compensation leisure, to follow my romantic inspiration—Hebraic bardic breath. I thought I wouldn't write a *poem*, but just write what I wanted to without fear, let my imagination go, open secrecy, and scribble magic lines from my real mind—sum up my life." Perhaps the mixture was spiced by a dash of Walt Whitman too, for the results included "Howl," the poem whose long lines first established Ginsberg's poetic presence; "The Supermarket in California," which records the poet's actual vision of Whitman's return to a contemporary setting; and "America," which concludes with that fantastic line, "America, I'm putting my queer shoulder to the wheel." As early as 1955, Ginsberg was declaiming "Howl" to small gatherings, mostly on the West Coast; but not until October 1956 did San Francisco's City Lights Books, run by the poet Lawrence Ferlinghetti, issue *Howl and Other Poems*.

Reactions were immediate and nation-wide, including polemical reviews for or against the poet and/or his poems, a number of slick-magazine pieces on Ginsberg and his colorful colleagues, and a San Francisco "obscenity" trial that implicitly afforded "Howl" the best publicity money could not buy; and in the late fifties, the world of American poetry had polarized into two camps at war over the significance of the "beats"—in particular, over Ginsberg's almost systematic rejection of the guiding poetic canons (ironic, non-urban, impersonal, mythic, and so on) of the post-T. S. Eliot academic establishment. Turned bitter by the attacks of conservatives, most of them resident in the universities, Ginsberg wrote in 1959, "A word on the Academies: poetry has been attacked by an ignorant and frightened bunch of bores who don't understand how it's made, and the trouble with these creeps is they wouldn't know poetry if it came up and buggered them in broad daylight." Nonetheless, perhaps because Ginsberg was the sole potentially great poet in his band, the only one to author widely memorable poems, his leadership coalesced a number of disparate talents—with Kerouac, Ferlinghetti, and Gregory Corso at the center; indeed, without him there might well not have been any "beat" movement at all. Within a dozen years, the City Lights edition alone went through twelve printings and over one hundred fifty thousand copies; and not only do nearly all the anthologies and college surveys of modern poetry by now include samples of Ginsberg's work, but the doggedly anti-academic poet of a decade ago has become a successful lecturer on the university circuits.

In the years since the opening salvos, most of the critics and poet-critics who objected to Ginsberg's work have made peace with him, a few of them admitting outright in his presence that "I was wrong in 1956," another few even rejecting the ironic, formalist mode for Ginsberg's freer, more personal style; and his poetry alone places him among the dozen major American writers of the post-1945 period. As, in Karl Shapiro's phrase, "not a poet but an overthrower of poets," Ginsberg singlehandedly changed American poetry and the appearance of the American poet (many of whom now sport full-faced beards); and not only did he dispose of the restrictions against the use of four-letter words, in both poetry itself and the public speech of poets, but his impact has also removed from common discourse about poetry such fifties epithets as "art," "critical," "successful," "strict," and "intricate." As Leslie Fiedler put it, "He has not destroyed a world, but only displaced a tired style; has not created a new heaven and a new earth, but only made a school." Since 1957, too, City Lights has been his primary publisher, issuing *Kaddish and Other Poems* (1961), collecting the work of 1958–60; *Reality Sandwiches* (1963), which contains miscellaneous pieces written between 1953 and 1960; and the recent *Planet News* (1968), which collects the work 1961–7, in addition to a book of epistolary remarks on hallucinogens in South America written in collaboration with William Burroughs, *The Yage Letters* (1963). (Another book, *Empty Mirror* [1961], collected his earliest poems, those written prior to 1953; *Airplane Dream* [1968] contains a short story and three poems not collected elsewhere; while two recent limited editions— *Wichita Vortex Sutra* [1966] and *T. V. Baby Poems* [1968] contain material incorporated into *Planet News*.) In line with his autobiographical processes, in these books, as elsewhere, Ginsberg insists upon the precise dating of his poems; and the forthcoming Anglo-American edition of his complete poems will, at his insistence, print all his work in chronological order. His poems have also been translated into Italian, German, French, Spanish, Bengali, Russian, Czech, Japanese, Hindu, and so on; and although other poets may have greater reputations at home, to the world at large Ginsberg is the most famous and most admired of living American poets.

Over the years, his poetry has ranged in style from conventionally rhymed lyrics to the freest of poetic structures. "Trouble with conventional form (fixed line count and stanza form) is," he wrote in a published extract from his journal, "it's too symmetrical, geometrical, numbered and pre-fixed—unlike my own mind which has no beginning and end, nor fixed measure of thought (or speech—or writing) other than its own cornerless mystery." In purpose, the poems range from meditation to remembrance to polemic; in tone, from Apollinairean surrealism to uncompromising negation to anarchic humor; and in stance, from narrative factual statements to the hysterical personal confession of "Kaddish," the lament for his dead mother, which is probably his best single work. The whole of Ginsberg's work, however, is uneven in quality, full of confused, flaccid, impenetrable, or outright bad poems, which, as he knows quite well, probably should have remained in the notebooks; yet like Whitman before him, Ginsberg is a poet of the great line and the sustained vision, social resonance and open-ended energy. "He is a sort of Theodore Dreiser of American poetry," writes the critic Stephen Stepanchev. "He is awkward in phrase and ungainly in manner as that novelist often was. His poems find their shape only after fighting almost insuperable obstacles in rhythm, grammar, and diction." Nonetheless, the measure of a poet's reputation is ultimately not his worst work but his best; and among the masterpieces most critics (as well as myself) would nominate are "Howl," "A Supermarket in California," "In the Baggage Room at Greyhound," "America" (all included in *Howl and Other Poems*), "Kaddish," "Aether," "Wichita Vortex Sutra"—a selection that more or less agrees with Ginsberg's own evaluation of his works.

More important perhaps is Ginsberg's indubitable success at becoming the truly popular poet that Whitman only imagined himself to be—the author of lines that have the status of scripture, that live in the minds of the literary young in America and, increasingly, in Europe and the Orient:

> *I saw the best minds of my generation destroyed by madness, starving hysterical naked,*
> *dragging themselves through the negro streets at dawn looking for an angry fix, . . .*
> *who bared their brains to Heaven under the El and saw Mohammedan angels staggering on tenement roofs illuminated, . . .*
> *who chained themselves to subways for the endless ride from Battery to holy Bronx on benzedrine until the noise of wheels and children brought them down shuddering mouth-wracked and battered bleak of brain all drained of brilliance in the drear light of Zoo, . . .*
> *who talked continuously seventy hours from park to pad to bar to Bellevue to museum to the Brooklyn Bridge, . . .*
> *who lit cigarettes in boxcars boxcars boxcars racketing through snow toward lonesome farms in grandfather night, . . .*

and who were given instead the concrete void of insulin metasol electricity hydrotherapy psychotherapy occupational therapy pingpong & amnesia. . . .

And anyone who has ever heard Ginsberg read aloud these lines from "Howl," whether live or on record—he does not mind reciting the same poem over and over again—will not forget their distinct cadences, the sound of their images, or the inimitably cigaretty, yet youthful, timbre of Ginsberg's voice. Indeed, few contemporary poets can declaim their own work so well—as the poet-critic Tom Clark put it, "He seemed to enter each of his poems emotionally while reading them." Or as Paul Carroll movingly wrote of a later performance of "Wichita Vortex Sutra": "Here was an American poet calling —for the first time in our literature perhaps and certainly for the first time since Whitman—for the possibility of the existence of the ancient verities in the life of these States. Ginsberg was calling for communion with the gods and for release of love and peace in the souls of Americans. He was calling, in truth, for the realization of himself and by all of us that the Kingdom of God is within everybody." This is the kind of power, of words and person, that has made Ginsberg, in Leslie Fiedler's words, "the nearest thing to a best-selling poet we have had since Frost (though his audience consists of bad boys rather than good ones)."

Ginsberg's poetry divides into a succession of periods, each of which represents a slightly different way of working with the materials of his art. The earliest era was at Columbia, where his poems, as noted before, were very much in the pre-Elizabethan, Renaissance mode. The next was closer to the idiomatic, perceptual short-line verse of William Carlos Williams. A poem written early in 1953, "My Alba," opens with the following circumspect lines:

Now that I've wasted
five years in Manhattan
life decaying
talent a blank

By the following year, however, in a poem like "Siesta in Xblaba," the line has become longer, the imagination more exotic, the cadences more various. "I became more wordly skilled," he explained to me, "at the question of finding form to articulate awe-full perceptions." By "Howl," written in 1955–6, the visionary sensibility fused with a sense of social commentary and, as Ginsberg characterizes it, "hallucinogenic terror rhetoric" that eventually fed into "Kaddish," which is, in contrast, however, a searingly intense and courageously personal poem.

In the sixties, Ginsberg's best poetry turned outward, commenting upon the world situation and the milieus through which he traveled. "Television Was a Baby Crawling Toward that Death Chamber," written in the winter of 1961, is, as its title suggests, an attack on the electronic world; "The Change" (1963), which Ginsberg considers a crucially important poem, was written just after his extended sojourn in India; "Kral Majales," as noted before, was composed on the plane out of Prague; "I Am A Victim of Telephone" (1964) is about the interruptions of a typical day at home in New York; "City Midnight Junk Strains" (1966), written for Frank O'Hara just after his death, reveals that kind of bitter, penetrating criticism that Ginsberg previously directed upon society, rather than individuals, living or dead:

and I stare into my head & look for your/ broken roman nose
your wet mouth-smell of martinis
& a big artistic tipsy kiss.

Throughout the sixties, Ginsberg has been moving toward a more immediate, if not instantaneous, poetry; and once Bob Dylan gave him a high-class tape recorder for Christmas, 1965, he began to dictate poems rather than scribble them into his notebook. The magnificent "Wichita Vortex Sutra" was created, in the spring of 1966, out of words observed or sprung into his head during eighteen hours of traveling through the Middle West. "This poem," he wrote in a letter that Paul

Carroll reprints in *The Poem and Its Skin* (1968) "is a collage of news radio optical phenomena observed & noted in a field of vision outside car window, at stops, etc. + fantasy + imagination, memory of history, desire, etc." Particularly brilliant at evoking the contraries and space of the American landscape and at dealing with the magical properties of mundane language, "Wichita Vortex Sutra" is the first of a projected cycle of poems Ginsberg plans to call "These States." (A contrary recent poem has been "Wales Visitation," which is about communing with the English earth and the tradition of English nature poetry while high on LSD in Wales; and Ginsberg told me that this poem, which cracked *The New Yorker*, went through more revisions than is usual for his poetry, partly because he wanted the poem "to exist simultaneously or identically in acid consciousness and normal consciousness and mediate between them.")

The personal, if not confessional, character of his poetry stems partly from several experiences with psychoanalysis, which left him skeptical about Freudian methodology and more sure of the value of the analysis as a human relationship. The first of his many analyses was with William Burroughs, on a couch in the latter's living room, back in the Columbia days. The second, for three months, with "a Reichian who is no longer a Reichian." The third, for eight months, with "dreary Freudians" at the New York State Psychiatric Institute; the fourth, for two and one-half years, with a doctor formerly attached to the institute. Then, "in 1955, in San Francisco, I did a year with a good doctor from the Washington School—you know, Harry Stack Sullivan's—he was the best," and it was this doctor, I later found out, who urged Ginsberg to abandon the square life of a market researcher for Peter, poetry, and pleasure. After pausing to light another cigarette, he summarized, "If an analyst is a good man, then the analysis will be good. Dig? What's necessary is tender communication between two people—in analysis or life." So his outlook remains closer to that of Martin Buber and Hasidism than to the Jewish rationalistic tradition exemplified by Freud.

Ginsberg would like to think of himself as espousing a

message above earthly politics, as consciousness stands above society. "We're in science fiction now. All the revolutions and the old methods and techniques for changing consciousness are bankrupt, like the Democratic Party. We're back to magic, to psychic life. Like the civil-rights movement hasn't succeeded in altering the fear consciousness of the white Southern middle class, but the hippies might." And he said in 1968 that his current politics derived largely from a book on top of his plywood table, Mircea Eliade's esoteric study of *Shamanism*. Nonetheless, over the years he has signed advertisements in support of the pro-Castro Fair Play for Cuba Committee (only to be expelled from Cuba) and petitions against American involvement in Vietnam (and yet been expelled from Czechoslovakia as well); and he has continually brought ecological problems, particularly concerning the poisoning of food and air, to the attention of anyone who will listen, including the late Senator Robert F. Kennedy, with whom the poet spoke early in 1968. More recently, his experiences at the Chicago Democratic Convention, as well as persistent harassment by narcotics authorities (largely in response to his pro-pot publicity), persuade Ginsberg to regard America as an incipient police state; and he fears that unless people wake up to the threat, there will be a series of paramilitaristic putsches across America.

In all, he is less anti-American than, as an anarchist by temper and persuasion, opposed to certain forces and ideas in the superpowers. "America," he explained to me, "is one of the main Judases of the contemporary world. As things are going now, it seems to me that dogmatic cold-war types in the U.S. and the Socialist countries are mirror images of each other and are bent on world destruction. Everything the Communists say about the U.S. is right; everything we say about the Communists is right, too, give or take a little bit of inaccurate reporting here and there. Everybody's bankrupt except for the long-haired young and the peaceful old." Inevitably, when Czechoslovakian authorities, in inviting him to Prague, expected him to make statements critical of America, Ginsberg, the truest of anarchists, surprised them by making anti-Communist ones too; and few can testify from personal authority to the similarity of police-state methods in Havana, Prague, and Chicago, all directed against him, as he puts it, for "the same sort of thing—performing an exorcism in public at the wrong time."

Another of Ginsberg's major interests has been the politics of pot; and here as elsewhere, he is the best publicist for his own passions. He discovered early in life that drugs afforded a means of experimenting with consciousness; and always willing to be the courageous guinea pig of persuasive ideas, he has since experimented with practically everything, typically remembering which drug inspired which poem. Throughout the sixties, he has been an active participant at pro-pot demonstrations, as well as a witness at Congressional hearings, and the author of one of the most comprehensive and elegantly written pro-pot polemics in print, "The Great Marijuana Hoax," submitted to several magazines before it appeared in the *Atlantic Monthly* and since reprinted in *The Marijuana Papers* (1966). Here he argued, as "a mature middle-aged gentleman, the holder at present of a Guggenheim Fellowship," that pot is less deleterious than alcohol, that it is not habit-forming, that it does not necessarily lead to habit-forming drugs, that a huge, pernicious, and self-seeking law-enforcement bureaucracy has grown around the idea of marijuana as a "menace," that millions of respectable Americans were smoking pot (and therefore disobeying the law), that pot is a legitimate pleasure in respectable circles around the world, that most disorders following marijuana usage were due to fear of arrest, and, in conclusion, "that it is time to end Prohibition again. And with it put an end to the gangsterism, police mania, hypocrisy, anxiety, and national stupidity generated by administrative abuse of the Marijuana Tax Act of 1937." As sophisticated as ever, he is also toying with a suit claiming the existing anti-marijuana laws violate the artist's right to the materials of his trade.

Back in the middle fifties, Ginsberg became a public issue that nearly all self-styled decent men found objectionable; but by the late sixties, he has become an established cultural figure, a friend of the eminent, a success with an upper-middle-class income, who has posed for respectful profiles in *Life*, *The New York Times Magazine*, *The New Yorker*, and other square periodicals. He has received a listing in *Who's Who* (whose publisher bowdlerized his common-law marriage, as well as other unusual details), as well as a Guggenheim Fellowship and a prize from the National Council on the Arts, among other cultural honors. (All that awaits him in this sweepstakes is initiation into the august National Institute of Arts and Letters and perhaps the cover of *Time*.) A poster of him dressed in the costume of Uncle Sam was a best seller in 1966, and from time to time there is talk of running him for President—not only the first Jew, but the first bisexual and the first pot-head. Nearly every campus in America is open to his visit—exceptions usually being Catholic colleges, where the students who invite him invariably protest the administration's ban; and he even got onto the floor of the 1968 Chicago Democratic Convention as a reporter for Hearst's *Eye* magazine, only to perform in the balcony a public exorcism while a priest was uttering a benediction and then be hustled out of the auditorium by the Secret Service. Regarding his own celebrity, he told me in 1965, "It's a Kafkian situation, like a repetition of consciousness. If one takes one's identity from a vague idea of oneself, fame can cause confusion of identity. If one takes one's identity from one's desire and the feeling of desire in the body, then one is stabilized." He stopped for a moment, fumbled for words. "If your soul is your belly, nobody can drive you out of your skull." At the time, I asked him about a decade hence. "I'll be living in a little cottage in the country," he declared, "with a wife and twelve children." He paused, then added, "I'll be scribbling poems." However, though he often speaks of wanting to propagate, he has yet to take a female wife.

Around the world, Ginsberg is also, it seems, the most widely acclaimed unofficial American cultural ambassador, hailed particularly by the young, which is to say the Future; and at times I suspect that a decade hence he may well be a permanent, but uncompromised, employee of the State Department. For one thing, his presence abroad symbolizes persuasively the genuine variousness and tolerance of America, as well as contradicting the common images of both native totalitarianism, suggested by certain anti-American propaganda, and the endless, mindless vulgar suburb that our movies present to Europe and too many of our official representatives confirm. In America, too, Ginsberg particularly appeals to that element of the younger generation with values and aspirations different from their elders'; and not only do they take heart, rather than offense, with the poet when square authorities restrict or condemn him, but unlike, say, Paul Goodman, who does not say yes to everything, Ginsberg condones, or encourages, nearly the entire gamut of youthful, anti-social behavior. By doing and saying publicly what many of the world's young do and say privately, he becomes their spokesman; and as perhaps the only major cultural figure to successfully make the transition from Beat to Hip, he has miraculously managed to influence, by now, several generations of the young. Fulfilling Whitman's dream, he is, like his friend Yevgeny Yevtushenko, a public poet whose best lines have infiltrated the public consciousness, who has attained a cultural importance beyond the merit of his poetry. "There is no way," writes the Canadian poet Irving Layton, inadvertently characterizing Ginsberg, "for the poet to avoid misunderstanding, even abuse, when he follows his prophetic vocation to lead his fellowmen toward sanity and light." As a truth teller, and author of some of the greatest lines of our time, Ginsberg ought to become the first American poet to win the Nobel Prize. As a prophet for youth and other avant-garde minorities, he is also one of Shelley's "unacknowledged legislators" or a harbinger of a new kind of existence in an age of cybernation and increased leisure, when many more people will be able to devote a larger portion of their lives, as Ginsberg does, not only to poetry and the arts but also to the cultivation of an uninhibited variety of possible pleasures.

MILTON BABBITT: Champion of a Complex Musical Art

I write the kind of music which does not appeal to those who understand nothing about it. But one must admit that it appeals to those who understand it.—ARNOLD SCHOENBERG

"Some people say my music is 'too cerebral.' Actually, I believe in cerebral music—in the application of intellect to relevant matters. I never choose a note unless I know precisely why I want it there and can give several reasons why it and not another." Indeed, the importance of Milton Babbitt stems largely from the diverse impact of his extraordinary mind. As a composer, he assimilated the serial revolution of modern music, initiated by Arnold Schoenberg, and then later, in an intellectual leap, extended its organizing principles into other musical dimensions, producing what is usually, but inappropriately, called "total serialization." In addition, he was among the first American composers to realize the potentialities of electronic machines; and several of his pieces for the RCA Synthesizer, such as *Philomel* (1963) and Ensembles for Synthesizer (1961, 1963), are among the most acclaimed examples of electronic music.

As a scholar and critic, Babbitt has offered a steady stream of articles, book reviews, lectures, and symposia contributions, particularly on the achievements and possibilities of modern music; and no one else in America has done as much to institutionalize Schoenberg's innovation. As an admired teacher, now the Conant Professor of Music at Princeton University, Babbitt fathered a school of rigorously serial composers, instructed well-known musicians as varied as the Broadway song writer Stephen Sondheim (a private pupil) and the jazz pianist Johnny Eaton (who once composed a *Babbittry*) and influenced numerous important young critics and musicologists. Although his reputation is hardly as public as John Cage's or Elliott Carter's, few would dispute that Babbitt's multifarious presence lends a particular scale to the current American musical scene.

The mind of Milton Babbit forms everything he does; and since he possesses one of the most overwhelming intellects of our day, his thought processes all but radiate through his work. Immensely learned in both the sciences and the humanities, and intensely curious about all facets of life, he exudes brilliance as his conversation travels, if not leaps, from music to criticism to literature to philosophy to acoustics to, his favorite pasttimes, movies and football; and perhaps because one-upmanship is among his penchants, there seems nothing, from the merits of the world's Chinese restaurants to female beauty, that he cannot discuss with considerable knowledge and decisive distinctions. He patently finds the expression and exchange of ideas among the primary pleasures, as well as possessing the capacity, if not the desire, to talk forever in an emphatic style somewhat inclined to hyperbole; and thanks to a fine sense of rhythm and an infallible knack for appropriate emphasis, he lets his listeners know which phrases are the most important, even if they do not entirely understand what he means. His fast mind never fails to rapidly provide him with words, sentences, paragraphs, and even memorable aphorisms spoken with an enthusiasm that suggests he discovered all these ideas just yesterday and yet so perfectly articulated that listeners often suspect Babbitt is remembering a prepared talk. He is asked to lecture so often that he is perhaps the only American composer who could live entirely off his chatter.

Medium in height, balding with a blondish gray fringe,

compactly built, pale-complexioned, bespectacled, modest in dress, Babbitt looks like a school teacher or perhaps a small businessman; however, once he speaks, he all but reveals his identity and instantly becomes a commanding, if not intimidating, presence. Extremely friendly, he has a cheery word for everyone; and during his biweekly excursion from New York City to Princeton, he resoundingly chimed "Hi, how are you" to the bus driver, the secretary of the Music Department, his colleagues, the custodial help, several fellow professors in other fields, all the graduate students he encountered, the manager of the restaurant where he lunched, and a few unidentified passers-by. He has a notorious reputation for making several times more generous promises than he (or any other mortal) could possibly fulfill; and the paradox his friends find inexplicable is that such a ferocious intellect should be so incorrigibly cordial.

Talk and friendship are his virtues, as well as his vices, as he cannot resist, for instance, chatting at least half an hour with every friend who telephones him. He has dozens of intellectual children (not all of whom were once his students) who regularly report to him; and like all good fathers, he checks on their current activities, remembers small details about their lives, and passes relevant messages from child to child. Because he gives so easily of himself in conversation, listening as well as speaking, enthusiastically answering the familiar standard questions for the thousandth time, Babbitt is generally admired by his pupils and popular among his peers; indicatively, his 1968 lectures for undergraduates at Princeton attracted over one hundred registrants, perhaps the largest number ever to attend a music course there. By now, he has met practically everyone on the academic musical scene; so that whenever any of his colleagues needs to visit an esoteric place, he always asks Babbitt for the name of the local V.I.P.—the college dean, the chairman of the Music Department, the head of the arts council; Babbit never forgets.

Though possessed of a passionate, if not somewhat impulsive, nature, Babbitt is intellectually a scrupulous rationalist and empiricist, with strong sympathies toward analytic philosophy. If he hears someone say that a piece of music "expresses" a certain experience or emotion, Babbitt will run him ragged by asking, "Precisely *what* does the music express?" Usually, since his interlocutor finds himself unable to make a statement so definite that it is universally verifiable, he inevitably retreats to the solipsistic position of admitting that the music "expresses" something *to him,* a conclusion that generally reveals more about the listener than the music. To Babbitt, the essence of music is the notes; the stuff of the composer's "inspiration" is discovering patterns that are more complex, coherent, and original than others; and the task of criticism consists of making substantive statements that all subsequent investigators can empirically verify. The result is, as he cheerfully admits, a wholly cerebral musical discourse.

Perhaps because he is a very passionate rationalist, he is everything but a square; and some mysterious impulse, which is perhaps innate, lends dimensions of originality, or eccentricity, to all he thinks and does. He used to be a chain smoker of esoteric southern brands such as "Picayunes" and "Home Runs," though he now objects to smoking; and his taste in beer runs to foreign labels no one else has seen before or since. Politically he is a "conservative anarchist" with a distrust of all authority, a disillusioned liberal's distaste for leftist hypocrisy, and more admiration for certain young English tories than any American right-wing publicists; and since he regards substantive expression as a primary virtue, he rarely finds a candidate rational and intelligent enough to earn his vote. On more mundane matters, he always wears colored shirts "because white ones get dirty too easily"; and he lives in a modest apartment near Gramercy Park, an area of New York somewhat unlikely for a radical composer, "because my wife Sylvia's folks had the apartment before us." He enthusiastically bets the going odds on major sports events; and rumor has it that two decades ago he developed a fantastically successful system for the horses.

Babbitt's conversation has a quick, engaging, informal, almost "hip" quality which contrasts with the academic weightiness of both his words and his written prose, as well as the notorious style of the "eminent professor" whose pretense to wisdom increases in direct proportion to the silences that precede his utterance; and slow questions and replies to him rarely reach their end. As he usually manages to distinguish people from ideas, becoming personally generous without compromising his intellectual principles, in conversation he practices the ethic of the "southern gentleman," asserting, "I can never speak badly to someone's face." However, once the person has departed, Babbitt has no qualms about blasting his ideas as "utterly idiotic."

Few subjects inspire his passionate words more than the state of serious modern music in America. "The situation has never been worse," he says, "less because of its general neglect than the ignorance of people of influence and power." The musical illiteracy of literary people never ceases to astonish Babbitt; for not only does no serious general magazine in the country (except *The Nation*), in his opinion, publish substantial essays on music, but he is continually appalled at what passes for music "criticism" among serious, non-musical people. "In the country of the blind, the one-eyed man speaks gibberish." The major foundations, he notes, have not been successful in their attempts to aid composition; for in giving too much money to composers not seriously respected (and neglecting more promising talents), they invariably become disappointed with the results and then refuse to enter the area again. When the National Foundation on the Humanities, in 1966, appointed Meredith Willson, noted primarily for writing *The Music Man*, as the only musician on its top selection committee, Babbitt got so angry that he joined other composers and musicologists in petitioning President Johnson; and the following year, Willson found reasons to step down.

Because the general public is so apathetic and patronage so scanty, serious contemporary composers must draw their incomes from elsewhere; and Babbit was among the first to find, as many creative artists also discovered after him, that the most propitious compromise was a permanent teaching position on a university faculty. The primary disadvantage, he admits, is the infrequency of those sabbaticals which the composer needs for the time-consuming work of contemporary composition, although he notes that academic composers have more free time than musicians holding nine-to-five jobs. Moreover, as they find it almost impossible to publish their latest music (not even all of Babbitt's finished compositions are in print), "we have no means of professionally communicating." He adds, his emphatic tones evincing a visceral concern, "I can't find out what composers are doing in various parts of the country. We can't infer a score from the tape of a performance, though we can imagine a performance from a score. The score must come first." To remedy the situation, Babbitt looks to the technological palliative of computer-assisted music-printing, as well as proposes that university presses should take the initiative; but neither a publisher, a foundation nor the government has so far supported this latter effort. The recording situation is hardly more encouraging, as commercial companies favor marginally different arrangements of the old sure-fire war horses to the best contemporary works, some of which, such as Stepan Wolpe's recent pieces or Babbitt's own Composition for Tenor and Six Instruments (1960), have never been recorded at all.

The shape of Babbitt's sensibility, as well as the variety of his interests, probably reflects his culturally diverse, but thoroughly American, background. Born in Philadelphia, Pennsylvania, May 10, 1916, Milton Byron Babbitt grew up in Jackson, Mississippi, where his father worked as an insurance actuary. Albert Babbitt, Sr., emigrated from Russia, and Milton's mother belonged to the well-established Potamkin family of Philadelphia. Her brother, Milton's uncle, was Harry Alan Potamkin (1900–1933), perhaps the first serious film critic in America; and the composer dates his prodigious interest in films to staying with "Uncle Harry" in New York. "Nobody believes this," Babbitt continues, "but one of my great-grandfathers was a rabbi; another was a Metropolitan [of the Russian Orthodox Church]." He counts the novelist Eudora Welty among his oldest friends; "Her father was the president of the insurance company of which my father was vice-president." Although he did not encounter much anti-Semitism until he came North ("The Klan down there worried more about Catholics"), he blames a famous novel by Sinclair Lewis for "some unpleasant experiences in my youth." Idiosyncratic in his sentimentalities, he warms over people and things relating to Israel and Mississippi.

Having learned to read music, as he puts it, "soon after I learned to read books, around four or so," he studied various instruments, eventually specializing in reeds. "I was doing gigs at ten years old," he remembers, "and I played in a jazz orchestra." He began to compose before he turned ten; in 1929, when he was thirteen and one of his popular songs won a national contest, Babbitt became a professional composer. By the time he graduated the public school in Jackson, "I had done so much work for Harms [the pop-song publisher] that I faced the choice of serious composition or popular." (Indeed, to this day, he claims to remember every pop hit between 1925 and 1935.) He opted for serious music, attending the University of Pennsylvania briefly and later transferring to New York University's Washington Square College. Well into the forties, however, he continued to write "gobs of popular songs, to see if I could make a living at it. I couldn't." He also did the score for the film *Into the Good Ground* (1949), today becoming grateful that the print shown on television omits his name from the credits; and in 1946, he drafted the score and some lyrics for a musical adaptation of Homer's *Odyssey*, tentatively entitled *Fabulous Voyager*, that never got off the ropes.

After his 1935 graduation from N.Y.U., at the age of nineteen, Babbitt worked as a critic for the *Musical Leader* and studied privately with the composer Roger Sessions, who, he recently remarked, "was the only good teacher of serious composition in America at the time." His first token of professional recognition was the Joseph Bearns Prize in 1941 for "a large, very distinctly not-twelve-tone mass. It has never been performed and now sits in the Columbia University library." After the War, Babbitt decided to retire all his pre-War music, including a symphony composed in the serial language. Like Cage, who is a few years older, Babbitt took all of his musical education here; and to this day, he rarely goes to Europe and advises his own students to travel there for the food rather than the professional instruction. In 1939, he married Sylvia Miller, whom he had known from N.Y.U., where they met in a geology class and took music courses together; and she is today his chauffeur and secretary, as well as an elegant and charming Manhattan lady.

After Princeton asked Sessions to join a brand-new Department of Music, he recommended his pupil, then twenty-two, to the faculty; and in retrospect, Babbitt considers this the biggest break in his career. "If not for Roger, I might have spent my entire life teaching in South Dakota." In 1942, he received an M.F.A. from Princeton; but his elders in the department found themselves insufficiently knowledgeable to judge the merits of the book-length essay on twelve-tone theory that he later submitted for a Ph.D. Nonetheless, he has since taught exclusively at Princeton, commuting a few days each week from the apartment in New York or, more recently, spending some nights at their new Princeton home. His academic office in the new Woolworth Center for Musical Studies is modest and cluttered, decorated with a Mondrian print and some Peanuts cartoons and a poster-sized photograph of his beautiful daughter, Betty Ann, as Liza Doolittle. He teaches courses in twentieth-century music, orchestration, the history of musical theory and musical acoustics, as well as seminars in composition. His pedagogical forte is giving two and one-half hour uninterrupted lectures from a small sheet of notes.

Like all eminent American professors, he has accepted many short-term guest appointments all over the world; and he sits on numerous "advisory committees" along with Elliott Carter, Leonard Bernstein, and other musical eminences. He suffers the distractions of the composer's life with the complaint that "we all get asked to participate in symposia, to lecture and to do articles and reviews twenty times more than to write a composition." To cope with this situation, he has learned to compose in his head, on subways as well as on airplanes, jotting down notes in pocket-sized books of staves he carries in his jacket; and what composition he manages at home is done late at night—for years over a three-legged folding bridge table, now over a more sturdy folding table—while old movies or, preferably, sports events flash across the television screen.

The son and brother of accomplished professional mathematicians, Babbitt has always identified mathematics as his second love, although antagonists sometimes make too much of this. Indeed, to those who charge that he glibly selects his notes according to some mathematical system, Babbitt retorts, "Would God I could. It would make writing music a great deal easier for me than it is now." In fact, he studied math extensively at college, even doing some graduate work in logic and algebra and then teaching a few math courses at Princeton, and during the Second World War he earned his military exemption first by becoming a full-time member of the Princeton Mathematics Department, where he taught mostly advanced calculus, and then commencing "activities associated with the military effort I still am not, and shall never be, at liberty to reveal." (Suffering from poor eyesight, he would not have made an auspicious foot soldier.) To this day, Babbitt sprinkles both his lecturing and writing with elementary mathematical terms ("set," "determinant," "permutation," "invariant"); and some peers find this so intimidating that, rumor has it, the music professors at another Eastern school hired a math graduate student as a tutor "so that we can talk with Babbitt." Nonetheless, music is clearly his vocational choice. "If not for Schoenberg," he once confessed, "I would have gone into mathematics. Schoenberg hit upon a technique that made composition more interesting and challenging."

In fact, Arnold Schoenberg was the greatest early influence on Babbitt's compositional career, although he was not, unlike some of his contemporaries, fortunate enough to study directly under the master. Schoenberg's innovation, known as "the twelve-tone system," implied a revolutionary reordering of tonal possibilities into a new musical language which was radically different from the seven-tone scale that informed the dominant language in the post-Renaissance West. Although the familiar grammars of this "tonal" music sound "natural" to Western ears, they are in fact no more "natural" to nature than East Indian or medieval tonal systems. Previous to Schoenberg, several modern composers, including Claude Debussy, Erik Satie, Richard Wagner, and Charles Ives, repudiated this language by consciously avoiding tonics and dominants, the keystones of Western tonality; and they developed a music of freer tonal possibilities—what we call "atonal" or "polytonal" with respect to traditional Western tonality. It follows that sounds classified as "dissonance" in the tonal system would be regarded as perfectly consonant in the atonal grammar, just as, in the history of literary style, Walt Whitman's unrhymed and uneven lines, though they violated the strictures of traditional verse, created their own kind of unprecedented yet valid forms.

Tonal chaos was the state of advanced music at the turn of the century, when Schoenberg started to compose; and he transcended this by devising an entirely new musical language with its own forms of order. For this new language, he developed its own radically original rules for organizing musical material (its own "grammar," so to speak), its own patterns of interrelationship (syntax), and its own kinds of structures (sentences). In brief, Schoenberg suggested that the composer could, working within the open range of twelve tones to an octave, organize any number of tones (up to twelve), without repeating a tone, into a certain order called, variously, the "row" or "set" or "series."

This ordering of intervalic relations would become fixed as the basic pattern that the composer could then use in one of four ways: (1) in its original form; (2) in a reversed order (working from the last note to the first); (3) in an inverted order (if the second note, in the original row, was three steps up, now it is three steps down, and so on); and (4) in an inverted, reverse order. Now this row is, to repeat, not a series of musical notes but a pattern of intervalic relations; therefore, perhaps the best way to illustrate a particular row's essential character would be to use not musical notation but a graph:

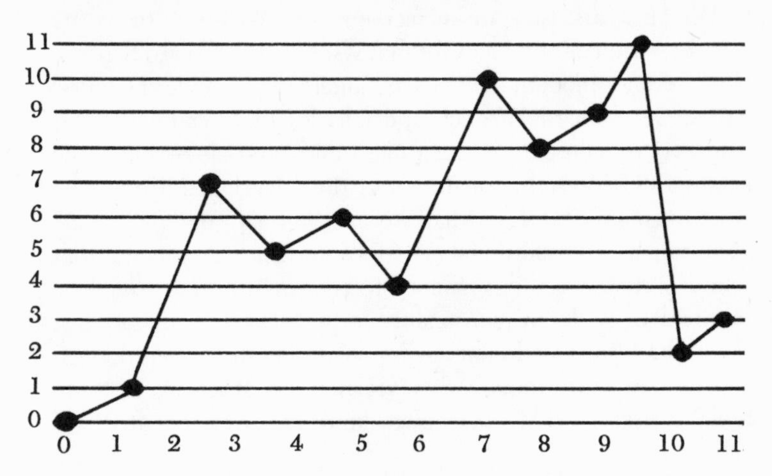

When such a row is imposed upon a musical clef and C-natural is chosen as the first note, the row produces the following notes, in a pattern similar to the graph:

When this row is reversed, the result is these notes:

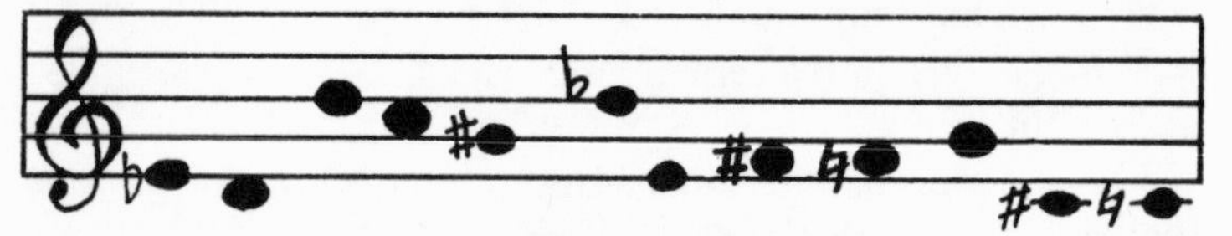

When the row is inverted and D-natural (above high-C on the G-clef) is chosen as the basic note, the result is these notes:

The row can also be transposed, up or down, as long as the pattern of intervalic relations is maintained. Here is the same inverted row transposed up two steps to E-natural:

To avoid certain confusions caused by traditional notation, Babbitt proposes that instead we represent the above set in the following binary terms (that he, in fact, uses in many preliminary drafts of his own compositions):

0,0; 1,1; 2,7; 3,5; 4,6; 5,4; 6,10; 7,8; 8,9; 9,11; 10,2; 11,3.

Here the first number in each pair marks the individual note's position in the entire set; therefore, the left-hand numbers in the pairs successively escalate from zero to eleven. The second number in each pair refers to that particular note's intervalic relation to the first or base note of the row; therefore, where the second note (marked 1,1) is one step away (up in the original form, down in the inverted form), the third note is seven steps away, the fourth only five, and so forth.

Were we to transpose this row up two intervals, we would then annotate it as follows:

1,2; 1,3; 2,9; 3,7; 4,8; 5,6; 6,0; 7,10; 8,11; 9,1; 10,4; 11,5.

Since the note number 6 in the original form has the interval designation of 10, now it becomes 0; for all that adds up to twelve becomes an octave to the base or 0 (as 11 plus 2 becomes 13, in note number 9 becomes 1 in the transposition), because once the row's pattern is imposed upon musical notes, the numbers refer not just to specific notes but also to what Babbitt calls "pitch classes." That is, if note number 6 in this row produces C-sharp, then the serial composer can use any of the C-sharps available to his instruments. Second, the notes of a row can be strung out in a line:

Or any succession of them may be bunched into a single chord:

These are among the elementary grammatical principles informing the twelve-tone composer's manipulation of the basic row.

In the following chart, Babbitt invents what is perhaps the most definitive way known of illustrating the possibilities of this particular row of intervalic relations:

	I	II	III	IV	V	VI	VII	VIII	IX	X	XI	XII
1	C#	D	G#	F#	G	F	B	A	Bb	C	Eb	E
2	C	C#	G	F	F#	E	Bb	G#	A	B	D	Eb
3	F#	G	C#	B	C	Bb	E	D	Eb	F	G#	A
4	G#	A	Eb	C#	D	C	F#	E	F	G	Bb	B
5	G	G#	D	C	C#	B	F	Eb	E	F#	A	Bb
6	A	Bb	E	D	Eb	C#	G	F	F#	G#	B	C
7	Eb	E	Bb	G#	A	G	C#	B	C	D	F	F#
8	F	F#	C	Bb	B	A	Eb	C#	D	E	G	G#
9	E	F	B	A	Bb	G#	D	C	C#	Eb	F#	G
10	D	Eb	A	G	G#	F#	C	Bb	B	C#	E	F
11	B	C	F#	E	F	Eb	A	G	G#	Bb	C#	D
12	Bb	B	F	Eb	E	D	G#	F#	G	A	C	C#

"Each row of this table," he explains, "read from left to right, contains one of the twelve transpositions of the prime set, and read from right to left, one of the twelve transpositions of the retrograde form of the set. Each column, read from top to bottom, contains one of the twelve transpositions of the inverted form of the set, and, read from bottom to top, one of the twelve transpositions of the retrograde-inverted form of the set."

This particular pattern of intervalic relations was the only row Arnold Schoenberg ever used in his magnificent opera *Moses and Aaron* (and the chart is taken from Babbitt's notes to the Columbia recording of that work); and the fact that the row's originator could successfully transform this basic material into continuously various structures illustrates that the serial language is not as constricting as all the rules might superficially suggest—tonal music, one remembers, had its rules too. Instead, even though twelve-tone procedure discourages the kind of repetition endemic in tonal music, it nonetheless creates its own kind of syntactical and grammatical possibilities. "Simple in its principles of formation and transformation," Babbitt once wrote, "twelve-tone technique is enormously complex and deep in its ramifications." Most of the brightest young composers find the twelve-tone system the most attractive of the contemporary musical languages; indeed, since the middle fifties, even Stravinsky, previously the figurehead of anti-Schoenberg neo-classicism, employs serial procedure. So, occasionally, does Aaron Copland.

Babbitt contends that the twelve-tone system represents one of the great achievements of modern thinking, "the result of a half-century of revolution in musical thought, a revolution whose nature and consequences can be compared only with those of the mid-nineteenth-century revolution in mathematics or the twentieth-century revolution in theoretical physics." Although he prefers to compose in the radically different serial language, he does not believe that the new language should or will replace the old. "Ideally," he declares, his words approaching the pace of a machine gun, "composers, as well as performers and listeners, should be multilingual. However, musicians and critics solely familiar with tonal music should no more judge a serial composition than people solely familiar with English can comment upon writing in French." Precisely to combat such illiteracy within the musical trade, Babbitt has become increasingly concerned with musical education, not only writing essays that, in the pianist Glenn Gould's words, "explain in an enormously elaborate way the actual operational procedures of twelve-tone music," but also becoming a guiding intelligence behind the new critical journal, *Perspective of New Music,* and the recently organized American Society of University Composers.

In the late forties, after his return to Princeton, Babbitt developed the logical extension of further serializing the dimensions of musical structure—the conception he christened "combinatoriality," and by which he first became widely known. He applied the serial principles of order not only to pitches, as Schoenberg had done, but to other elements of composed sound—duration, register, dynamics (attacks), and timbre—producing a twelve-tone music of unprecedented structural complexity, in which each and every note contributes to several lines of serial relationships. "The whole twelve-tone conception must concern the composer with order in every aspect of the musical domain, particularly ordering in time." (The German composer Karlheinz Stockhausen once claimed to serialize even more dimensions, such as harmonics and the rate of change in timbre; but perhaps because his scheme inevitably disintegrated in the course of the piece, Stockhausen has since moved on to other ideas.)

From this principle of composition Babbitt develops a rather revolutionary esthetic which equates excellence with "the multiplicity of function of every event"—with the variety of significant relationships each note simultaneously develops. In other words, every moment in the piece should ideally "say" several things in relation to what has already been said. "I want a piece of music to be literally as much as possible," he once declared; and among his favorite words of praise are such cerebral epithets as "profoundly organized" and "structurally intricate." (Indeed, a young composer within this ambience once boasted that his six-minute piece contained "over 900 musical events.") When the televised football game (actually, the Superbowl) was slow in starting, Babbitt audibly moaned, "I could have gotten in another sixteenth note."

In contrast to European examples of "totally organized" music—the early fifties pieces of Stockhausen and the Frenchman Pierre Boulez, for instance—whose sounds inhabit rather open spaces, the immediate impression conveyed by Babbitt's work is a wealth of rapidly interweaving activity; if the visual analogue for the Europeans is the paintings of Paul Klee, Babbitt seems closer to the rich multiplicity of Jackson Pollock and Willem de Kooning. Recorded examples of this phase of his compositional career include *Du* (1951), a song cycle; Composition for Four Instruments (1948); and *All-Set* (1957), written for a fourteen-piece jazz combo. The most obvious objections to Babbitt's practice hold that most ears cannot comprehend such complex simultaneity and that even professional ears cannot appreciate every discrete event; and to these Babbitt retorts, first, that his difficult music is not for the populace of concert-goers; second, that textural complexity itself is accessible to untutored perception; and, third, that progressively more thorough comprehension can be developed through training and experience.

To characterize the unprecedented intensity of Babbitt's music, the music critic Benjamin Boretz, once a Babbitt pupil, has observed, "Every musical event is given a multiple function and the resulting syntax is so efficient that a single sound may convey as much information [that is, musical action] as, say, a whole section of a Mozart symphony." In the other arts, the precise analogies to this multiple conception include symbolist poetry (Mallarmé, Apollinaire), in which, ideally, each word relates to other words in a maximum number of ways; *Finnegans Wake* (Babbitt's favorite novel), in which James Joyce tells several stories at once on the same page and creates individual words that embody several possible meanings; and the early films of Orson Welles, where, according to Babbitt, "each event has many perceptual dimensions."

Like other advanced composers concerned with the precise articulation of their intricate musical ideas, Babbitt became depressed by what happened to his pieces in performance; only a few musicians were able to cope with the rhythmic complexity of his scores. "Conventional instruments," he explains, "provide automatic, or semi-automatic, means of pitch-control, but no comparable means of rhythmic control." This dejection, as well as heavy academic duties at Princeton, are among the reasons why he composed so little during the middle fifties. Toward the end of that decade, rather than submit to further sabotage by performers, Babbitt turned to the electronic music-making machines, not for new sounds ("Nothing becomes old as quickly as a new sound.") but for the twofold possibility of achieving precisely all the complicated effects he desired and of fixing a "performance" for all time. Just as print is more efficient than human lecturers in repeating a definitive exposition of complex scholarly ideas, so a tape, Babbitt recognized, would always be more efficient than human musicians in precisely articulating a complex musical pattern. As his tape-making instrument, he chose the Mark II Electronic Music Synthesizer, constructed, with Babbitt among the consultants, at RCA's David Sarnoff Research Center.

The impact of electronics on music, it should be pointed out, has taken several forms. In the most elementary uses of electronic machinery, the composer and/or performers employ amplification equipment to raise significantly the amplitude and often change the timbre of a live sound. The most popular form of electronic composition is essentially sophisticated tape-doctoring, where, since tape machines do not generate their own noise, a composer must first tape a sound, either live- or machine-produced (often oscillators or signal generators), and then tamper with it in various ways. By speeding up the tape, for instance, he can raise its pitch; by using a third machine to record the sounds from two others, he can combine sounds. By splicing his phrases together, the composer produces a final, fixed piece. Professors Otto Luening and Vladimir Ussachevsky, who founded the Columbia Electronic Music Center in 1951, were among the first Americans to compose in this manner; and among the better tape compositions are Edgard Varèse's *Deserts* (1954) and *Poème électronique* (1958) and Bulent Arel's *Music for a Sacred Service* (1961).

Babbitt's electronic pieces, in contrast, are composed directly on the RCA Synthesizer, a singular instrument whose huge cost of approximately $250,000 permanently discourages imitation. Some twenty feet across, seven feet high, and a few feet deep, the Synthesizer contains various sound-generating devices (tuning forks, oscillators, signal generators, frequency multipliers, etc.) and about 1700 tubes, all of which make it capable of producing sounds precisely to the composer's instructions. Potentially, Babbitt says, the machine can create "any kind of acoustical event known to man"; however, certain sounds, he admits, remain for the moment beyond his capacity to specify their components. Since it does not compose, but responds, like conventional instruments, to the musician's instructions, the Synthesizer is in no sense "a composing machine"; and since it computes nothing, it is not a computer either. This Mark II Synthesizer is currently housed in the Columbia-Princeton Electronic Music Center, which is located in a most unlikely neighborhood for artistic creation—on 125th Street in Manhattan, west of Broadway, in a warehouse area; and as the building also houses naval research equipment, it has a guard and a sign-in book at the door.

On the face of the machine are switches that program the following dimensions of a musical sound—frequency (pitch), octave, volume, timbre, and envelope (degree of attack and decay); and all of these dimensions, appropriately enough, are subject to serial permutation in Babbitt's system. The composer can either set the individual switches by hand or, more conveniently, use a typewriter-like instrument attached to the Synthesizer's face to punch holes in a roll of broad paper tape that feeds into the machine; and once he assigns all the attributes of a note, the machine can immediately produce the specified sound, while an oscilloscope on its face indicates visual analogue to the aural experience (that is, for practical compositional purposes, absolutely useless). If the composer finds that the result suits his intentions, he can then affix it to a tape which, as the storage medium, will contain the piece's final version; if the result is unsatisfactory, he can readjust his specifications to make a new sound.

The composer can also place one sound atop another (as is standard practice in tape-doctoring), transform live sounds, and even program wholly original scales. By these methods, he affixes sound to as many as four separate tracks of the tape—in performance, in better situations, each track has its own speaker or brace of speakers; and in all, the composing process can be so painstaking that several months is fast time for a medium-length piece. Another handicap is that the center, which also houses a thriving tape studio, is so crowded during the working day that Babbitt goes there on weekends and at odd hours, sometimes staying until three or four in the morning. He uses the machine for such serial compositions as *Philomel* and Ensembles for Synthesizer; but as it lacks an esthetic conscience, the Synthesizer could theoretically just as well produce rock 'n roll. In practice, however, "The Synthesizer is most useful for what it can uniquely do." Babbitt grinned. "It would take me over an hour to imitate a long glissando on the piano; and if someone wants to do a jingle, he'd be wiser to hire people." In all, he regards the Synthesizer as supplementing the traditional instruments rather than replacing them; and devoting perhaps only half of his compositional activity to works for the machine, he recently did a work for string orchestra and Synthesizer, *Correspondences* (1968), and a pair of related pieces, *Relata I* (1965) and *Relata II* (1968), wholly for live orchestra.

In sharp contrast to tape laboratories that require that sound be transferred from one machine to another, the Synthesizer does all its work itself. "It is as if in copying the parts," Babbitt enthuses, "you can hear them performed at the same time. Better, it is a wonderful opportunity to walk into the studio, close the door and know that in one series of steps I'm going to be specifying what I have composed, copying the parts, proofreading, rehearsing and walking out of that studio with the final performance for which I'm totally responsible. This is a very unique and satisfying experience." Along with other composers, Babbitt is eagerly interested in a wholly new adaptation of electronics to music composition—the use of computers; and for a projected chamber opera, he is toying with the idea of using a computer to compose visual patterns directly on film.

If only to convey Babbitt's conception of his purposes, as well as his inimitable prose style—at once energetic and stolid, complicated and generalized, overbearing and witty—here is the program note he supplied to the Lincoln Center 1966 performance of Ensembles for Synthesizer: "The title *Ensembles* refers multiply to characteristics of the work. In both its customary musical meaning and its more general one signifying 'collections,' the term refers more immediately to the different pitch, rhythmic, registral, textural, and timbral 'ensembles' associated with each of the many so delineated sections of the composition, no two of which are identical, and no one of which is of more than a few seconds' duration in this ten-minute work. This speed and flexibility of succession in all musical dimensions which are made uniquely available by electronic media reflect, in turn, the particular and vast resources of these media in every aspect of the time domain. Also, in its meaning as a 'set,' the word 'ensemble' relevantly suggests the, I trust, familiar principles of tonal and temporal organization which are employed in this work, as in other of my compositions."

In some discussions of contemporary music, Babbitt's name is frequently mentioned with John Cage's, not because they are artistically close—instead, they are in most respects diametrically opposed—but because each in his own way took an extreme leap and became the primary exponent of an avant-garde direction. As Babbitt represents total control over all musical dimensions, Cage espouses the abdication of all control; whereas Cage would miscegenate music with the other arts and even life, Babbitt would isolate the indigenous qualities of sound—pitch, duration, timbre, dynamics; yet they are often blamed jointly for making the composition of serious music today unprecedently difficult. As Babbitt makes composing so extraordinarily complicated that few can successfully emulate his demanding methods, so Cage's theories make musical creation so ridiculously easy in principle that few serious composers would dare imitate him. Beyond that, however, they are similar in many ways. Each is indubitably American, not only in his musical education but his intellectual style; and both would reject expressionistic theories of musical creation and musical experience, as well as regard music as both an art *and* a science. Moreover, each is the leader of an entourage of avant-garde music so parochial that neither will acknowledge the relevance, or even the validity, of the other's work.

Furthermore, just as Cage's music implies a revolution in listening, where one hears everything in a performance situation, Babbitt's implies that the content of a piece is not a single line of sound but a brace of simultaneously developing structures. Ideally, rather than perceiving only one line of development, the trained listener should be able to appreciate how each note contributes to several serial patterns—in all, to recognize various kinds of relations developing at once. To both Babbitt and Cage, then, the compositional methods become the core subject of the piece; for just as Cage's recent works are all essentially explorations of indeterminacy, so Babbitt's subject is literally the permutations of serial patterns. Furthermore, both Cage and Babbitt write prose essays, each achieving a stylistically distinctive and intellectually appropriate expository language; and just as Cage collected his fugitive pieces into two books, Babbitt is currently compiling a collection of those papers graduate students now dredge out of esoteric professional journals.

Although this champion of a complex musical art admits that his works are written for a specialist audience, consisting largely of other professor-composers, he still believes, perhaps too optimistically, that "anyone who hears well can be educated to appreciate my music. The more you listen to serial music, the better able you are to recognize its grammar, its configurations, its modes of procedure." Finally, Cage's millennialism parallels Babbitt's, for whereas the former believes that music had a new birth once man recognized that everywhere was music, so Babbitt says, "Sometimes I think that music is just beginning, reborn with such an utterly different musical language. Electronic instruments, I also believe, have shifted the boundaries of music away from the limitations of the acoustical [musical] instrument and the performer's coordinating capacities. The limitations for the future are the human ones of perception."

Babbitt and Cage also share that American quality of assimilating certain European ideas—atonality and twelve-tone serial tonality, respectively—and pushing them to extreme conclusions; and what they also have in common is an unwillingness to accept the other. Babbitt, who frequently denies making the nasty remarks that many other people remember hearing, in his more gentlemanly moments will say that Cage "is less concerned with musical structure than with theater." In turn, Cage, who long ago complimented Babbitt as the "most accomplished and adventurous representative" of serial composition in America, now says that Babbitt's music represents "an escape from one's experience, rather than an engagement with it." Although they continue to exchange cordial pleasantries, Cage and Babbitt talked extensively just once—nearly twenty years ago, when Cage had just returned from Paris with some fresh scores of young European composers; today each admits that he has "little to say" to the other.

In spite of his extreme emphasis upon unifying structure, Babbitt cannot erase the fact that music does make sounds which contain their own appeal independently of how they are organized; and the qualities of this surface sound entices a listener's interest in a piece, particularly if the serial multiplicity is not immediately accessible to him, just as an effective use of color can provide an entree into the structural intricacies of a particular painting. Early examples of Babbitt's efforts at a more pervasive serialization, such as *Du* or the Composition for Twelve Instruments (1948), realize an immense structural complexity "at the sacrifice of a certain scope and variety in its line, texture and articulation," as Benjamin Boretz puts it—at the price of a sound level too stubbornly constant for Babbitt's multiple purposes. However, in his recent work with the Synthesizer, particularly *Philomel,* Babbitt exploits the machine's ability to produce unprecedented sounds (although he frequently declares they hardly interest him) to create works that, to Boretz, "seem as beautiful in the conventional sense as [they are] effective as a medium for the transmission of subtle new ideas of reference and relation."

Philomel, using a text especially written by the poet John Hollander, retells the Philomel-Procne legend of the acquisition of speech by drawing upon the unprecedented potentialities of live voice, the soprano Bethany Beardslee, in combination with transformed recordings of her voice and a range of sounds wholly produced on the Synthesizer. "The strangled cries of the voice at the opening," writes Boretz, "gradually merge into a sustained vocal line that seems to trace a wider arc at each of its appearances, successions of pitches in the tape accompaniment gradually accelerate into beating and chattering wood noises; and the single voice of the soprano is first counterpointed against its recorded sound . . . which then is subdivided into choruses of Beardslees, transmuted into bass, alto and piccolo Beardslees, and finally merged again into the single sound that sustains the 'live' soprano's final note with a breath capacity uniquely available to synthesizers." To every ear, both trained and amateur, the result is nothing but stunning, although, one must add, the piece stuns various listeners in different ways. *Philomel* is admired by Babbitt's peers and yet accessible to the perceptive layman; it achieves a measure of popularity without compromising that immense musical integrity that has always been Babbitt's trademark.

The standard professional criticism of Babbitt holds that "he talks a better piece than he writes." Another musician, with little sympathy for the serial language, charged, "He is said to have the greatest articulateness and the least compositional talent of any composer in America today." Goddard Lieberson, formerly chief of Columbia Records and now assistant lord of the CBS empire, says for the defense, "The serious composers of each generation, whether Beethoven or Schoenberg, are always, with few exceptions, accused of over-intellectuality; and it is a charge that comes most frequently from those people who have read about Milton Babbitt's music without hearing it." The experience of *Philomel* in particular is eminently persuasive.

It is precisely his belief that complex structures are more important than mellifluous or original sounds that makes Babbitt an extremist on the contemporary musical scene—the leader of the "academic avant-garde," as Morton Feldman, of the unacademic, Cagean avant-garde put it. Indeed, although one may disagree with his ideas or dislike the musical creations of his thought, it is impossible to deny that Babbitt as a man demonstrates what immense power a great intelligence has over the new language of musical composition, over intellectual laxity, over dozens of students and scores of admirers, over philosophical discourse, over the challenges of contemporary artistic creation, over the new machines, and over much, much else.

REINHOLD NIEBUHR: Colossus of Religion and Politics

The office of the intellectual, Lippmann has generally proposed, is to articulate the guiding faith which will enable society so to discipline itself and focus its purposes that its members can live effective, coherent, and fulfilled lives.—ARTHUR M. SCHLESINGER, JR.

Several years ago, Reinhold Niebuhr, then Professor of Christian Ethics at New York's Union Theological Seminary, spent a year teaching at Harvard University, where he passed the first semester lecturing in the Divinity School and the second addressing classes in government. "That was symbolic of my lifetime interests," he says in retrospect; and no one else in his time has straddled the two cultures of religion and politics so effectively and influentially. To a fellow master of one realm, the political scientist Hans J. Morgenthau, Niebuhr is "the greatest living political philosopher of America, perhaps the only creative political philosopher since Calhoun," and no other philosophical name was cited more often by the intellectuals of the Kennedy administration. By common professional consent in the other realm, as the theologian Rev. Nathan A. Scott, Jr., put it, "Among Americans, he alone belongs to the great circle of modern theologians." Niebuhr's books and ideas have had a huge impact upon both religious thinking and political activity, not only in America but elsewhere in the world; and his personal example of a twofold involvement has influenced generations of younger ministers, even those who may quarrel with the gist or details of his thought.

Well into his seventies, Niebuhr today is less of an activist than before; but since "responsibility" has always been a key word in his vocabulary, he has by no means retired from all the controversies and commitments he initiated. A series of small strokes in 1952 handicapped him considerably—his left hand becoming palsied and his entire left side weakened; subsequent attacks that in 1965 upset his colon prevent him from sitting down as long as he should like; and an assortment of other medical problems progressively worsened his condition over the years. Nonetheless, though officially emeritus at Union and though continually in pain at the time we met, early in 1967, he still taught a weekly seminar, handled much of his own correspondence, at times answered his own phone, served as a research associate of Columbia University's Institute for War and Peace Studies, and wrote an occasional essay or review. Despite the fact that he was born left-handed and then forced to hand-write with his right, he would sooner write his words than dictate them, typing his own prose with one right-hand finger on an electric machine especially equipped with a foot pedal to make capitals; and although he misses individual letters, particularly making too many s's where a's should be, much of what he writes does not need to be rewritten or retyped. At times he refers to himself, with some irony, as "only an invalid retired academic, who has ceased to have even minimal influence on our thought," but no one really believes him. Indeed, his determination today is not merely courageous but sheerly heroic, as well as the most immediate sign of his continuing greatness.

Over six feet tall and basically slender, Niebuhr is now more stooped and rounded than before; but the breadth of his good hand, his shoulders, and chest still reflect the immense physical vitality that in his prime years was legendary. He has clear blue eyes that are piercing and somber until he smiles, when they twinkle; and his nose hooks out of its bridge in an arc that sweeps down to its end. The compelling command of his glance is accentuated by the lines of his long face, for they all flow to his eyes—down the middle of his forehead, across the tops of his cheeks to the base of his nose, and up from his chin through the end of his mouth to the sides of his nose. A bout of scarlet fever over fifty years ago took much of his hair; and what gray fringe he has is cropped quite short. His face is, nonetheless, so indefinite in visual identity that it resembles pictures of T. S. Eliot from one angle, Isaac Bashevis Singer from another, and Vladimir Nabokov from a third; yet his general appearance exudes a twofold presence of strong character and personal charisma that his reputation confirms.

His speech, like that of most intellectuals raised west of the East Coast, mixes formal words and inflections with informal ones, as well as shifts between oracular tones and more intimate sounds; and at times, he embarrassingly mispronounces foreign words and names (Albert Camus as "Ka-moose," for instance). His remarks inevitably reflect his instinctive impatience and directness, as they are invariably more forthright than circumspect, more determined than polite. A Catholic clergyman interviewing him recently for *Commonweal* was surprised to hear Niebuhr snort, "Now I don't think that anybody really believes in the resurrection of the body," and he later added that the "Death of God" theologians were "stupid because they don't realize that all religious convictions and affirmations are symbolic." (Similarly, as an inveterate independent, he used to make a practice of marrying couples whom, for reasons usually of religious difference, their own ministers would not honor; and too free of self-consciousness for snobbery, he is still all but oblivious to the prestige, position, or credentials of people he meets.) When he talks, his hand moves sideways in front of his chest and horizontal lines cut nervously across his forehead, while words sputter out in irregular patterns.

He lives with his wife, Ursula, who is small, blond, endearing, youthfully attractive, and still very English, and a shaggily manicured French poodle named Miranda, in a high-ceilinged three-room apartment that overlooks the Hudson River from Riverside Drive; and except for several impressive medals inconspicuously displayed, the furnishings are modest and unremarkable. An early riser by long habit, Niebuhr reads *The New York Times* over breakfast and then goes to his desk to handle the mail and do some writing. Lunch he usually eats at home quite early; and in the afternoon he prefers to handle such outside business as formal visitors and, on Wednesday, the graduate seminar from Union. As his palsied hand falls asleep and his colon becomes irritable, once every half hour or so Niebuhr gets up and moves around; and in the course of the day he generally takes several short walks outside, often with friends who drop by for consultations during these slow-motion rambles. A large limousine parked in front of his apartment house during the day sometimes signifies that an official dignitary, such as Hubert Humphrey, is paying a call; and he frequently gives brief advice over the telephone. Although his health is a constant preoccupation, he often forgets doctor's orders, physically exceeds his limits, and sometimes hurts himself seriously. He generally naps before dinner, takes a drink before eating, watches the news on television, and reads in the evening; political biography has recently been his favorite genre. Most of his days, as well as most of each day, he spends in and around his house; and he generally enjoys the summer and much of the fall at a large home in Stockbridge, Massachusetts.

Actually, since the afflictions he has suffered are far from negligible, Niebuhr's resilience and capacity for work continually amaze his friends. "Before he took ill," an old acquaintance remembers, "Reinie did the work of three men; now he does as much as a normal person." To get his work done, he has devised the best possible compromise between the responsibilities of his life and the condition of his health. He has, in general, a far firmer command of the professional dimensions of his existence than most others, perhaps because his wife takes care of the latter well. Indeed, he would sooner talk about politics than anything else; and more than once I noticed that whereas my more personal questions usually went neglected, certain queries about the current scene awoke him from his pain. He would stand straight, start moving his arm, and then offer a perfectly organized, passionately expressed, beautifully argued, and knowledgeably relevant critique, only to sink back into the shadow of his more powerful self. Since the original "episodes" of 1952, Niebuhr has taught classes, served Union as its vice-president, given lectures, written several books and scores of articles—a remarkable achievement for even a totally healthy man in his sixties and seventies. Nonetheless, lacking pretention, he is not pious; and personal humility forbids him pride in his extraordinary achievements over adversity. Rather, he regrets he cannot do more. The discomforts he suffers are so great that he has no fear of death; he knows that friends have been counting his days for years; yet there are still books he plans to finish. "When you are seventy-five," he told me before his birthday in 1967, "you don't celebrate a birthday; you feel it passing over you. The late Arthur Schlesinger, Senior, once told me that every time he read the obituaries in the newspaper he calculated how many people died before his age and how many died after. I replied that I do the same thing."

His indestructible commitment to the most active possible life seems embedded in his spirit, perhaps too in his inheritance. Karl Paul Reinhold Niebuhr, as he was christened, was born June 21, 1892, in Wright City, Missouri, about fifty miles northwest of St. Louis; and his father was a Lutheran Evangelical minister who emigrated to America as a teen-ager. Gustav Niebuhr must have taught his children well; for out of his small-town German-speaking Midwestern home came four distinguished Americans. Where Reinhold's elder brother, Walter, was a pioneer producer of documentary films, his sister Hulda became Professor of Christian Education at Chicago's McCormick Theological Seminary, and his slightly younger brother, H. Richard Niebuhr, taught in the Divinity School of Yale University and authored several important books, which likewise preached against the pietistic, fundamentalist strain in Protestantism. "Richard was a more scrupulous scholar and a more profound theologian than I," his brother says today; but others would add that "systematic" is probably a more appropriate word than profound. Today only Reinhold has survived; but H. Richard's son, Richard Reinhold Niebuhr, now teaching at Harvard, sustains the tradition of, as *Time* waggishly put it, "the Trapp family of American theology."

Young Reinhold, after his graduation from the local high school, attended his denomination's college, Elmhurst, a school so improvised it then lacked sufficient authorization to award an American B.A., and later Eden Theological Seminary in St. Louis. When his father died, early in 1913, the son felt sufficiently prepared to assume the ministerial duties for the spring and summer. To this day, Niebuhr belongs to the same Evangelical denomination (now merged within the Church of Christ) into which he was born. A moderately good student and, more important, an acknowledged leader, he won a scholarship to Yale's Divinity School, where he received his Bachelor of Divinity in 1914, just before he turned twenty-two, and his M.A. the following year. Few living thinkers have been the subject of as many Ph.D. theses, few have received so many honorary Doctorates of Divinity (Harvard, Yale, Princeton, Columbia, Oxford, etc.); yet Niebuhr himself never worked for a doctoral degree.

The Home Mission Board of his denomination assigned young Niebuhr to a newly organized parish in Detroit, where he eventually served for thirteen years. "There must be something ludicrous about a callow young fool like myself standing up to preach a sermon to these good folks," he wrote in his journal at the time. "I talk wisely about life and know little about life's problems." Nonetheless, he was an inordinately successful pastor, whose church's membership increased from several families to over eight hundred during his tenure; and his parishioners ranged from millionaires to automotive laborers. Niebuhr began to explore the inequities of his industrial environment, particularly exposing the moral hypocrisies of Henry Ford. "His five-dollar-a-day wage created a worldwide reputation for humanitarianism," Niebuhr remembers, "but this obscured the fact that his speed-ups exhausted his workers, he fired people in an arbitrary, high-handed way, and created enforced [unpaid] vacations while he retooled the factory." Niebuhr joined the Detroit Council of Churches' Industrial Relations Commission, which was investigating the situation; and many of its researches and suggestions guided subsequent business-union policy. "I was converted to socialism by Henry Ford," Niebuhr has often joked; and at the time, he coined an aphorism that became popular, "When private property ceases to be private, it no longer ought to be private." During his Detroit pastorate, Niebuhr also began to contribute several articles each year to such American magazines as *Atlantic Monthly* and *Christian Century*; and these, along with the success of his pastorate, brought him the attention of strangers. Sherwood Eddy, then an official of the YMCA, became Niebuhr's prime professional benefactor, first providing him with an assistant minister (thereby leaving Niebuhr more time to write and lecture) and then recommending him in 1928 to the newly created chair in Christian Ethics at Union Theological Seminary.

His spotty education and years of field experience hardly prepared him to assume an academic specialty; so like other men of affairs who became professors, Niebuhr successfully transformed his previous interests into his "field." "It was," he once wrote, "a full decade before I could stand before a class and answer the searching questions of the students at the end of a lecture without the sense of being a fraud who pretended to a larger and more comprehensive knowledge than I possessed." In his classes and seminars in "social ethics" he initiated the dialogues that produced the ideas which subsequently informed his books and essays; and by the thirties, hundreds of incipient ministers came to Union especially to study with him. Soon after he arrived, he met his wife-to-be, née Ursula Keppel-Compton, an Oxford alumna who had matriculated at Union for graduate study; and the Niebuhrs became one of the most attractive and loquacious couples ever to dominate the late-afternoon social circles of New York's uptown university neighborhood, Morningside Heights. A writer and teacher in her own right and perhaps a more conservative figure than her husband, Mrs. Niebuhr was a professor in the religion department at Barnard for fifteen years. The Niebuhrs have two children, Christopher, in his early thirties, an alumnus of Groton and Harvard who works for housing development organizations, and Elisabeth, in her late twenties, a Radcliffe girl now in New York publishing. So entrenched were the Niebuhrs at Union that he turned down numerous more lucrative offers, including a university professorship at Harvard.

Between 1931, the year of his marriage, and 1952, the onset of his illnesses, Niebuhr was endlessly active on behalf of all his chosen tasks; by rough estimate he achieved as much as four great men. In addition to teaching, correcting papers, conducting a weekly "at home," handling his correspondence, opening his office hours to people outside the Seminary, he spent nearly every weekend lecturing, "as a kind of circuit rider in the colleges and universities." Victim, or beneficiary, of a drive to assert himself all the time, he helped establish several organizations and lent his name to scores more. He founded the short-lived journal *Radical Religion* and then the fortnightly *Christianity and Crisis*, which celebrated its twenty-fifth anniversary in 1966, and served on the editorial boards of both magazines. A 1930 Socialist Party candidate for Congress (he lost), in 1936 and 1940 he actively supported Norman Thomas for the Presidency; and in the forties, Niebuhr became a Founding Member of the Liberal Party, to which he still officially belongs, as well as the Americans for Democratic Action. Perhaps because he disavows pomposity, he seems embarrassed by the appelation of "theologian," and he often says that could he live his life over again he would probably become a historian.

In this time, he also produced scores of essays and editorials each year—for 1948 alone, his bibliographer, Professor D. B. Robertson, counts eighty-one pieces—which appeared all over the intellectual map, even in the Luce magazines, where, in that year, he was honored with a *Time* cover story. "Henry

Luce," he remembers, "liked me because I was religious and hated me because I was a radical." In this period, Niebuhr also wrote his most important and influential books: *Moral Man and Immoral Society* (1932), the first to attract widespread interest; *An Interpretation of Christian Ethics* (1935), which became a cornerstone of American neo-orthodox Protestant theology; *Beyond Tragedy* (1937), sermonic essays that contain some of his very best prose; *The Nature and Destiny of Man* (1941), his two-volume magnum opus; and *The Children of Light and the Children of Darkness* (1944), a primary work in post-World War II neo-liberal political philosophy. As an activist intellectual, Niebuhr has always been less interested in power than influence; and because his ideas won their following, his writings significantly changed the thought, if not the action, of his era. (Indeed, though scarcely a Christian, I count *Christian Ethics* among the few great books in my own reading life.)

His wife remembers that by the late forties Niebuhr was working on something all the time, often executing two or even three tasks simultaneously. "Sometimes we would get the same book to review; and not only did he always finish his assignment before I did, but he sometimes nearly completed the review before he finished the book." Too much of an activist to be much of a scholar, or even a reader, he generally asked his wife to check the quotations and garner the citations; and he also let her collect and file the correspondence he would have otherwise thrown away. To shift between public activity and private work, he frequently took naps, his wife relates; always a high-strung man, "he would literally clench himself to sleep." He adds, "I guess I was a compulsive writer in those days. My wife tells me that I used to put a typewriter on my knees in the train." His daughter remembers that he could write anywhere, anytime, even while his noisy children ran through the apartment; and he never protested the fact that the family television set was in his study. Nearly everything he published was a first draft; and like other productive professors, he did his more extended writings, particularly his books, in the summertime. The pace was so murderous that his strokes, he now admits, were probably inevitable; and wondering about his earlier motivations was among the causes of his fifties psychological depressions. (His daughter adds that he then saw American Protestantism from the congregant's perspective; and this disappointed him too.) On the more positive side, he recognizes that his recent condition kept him home and made him more appreciative of his family.

Niebuhr is unusual not only because he combines a religious vocation with political activism but also because his religious ideas, generally classified as "neo-orthodoxy" (against his occasional objections), strike many an observer as contrary to his radical-liberal political persuasions. As Sidney Hook once bluntly put it, "Logically, not a single one of Reinhold Niebuhr's social, political and ethical views can be derived from his theology." In practice, many admirers of his theological positions do not at all subscribe to his political ideas, and so few of his political associates bother with his theology that his biographer June Bingham remembers him joking, "Some of my friends think I teach Christian Ethics as a sort of 'front' to make my politics more respectable." Hook's criticism notwithstanding, Niebuhr's views on politics and theology complement each other; but as he regards the Bible as the source of primary truth, his political ideas follow from his theological understanding of human nature.

His neo-orthodoxy evolved, historically, from his critique of individualist Protestantism, on one hand, and, on the other, the more serious liberal Protestant theology prevalent in the major seminaries during his youth. Regarding the first, he wrote critically in 1926, "The church honestly regards it of greater moment to prevent women from smoking cigarettes than to establish more Christian standards in industrial enterprise," and to this day he scorns such evangelical individualists as Billy Graham. The Social Gospel, as the second was called, believed, in general, that God was basically benevolent, that history demonstrated moral and social progress, that education could overcome ignorance, that good men capable of good works would produce a better society, and that human will power could overcome the impulse to sin. In its most exemplary form—say, the thought and career of the clergyman Walter Rauschenbusch (1861–1918)—the Social Gospel contributed to progressive politics; in more popular versions, it also informed the sentimental Protestantism of sweetness and light. The secular ally of the Social Gospel was the pragmatism of John Dewey, which also received Niebuhr's constant scorn; for both very deeply believed that a kingdom more godly could be created on earth.

Niebuhr as a young man had assimilated both streams of these ideas; but his observations of World War I and its aftermath, along with his experiences in Detroit and his rereading of St. Augustine and the Bible, led him to doubt the philosophical assumptions of liberal Protestantism. "When one deals with the affairs of a civilization," he wrote in *Leaves from the Notebook of a Tamed Cynic* (1929), "one is trying to make the principle of love effective as far as possible, but one cannot escape the conclusion that society as such is brutal, and that the Christian principle may never be more than a leaven in it." Soon after he came to Union, he translated his new attitudes into more systematic thought. Like so many radically original American intellectuals, Niebuhr was well into his thirties before he presented his major ideas and over forty before the world took cognizance of them.

In such books as *Christian Ethics*, drawn (ironically) from his Rauschenbusch Memorial Lectures at the Colgate-Rochester Divinity School in 1934, Niebuhr suggested that ultimate wisdom lay not in history but in the Bible, "that the Biblical view of man was superior to both classical and modern views," that the events in the Garden of Eden had a legendary rather than a historical truth, that man's inclination to sin is fundamentally ineradicable, that no human being could be absolutely virtuous, that man's primary sin, as illustrated in the myth of the Fall, lay in his rebellion against God or his pride in presuming "finite man to be more than finite." From these ideas followed his assertions that "the ideal in its perfect form lies beyond the capacities of human virtue," that even the most devout and moral man is capable of causing the worst evils (or that faith did not necessarily bestow goodness), and, most vividly, that man lives torn between his aspirations to the idea of altruistic love—the agape symbolized by Christ on the Cross—and his inclination to sin. This theology can be characterized as "dialectical," or more appropriately, "paradoxical," because it regards man as suspended in tension between the contraries of finity and infinity, history and eternity, justice and injustice, grace and greed.

Over the years, Niebuhr has softened his sense of sin, now defining it as "a persistence or universality of self-regard in everybody's motives, whether they are idealists or realists or whether they are benevolent or not." Nonetheless, from this general definition of human nature, Niebuhr concludes that all human life is inherently tragic, for just as an individual never wholly fulfills the goals and ideals he sets for himself, so the activities of nations, or even religious groups, can never equal their aspirations or even their claims. In history itself Niebuhr finds confirmation of his theological position. "That the basic motif of the myth of the Fall, expressed in the idea of the jealous God and the human rebellion against the divine, is not the fruit of primitive fantasy but a revelation of a tragic reality of life, is attested by every page of human history." By assenting to this observation, secularists can here enter the path of Niebuhr's thought.

Such an awareness of the tragic character of history and the sinfulness of men generally induces a conservative political philosophy, which regards man's delinquency as sufficient reason to suppress his freedom; however, Niebuhr gives the traditional logic an original twist. His intellectual leap comes from pointing out that since a nation's leaders are not exempt from the human condition, they are as inevitably subject to sinful behavior as the next citizen; therefore, the populace needs some protection from, as well as control over, the excesses of its kings and politicians. From this paradoxical understanding Niebuhr derives, in *The Children of Light*, one of his most famous aphorisms: "Man's capacity for justice makes democracy possible, but man's inclination to injustice makes democracy necessary. The democratic techniques of a free society place checks upon the power of the rulers and administration." That is, whereas classic liberalism justifies democracy with an optimistic conception of human nature and man's potential progress, Niebuhr posits his political values upon a wholly different, more skeptical image of human experience. Pluralism becomes as essential a value in his political thinking as "social justice," because only through the dispersion of power can the latter be insured. "I would say," he once generalized, "that the whole art of politics consists in directing rationally the irrationalities of men." On more immediate objectives, Niebuhr has over the years usually concurred, nonetheless, with the more radical strains of American liberalism; for instance, all through the thirties he criticized FDR for his resistance to necessary change. "The ideal possibility for men involved in any social situation," he wrote in 1935, "may always be defined in terms of freedom and equality," and his basic principles have not changed since then.

Just as an individual errs by making claims greater or more pretentious than his finite status allows, nations sin, Niebuhr believes, by asserting their destiny beyond appropriate or natural bounds; and because collective bodies usually deflect the power of individual consciences, all organizations, particularly governments, can be expected to function with inherently less morality than individuals. In this respect, Niebuhr has always been a vehement critic of American presumption, especially as it is channeled into economic and philosophical imperialism; standing tall and shaking his arm, he told me in 1967, "President Johnson's domestic program is fantastic; it's superior to anything Kennedy could have done. But in foreign affairs, he is an inept, stubborn man, who espouses the worst ideas of American self-righteousness. Our essentially futile involvement in a civil war in Vietnam is a needless expenditure of money and blood—American blood—to establish a democracy in a peasant culture. The trouble with America today is that it tries to project its innocent sense of mission, gained over a century ago, into its maturity." Nonetheless, as he is no longer a pacifist, Niebuhr hardly favors complete unilateral withdrawal, believing that a balance of potential power must be preserved in Southeast Asia. With characteristically broad strokes, he explained, "American military presence might be better justified if it didn't involve war and bloodshed." Here, as elsewhere, Niebuhr profoundly discerns that so much of the greatest destruction in our time is caused not by cynics but by men and nations who sincerely believe they are doing the Lord's work; the ultimate curse of modern life is not nihilism but fanaticism.

It also follows that Niebuhr insists the religious domain and the political are inevitably separate, just as "a sharp distinction must be drawn between the moral and social behavior of individuals and that of social groups, national, racial and economic." Since the values that religion regards as absolute can function in politics only in a proximate and pragmatic way, the "prophet" and "statesman" can never be identical. Therefore, as politics can only corrupt the ideals of religions, so scrupulous religiosity can only disrupt the essential and necessary practicality of humane and democratic politics. "The relations between groups must, therefore," Niebuhr wrote in *Moral Man,* "always be predominantly political rather than ethical." For this reason, he has always been a severe critic of millennialism, whether religious or secular. By importing absolutist values characteristic of religion into a political context, all millennialists commit the sin of pride on behalf of their vision, becoming intolerant of cultural pluralism, if not antidemocratic; indicatively, from the time of his visit there in the early thirties, Niebuhr never had any illusions about Soviet Russia.

His commitment to pragmatic politics forced him long ago to abandon his youthful pacifism; for some conflicts between nations, he thinks, can only be resolved by force. Indeed, his support of America's entrance into World War II led to his official resignation from the Socialist Party in 1940, as well as a polemical debate with established Protestant opinion which was then pacifist too; and today he regards Russia and America as preserving an undeclared peace through recognition of mutual deterrence. To Niebuhr, the most crucially relevant fact about the Vietnam War is not that it is such a terrible waste but that the major powers have implicitly agreed to curb its size and isolate its bloodshed; yet he fears the war's escalation more than its continuance. "For the first time in my life," he told me in 1967, "I'm frightened about the future. We're liable to shake the tacit partnership between ourselves and Russia." Just before his seventy-fifth birthday, he wrote me, "My weakness is neither better nor worse, for which a man of 75 years must be thankful; but the world, whether in Vietnam or the Middle East, is in foul shape."

Few living writers and lecturers have influenced as many people as deeply as Niebuhr. On one hand, he had ministerial contact with many individuals at crucial points in their lives—marriage, death, and such; on the other, his broader impact can be attributed to his personal style as well as the persuasiveness of his ideas. "I swear that I will never aspire to be a preacher of pretty sermons," he wrote in his journal, back in 1916, at the beginning of his career. "I'll keep them rough just to escape the temptation of degenerating into an elocutionist." He has always fulfilled the American Protestant ideal of a powerful and dramatic speaker, able in his prime to command a large audience without a microphone; and when he came to a college campus, for instance, his audience included many who did not usually come to hear the men of God. There was excitement and authority in his talk; and even his wife attests, with some amazement, "I never got bored at his sermons and lectures." (On second thought, his journalistic career, which included a short stint as a regular columnist, resembles the preacher's habit of working up something fresh in a regular way, even though it echoes what he said the previous Sunday.) Although he spoke passionately, his ideas invariably assumed the air of disinterested wisdom—they were at once polemical and yet above the petty quarrels of polemicism; even his earliest books create the image of an elder wise man. Above that, he dramatizes his ideas effectively as well as identifies their relevance to everyone's immediate experience. In general, he aims his argument directly at his audience, not to assuage their prejudices but to change their minds, since he is less concerned with obvious evils than closer, more hidden deficiencies—the enemies within ourselves; for he is usually less of a critic of mischievous individuals than of bad ideas. Perhaps because the grain of his thought discourages smug piety, his words rarely sink into platitudes. Beyond that, he has the paradoxical knack for being intellectually controversial but immune to personal criticism.

An important dimension of Niebuhr's immense influence stems, I suspect, from his extraordinary gift for aphorism—nuggets of evident wisdom longer than slogans and still short enough to be memorable; and over the years he wrote a number of prayers that organizations have formally adopted. Although Niebuhr's style is generally far from either concise or elegant, his prose occasionally throws up cogent lines that combine generalization with persuasive insight:

> All justice in human society rests upon some kind of balance of power.
>
> The Gospel gives no special securities or exemptions from the frailties of men and the tragedies of life.
>
> Every growth of human freedom may have evil as well as virtuous consequences.
>
> [America is] at once the most religious and the most secular of Western nations.
>
> Perhaps the most significant moral characteristic of a nation is its hypocrisy.
>
> The Church does not seem to realize how unethical a conventionally respectable life may be.
>
> The law of love is an impossible possibility.
>
> The power which prevents anarchy in intra-group relations encourages anarchy in inter-group relations.
>
> No religion can guarantee personal integrity. Religion is a good thing for honest people but a bad thing for dishonest people.
>
> Democracy is a method for finding proximate solutions for insoluble problems.
>
> I make no apology for being critical of what I love. No one wants a love which is based on illusion.
>
> Most of the evil in this world does not come from evil people. It comes from people who consider themselves good.

Although the structure of his thought is essentially complex—paradox is after all not the most accessible mode of understanding—Niebuhr's talents with words make him his own best popularizer; and no one has yet produced an effective trot through his philosophy. (However, two professors, Harry R. Davis and Robert C. Good, have placed together an expository anthology from a multitude of sources, *Reinhold Niebuhr on Politics* [1960], which remains probably the most successful introduction to his social thought.) Furthermore, because Niebuhr has always preferred to confront new issues and problems, rather than proudly defend earlier positions, he always wrote in abundance, continually developing his thought and singlehandedly stirring ferment on a spectrum of political and theological subjects. Indeed, his variousness and aspirations for relevance probably explain why, in a culture that renders its fashionable intellectuals obsolete as rapidly as automobiles, Niebuhr has remained an acknowledged influence for four decades.

Over the years, he has been honored as much for his ideas as his example; perhaps he is one of those rare people who radiate an envelope of greatness and significance. "During my last year in theological school, I began to read the works of Reinhold Niebuhr," the late Martin Luther King wrote in *Stride Toward Freedom* (1956), echoing the thoughts of many others. "While I still believed in man's potential for good, Niebuhr made me realize his potential for evil as well." Another young minister told me, "All of us were deeply influenced by Niebuhr because he took secular affairs seriously, on their own terms." Arthur Schlesinger, Jr., who was very much a Niebuhrian-in-residence during the Kennedy administration, attributes the theologian's untarnished reputation to "such evident seriousness, good will, and basic intellectual achievement." A decade before Schlesinger told me this, he wrote, "If his searching realism gave new strength to American liberal democracy, his own life and example have shown in compelling terms the possibilities of human contrition and human creativity within the tragedy of history."

ROBERT RAUSCHENBERG
Painting in Four Dimensions

> *Every fresh and productive impulse in painting since Monet . . . has repudiated received notions of unity and finish—has manhandled into art what seemed until then too intractable, too raw and accidental, to be brought within the scope of esthetic purpose.*—CLEMENT GREENBERG

Robert Rauschenberg once said that as soon as working in a certain way became too easy for him, he would give it up to try something else; for the past few years, he has been mostly a theater man. While traveling abroad late in 1964, just after he received the coveted grand prize for painting at the Venice Biennale, he instructed a friend to destroy all the unfinished (mostly silk-screen) projects left in his New York studio, even though his fresh canvases were commanding between $10,000 and $50,000. Upon returning home, he began to explore a territory only peripherally touched before—the creation of performance pieces lying between dance and plotless plays, such as *Map Room I* (1965), *Map Room II* (1965), *Spring Training* (1965), *Linoleum* (1966), *Open Score* (1966), and *Urban Round* (1967).

Rauschenberg has long been attracted to the idea of using the new electronic technologies for artistic purposes; and not only has he employed radios and amplifying apparatus in his sculptures, but he has also purchased a sound movie camera, closed-circuit television system, and infrared equipment. When we first met, late in the summer of 1966, he was preparing *Open Score,* which used the television system with infrared attachments, for the Theater and Engineering Festival, in the huge cavernous chamber of New York's 69th Regiment Armory. "My theater piece," he explained to me in advance, "begins with an authentic tennis game with rackets wired for the transmission of sound. The sounds of balls hitting rackets will control the lights. During the game, the sounds will turn out the lights one by one. At the game's end, the hall will be totally dark, but the darkness will be illusory. The hall is actually flooded with infrared light invisible to the human eye." At that point in the performance, a crowd of people poured onto the darkened floor—their presence was better perceived by ear than eye; and a tape began to play in which people repetitiously declared, "My name is XYZ." The seats were so strategically placed that the audience could see both the performance area and large screens suspended over the floor; and onto them were projected live Bosch-like images of people milling about. In the second and more successful of the piece's two performances, electronic sounds chimed atonally, as the earlier tape had been inadvertently erased; and Rauschenberg concluded this later presentation with an effective coda regrettably not used before—carrying a live singing figure wrapped in a blanket across the armory floor. In the artist's own mind, the subject of *Open Score* was "seeing without light."

The Theater and Engineering Festival was the result of many months of collaboration involving dancers, musicians and artists, and about thirty technicians from Bell Telephone Laboratories, all of them working in their spare time. Rauschenberg personally found the collaboration so suggestive that he arranged for its continuance, in spite of the unfavorable reviews the festival received. "Part of the responsibility an artist has is to acknowledge the resources of his own time. We are surrounded by materials and technologies that are too refined to be commonly known. So several artists had bull sessions with scientists, and out of those talks came machinery which we built ourselves. The motivation for all the works has been to use technology without letting technology be the theme itself; it doesn't control the work." With the profits and publicity, the artists, under Rauschenberg's leadership, established a foundation, entitled "Experiments in Art and Technology," to buy and house machinery for artistic purposes, as well as arrange further collaborations between artists and technicians.

Historically, Rauschenberg's involvement with theater is hardly new; it dates back to his high school years in Port Arthur, Texas, in the early forties. "I worked with a repertory after hours," he recalls. "I was too shy to act, but I did all the *schlepping*. I painted posters and scenery and stuff like that." In the summer of 1952, he participated in John Cage's untitled mixed-means performance piece—the first American happening—at Black Mountain College. In 1955, he began a decade-long association with The Merce Cunningham Dance Company, first designing costumes and the décor and then handling the lights. At times, the situation demanded that he become a performer. One of Cunningham's pieces, entitled *Story* (1963), requires that a set be made for each performance from miscellaneous scraps found in and around the theater. Once, in Dartington, England, Rauschenberg could find nothing suitable, so he and his assistant, Alex Hay, set up ironing boards and ironed shirts at the back of the stage while blue lights in the stage floor flashed up and the dancers performed in the front. "From what I could feel about the way it looked and the lights coming up through the shirts, I suspect it was like a live, passive set, like live décor."

What *is* new, however, is that Rauschenberg has now become the author of his own pieces; and the same qualities that distinguished his painting from conventional works (his unfettered attitude toward his materials and his acute eye for effective visual composition) also mark this theater activity. His work now is very much part of the Theatre of Mixed Means, in which artists use movements, sounds, lights, props, sculpture, décor and whatnot to create a theater that is distinctly different from literary drama; and like other major mixed-means practitioners—John Cage and Robert Whitman, Allan Kaprow and Ken Dewey—Rauschenberg works not only within the proscenium arch but outside it. In artistic purposes, as well as technology, he is well into the last third of the twentieth century.

In his first mixed-means theatrical piece, *Pelican* (1963), the performers wore roller skates and had parachutes attached to their backs. "When I heard the piece would take place in a rink. I said, why not use roller skates? I favor a physical encounter of materials with ideas on a very literal, almost simple-minded plane." In *Spring Training*, done two years later, he attached flashlights to the backs of turtles. "I like the idea of light being controlled by something literally alive and the incongruities of a small animal actually assuming that responsibility." He looks upon his theater pieces as animated compositions that can draw upon as wide a range of materials as possible. "I don't find theater that different from painting, and it's not that I think of painting as theater or vice versa. I think of working as a kind of involvement with materials." He added, "You see there is really very little difference between the action of paint and the action of people except that paint is a nuisance because it keeps drying and setting." He also favors loose collaboration more than closely programmed action; and in more than one theater piece, his associates never managed a complete rehearsal before the opening night, not that Rauschenberg necessarily wanted them to do so. "My life is built upon the assumption that everybody is trying to do what they do as well as they possibly can. That's the seed of the confidence I have in people and, ultimately, myself." However critics who have admired his theatrical images, which are invariably original and memorably striking, have found his performance pieces needlessly slack, as well as deficient in that quality that separates theater from painting—a sense of articulate time.

Contrary to an occasional rumor, Rauschenberg has not abandoned painting, although he has finished only a few drawings in the past few years, mostly to repay a favor or debt, or to include in an exhibition. Between his theatrical commitments and the pains of moving into a new house, he has not had much time. Way back in 1965 he finished *Oracle,* an environmental sculpture of five pieces, each of which contains a radio whose dials move automatically or respond to the spectator's adjustments and he envisioned a work where "the relationship of visual images can be determined by the activity of the viewer, who acts in collision with a manufactured situation that is responsive not only to his presence but also, perhaps, to the weather and incidental noises—a construction in which no two people will ever see the same thing." The exploration of previously unknown territory does not, to his mind, necessitate "the dramatic gesture" of relinquishing the old. Opposing the traditional equation of seriousness with concentration, Rauschenberg prefers doing several things at once—to work on theater pieces while he paints and/or makes constructions. "That's why I'm no more interested in giving up painting than continuing painting, or vice versa," he told me in 1966, "I don't find these things in competition with each other. If we are to get the most out of given time, it will be because we have applied ourselves as broadly as possibly, not as singlemindedly as possible." More recently, he has finished three massive and complex technological sculptures, entitled respectively *Revolver* (1967), *Soundings* (1968), and *Solstice* (1968); a "drawing" in neon tubing for Expo '67; a huge two-dimensional *Visual Autobiography* (1967), which was issued in two thousand initialed photo-offset copies (at a husky price); and *Reels (B plus C)* (1968), a series of lithographs using images drawn from the film *Bonnie and Clyde,* among other projects.

Just as Rauschenberg's art today is considerably different from a decade ago, so is his life. Where he was once an impoverished eccentric, taken only half-seriously by his peers and unable to sell his work, now he is an international celebrity, who has won numerous prizes around the world, whose 1964 show at the Whitechapel Gallery in London drew record-breaking crowds. Similarly, while he once lived near Fulton

Street on less than $25 a month, unable to afford either kerosene or canvas, he now commands a grand income, some of which went to purchasing and remodeling a Lower East Side palace, a five-story abandoned mission-orphanage that fulfills every New York artist's dream of abundant space. Today Rauschenberg the man presents a singular mixture of Bohemian taste and conspicuous signs of opulence. During our conversations in his house, he usually wore corduroy Bermuda-length shorts that he cut from long trousers, an Ivy-League short-sleeved shirt and sandals; yet his personal appearance is clean-shaven and impeccably immaculate and he dons a well-tailored, freshly pressed suit to lunch with uptown people and other dignitaries. He drinks the best hard liquor in chipped cups and glasses. Although he has hardly lost his Southwestern twang, he speaks with the cultivated modulations that Easterners associate with culture and education. His slow, halting speech, his idiosyncratic vocabulary and clumsy syntax, his evident difficulties in organizing a sustained exposition all at first suggest an "artist's inarticulateness," as though he is not entirely sure what words mean or how they function; and, in fact, he does not know many of the things most artists learn in college, which he attended only briefly, or by reading, which he does not like to do. Nonetheless, in conversation, his words and metaphors are sometimes informed by flashes of unusual perception and high elegance.

Although open in demeanor, Rauschenberg cuts a rather anomalous, inscrutable figure in the community of art. On one hand, he eschews the temptation to make grandiose claims about his work and career, often declaring, "I don't feel that being an artist is that special." Outwardly, he is not at all haughty or pompous, being rather the sort who once got easily lost in the crowd at an art opening. He says he dislikes to read articles about himself, because, "When I see my name for the third time, I get embarrassed and stop." Most of the time, he lives a leisurely, unambitious life; but when a deadline looms, he puts everything else aside, lets the telephone ring unanswered, and works twenty hours a day, taking occasional naps until his task is done—a bout he undergoes but few times each year. Still, since he hardly disclaims his reputation for excellence or refuses the spoils of eminence, his professions of extreme modesty sometimes seem a bit forced, if not disingenuous; and in artistic society, his fame inevitably makes him a commanding figure in spite of his lack of personal presence. Furthermore, his success has turned Rauschenberg into something of an implicit snob, who is very sensitive to the relative importance of the many strangers and passing people who make claims upon his time and attention; and nowadays he tends to cultivate friendships with the rich, eminent, and influential more avidly than, say, his fellow artists. His intelligence mixes innocence and sophistication in circuitous ways that all but defy clear explanation. His innocence allows him to accept his eccentric ideas as perfectly reasonable, if not normal, and to pursue paths that others would condemn in advance as ridiculous; yet precisely in his constant willingness to take such risks lies his sophistication and his success. For instance, he has a negligible sense of art's history; yet many of his works stand distinctly on the contemporary frontier of several distinct historical tendencies. Rauschenberg has an intense curiosity about many areas of life, a keen intelligence, a consistent esthetic attitude, a strong memory, and an unusually tenacious capacity for concentration; yet his perceptions about non-artistic matters are distinctly unexceptional, if not embarrassingly common, and he is somewhat intimidated by intellectual conversation. Nonetheless, his personality displays so little of the superlative inventiveness reflected in his work and career that even his friends are somewhat mystified by his achievement; and one new acquaintance doubted "if such a nice, simple guy as Bob could do all those gritty, brilliant things." For another instance, at the same time, in 1955, that he was constructing lucrative midtown Manhattan window displays, mostly in collaboration with the painter Jasper Johns, he was initiating the innovative collages and assemblages that were eventually interpreted as repudiating abstract expressionism, as well as much else in traditional Western art, let alone the conventions of window display. Another apparent contradiction stems from a hard pragmatism that is not likely to get conned into anything contrary to his interests and aspirations; yet more than one admirer thinks Rauschenberg has innocently followed Billy Klüver, a Bell Labs research scientist, along an art-technological expedition that has yet, except perhaps for *Soundings*, to return any golden eggs. For the past few years, the artist has had every reason to be immensely contented with his life and position; yet he pushes on to new things with the restlessness of a perpetually bored man. In the end, he blends acceptance with rebellion, generosity with possessiveness, empathy and unconcern, simplicity with complexity, kindness and malevolence, as well as innocence and sophistication, in singular, if not unpredictable, measures.

His clear skin, ready smile, relatively unlined neck, protruding Adam's apple, full head of wholly light-brown hair, and slender build all make him look far younger than his forty-plus years; and when he lets the sides of his gently curling hair grow long, he looks even more youthful. Of medium height and fair complexion, he has a prominent brown mole on his right cheek and unusual eyes he describes as "brownish green with orange spots"; and out of a vain distaste for eyeglasses, he squints often enough to have distinct crow's feet. In profile, particularly in his nose, he reveals fractional traces of Cherokee ancestry. His sense of humor favors wry remarks, and he enjoys laughing at his own jokes as well. Shy by nature, he drinks a good deal, even during the day; and this loosens the reins on his expression. His cheerful and optimistic demeanor makes him seem younger too, perhaps because he still innocently regards life as an endless adventure into untested possibilities. His capacity to charm everyone from fellow artists to Philistines is legendary; yet that ready smile masks an underlying reserve.

His recent activities have made his life more complicated, and he handles his varied commitments with the calm and competence of a seasoned executive. Unlike paintings, theater pieces cannot be created alone; and prior, say, to the Theater and Engineering Festival, Rauschenberg spent his day talking to his producers, public relations agents, repairmen, fellow performers, architects, technicians, electricians, politicians, patrons, reporters, and communications officials, some of whom were continually milling about his house. Contained in spirit, he possesses the executive's ability to make decisions rapidly, to keep his appointments and conversations in his head, to handle intrusions and crises gracefully, and to quickly shift his concentration from one problem to another. Sometimes he seems so comfortable in this new role that I got the impression he could deemphasize painting and theater to become a producer of cultural activities; and since he has never been much of a worshiper at the Temple of Art, he probably would not feel much of a loss. (Years ago, when an antagonistic French critic asked if he would accept an offer to become President of the United States or General Motors, Rauschenberg replied, only partly in irony, "Those are good jobs. I'd think seriously about it.") He lent his name and money to Senator Eugene McCarthy's Presidential designs, as well as accepted a five-year appointment to the Mayor's Cultural Committee; still, his politics are finally as undogmatic as his esthetics. "I'm only against the most obvious things, like wars and stuff like that," he told me. "I don't have any particular concept about a utopian way things should be. If I have a prejudice or bias, it is that there shouldn't be any particular way." By principle, he has always been open to the world, and right now the world is wide open to him.

Le Palais Rauschenberg suits its owner's singular mixture of dowdiness and success; with its spacious grandeur, institutional ambience, and modest furnishing, it is one of the most spectacular private residences in New York City. Rauschenberg bought the building in 1965 from a man who in turn got it from the Catholic Church. Situated in a factory neighborhood, between a gas station and an office building, it reveals its orphanage origins with a dirty red-brick exterior, linoleum floors, high ceilings, and wide stairways; and there are five floors, a basement and subbasement, a usable roof, as well as a small chapel about forty feet high at its nave, that extends from the back of the ground floor. Along the top of the open outside wall runs a large indelibly painted advertisement with two smiling kids, a boy and a girl and an inscription which reads, "Help Us Provide Home and Education for Neglected Children, St. Joseph's Union Mission of the Immaculate Virgin."

Its current occupant converted the chapel and high-ceilinged ground floor into two immense studios; the second floor contains a reception room with a small library of books and a large table full of miscellaneous papers, as well as a bedroom; the third floor has a kitchen, a living room, and a small office. Storage space and a large study to house his art collection fill the fourth floor, and the fifth provides rehearsal space for dance and theater pieces. The open roof he set with tile and equipped with a shower, a collection of plants, and a telephone. Most of the furniture came from the neighborhood second-hand stores, the stove is a relic from orphanage days, and the dishes do not match. Out of a childhood love of animals, he keeps a ménage of pets, including a dog or two, several cats, occasional chickens, and even a tame rabbit.

In Port Arthur, Texas, where Rauschenberg was born in 1925, he knew nothing about art and less about culture. A poor student, who graduated in the bottom quarter of his high school class, he remembers that instead of studying he preferred to draw, looking upon this interest less as an artistic talent than a mere technical facility, like weight-lifting or penny-pitching. "I thought everybody could do it a little bit, and I never took it more seriously than that." While in the Navy, he discovered "Art" at the Huntington Museum in California; and once discharged, he attended the Kansas City Art Institute. The myth of Paris wooed him a year later, 1947, but language difficulties hampered his education. Returning to America, he registered at Black Mountain College, the now-defunct progressive school in North Carolina, where he studied under Josef Albers, a tough Bauhaus disciplinarian. "I had an awful time pleasing him," Rauschenberg remembers, "I was too messy for collage, and I was too heavy-handed in my drawings." Despite such persistent failure, he continued on his chosen path, winning some recognition in the early fifties for his work with blueprint paper. Most pieces from this period were regrettably destroyed in a fire.

In the summer of 1952, after the break-up of a brief marriage and the birth of his son Christopher, Rauschenberg returned to Black Mountain as an unofficial artist-in-residence; and here he met the composer John Cage, who became one of his closest friends and artistic associates. Rauschenberg's famous White Paintings of this period resemble in purpose Cage's silent piece *4′ 33″*, in that both attempt to incorporate the live activity of the environment into the field of art. "A canvas is never empty," he has since declared; and whereas the "music" of Cage's piece consisted of all the sounds that happened to arise in a concert hall in four minutes and thirty-three seconds, Rauschenberg created a field so thoroughly white it reflected and even reproduced the lights and shadows within its surroundings. "After I painted one, two, three and four of the white ones, I jumped to an arbitrary large number, which would imply that they could just go on and on. I had no interest in exploiting the fact or establishing a reputation as the artist who paints those white canvases. It wasn't an obsession." He paused, took a swallow from his drink, and alluded to artists like the late Ad Reinhardt, "I try to avoid obsessions." At last count, not one White Painting has found a buyer, but Rauschenberg's example stands as a major precursor to recent "minimal" tendencies in art.

With this work Rauschenberg opened his painting to the environment, and he has subsequently incorporated more of the environment in his painting. Not only did he use flat images that his elders thought unfeasible—pictures of his relatives, newspaper headlines, calendars, reproductions of classic paintings—but he also incorporated three-dimensional "found objects" such as an automobile tire, an umbrella, a quilted bed, Coke bottles, hand-painted neckties, a stuffed Angora goat. The result was an endless series of stunning collages (mixtures of diverse material) and assemblages (three-dimensional collages). Indeed, to the curator Henry Geldzahler, a work as early as

Rebus (1955) "is close to an anthology of the techniques of contemporary painting: dripped paint, hard rectangles of primary colors, cloth, torn posters, comic strips, children's drawings, graffiti and the commercial reproduction of art." Still, even to this day the compositional style reveals Rauschenberg's characteristic forte. "The ensemble," Geldzahler continues, "is organized with an uncanny aptness of placement into a composition that remains harmonious and spare despite its complexities." Indeed, contrary to the radical and offhanded character of his visual materials, Rauschenberg's pictures are rather precisely composed, revealing the classic qualities of symmetry and balance, so that everything seems in its proper place. Moreover, because the images have an interchangeable quality (why not a German shepherd instead of a goat?) and because he rarely allows one to dominate the other, Rauschenberg contributed to abolishing the traditional hierarchy of images (with the female nude at the top and junk at the bottom). His work states, in effect, that one image is as feasible as any other, and this playful attitude toward his materials established Rauschenberg as father to both "pop art" and "junk sculpture."

Pursuing these themes, Rauschenberg also denies that there is a distinct wall separating Sacred Art from Profane Life, believing instead that they are hardly exclusive entities and that one can be as interesting as the other. His most-quoted aphorism holds, "Painting relates to both art and life. Neither can be made. (I try to act in that gap between the two.)" One of the reasons he uses real materials, rather than painting or constructing imitations, is that he wants to enhance the spectator's visual perception of familiar objects and experiences and to this end he sometimes succeeds in spite of the spectator's esthetic resistances. "Though I happen to dislike Rauschenberg," writes the eminent art historian E. H. Gombrich, "I notice to my chagrin that I cannot help being aware of such sights in a different way since seeing his pictures. Perhaps if I had disliked his exhibition less, the memory would have faded more quickly." By incorporating so much popular imagery into his art, Rauschenberg insists that considerable art exists in ordinary life, if we would only learn to appreciate it. "There is no reason," he once remarked, "not to consider the world one gigantic painting." His inspirations and intentions are exterior to himself; for unlike the action painter, whose purposes were partially cathartic, Rauschenberg says, "I'm not interested in the second-hand quality that comes from expressing emotion directly," while his work presumes a viewer whose preconceptions are taunted and patterns of response instructed. Indeed, he so much wants his audience to get involved with his works that he will sometimes appear at his exhibitions to talk with the befuddled. In these conversations, he gently questions their dogmatic assertions (usually dissuading them), helps ask probing questions about the materials in a particular work, or relates the concerns of the painting to extrinsic experience; yet just as he is not one to explain the mysterious titles of his pieces, so he resists critical interpretations that are any more elaborate than general description.

All this means that his pictures demand viewing habits different from action paintings, or even classic works. In the painting *Tracer* (1964), for instance, the images include army helicopters, a Rubens nude Venus whose head is reflected in a mirror, an eagle, the outlines of boxes, a taxicab, a slummy street scene, two small birds in a cage. The colors in the picture gravitate toward four shades—red, dull blue, black, and white. What is remarkable about this picture is the way Rauschenberg transforms rather ordinary, esthetically recalcitrant visual material into visionary art. ("There is no poor subject," he once declared, "A pair of socks is no less suitable to make a painting than wood, nails, turpentine, oil and fabrics.") First, he superimposes unnatural colors upon the photographic, highly realistic images and then arranges these miscellaneous materials in an appropriate way (and with all the images right side up); despite the mundane quality of the individual images, the result has the visual elegance of something that clearly belongs in a museum.

Rather than ask straight out what does *Tracer* mean and what is Rauschenberg trying to express, let us start with the question of why a Rubens nude next to a picture of a shabby neighborhood. Is Rauschenberg blaspheming a classic work by placing it in such a dingy setting? That is unlikely, because he also puts it in a prominent, flattering position. What is the artistic status of a reproduced reproduction of a classic? The images offer symbolic contrasts—classical grandeur versus contemporary squalor, the incipient violence of Army helicopters versus the serenity of the owl; but the other objects do not contribute to either of these allegorical themes. All the images seem equally viable, because compositionally they balance each other just as the smeared paint on the lower-middle left balances the flowing hair on the upper-middle right; similarly, the four black-and-white images in the work all serve to pull the miscellaneous surface together. Therefore, what is the purpose of this painting? What might be its relation to life? In another sense, the balance of a Rubens nude and a street scene suggests that one is as familiar and immediate to Rauschenberg as the other; and the entire canvas suggests a vision of life as full of complex and incongruous juxtapositions, where elements have relations that are at once rational and irrational. "The more we look," writes the curator Alan Solomon, "the more we are faced with complexities of meaning." In the end, *Tracer*, as an ordered chaos of unconventional, mostly representational imagery, looks stylistically different from all previous art.

"I work very hard to be acted upon by as many things as I can," Rauschenberg told me. "That's what I call being awake." And as formal arrangements, his paintings are about living in New York, where he sees "this constant irrational juxtaposition of things that one doesn't find in the countryside." He once defined his overall themes as "multiplicity, variation and inclusion"; yet few painters can treat the theme of chaos with such visual coherence—a technique usually based on approximate verticals and horizontals. The point is that once these basic questions of relation are pursued the painting assumes a consistency and purpose that may at first escape the lazy or unperceptive viewer; and one's inquisitive involvement with the painting becomes profitable. This bias toward challenging perception leads Rauschenberg to defend works, not always his own, that most spectators find interminable. "I've never deliberately thought about boring anyone; but I'm also interested in that kind of theater activity that provides a minimum of guarantees," he rationalized over a dinner he cooked. "I suspect there is a lot of work right now in theater, described as boring, which is simply the awkward reorientation of the function of theater and even the purpose of the audience." Beyond that Rauschenberg is more concerned with processes than products, more interested in creating than creations; and this explains why his paintings, unlike Jasper John's work, have a faintly unfinished quality. "It's almost as if art, in painting and music and stuff, is the leftovers of some activity," he says. "The activity is the thing that I'm most interested in."

This emphasis upon unending process accounts for the great variety of his work as well as the exploratory motif of his entire career. "I think," he once told me, "that a person like Leonardo da Vinci had not a technique or a style in common with other artists but a kind of curiosity about life that enabled him to change his medium so easily and so successfully." After that, Rauschenberg is very much an intellectual painter, and each series of pictures represents, to his mind, a number of tests of a particular idea. However, these ideas are usually neither esthetic (challenges to the history of art) nor even literary but outright physical experiments—to see what would happen if he did a certain thing. In the White Paintings, for instance, he wanted to discover if he could incorporate the immediate environment into the painting; in *Bed* (1955), he attempted to transform his own bed into a work of art. In *Factum I* and *Factum II* (1957) he tried to paint two pictures as identical as possible. "I wanted to see," he declared, "how different, and in what way, would be two paintings that looked that much alike." In *Summer Rental* (*Versions I–IV*) (1960), he did four different pictures, as Calvin Tomkins reports, "using exactly the same materials—the same colors, the same amount of each color, the same collage elements, all carefully measured out." In these examples, the ideas were, respectively, painting a reflecting field, working with a bed, creating duplicates wholly by hand, making dissimilar paintings out of identical materials; and in each of those experiments, the act of testing the physical idea was part of the process.

Still, what holds all his work together are, first, stylistic qualities so common that his pictures do resemble each other and, second, a certain kind of autobiographical impulse. That is, his paintings (his silk screenings, even his distinctly contemporary drawings for Dante's *Inferno*) contain images, objects and impressions recently gathered—from newspapers, from the street, from a conversation, from a chance perception, and these are arranged so vertically and horizontally that they are distinctly reminiscent of Mondrian and so diffusely that all the elements tend to seem of equal visual importance—even in *Monogram* (1959), the predominant goat competes with other articulated images. This achieves that paradox of ordered disorder that became a distinctly Rauschenbergian trademark. "What is extraordinary," writes the English critic Andrew Forge, "is the way in which such powerful, aggressive forms as the (goat), as the umbrella (in *Charlene* [1954] and elsewhere) are brought to terms with the painting's surface. And they remain self-contained, intact." In his work of the fifties, paint was evidently applied in rough swatches typical of abstract expressionism; but by the sixties he developed the more personal style of discrete pools of color. Beyond these particular qualities are the recurring facts of an autobiography, for *Bed*, which is after all his own bed, is a permanent record of his 1955 decision that since he had no money to buy canvas and the time was late enough in May to forget about the cold, he would paint his own sack. "His *Bed* is the equivalent of *Vincent's Room at Arles* by Van Gogh," writes the critic Harris Dienstfrey, "but the means of expression have been radically compressed and foreshortened, because the object has become the entire canvas." However, in contrast to artists who interpret the materials of their experience, Rauschenberg sees himself more as a reporter, hypersensitive to his environment, which in turn has a huge influence upon his work. His assemblages are full of discarded automobile tires, for instance, because they are plentiful in his Lower East Side neighborhood. He mixes images drawn from advertisements with reproductions of classic paintings, because both have an immediate existence in his visual experience and memory (just as the American composer Charles Ives, perhaps the first pop artist, long before mixed snatches of folk and hymn tunes with the phrases from Beethoven's Fifth). "Superficially, Rauschenberg's attitude toward objects seems rather like that of the traditional Surrealist painters who frequently located familiar objects in bizarre settings," writes Dean Swanson of Minneapolis's Walker Art Center. "But, unlike the Surrealists, Rauschenberg constantly reminds us of the real world from which the objects in his combine paintings came; he never transmutes them into props in a dream-world of his own making."

Toward the late fifties, Rauschenberg's art took on a greater dimensionality, incorporating objects that conspicuously emerged from a flat painted canvas, such as genuine Coca-Cola bottles in *Coca-Cola Plan* (1958) and *Curfew* (1958), or broke the painting's rectangular shape, like *Winter Pool* (1959), where a real ladder bridges two canvases, or *Pilgrim* (1960), where a chain rests on the floor in front of the canvas, as well as platforms that took them off the wall, implicitly breaking down the traditional distinction between painting and sculpture. "What to call them—painting or sculpture—got for some people to be a very interesting point, which I did not find interesting at all," he declared after dinner. "Almost as a joke, I thought I'd call them something, as Calder was supposed to have done with 'mobiles'; and once I came up with 'combines,' people were confronted with the work itself, not with what it wasn't." For instance, *Monogram,* perhaps his most famous assemblage, has a stuffed angora goat with a discarded tire around his middle and paint across his face, all mounted on a platform of paint and collage. "I had always worked with stuffed animals," Rauschenberg explained, "but a goat was special in the way that a stuffed goat is special, and I wanted to see if I could integrate an animal or an object as exotic as that. I've always been more attracted to familiar or ordinary things, because I find them a lot more mysterious. The exotic has a tendency to be immediately strange." And in fact, the goat went through several tentative combines before Rauschenberg arrived at its final form. In *Pantomime* (1961), he placed two opposed fans in front of the picture to show that "any physical situation is an influence on not only how you see and if you look but also what you think when you see it. I just knew that if you were standing in the strong breeze, which is part of the painting, that something different would happen. Even the air around you is an influence." Later pieces such as *Broadcast* (1959) and *Third Time Painting* (1961) introduced elements which contained time—both clocks and radios—literally bestowing the fourth dimension into his collage. Indeed, his present theater activity could be defined as impermanent fourth-dimensional painting, and Rauschenberg, we remember, has always insisted that his theater is not much different from his painting.

The variousness of his artistic history has created the Myth of Rauschenberg as the master adventurer who continually moves beyond past and current successes for new territory, constantly risking utter failure. His close friend, the sometime painter and mixed-means artist Robert Whitman, characterized this quality in comparing him to Jackson Pollock. "The first time I saw Pollock's big paintings I thought they were the most incredible things. Now that I think about them for a while, I wonder why in the hell he kept on doing them. It doesn't seem very interesting to do a whole lot of those after you do one or ten of them. In contrast, think of what Bob does. He might do some all-black paintings, then some all-white paintings, and then do paintings with collage and then do combines and then reject that and have things coming out of the canvas into the space, and then do works that are on Plexiglas and then go on to theater work, which so far seems to be much less defined than his visual work. It's more dangerous for him personally to do that." What complements this Rauschenbergian myth is, as Lucy R. Lippard puts it, "his fondness for iconoclastic gestures." Among the more famous, Lippard continues, were "the acquisition from de Kooning of a de Kooning drawing which was then erased with some difficulty, and exhibited as "erased de Kooning by Robert Rauschenberg 1953"; and the cabled reply to a request to make Iris Clert's portrait, which read, "This is a portrait of Iris Clert if I say so." (Regarding the symbolic import of the first gesture, John Cage has written, "In preparation he erases de Kooning.") This penchant for originality is remarkable; but even more extraordinary is the fact that, whereas an older generation of American artists consciously emulated the styles of the classic moderns before arriving at their own breakthrough, Rauschenberg created innovative works almost from the beginning of his professional career.

Rauschenberg is a conscious avant-gardist, creating a bold new step with every manifesto-backed gesture. His originality stems from curiosity about perception and organization, as well as from willingness to follow his curiosity wherever it takes him. In the end, the achievement of his earlier steps ahead gave Rauschenberg a decided place between the abstract expressionism dominant in the fifties and the various styles of the middle sixties, most of which drew upon one or another of his artistic examples; and while he is haunted by the recognition that artistic inspiration, as well as luck, sometimes runs out, he takes his current steps with the tenuous confidence that his talent has yet, not yet, to fail his ambition. "Art critics look at my work right now and say, 'Why are you wasting your time?' I am damn well continuing to do what I please." As the Texan of yore hardly thought of himself as a frontiersman—that was an Easterner's myth—but a man doing the work that his life required, so this Texan pursues the paths that suit him, only to hear eastern critics, as well as Europeans, discover that his works have created a frontier for art in our time.

PAUL GOODMAN:
Persistence and Prevalence

The old masters, then, in order to prevent themselves from being displaced . . . deliberately went to work taking the young bright ones as they came along, and divided them up anticipatorily into non-self-integratable specializations, which made them completely innocuous as challengers to comprehensive grand strategy thinking and practical affairs integration.—R. BUCKMINSTER FULLER

There must be several Paul Goodmans, to judge from how often and how variously that name appears in print. The most famous is Paul Goodman, the social critic, author of *Growing Up Absurd* (1960) and *People or Personnel* (1965); and this is surely the same Paul Goodman who was non-resident philosopher of the Berkeley Free Speech Movement, who stands as father figure to many academic dropouts, who is a leading participant in peace demonstrations, the guiding spirit behind the "Free Universities," the acknowledged exemplar of anti-bureaucratic existence, and the same Goodman who frequently writes moralistic essays and epistles to public figures. It is to this Goodman that Adlai Stevenson, just before his death, addressed a major letter on foreign policy. (Never sent, the letter was published posthumously.) The American Place Theater in New York presented Paul Goodman's play *Jonah* in February 1966, and a recent issue of the little magazine *Salmagundi* contains a poem by a Paul Goodman whose verse was collected as *The Lordly Hudson* (1962) and *Hawkweed* (1967). Then there's the novelist Paul Goodman, author of the tetralogy *The Empire City* (1959) and *Making Do* (1963), who must be related to Paul Goodman the short-story writer—*Our Visit to Niagara* (1960) and *The Break-Up of Our Camp* (1949). These two men are quite likely connected with Paul Goodman the literary critic, who wrote *The Structure of Literature* (1954) and *Kafka's Prayer* (1947), and close to the perceptive man of the same name who was television critic of *The New Republic* a few seasons back. But where else can one find "Paul Goodman, Ph.D.," coauthor of a mammoth treatise, *Gestalt Therapy* (1951)? Or Paul Goodman, coauthor of *Communitas* (1947; revised 1960), a classic of city planning?

They are all the same Paul Goodman, born in New York City in 1911, now a resident of its lower West Side—a man of many highly developed interests but, to himself, of only two distinct personalities. "First, I'm a humanist," he says. "Everything I do has exactly the same subject—the organism and the environment. Anything I write on society is pragmatic—it aims to accomplish something. I don't write on psychiatry; that book's on therapy. That universities should divide my interests into different fields doesn't make them separate in fact. Apart from that, I'm also an artist. That's a different internal spring. You don't create an artwork from the same motivation. I write songs, for instance, but that's the same as writing a poem. Also, it's impossible to be a dramatist without being a musician or a choreographer." Pausing, he concluded, "I'm a man of letters . . . or an artist-humanist."

Equally fantastic is how Paul Goodman became "Paul Goodman." Soon after his birth, his father suffered a setback in business and deserted the family. His mother moved her three children from Washington Square to a slum area near Mount Sinai Hospital. Goodman remembers that since his mother worked as a saleswoman, and his older sister had a job and his older brother Percival (now a famous architect) had run away from home, he was "a latchkey boy—someone who let himself into his own house." Contrary to currently popular belief, Goodman believes that the absence of a father has its advantages as well as disadvantages. "It means more freedom for the kid to discover himself and the removal of a certain competitiveness. Remember, a good father can be difficult for a kid; he has nothing to revolt against. On the other hand, a fatherless kid is likely to be poor, also to be lonely; his house is nearly always empty. The real meaning of being fatherless, however, is that you have no one to show you the basic ropes through life, such as, in my case, of applying for a scholarship to college or graduate school."

Goodman's education was the best that American poverty could buy. "I had a thorough religious training," he remembers. "I went to Hebrew School forever, and I still have a strong theological interest." He also went to the then-legendary, now-defunct Townsend Harris, a high-pressure high school near the campus of City College that was the liberal-arts version of Bronx Science but tougher and quicker—of the three hundred accepted at entrance, only eighty graduated three years later. Goodman, who characterizes his younger self as "a great test-athlete," graduated at the top of his class in 1927. The year-book lists a collection of honors and prizes, and a classmate remembers: "Those bona fide geniuses like Goodman and Konrad Gries [now Professor of Classical Languages at Queens College] loused it up for all the normal geniuses, because they got such high scores on the exams." From there, Goodman went to City College, where he earned a straight A average, except for a D in public speaking (an art he later mastered); but since he neglected to apply for a graduate fellowship, he had to find a job. The best he could do in 1931 was "outside reading" at $10 per week for M-G-M, where his older sister Alice, with whom he lived, was working full time. (This phase of Goodman's life is described in Delmore Schwartz's marvelous short story, "The World Is a Wedding.")

One day, he bicycled to Columbia University; and although

too poor to register as a student, he took a seat in Richard McKeon's lectures in philosophy. Before long, McKeon informally accepted him as a member of the class and invited him to submit papers—one of which, "Neo-Classicism, Platonism and Romanticism," was published in the *Journal of Philosophy* in 1934. Once in a while, Goodman remembers, he would take the boat to Fall River, Massachusetts (round trip, $1.70) and hitchhike to Cambridge to attend Irving Babbitt's lectures at Harvard. To this day, Goodman insists, "Anybody who really wants an education can always get one. Just go in and sit down." He also admires the attitude of his great professor, the philosopher Morris Raphael Cohen who, faced by a class three times the number of officially registered, shrugged, "Well, I'm not a constable." In 1935, McKeon, then a dean at the University of Chicago, invited Goodman to lecture on English literature; and by 1940, Goodman had finished a Ph.D. thesis. He was fired from the faculty, however—for non-conformist sexual behavior—and, because he was too indigent to present his research in the proper form, he did not officially receive the degree until 1954, when the University of Chicago Press published the thesis as *The Structure of Literature*. Partly from this experience, Goodman derives his incisive distinction, in *The Community of Scholars* (1962), between intellectual "commencement"—admittance into the company of one's peers—and academic licensing.

His official career since then has been sporadic at best. Twice more he held teaching positions—at Manumit, a progressive school in Pawling, New York (where he taught Greek, physics, history, and math), and at Black Mountain College in North Carolina. In both places, sexual irregularities again hastened his departure. In the fifties, he converted an informal habit of helping people who came to him into a profession and became a lay psychotherapist. His credentials were two years of therapy with his college classmate, Alexander Lowen, M.D., author of *Love and Orgasm*, (1965), and three years of group therapy in a circle of psychiatrists. In other words, although unlicensed, Goodman had gained the acceptance of both his psychiatric peers and his patients; and that authority, to his mind, was sufficient. Twenty-five hours a week of therapy raised his family's income to $100 or so per week, although many of his patients were treated gratis. By 1958, he found himself both too busy and too depressed to keep regular contact with his patients. For most of his adult life Goodman's sole profession has been writing—a trade which only rarely, until recently, brought him any monetary support.

During the early thirties, he wrote about one hundred short stories; too poor to purchase stamps, he bicycled downtown now and then and by his own hand moved his manuscripts from one magazine to another. Not one was published until, after Goodman had left New York for Chicago, James Laughlin selected some for his New Directions annuals. Goodman also contributed essays to a short-lived, eclectic little magazine edited by James Burnham and Philip Wheelwright, *Symposium;* and by the late thirties he had become a regular contributor to *Partisan Review* (first as a cinema editor). "If you have enough to eat," he believes, "depression times are good, for you have lots of leisure. If there's no chance to get a job, the competitive sense to get ahead disappears. Decent poverty is really an ideal environment for serious people."

Goodman's poverty lasted beyond the Depression and beyond his acquisition of a family. "Until 1953, we lived in the lowest tenth—like Southern sharecroppers—at $1500 to $2000 a year. Every time I explained our situation to intelligent people, even economists, they insisted no one could live on so little money." (As recently as 1965, Goodman wrote, "independent, educated people with connections" should be able to subsist on $2000.) In the forties, anarchist publications, like *Resistance* and *Why?* and Dwight Macdonald's *Politics,* paid its contributors little or nothing, while *The New Republic* offered modest sums, as did John Crow Ransom's *Kenyon Review.* Indeed, Goodman acknowledges Ransom, very much a conservative southern gentleman, as a "decent, honorable editor" who published manuscripts with whose point of view he personally disagreed. "There are no more like him around, for none of them have any ability as writers." In 1948, he could speak of possessing a trunkful of unpublished manuscripts, and what Goodman considers "my best single book," the novel *The Dead Spring* (later incorporated into *The Empire City*), he privately published in 1950 by unashamedly soliciting money from friends. In 1959, at the nadir of his adult life, his poetry was riddled by self-pity:

> *What I will I can't*
> *and what I wish I mayn't*
> *what I ought I won't*
> *and what I must I don't.*
>
> . . .
>
> *Heavy silence has grown*
> *around me like a wall*
> *and I feel early*
> *shut in my narrow room. . . .*

And the despairs of this period are remembered in the courageously honest memoir *Five Years,* published in 1966.

The turning point in Goodman's career—from scorned outsider to respected thinker, from poor man to wealthy one—was the publication of *Growing Up Absurd* in 1960. Even this book was rejected by the publisher who originally commissioned it; but after *Commentary* started publishing chapters, Random House purchased it. Moderately acclaimed upon its appearance, it has since become the major book by which the more sensitive of American youth, between fifteen and twenty-five, understands itself. Indeed, I rather vividly remember how, early in 1960, my college friends and myself found the inarticulate truths of our existence vividly and persuasively explained.

Today, Goodman has one book-a-year publisher and several less regular sponsors of his manuscripts (he published five books in 1962); and nearly every important experience he has eventually gets turned into print. ("The prophet-hero," writes Adrienne Rich, "believes that what has been touched or known by him has, implicitly, significance.") More remunerative are the lectures, for which he gets "anywhere from nothing to $1000." His schedule nowadays is the nightmare of the intellectual in demand—an endless series of lectures, readings, symposiums, conferences, interviews, rehearsals of his plays, even dedications at churches built by his brother. He admits he has learned to write on airplanes, which he doesn't mind. "But it's the waiting and so forth that's a pain." Once every three weeks during the middle sixties he conducted a seminar at the Institute for Policy Studies in Washington. In the spring of 1964, he was the Knapp Distinguished Scholar (in Urban Affairs) at the University of Wisconsin in Milwaukee; the following spring, he became the first occupant of a new chair at San Francisco State College, where the student government has worked out a self-imposed tax plan through which it can hire a teacher of its choice each semester, totally independent of administrative control.

All this success has hardly changed Goodman, perhaps because he was so poor and so neglected for so long. He could still write, in 1962, with a self-honesty rare in such public personalities, "Lately I have been too exhausted to invent new speeches, and I repeat myself, sick of the sound of my voice." Medium of height, still thin of build, he looks at least a dozen years younger than he is. Perceptibly melancholic and remarkably relaxed for a man so active and productive, he talks easily and engagingly, occasionally filling his pipe or exchanging it for a new one, sometimes cracking a walnut or peeling an orange. His graying brown hair is long, dry, stiff, and unruly; his dress generally as informal as his language and habits. "Every Saturday I can, I go out and play handball with a bunch of kids on East First Street. I like handball; it's a real city game, for city kids." (Goodman's own son Mathew, an alumnus of Bronx High School of Science, was a student at Cornell in 1967, when he died in a mountain-climbing accident—a tragedy his father suffered severely. Susan, a daughter by his first wife, teaches at the First Street School, a Summerhill-style progressive school on New York's Lower East Side.) "Now my income falls in the highest tenth," he says, "but we hardly live differently." He and his present wife, Sally, and their young daughter, Daisy Jane, resided through the middle sixties in a modest Upper West Side apartment with nary a carpet on the floor. The piano in the living room is a battered upright. On the whitish walls are numerous paintings—one by his first wife, another inscribed "Souvenir to Paul" by William de Kooning. The single table in the living room has a bare wood surface; the easy chair's upholstery is taped together; another nondescript chair is the pet beagle's favorite napping place; the "couch" is essentially a single cot with some pillows strewn across it. Nothing matches, not even the silverware or the china. Only a sparkling television set, atop a small bookcase, seems incongruous. A 1953 Chevy sits on the street, and the family has a small farm in North Stratford, New Hampshire, near the Canadian border.

Unlike nearly all the intellectuals of his generation who have flip-flopped through various political positions, Goodman, to his credit, has remained what he calls "a community anarchist" (rather than a philosophical, or individualist, anarchist) ever since he read Prince Peter Kropotkin as an undergraduate. These anarchist sympathies, which are pragmatic and reformist rather than apocalyptic, continue to infuse all his writings. As an anarchist, he has always been anti-Communist, and American Communists and their fellow-travelers have never honored Goodman or his work. Beyond that, he eschews the Marxist dialectical bias that regards the worse in society as really ("objectively") better; and he never indulges in pious anti-Americanism, instead referring jocularly to himself as "an anarchist patriot" and speaking warmly of "our beautiful libertarian, pluralist and populist experiment." In brief, Goodman believes that man is essentially creative, loving, and communal; but often the institutions and roles of behavior that he creates serve to alienate him from his natural self. Moreover, once society's organizations become more important than the individuals who comprise them, then man must suppress his humanity to suit the autonomous, inhuman system. As an anarchist, Goodman generally wants less order and organization, rather than more; and he favors rejecting institutional life and working toward decentralization of social functions into smaller units—functioning communities that suit the needs of men. Underlying both his life and writings, then, has been this basic anarchist principle: human beings are innocent; bureaucracies create evil.

In his recent spate of books, Goodman has steadily moved from criticism—defining how society corrupts its citizens—to the inevitable next step of offering both specific and general remedies. *Growing Up Absurd* explains why it is so difficult today to grow up in America, in this "best of all possible worlds," why the young drop out of school, why they steal cars, why they cannot choose careers, why they seem to care about so little. Arguing on their behalf, Goodman believes that the man-made environment has become antagonistic to human resources. It no longer offers satisfactory outlets for human capability or a scrupulous attention to psychological needs. To explain its functioning, Goodman constructs the "model" or metaphor of a rat race—people competing in an "apparently closed room" with no value higher than self-perpetuation. "Absurdity," in this context, refers to the discrepancy between purpose and effect—the awareness of the young that society, the creation of people, no longer exists for the sake of people, but for the sake of preserving its own systems. The young like the book (here I speak again from personal experience) because it defines the anomalies of society that they sense but cannot clarify.

What Goodman desires is a world that attains a unity of purpose and effect, and in the following sentences he outlines his vision, clearly utopian, of a possible America, where: "A premium is placed on technical improvement and on the engineering style of functional simplicity and clarity. Where workers are technically educated and have a say in management. Where no one drops out of society and there is mobility between classes. Where the community is planned as a whole with an organic integration of work, living, and play. Where production is primarily for use. Where it is the policy to give an adequate voice to the unusual and unpopular opinion and to give a trial and a market to new enterprise. Where people are not afraid to make friends. Where sexuality is taken for granted. And where education is concerned with fostering human powers as they develop in the growing child."

Over the years, Goodman has continually posited a plethora of remarkably imaginative notions which, if realized, he insists will bring us closer to this desirable existence. Indeed, few utopian minds are as fertile with specific proposals. In the revised edition of *Communitas*, written with his brother Percival, he envisions that the economy be divided into two sectors—subsistence and luxury. Whatever is essential for life—food, basic clothing, shelter, medical service, and transportation—would be given free to everyone. In exchange, the state would require that every citizen devote only six years of his working life to produce subsistence goods; and given modern production techniques, such a minimal estimate, Goodman believes, is not too modest. The remainder of one's life would become one's own. If he wishes luxuries—wealth, power, extensive travel, or other "extra" items—a person is free to work in the luxury economy completely outside of government control; and here he would earn a different kind of money to purchase supra-subsistence goods and services. However, if a person is content with minimum subsistence, he is free not to do extra work at all. In contrast to the present economy, in which bread cannot be produced unless cars are sold, such a two-sided economy, Goodman argues, has the advantage of always providing everyone with essentials without requiring the production or consumption of inessential objects. "There is a dilemma in *any* High Standard of Living in a profit economy," he once wrote. "I am referring to the embarrassing truth that the best things in life are free—things like friendly competitive sports, friendly gambling, love-making and sex, solitary study and reading, contemplation of nature and cosmos, art-working, music, religion. . . ."

In his two books on education, *The Community of Scholars* (1962) and *Compulsory Mis-Education* (1964), Goodman favors abandoning the myth of compulsory education for a system comprising various kinds of schooling which would allow every child a choice of the kind that suits his taste (or, if he wishes, of no schooling at all). Moreover, Goodman complains that academic high schools give their students so much work to do, as well as coercing them into extracurricular activities, that they have no time to develop their own interests. Indeed, he thinks it would be wise to require students preparing for university study in the liberal arts to spend at least two years outside of school before entering college. Transcending a major quarrel in contemporary educational thought, Goodman espouses an education richer in both classical knowledge *and* contemporary experience. As for the universities, he favors dismantling the larger ones and making them into federations of small colleges, each with a student body of roughly 450 and a faculty of approximately 50.

Goodman's most recent book, *People or Personnel*, is essentially a manual in decentralization. Whereas he is willing to admit that certain functions in society should be centrally organized, such as the water supply or the telephone system, Goodman finds nothing to justify radio networks, motor-car combines, chains of supermarkets, or any other "enterprises extrinsically motivated and interlocked with other centralized systems"; for not only do they make expensive what should be cheap, but they also transform the people within them into personnel—automatons contributing to an on-going process over which they have negligible personal control. As an active pacifist who believes in "waging peace," Goodman insists that peace can be finally achieved only through a systematic decentralization of overorganized systems. "As soon as you have a massing of technological power in a few hands and the existence of national boundaries," he remarks, "you will have expansionism and war. I'm against the concept of great powers—the U.S., the Soviet Union, and China will all act in the same way. Instead, I'm for the decentralizing of power and the returning of boundaries to the natural contours of the land. This is an anarchist position. I am also a Taoist in that I believe that if a man lives in accordance with nature, then the state will be ruled well."

Despite his contorted prose, which suggests the processes of chasing a difficult truth, Goodman has an essentially didactic mind which is imaginative, insightful, schematic, and moralistic before it is profound, skeptical, analytical, or empirical. His intellectual forte is applying his anarchist sympathies and ideas to all kinds of pressing problems to produce unconventional, appealing solutions to pressing problems. In his books are such original public proposals as the following: (1) Banning private automobiles from Manhattan and converting most of the side streets into public parks; (2) using city funds to encourage permanent and temporary emigration to the countryside; (3) constructing wall-to-wall ramps above the traffic of Fifth Avenue "to revive the amenity of New York's great shopping and promenade street"; (4) taxing commuters who use New York City but do not contribute to its upkeep and diminishing commutation through "a bureau of apartment exchanges to bring people nearer to their jobs"; (5) building dormitories in all public housing projects to allow kids over eleven safely to get away from home; (6) encouraging children to observe their parents' love-making; (7) replacing physical education with "eurhythmics" (performing bodily movements to rhythmic accompaniment) which "works on incipient neurosis by unblocking emotion through muscular release"; (8) creating programs of apprenticeship to small enterprises for those who wish to drop out of school (and then allowing them to reenter the academic system at will); (9) decentralizing "the policing of run-of-the-mill delinquencies to (members of) the neighborhoods themselves"; (10) allocating one half of the research budgets of the National Science Foundation and Institute of Health for "subsistence incomes of $5000 to any and all who demonstrate a concern for scientific tinkering and speculation," especially since so much recent invention comes from lone adventurers; (11) instituting psychiatry in public high schools and group therapy as a required course for the senior year at college. "Like medicine" he explains, "psychiatry should be preventive; for by the time the neurotic is an adult, his problems have hardened and therapy is more difficult."

To implement his utopian thoughts, Goodman becomes a man of intellectual action who actively propagates his ideas by contributing to all sorts of periodicals an endless flow of essays and reviews (which often repeat or elaborate themes already presented in his books), writing letters to major publications and eminent people and then publishing copies of them wherever possible (some of these were collected in 1962 in *The Society I Live In Is Mine*), lecturing everywhere and under all kinds of auspices and circumstances, appearing on radio and television, participating in public symposia, accepting such appointments as membership on the local school board in his Manhattan neighborhood, and publicly supporting the rare political candidate who merits his scrupled favor, such as John Lindsay. Although he often clowns excessively, perhaps becoming too much of "a jester" for the comfort of solemnly serious people, rarely does Goodman compromise his attitudes to suit either his audience or the occasion; and more than once he has courageously offended his sponsors and supporters. Long ago, he exposed in print the CIA's backing of journals to which he had contributed or which had favorably appraised his books; and once wrote in *Dissent*, "*Esquire* magazine has used me as an instrument, a kind of jester to manfacture conversation-pieces, while I was nevertheless expressing my 'free' ideas and decisions and hoping that a few of the many hundred thousand readers would take them seriously." More recently, he made certain severe remarks about the intellectual disorientation of the student rebels, and these have produced a backlash of *ad hominem* criticisms from his most likely supporters. In the end, this twofold willingness to take the personal risk and give of himself so easily is among the reasons why Goodman's books are not as excellent as perhaps they could be (the prose, in particular, is sloppy, if not occasionally impenetrable) and yet also why he is so pervasively influential and admired among his radical peers.

In his report from Berkeley, Calvin Trillin noted in *The*

New Yorker that "The only writer who was quoted consistently by the Free Speech Movement . . . was Paul Goodman." Jocularly calling himself "the Joan of Arc of the free student movement," Goodman added, "I'm invited to be on the staff of every free university in the land. I wish I could; but I don't have the time." The Berkeley F.S.M. frequently cited Goodman's statement: "At present in the United States, students—middle-class youth—are the major exploited class. The labor of intelligent youth *is* needed and they are accordingly subjected to tight scheduling, speed-up and other factory methods." Later he elaborated that their education "has become mere exploitation—the abuse of the abilities and the time of school youth for other purposes." To explain his impact upon the young, Goodman suggests, "I love kids. I really do. I listen to them. I don't want to impose my ideas on them, for I'm sure the ideas they will have will be ideas I've never thought of. I want to teach, but I don't want to lead." Goodman believes that not only are his ideas sympathetic but that university students find the immediacy of his classical learning appealing. "They suffer from no bridge to the great cultures of the past, for its exponents on their campuses are too square. I'm able to show how you can relate Aristotle to the correct position on Vietnam." Perhaps even more, however, the young today admire Goodman as the prophet and exemplar of a free life in a bureaucratic society.

Goodman is a willing picketer at everything from anti-Vietnam War rallies (recently, his strongest political passion) to the General Strike for Peace. During World War II, "When they tried to draft me, I made such a pain of myself they rejected me as not military material—a 'stinker case.' I believe that the cause of this war was less Hitler himself than the whole international power structure of nation-states; and although I do not criticize those who stopped an immediate evil, I believed you had to be a pacifist in order to prevent the next war. Unless some of us stuck to our pacifist guns and tried to stop the war altogether, there wouldn't be any future." The Vietnam situation, he believes, is "immoral, unjust and disadvantageous. You don't send mechanical bombers to kill peasants. We should get the hell out, period." In the summer of 1965, he joined a group of intellectuals, including Dwight Macdonald and David McReynolds, in personally asking Adlai Stevenson to resign in protest over American foreign policy. Goodman also serves as an associate editor of *Liberation* magazine, recently culling an anthology from its pages, *Seeds of Liberation* (1965); and all through 1966, he was particularly active as a lecturer, largely because he feels he cannot refuse pacifist groups. "If these guys can burn themselves to death," he explained then, "I can run myself ragged. One can never fight too much for social justice."

All this public activity has hardly dampened Goodman's cultivation of his other self. In 1963, he published another novel, *Making Do*, which many reviewers took as all but autobiographical; most of his recent poems have been collected in *Hawkweed* (1967); and the scripts of new plays are currently in circulation. His professional interest in theater dates back to his first encounter with Julian Beck in 1940, when Beck, then a teen-ager, was more interested in painting; for when Beck and his wife Judith Malina later formed The Living Theatre, not only did Goodman become, as he puts it, "a kind of company psychiatrist," but he also wrote plays for them. For years their standard program declared that Goodman "uncompromisingly leads the vanguard of American playwrights," and perhaps their most extravagant early venture was the cruelly reviewed production, in the summer of 1959, of his play *The Cave at Machpelah*. To the director Lawrence Kornfeld, who has staged many of Goodman's plays, "They're simply beautiful, and significant. He was among the first playwrights concerned with both poetic and non-linguistic statements—sounds, screams, movements and such." Partly in gratitude, Goodman has frequently written on behalf of The Living Theatre, both lamenting their recent exile and insisting that such respected noncommercial organizations should be supported by funds accrued from taxing the commercial theater and the mass media. "I want to be a theater-man more than any other kind of creative writer," he remarked wistfully, "but you got to have a company to write for, so that you can hear their individual voices."

Although Goodman is rarely grouped among America's most significant imaginative writers, in those polls that serve as Guides to Fashionable Taste, his creative work has earned respectful reviews and some vociferous admirers. His extravagant tetralogy *The Empire City* is, to my mind, his most impressive fiction, indubitably more spectacular in its conception than its execution, which tends to be intolerably sloppy, lumpy, and at worst, self-indulgent. The critic Harold Rosenberg, long a close friend, wrote in *Partisan Review* that "*The Empire City* is not a good novel but it is a great book, as one might say of Melville's *Mardi* that it is a great book though by no means a pleasure." Of *The Lordly Hudson,* Goodman's first one-man collection of poetry, his fellow urban poet Harvey Shapiro has written, "His verse is probably the purest version of his thought and, to my mind, the most successful. . . . Always serviceable, sometimes awkward ('gaunt and fumbling' by design, but sometimes merely awkward) [it is] then by rips and starts brilliant." Goodman usually employs rather traditional formats in a loose manner (perhaps out of homage to his Aristotelian education) to write directly of personal experiences and observations, in language closer to heightened speech than modernist ellipses; and among his most memorable lines are those concluding the title lyric:

> *This is our Lordly Hudson hardly flowing*
> *under the green-grown cliffs*
> *and has no peer in Europe or the East.*
> *Be quiet, heart! Home! Home!*

Like his fiction, his poetry at its best is thoroughly personal, concerned with *his* city, *his* family, and *his* experience.

Both his art and his politics relate to his views on drugs and sex. He vehemently opposes the use of hallucinogenic drugs for the principled reason that "unless taken in concert, as in a religious rite, they alienate a man from his fellows." On the other issue, he espouses Wilhelm Reich's position that bodily satisfaction determines mental health, whereas Freud posited the opposite causality. "As St. Thomas said, a chief use of sex is to know someone intimately," he has written. "Some people perversely want to be 'understood,' 'loved,' 'esteemed' before they make love, whereas it is love-making that leads to understanding, love, and esteem." He also vehemently thinks that society's rules and attitudes toward sexuality are irrelevant. Although he has lived with his wife, Sally, a robust, quiet, handsome woman, for over twenty-three years and they have had and raised two children, they were never legally married. "I don't think that people's sexual lives are any business of the state; to license sex is absurd. On the other hand I have no objection to a religious ceremony." Monogamous at home, he cultivates girl friends on the outside; and in his conversation he often speaks fondly of men he has known, explaining, "Ever since I was twelve, I have been bisexual. My desperate efforts at homosexual satisfaction have given me some beautiful experiences and friendships, but much more frustration and unhappiness." One friend adds, a bit peevishly, "Paul tries to keep a girl friend, a boy friend, and a wife; but rarely does he manage to have all three and then keep everybody happy."

Goodman's radical career and thought have been subject to unending criticism, only some of which is justified. Occasional evidences of intellectual snobbery and personal pretention compromise his espoused egalitarianism, and impatient imperviousness blunts his reputation for human concern, while his unabashed homosexuality is still perhaps too aggressive for even enlightened circles, repelling many people who might otherwise honor his presence; in the eighteenth stanza of his poem "Little Prayers," Goodman revealingly bemoans,

At last I know—for friends have said—
my shameless public ways have made
me scorned and frail and lonely in
this teeming city.

Some critics assert, usually vaguely, that his thought is too utopian. Others, like the philosopher Stuart Hampshire, knock

Goodman as too scornful of the genuine achievements of modern technological society; and even sociologists sympathetic to Goodman's critical purposes, like N.Y.U.'s Dennis H. Wrong, suggest that he does not see why bureaucracies are necessary in a modern society of 200 million people. Although Goodman extolls the worth of individual labor, he does not understand (and perhaps has not bothered to find out) how complex work gets done in the contemporary world; nor does he know, as Bernard Muller-Thym has pointed out, how the structure of bureaucracy has changed in the past decades. Moreover, every specialist can say that Goodman spreads himself too thinly; yet he claims not professional expertise but the application of his organic sensibility to various areas of human endeavor. More substantially, he can be faulted for his failure to judge morally his more loyal professional benefactors, which include what is perhaps the most venal cabal in American cultural history, the New York literary mob, whose sins demand persistent exposure, if not correction from within. The most serious intellectual charge is Harold Rosenberg's—that Goodman refuses to allow for failures or deficiences in human intelligence. To this, Goodman replies, "I have a democratic faith—it's a religion with me —that everybody is really able to take care of himself, to get on with people, and to make a good society. If it's not so, I don't want to hear of it."

Of the many roles Goodman has assumed in recent history, none is as significant as father-figure to the vanguard—the representative minority—of the young. "Most of my intellectual generation sold out," he surmises, "first to the Communists and then to the organized system, so that there are very few independents around that a young man can accept as a hero. The next generation must have fathers more ideal than their own." What particularly impresses the young (and perhaps disturbs the old) is Goodman's personal integrity. He has always lived by his ideals, defying whatever bureaucratic systems he touched, practicing conspicuously the sexual libertarianism he preached, forbidding editors to bowdlerize what he had written, attaining such a mastery over poverty that he could never succumb to money, and having a sense of purpose that made him largely resistant to flattery or vanity.

Goodman largely joins Ginsberg as a prophet of the new age where increasing leisure will allow men a greater cultivation of artistic pursuits and bodily pleasures.

For the beautiful arts
are made of cheap stuff,
of mud and speech
and guts and gestures

of animal gaits
and humming and drumming
daylight and rock
available to anybody.

As a man of letters, Goodman sacrifices the necessities of excellence for the capacity to influence; and as the humanist finally takes precedence over the artist, so the man himself and the ideas he espouses are perhaps finally more durable than his work. For his own future, he has few ambitions but, rather, great hopes for "happiness, which means more sexual happiness, a community to work for, and a world at peace."

ELLIOTT CARTER:
Effort and Excellence

To be a new man is not a condition but an effort—an effort that follows a revelation in behalf of which existing forms are discarded as irrelevant or radically revised.—HAROLD ROSENBERG

Among the professionals of contemporary music, who comprise a scene riddled with personal and artistic conflicts, no positive opinion seems more diversely accepted, if not more ecumenical, than Elliott Carter's excellence as a composer. To Milton Babbitt, definitely of the twelve-tone persuasion, Carter is "one of our two best composers, Roger Sessions being the other. It's a remarkable achievement and accomplishment." Aaron Copland, totem figure of the musical mainstream, declares, "Everybody agrees that he is in complete command of what he wants to do. You can hear any new work of his with confidence." The Polish-born conductor, Stanislaw Skrowaczewski, who is particularly noted for his performances of contemporary orchestral works, unequivocally testifies, "Objectively, Elliott Carter is certainly one of the greatest composers of our time." The composer-critic Benjamin Boretz observes that Carter and Babbitt have "made the decisive discoveries, and have developed musical languages which are not only unmistakably their own, but which have also crystallized the musical thinking of most of their younger colleagues, as those of Schoenberg and Stravinsky did in the twenties." That sophisticated and discriminating American audience that, for various reasons, finds Babbitt too difficult, Copland too easy, and Cage too trivial generally tends to acknowledge Carter as the greatest living native composer; and remarkably enough, Carter forges a position that is at once between the extremes and yet artistically avant-garde.

A small and slight man, with longish, somewhat unruly gray hair, clearly demarked scalp line, wide smile, and a broad, open, and handsome face, Carter lives in a moderately spacious apartment in a Stanford White-designed 1890's building a few blocks north of New York's Washington Square. Looking younger than his fifty-nine years and flipping on and off two pairs of glasses, Carter was dressed as casually as usual the day we met—baggy and cuffless trousers, scruffy shoes. Neither as dominating nor prepossessing as his awesome reputation might suggest, he is by turns lively and reticent, sometimes engaging but usually quite diffident. He speaks animatedly in an indefinable accent, overcoming a slight stutter; yet his sparkling blue eyes, topped by bushy reddish eyebrows, tend to turn away, as though he were too shy to look his guest straight in the eye. He frequently moves both hands in symmetrical gestures; yet he often lets the rhythm of conversation disintegrate completely. He can go on enthusiastically about certain subjects and nonetheless give the impression that he finds talk a bit boring. More contained than outgoing, he seemingly puts blocks between himself and the world, neither communicating facilely with others nor assimilating easily the information his experience continually throws across his eyes and ears.

"I became interested in contemporary music as a teen-ager, some years before I studied music in general," he reminisced. "At that time, this was a very drastic thing to do, since contemporary music was not an integral part of education and culture, as it is today." This was the first step in his explanation of a cultural mystery of his own creation: In a country where advanced minds do *not* come from the biggest cities, do *not* attend the "right" schools or study abroad, how did a young man of squarely mainline background—New York City-born and bred, college at Harvard, study in Paris with Nadia

Boulanger, and "neo-classical" beginnings—become one of the most innovative composers in the world today? That is, how did Elliott Carter manage to overcome all his disadvantageous advantages?

It seems that one of his classmates at New York's Horace Mann prep school was the late Eugene O'Neill, Jr.; and through him, as well as other sons of artistic parents, young Carter, then living near Columbia University, made the Greenwich Village scene in 1925–6, meeting the composers Charles Ives, Edgard Varèse, and Henry Cowell, the legendary harpist-composer Carlos Salzedo, and their patrons and critics. A frequent guest of the Iveses, Carter even played piano four hands with the master himself. Young Carter became so steeped in the avant-garde musical culture of the middle twenties that when his father took him to Vienna in the summer of 1926, the seventeen-year-old purchased all the scores by Schoenberg, Webern, and Alban Berg that he could find. Around that time, although his musical training consisted merely of piano lessons, he even started to write his own pieces, mostly song settings to passages from James Joyce's *Ulysses;* and he regarded his own efforts highly enough to submit them to Cowell, who was then editing New Music Editions. (Cowell returned them just before his own death in 1965 with a note assuring Carter that his juvenilia displayed precocious talent.)

Carter chose Harvard partially because Serge Koussevitzky's Boston Symphony Orchestra was predisposed to advanced music; but finding the university's Music Department too backward for his taste, Carter majored in English literature instead, letting music become his primary extracurricular interest. He graduated in 1930 and stayed two more years to take an M.A. in music, studying composition with the English musician Gustav Holst, then a guest professor at Harvard, who did not approve of the Hindemithian tastes that then informed Carter's work.

That was the first of many discouragements that would have retired a less determined composer. Thanks in part to a meager $500-a-year allowance from his father, Carter went abroad to study, choosing Paris largely because he had been able to speak

French fluently since childhood. He made extra money by copying scores, singing in church choirs, and even conducting a Parisian madrigal group. "It's hard to live on the margins of life," he says today, "and it's foolish for wealthy parents to be so difficult. My teeth have been bad ever since." For three years he studied with Nadia Boulanger; and even though he conscientiously executed all the laborious exercises she prescribed and "looked for constructive criticism," she was not particularly encouraging either. Returning home in 1935, still on the modest charity of his family, Carter labored in the compositional style most fashionable at the time, representational neo-classical American, becoming musical director of Lincoln Kirstein's Ballet Caravan; and then authoring, among other pieces, the ballet suite *Pocahontas* (1939; revised, 1941). He also worked hard at playing the oboe and piano, but he never became a particularly adept performer.

Carter's name at that time was hardly distinguishable from others working in the hyper-American idiom; indicatively, it is not even mentioned in either Aaron Copeland's 1936 or his 1949 survey of the native musical scene. His personal reputation was largely for multi-lingual literacy and a financial heritage above the professional norm; musically, his pieces were known to be slightly more difficult than what was common at the time. When he showed his *Holiday Overture* (1944) to an older, artistically similar, but more established composer, the latter dismissed it as "another typical Carter piece, too complicated to understand." From New York to Harvard to Paris to Cambridge (Massachusetts) for a year and then back to New York, Carter trod a rather "establishment" path; but not only did he miss becoming the protégé of either an influential elder or a reigning clique, but his work went unchampioned, if not neglected. When asked what distinguished him from other Boulangerites, he replied immediately, "I'm a radical, having a nature that leads me to perpetual revolt."

Carter says today that he was not particularly pleased with his compositions so far, and this perhaps explains why he is now neither overly embittered about this early neglect nor especially proud of putting down his former detractors. "There were many things that I wanted to achieve but couldn't do," he remarked, peering over the glasses that slid down his nose. "Like so many others who received the same university education, my comprehension, taste, and conceptual ability were much more developed than my musical craftsmanship." His first breakthrough was the Piano Sonata (1945–6), composed on Cape Cod and in New York City on his initial Guggenheim Fellowship; and there are few other examples in music history of great composers just starting to bloom in their late thirties.

Here, for the first time, he took the leap that connected his work to the avant-garde tradition he had assimilated as a youth, as well as exhibited the necessary extra dose of personal purpose that sprung him above a pack of peers. Since nearly everybody told him his work was not particularly good, he set about to be better than good; and as if to implicitly rebuke his pious advisors, along with their preoccupations and conventions, his work became more complicated rather than less. To the pianist Charles Rosen, the Piano Sonata "represents a new departure in piano writing that has few analogies in the literature of the past. The sonata is built upon, and constructed out of, the overtone possibilities of the piano." Particularly in Rosen's recording, played on good equipment, one can hear not only the various overtone sounds that notes in combination produce, but also the way in which the overtones create their own semblance of melodies. In this piece Carter also introduced the rapid changes in rhythm—here, Rosen estimates, one change every two or three measures—that later became a primary mark of his style.

The ballet score *The Minotaur* (1947) seems almost a step back into the neo-classical vein, while the Sonata for Cello and Piano (1948) incorporates a musical idea that he would subsequently develop—"a work that would emphasize the individuality of each instrument and that made a virtue of their inability to blend completely." The second breakthrough of Carter's compositional career was the First String Quartet, written in 1951–2 in Tucson, Arizona, on Carter's second token of confidence from the Guggenheim Foundation; and he now regards this piece as "the first time I really got there."

The score turned out to be so complicated that Carter has since written that he feared it "might never be played"—indeed, a well-known ensemble found it too difficult to do—and not until six months after he started sending the score around did the Walden Quartet of the University of Illinois offer to perform it. In this work, Carter bestows such individual identities on his four instruments that the piece, as Virgil Thomson put it, "sounds less like a classical string quartet than like four intrinsically integrated solos, all going on at the same time."

Crediting Charles Ives's Second String Quartet (1907–13) for a basic conception, Carter appropriates a theatrical metaphor to characterize his technique as the "simultaneous juxtaposition of different musical characters"; however, he adds that in contrast to Ives, who sometimes lets his "ensemble" disintegrate into aural chaos, Carter prefers to control constantly the interactions of the various parts. Always eclectically literate, Carter drew upon the movies for another artistic model. "The general plan of my First Quartet actually was suggested by Jean Cocteau's film 'Le Sang d'un poète' [*Blood of a Poet*], which opens with a shot of a large brick chimney being blown-up and beginning to fall and ends with the continuation of this sequence. In between the entire action of the film takes place, which appears to last for a long time but actually takes only a brief moment, as dreams always do. The falling chimney is the measure of time elapsing, just as, in my piece, the cadenza for cello carried on the end by the violin is interrupted by the 'dream' of the entire work." As the critic Benjamin Boretz defined another Carter innovation, which was likewise drawn from the non-musical arts, " 'Theatrical situations' could provide the basis for analogous instrumental situations. With instruments as 'characters' in more than a fanciful sense, then 'characteristic' sonorities and performance styles become primary molders of structure."

In the String Quartet, as in all his later works, Carter abolishes key signatures, as well as introduces the innovative technique that William Glock of the B.B.C. has since christened "metrical modulation." This is, Glock explains, "the idea of having continual changes of speed and character, and linking them into a convincing and novel continuity." Carter's rhythms are neither regular nor syncopated, but rather continually rearticulated, until that sense of perpetual rearticulation of the fundamental pulse becomes itself a major theme of the piece. Moreover, this and subsequent Carter pieces become an implicit illustration of the famous remarks about American music that the composer Roy Harris made in 1933: "Our rhythmic impulses are fundamentally different from the rhythmic impulses of Europeans; and from this unique rhythmic sense are generated different melodic and form values. Our sense of rhythm is less symmetrical than the European rhythmic sense. . . . This asymmetrical balancing of rhythmic phrases is in our blood. We do not employ unconventional rhythms as a sophisticated gesture; we cannot avoid them."

"My own thinking came out of this," Carter explained, his hands grasping for the rest of his thoughts, "and out of my own interest in Oriental (Near and Far Eastern), medieval, renaissance music and jazz. I've expanded the early twentieth-century techniques of irregular accentuation, polyrhythm, and written-out rubato into a personal rhythmic vocabulary that contrasts simultaneous speeds and complexes of polyrhythms." He paused, turned his blue eyes away and then back. "Although I was very interested in writing 'American music' when I first began, this has ceased to interest me as a goal; for one was doing it, whether he wanted to or not. To be an American is to be yourself; America is always in the process of being created by the acts, thoughts, and products of its citizens at any given moment. I try indeed to give expression to this notion of process in my music."

Indicatively, even though Carter studied abroad and traveled there extensively, he recently wrote of the European musical world as "rapidly losing its inner impetus and . . . fading into a lifeless shadow of what it was." In conversation, he elaborated, "I don't like Europe very much these days. Its musico-cultural pretentions are shallow, although they seem to be sweeping off their feet the chairmen of American university music departments. Science-fiction salon music blown up to messianic proportions seems to be the best they can manage. American composers, for the most part, are more involved with central issues, and they exhibit more fantasy and spirit and less adherence to the 'party line.' Still, the musical world is very international now and within the frame of the annual Warsaw Autumn one can see many fascinating things being done. The Swedish radio, which has incidentally played all my works, the British Broadcasting Corporation, the state-owned Italian, French, and German radios encourage their own as well as other European composers by extensive public presentation of their works. All this support is admirable; but if American composers had this kind of consistent and more or less intelligent interest, they would perhaps profit more by it than the Europeans."

Carter composed a few other works in the fifties; but not until his Second String Quartet (1959) did he make his third and most recent stylistic leap. By then, he was already acknowledged as one of the major composers—a trifle too elitist perhaps, but still a recognized master; so not only has the piece not lacked its performers—the Lenox Quartet has already presented it over a hundred times—but it also won the Pulitzer Prize six weeks after its debut. In this work, Carter imaginatively developed several principles broached before. First, he bestowed even more distinct identities upon the four instruments—indeed, the first violin he has characterized in print as "fantastic, ornate and mercurial"; the second violin, "laconic, orderly"; the viola as possessing a "repertory of expressive motifs"; and the cello as "somewhat impetuous." To enhance their individuality and their continually rearticulated relationships, Carter prescribes, in an Ivesian gesture, that in performance the instrumentalists should space themselves further apart than usual, eight feet to be exact. "I regard my scores as scenarios—auditory scenarios—for performers to act out with their instruments, dramatizing the players as individuals and participants in the ensemble." To those who consider performing it, the Second String Quartet is a terribly difficult work that can all too easily be done badly; to an attentive audience, the piece can provide an arresting and exhausting listening experience; and to my mind, it is unquestionably, by international standards, among the five greatest works of the past decade.

"My First String Quartet," he wrote me, a while after we had met, "is circular in form, like *Finnegans Wake*, ending with a beginning of an imagined next cycle of events. My Second Quartet, and in fact all of my recent works, are examples of forms which give the impression of coming into focus and then going out of focus. *in medias res*. This, along with many techniques for linking of sections and producing various designs in time, were deeply influenced by movie techniques, as well as by the choreography of George Balanchine, whose work has fascinated me ever since I first saw it in 1932." This strategy of continual decomposition and redefinition creates a sense of diffuse energy, encased within a tenuous order; and all this conveys what Carter calls, in another context, "the impression of that combination of freedom and control that I greatly admire in many works of art."

The two major works that Carter has subsequently composed—the Double Concerto for Harpsichord and Piano with Two Chamber Orchestras of 1961, which Igor Stravinsky judged in print "a masterpiece," and the Piano Concerto of 1966—have further explored this compositional idiom. In the spectrum of contemporary music, it lies indefinitely between the new serial language initiated by Schoenberg and more familiar mainstream music; for Carter's recent pieces combine the textural complexity and avoidance of repetition that we associate with the former along with the overall mellifluousness more typical of the mainstream tradition, as well as perhaps bowing slightly to the line of chaotically dissonant and spatial music that runs from Charles Ives through early Varèse to John Cage. As the pianist Paul Jacobs remarked of the Piano Concerto, "It looks like an open and spontaneous piece; but after you play it for a while, you suddenly realize that every note is accounted for." To insure that performers realize his precise conceptions, Carter has been known to oversee rehearsals and sometimes to return the following day with sheets of meticulous and specific handwritten notes for the musicians to consider.

Though he hesitates to use the phrase "avant-garde," he believes that his recent work achieves something new in music—in formal structures rather than timbral content. "There are," as he puts it, "more possibilities of experiment in design, particularly complex designs in time, than in sound effects which tend to be static items or very simple and obvious trajectories." To Carter, the primary medium of his music is not melody but time—not only how long the notes last but the articulated silences between them. "Pitch," he declares, his hands gesturing in unison, "is the population of time. I try to make many different kinds of temporal relations." Of classic influences, he credits "mostly Mozart and Haydn, because my music is concerned with rapid change, and it doesn't try to follow an argument point by point. It gives an impression of discontinuity while remaining coherent."

This subtle handling of unusual and complicated rhythms endows his work with a pedagogic dimension, which aims to enhance the listener's perceptual capabilities. "In my pieces, there are oppositions, such as four instruments playing four different parts, where one should hear each part as well as the ensemble," he explains, "and how the parts interact defines the quality of time in that piece. It takes a fairly aware listener to perceive all this." Even though the theme expressed in each recent work—almost, so to speak, its programmatic content—is "a distinct large statement about time," all his compositions of the past two decades exhibit a rhythmic sense so unique that an experienced listener needs only a few bars to recognize a particular piece as "a Carter."

Although he aims to weave the intricate structures characteristic of the best modern music, he will still discard a realized textural intensity merely "because it doesn't have an immediate appeal to the ear; both the first impression and the deeper context must be interesting." While this suggests that Carter might be trying to bridge the chasm between the musical profession—more or less the sole audience for quality contemporary music—and the more general public, he has hardly made the compromises that would win him greater attention. "Composition today," he says, again conducting both hands in unison, "has nothing to do with the economy, and with so little interest and so little public—here the difference between us and Europe is striking—the composer cannot help but do everything for himself." Nonetheless, some professionally respected composers do draw more interest from the non-professional audience; and Carter is among the few—others being Karlheinz Stockhausen, and Igor Stravinsky—to command a relatively large and enthusiastic lay following.

One reason why his new works are so intricate stems from his awareness of the recording medium. Not only does he explicitly state, "I write for records," but each of his three recent pieces runs about twenty-five minutes, the length of an LP side. Carter believes that if a record is to be played over and over again, the composer is obliged to construct a composition so rich that it will offer new perceptions to the listener each time he hears it, in addition to preserving the ambiguous qualities of art in a repetitive medium. They should offer "bits of mosaic that the listener ought to assemble," he said, then paused and smiled modestly, "I'm not sure I'm telling you the truth." This concern for the new medium, along with Carter's reputation, may explain why his records usually sell better than the three thousand copies considered the standard quota for contemporary music or why I have played my own copy of the Second String Quartet at least a hundred times. Besides, Carter informally notes of his works, "The harder a piece is, the more often it gets played," and that is also a wry comment on how different the performing scene today is from that of a decade or two ago.

Carter works at a small desk in a medium-sized room, separated only by an archway from the larger living room of his New York apartment. Manuscript score-sheets lie neatly on his desk; clipped on a cork board above are a few recent letters, reminders of appointments, and a small informal picture of the late Edgard Varèse. Smack in the middle of the room is a baby grand piano, but Carter uses it more as a testing machine than a source of compositional inspiration. Shelves of books on various subjects line the back wall, while a library of scores fills an inlaid cabinet of vertically slim drawers. The Carters also have a house on a lake in Waccabuc, New York, near Katonah, about one hour and a half north of New York City; here the composer generally works in a three-room garage-top studio away from the main house.

Even though he tries to set aside his entire morning for composing and he dabbles at his work throughout the day, Carter has in recent years hardly been a productive composer. On one hand, he seems to lack the physical, mental, and perceptual dexterity of more facile musicians; on the other, mounting levels of compositional complexity have reduced his output in the past decade to three major pieces, totaling about an hour and a quarter of playing time. (The fact that few composers in history have won such acclaim for such a small corpus of topnotch work should testify to the persuasive excellence of these pieces.) One reason for his patience, he explains, is that he uses contrapuntal techniques; another is that the necessities of the latest style are so demanding, and yet so unfamiliar, that Carter often feels the anxiety of an explorer in uncharted territory. "I want," he declares, "to invent something I haven't heard before." And this echoes a statement made several years ago. "Each piece is a kind of crisis in my life; it has to be something new, with an idea that is challenging." An empathetic listener can figuratively "hear" all the work that Carter puts into his pieces, as they evince no easy compromises with his very demanding conceptions.

Indicatively, the plans for writing these recent works have usually consumed more time than actually executing the compositions; so Carter is now systematically analyzing and collating the basic rhythmic and harmonic techniques that inform his recent work. "In classical music," he remarks wistfully, looking up and away, "this was all given." Once he gets this "musical vocabulary" into viable shape, he expects that future pieces will come more easily. Current major projects include a Concerto for Orchestra, commissioned for the New York Philharmonic's 125th anniversary (which has already passed), a Third String Quartet that the Julliard School of Music especially commissioned for the opening of its new quarters in Lincoln Center; and a Cello Concerto for the Russian musician Mtsislav Rostropovitch. On the side, so to speak, he has been revising many of his older pieces, particularly as performing groups saturated with the recent works have requested more Carter for their repertoires; and he recently completed two short pieces for four tympany, *Adagio* and *Canto* (1967), which he actually regards as numbers six and seven of a series written many years ago. "I have a lot of crazy ideas I want to get down on paper."

Carter's father, Elliott Cook Carter, Sr., persistently tried to convince his sole child to take over the prosperous family lace importing business that Carter, Sr., had himself inherited; but since his son just as persistently refused, the older Carter eventually sold E. C. Carter and Son, Inc., as it is still known, to his employees for a modest sum and set up trust funds for his heirs. Elliott, Sr., was, as his son remembers, so "violently opposed to my musical career" that even before his death in 1955, he hardly acknowledged his son's growing reputation, let alone appreciated his music. Ironically, the management of his father's estate became so complicated that Elliott, Jr., had to intervene, belatedly discovering a certain competence for business.

New England Spartans by heritage, Elliott Carter and his wife Helen live beneath their means—their furnishings for instance, are more tasteful than elegant, and they exercise all sorts of frugalities that amuse, if not infuriate, their friends. On the other hand, it is no secret that they surreptitiously support certain indigent musicians and generously lend their apartment or country place to needy friends. "Where their wealth shows," a New York friend remarks, "is in all the parties the Carters give, and in their disconcerting habit of taking off for somewhere far away with little advance notice."

Carter is in many ways an American aristocrat, whose inherited nature forbids him from being either too conspicuous about his inheritance or too assertive of his intelligence. Likewise, he does not display an overt pride in his achievements; but he does enumerate, in a matter of fact way, the considerable number of major prizes, grants, commissions, and, more recently, honorary degrees he has received. One does not need to scratch too far to find his innate haughtiness, but he conscientiously tries to keep it more implicit than explicit. He does not, for instance, mention any fellow composers as either artistically or emotionally close to himself, as though he regards himself as unquestionably unique as well as detached from the routine concerns of the professional *hoi polloi.*

Similarly, although he will speak critically of certain positions or trends in contemporary music—serial technique, for example, he considers "basically coarse, crude, and insensitive" —he refuses to make public his evaluative comments, either positive or negative, about other individual composers and/or their works. Perhaps because the neglect he once suffered makes him insecure, Carter prefers to remain above the wars within contemporary music, at the same time that the character of his pieces implies that he stands for certain values and compositional persuasions. "The work," he insists, "is what makes the position; the music takes a stand for me." He does, however, appear at professional meetings, where he sometimes innocently asks the embarrassing questions that no one else dares raise, and he likes to attend international conferences and festivals, partly because he is polylingual, partly because he enjoys cultivating friendships with such rising European composers as the Russian Edison Denisov (they converse in French) and the Pole Krzystof Penderecki (they speak German).

Over the years, Carter taught for brief spells at various institutions including St. John's College in Annapolis, Maryland, Peabody Conservatory of Music in Baltimore, Columbia University, and Yale, and he has recently been up to Juilliard one afternoon a week. Although he does not need the money or particularly enjoy the work, he has taken these positions partly to keep in touch with younger musicians. "Students teach you an awful lot," he remarked, then twinkled; "for one thing, you can see in them pitfalls you should avoid." The example of, say, Milton Babbitt has perhaps persuaded Carter that students well taught are often the established composer's best testaments and publicists; yet his aloof manner, together with his resistance to professional controversies (which the young invariably take more seriously than their elders), puts off pupils who might otherwise become his followers. Moreover, he has not stayed long enough at any one institution to create a continuity of students; those who come especially to study with him often find that by the time they arrive he has gone elsewhere.

Carter is more literary than his musical peers. Not only is he well versed in English literature but he also reads and speaks French, German, and Italian fluently, a few other languages more haltingly. He is also an insomniac who, according to a friend, "will while away the sleepless hours by conjugating irregular Italian verbs in his head." He acknowledges Proust and Joyce as the greatest influences upon his sense of rhythm, identifies the critic Edmund Wilson as his closest literary friend, and keeps up with contemporary literature. Carter has himself written many reviews and essays over the past thirty years, and he hopes to collect some of them into a book.

A man of varied interests, of even more varied tastes, he has produced scores in a diversity of sizes ranging from those for a solo pianist or percussionist through string quartets and chamber ensembles to full-sized orchestras; yet through this diversity runs a purposeful attempt to construct a compositional language appropriate to our time—an age shaped by recordings, chaotic or chance music, the twelve-tone language, and the gap between the professional composer and the larger musical audience. Although listeners can now discern how the Piano Sonata of 1945 fed into the excellences of his recent works, in looking back over his career we can also recognize how Carter made several courageous leaps above the conventional ways of composing to fashion a compositional style very much his own, yet today more widely admired and, in the highest kind of flattery, often imitated by younger American composers. The question of how Carter became a great composer deserves a profoundly American answer: Despite adverse advantages, he did it all by himself.

HERMAN KAHN:
Thermonuclear Santa Claus

The great speed of the computer enables us to test the outcome resulting from a variety of choices of initial actions and so to choose the course with the highest pay-off before the march of human events forces us to take some inadequately considered action. This ability to see into the future, as it were, by simulation on a computer . . . is sure to find application in more and more aspects of our daily lives.—ARTHUR L. SAMUEL

Soon after Herman Kahn's *On Thermonuclear War* first appeared, late in 1960, the late James R. Newman opened his review in *Scientific American* with, "Is there really a Herman Kahn? It is hard to believe. . . . No one could write like this; no one could think like this. Perhaps the whole thing is a staff hoax in bad taste." Not only is Herman Kahn alive and thriving, romping out into the world from his home turf of northwest Westchester, but in his fleshy flesh, he is considerably more amiable, if not downright endearing, than the persona that some readers found in one of the most notorious books of our time.

Slightly under six feet tall, moon-faced, bespectacled, rotund, balding and graying, effervescent and noddingly agreeable in manner, very friendly and insanely gregarious, Kahn looks more or less like a retired football tackle or perhaps a jovial neighborhood grocer. An imposing, yet not overbearing presence, this buttery ball of a man moves quite energetically and gracefully for someone of his huge size, dreading only restaurant booths and chairs (such as airplane seats) with excessively narrow arms; in small rooms, his presence generates a perceptible heat. Possessed of an open and responsive personality, Kahn gets on easily with people, cultivating first-name friendships with scientists, politicians, generals, and hippies, not only because he has a compulsive curiosity about everything important in his world, but also because he genuinely likes people (and they in turn genuinely like him). His geniality hardly resembles public relations charm, for he is several times too clumsy to be "smooth," as well as too spontaneous to be self-consciously slick and too argumentative to be falsely agreeable. Indeed, this accessible friendliness stands as the biggest block between his mind and all the work it would like to achieve. He said, when asked, that he could not think of a single person he hated for longer than a week; and considering how often Kahn himself and his work have been publicly pilloried, his conversation is remarkably free of vindictive bile.

Kahn, his wife Jane and their two children—Deborah, in her early teens; and David, four years younger—live in a long split-level, two-car suburban house at the apex of a dead-end road in Chappaqua, New York, about an hour north of New York City. Books and papers flood the place, filling shelves in the living room, the dining room, the bedrooms, the basement den, the guest room, and even the kitchen, where *The Joy of Cooking* camps next to Carroll Quigley's mammoth *Tragedy and Hope: A History of Our Time*. Other books lie piled on tables, while some sit neatly on the floor. Kahn claims to have read half of them, skimmed another quarter, peeked at the rest. The Kahns' furniture could be characterized as academic nondescript, inclining toward the modern; everything is more comfortable than elegant. The major frills are abundant electronic equipment (including two hi-fi sets) and an indoor heated swimming pool a few steps down from the living room. Jane

Kahn, bespectacled, dark-haired, and attractively slim, married Herman in 1953; and since he possesses one of the fastest metabolisms alive, the pace of her life slows down only when he goes off on a trip. Whether Herman Kahn is at home or in the office, books pass through him, ideas and words pour out, with a rapidity and quantity that are legendary.

One of the world's greatest talking machines, Kahn has been known to speak continuously from morning to night, confronting the same audience with only a minimum of notes and wholly without a repetition. His wife insists that he can sustain his normal rapid pace "indefinitely," but I heard him reduce speed around 11 P.M., after a sixteen-hour day. Acutely aware that talking is as much an art as an exercise, Kahn generally designs his lectures around an appropriate rhetorical strategy, occasionally using carousel-projected slides to organize his commentary and provide some cues. Perhaps because he conscientiously tries to use a mode of address and a frame of reference suitable to every audience he sees, Kahn can communicate as successfully to teen-agers as academics, foreigners as Americans, and probably to idiots as well as wise men; "talking down" is simply not a strategy he knows.

He is able to give exactly the same "extemporaneous" lecture twice, or even to offer successive audiences two wholly different discussions of the same subject. Possessed of three computer-like capacities—accurate and elephantine memory, random access to accumulated information, and instantaneous retrieval—Kahn in a public performance can reach into his prodigious repertoire-library for a series of appropriate "routines" —explanations, arguments, responses, dramatizations, and/or anecdotes that he has developed in previous lectures and conversations. As his enthusiasm for his pet routines is all but demonic, he suffers no taboos against using the same material over and over again. "I can't hear him too often," a colleague says, "because his lectures tend to repeat themselves; but six months from now he'll have ninety per cent new stuff." Like most first-rate transient intellectual vaudevillians, not only does Kahn carry everything in his head, but he can adeptly fit himself into two-, three-, or four-a-day formats; however, rare is the trooper who can lecture solo, as Kahn often does, continuously for a few days. "There will be three full days of lectures on thermonuclear war," he would tell friends in the late fifties. "Who will be speaking?" was their reply. "Me."

When an audience accumulates, Kahn invariably opens with a joke; for not only is his love of humor so irrepressible that he giggles generously at his own jokes, but his deliveries are so deft that he rarely fails his material. Nearly every minute contains at least one comic image and perception, usually more sympathetic than devastating; and like all great humorists, Kahn knows that the best jokes invariably include at least a swipe at himself. Rare is a speaking day without a crack at his obesity; and he often characterized the late Ché Guevara as "talented but a nut—a condition I know quite well." Once apprehensively looking behind the podium, Kahn asked, "Where did my briefcase go?" Suddenly a sparkle ignited his eyes, and his voice boomed, "Okay, lock the doors. Don't anyone leave this room." In praise of the Calvinist Puritanical ethics of the Black Muslims, he remarked parenthetically, "If I were the OEO, I'd subsidize their (and my) middle-class value system; but since government support might wreck them —bring charges of 'selling out'—I'd favor supporting them through the C.I.A."

He often boasts, "I can be really funny about thermonuclear war," appreciative of even his unintentional jokes. Indicatively, he recalls with great glee how late one evening a woman in the audience asked, "How much time do you give us Mr. Kahn?" and, worried about the hour, he inadvertently looked at his watch. His jocularity assuages his audience and perhaps distracts from the seriousness of his purpose, as well as probably aids Kahn's psyche in coping with the terrifying images of his chosen subject. As certain critics have noted, no other strategist could induce an audience of sane people to laugh at lines such as, "Of course, the system might blow up in the meantime; there's no point in glossing it over." On the other hand, because he has peered deeply into the contemporary hell, as well as imagined some horrendous possibilities, only to surface as a rather jovial fellow, Kahn all but represents an argument for the psychological therapy of mental descent.

Not only does Kahn's diction tend to be erratic and nasal, as his staccato words tumble over each other and his phrases march at an uneven pace; but Kahn is one of the few acclaimed lecturers who manages to overcome such otherwise debilitating speech deficiencies as a stammer, a stutter, and a slur. The last makes "submarine" invariably sound like "summary," "manned bomber" like "mad bomber," and "nonentity" like "nontity," as well as engulfs whole phrases, if not sentences, in a gushing sound. Some ears encounter trouble becoming accustomed to his inimitable delivery—a British television critic once wrote that he "could not understand a word"; and comprehending him over the telephone can be especially difficult. As an intellectual grasshopper, Kahn leaps so quickly from one point to another that his words barely keep pace with his mind, his themes are often misunderstood, and even his closest associates sometimes jump the track of his thought. Also, his explanations can become so convoluted that audiences sometimes take away an impression quite contrary to what Kahn actually intended, while his presentations are so loose-ended that a morass of extravagant examples often obscure his basic argument; yet the stuff of his lectures is, nonetheless, so original that if professionals in the field leave slightly shaken, literate laymen are invariably escalated into a new realm of thought and discourse. Although he finds his intelligence nothing but a pleasure, Kahn does not flaunt his fantastic intellect too ostentatiously, rather letting the quality of his enthusiastic talk create a persuasive and indelible impression upon everyone he meets.

Even if he has a lectern, Kahn prefers to perambulate across his stage, punctuating his points by pumping his thick right hand and pausing only to take a whale of a breath; and since he perspires easily, he likes to remove his suit jacket to reveal a short-sleeved white shirt and workingman's arms. When he uses slides and stalks in front of the two screens in a darkened room, words flash across his shirt and broad forehead, escalating Kahn into a self-contained mixed-media display; should he sit, he generally folds his hands across his ample tummy. His voice is so resonant that those words which are clearly articulated can be heard in crannies where lesser speakers would need amplification, and so successfully does Kahn project his warm personality over an audience that they usually have no fear of interrupting him, invariably to discover that his pick-up is enormously quick and that he never, yes never, suffers a loss of words or pauses to work out an answer. Like most compulsive intellectual chatterers, he will pontificate about most everything under the sun, always indicating some familiarity with a particular subject, even though his perception is sometimes not quite commensurate with his interest.

The speed of his delivery abets the grasshopping quality of his expansive style, full of modifiers, anecdotes, parenthetical statements, developing images, agile leaps to unusual examples, dramatized scenarios, and references to hordes of specific facts. Kahn invariably runs far over the time-span alotted to him—a pet source of standing jokes—and in a masterful self-parody he can even extemporize a Gettysburg Address in Kahnian style. "Four score and seven years ago," it starts, "(this is of course a more or less arbitrary selection of a salient point of what is essentially a continuous process) our forefathers (a simplification, but one that is reasonably valid) brought forth on this continent. . . ." One of his more spectacular devices for oneupsmanship in debates opens with him announcing, "I can make your argument more persuasive than you can. Let me show you how." After an extensive and reasonable sympathetic elaboration, Kahn counters, "But let me show you why it is wrong," and then expounds his own reply. In the end, talking becomes his principal obsession, if not a primary vanity, as, for instance, he usually makes sure that on the first day of a series of lectures with a fresh audience he should be heard speaking from early morning to nearly midnight.

Kahn's books and essays start as chats with one of several tape machines he owns; only when a secretary transcribes his words does he confront the reality of cold print. Rewriting and reorganizing, which is to say the process of making one's written text better than his spoken words, interests Kahn not at all; and this explains why most of his printed output seems conspicuously disorganized and unedited. (Like Marshall McLuhan, he expresses a distinct distrust of well-wrought prose.) Indeed, when a magazine asks for an essay, he is liable to arrive in its editorial offices and dictate his piece on the spot. Kahn insists that he actually learns by talking; for not only does he learn from his audience's responses, but he actually develops, or discovers, basic ideas in the process of lecturing. Ideally, in working out a major interest, he prefers to give a one-hour lecture one day, a two-hour lecture on the same subject the following day, progressively expanding his thoughts to "say, a three-day lecture, when I'll ask someone to write it all down." The 652-page *On Thermonuclear War*, which he culled from the transcripts of four sets of briefings, contains three sections entitled "First Lecture," "Second Lecture," and "Third Lecture," which run respectively 113, 189, and 256 crowded pages.

Kahn's personality is such an unusual mixture of intellectual hardheadedness and emotional softheartedness that it is hard to believe that he exists—that any mortal could combine both qualities to such an extreme degree. Intellectually a great objectivist who refuses to be partisan even in sports events, he is yet profoundly patriotic about America and sentimental toward Israel and all things Jewish. A man with a lot of work to do and deadlines to meet, he can succumb to the most trivial distractions and temptations and still not quite realize that valuable time is passing. He often makes lists of the working day's priorities, only to disregard his own advice by, say, killing the morning with an extended conversation. Although he keeps Classified Information secret, he is so inherently honest that to strangers as well as friends he will reveal "off the record" personal details and opinions that most men of his eminence would scrupulously keep to themselves. A scrupulous rationalist and highbrow, he nonetheless prefers rather syrupy music, such as Wagner's operas and Rimsky-Korsakov's "Scheherazade." Even though he loves abstract intellectual models, he also exhibits that "homely sense of the immediate and practical" that Alexis de Tocqueville characterized as peculiarly American. Another paradox is that the master strategist, who can talk so coolly about nuclear death, years ago got so ill from disposing of his wife's recently deceased cat that she has since done all such mortuary work herself. Desirous of comfort, yet generally impervious to his surroundings, he once, during his wife's absence, let bugs overrun the house without bothering to find out where they came from or how their invasion might be halted. He is so fond of people in general that even his friends do not regard him as a particularly shrewd judge of personal character. "Herman really doesn't find dull people dull," Jane Kahn judges, "for he manages to get something out of nearly everybody; and he accepts very eccentric people easily, partly bebause he doesn't realize they are strange. Sometimes I think Herman is in the world but not entirely of it.'"

Kahn became an intellectual celebrity in the mushroom cloud produced by *On Thermonuclear War*, a large, fat, university-press bomb-of-a-tome which is so clearly among the most extraordinary, if not terrifying, books of our time that it produced a fallout of sharply worded reviews. In this book Kahn coolly, rationally, and extensively explored many aspects of the thermonuclear (hydrogen bomb) reality that had superseded the nuclear (atomic bomb) threat, as he discussed at length and in detail such hair-raising dimensions as the leaping development of weapons technology, the most propitious deployment of armament, the various ways in which thermonuclear attack might begin, how wars in several sizes and shapes might then be conducted as well as terminated, the degrees of "victory" and "defeat," the magnitude of possible damage, the effects of fallout, the efficacy of shelters, the probable ways by which a devastated society might recover, and the possible kinds of future weaponry, including a hypothetical "Doomsday Machine" that left no reader unstunned.

As Kahn viewed the Soviet-American antagonism as less an ideological death-match than a "conflict of interest over mutual territories," he regarded both sides as rational enough to desire the avoidance of war unless not-war should, for some reason, become intolerable. In his Hobbesian vision of existence, the existence of an organized antagonist became his primary presupposition. While Kahn in principle "would rather have everybody Red than everybody dead," he also thought that far fewer than everybody would die in thermonuclear conflict and that Russian takeover would bring about more evil than a moderate war; in short, the option of preparing to fight and survive became his wager. His second assumption, likewise Hobbesian, was that deterrence provides the most effective defense. "The only safeguard against force, intentional or not, is a greater force." Still, perhaps because he envisioned situations where the United States might use thermonuclear weaponry and because he had been an employee of the infamous RAND Corporation, some hasty readers fallaciously tagged Kahn as advocating United States attack. In fact, not only has Kahn always opposed "tactical first use," but he concludes the book by advocating "world government" as an improbable ideal and arms control as a realizable expedient.

What also shocked the early readers of the book was Kahn's gleeful audacity in creating "scenarios" for such unlikely yet resonant possibilities as juvenile delinquent Eskimos sabotaging SAC bases. Some were also horrified by his willingness to talk about figures as high as forty million deaths without some pious words, for the magnitude of numbers, as in the following remark, could mask the genuine quality of Kahn's moral concern. "I have tried to make the point that if we have a posture which might result in 40 million dead in a general war, and as a result of poor planning, apathy, or other causes, our posture deteriorates and a war occurs with 80 million dead, we have suffered an additional disaster, an *unnecessary* disaster that is almost as bad as the original disaster." If Kahn had, instead, used the numbers *one* and *two* respectively, as well as perhaps spoke of automobiles rather than war, his humanism would have gone unquestioned; yet the new technologies, rather than Kahn, made the ante so large. His visions of holocaust also lack the conspicuous passion for gory detail that so patently inflames certain proponents of disarmament. The thread of Kahn's ethical position ran like this: If countries manufacture and nurture thermonuclear weapons, then their use is possible; and since usage can bring unprecedented devastation, then responsible readers must plan for confronting and surviving such a situation. "I think perhaps the most important notion he has come up with is this," said his Hudson colleague Edmund Stillman, by reputation not an easy man to persuade, "Because a button is pressed and a bomb detonated somewhere, that doesn't mean we must all commit suicide. All reason doesn't have to flee."

In one of his more spectacular insights, Kahn suggested that new generations of weaponry so superseded the old—at the rate of one complete overhaul every five years—that if the difference between World War I and World II (or between the American Civil War and World War I) represented one technological revolution, then by 1961 the U.S. and the S.U., to use his pet initialing shorthand, have not fought what would have been, hypothetically, World Wars III to V. From this observation followed Kahn's warning that defense preparations valid in 1959 would simply be technologically obsolete by 1968, because, "strategy and tactics change as technology changes." By 1968, according to Kahn's chart, we have not fought World War VI and are not about to fight number VII.

As a feat of intellectual pioneering, *On Thermonuclear War* simply jumped beyond all earlier discussions of its much-trodden subject, as Kahn overcame the barriers—partly imaginative, mostly psychological—that inhibited other strategic thinkers from contemplating hydrogen, as distinct from atomic, weaponry; for the book successfully illuminated dimensions that previously went invisible, as well as defining more comprehensively the new environment of thermonuclear possibility. Precisely because Kahn's analyses and speculations made the intellectual leaps appropriate to the unprecedented realities of the late 1950's, his work seemed at first more "crazy" than true, then more canny than eccentric, then more accurate than evasive, and finally more profound than obscure; as well, it evoked the paradoxical image of its author as a madman with a firm grip on an absurd reality. In the end, the book was, as one reviewer put it, indubitably "a contribution of real originality, humanity and intellectual courage," and even one of Kahn's most acerbic critics, Philip Green, regards it as "without doubt the most significant single contribution to arms policy discussion during the nuclear era." Thanks in part to its author's rhetorical gifts, in larger part to his fantastic intelligence, *On Thermonuclear War* propels its readers out of the past into the second half of the twentieth century—a quality it shares with such outstanding contemporary probes as Paul Goodman's *Growing Up Absurd* (1960) and Marshall McLuhan's *Understanding Media* (1964).

As no one before had so brutally yet objectively—so complexly yet unsubtly; so imaginatively yet realistically—exposed the literate world to the hell of a potential situation that the new weaponry had created, many front-line critics foolishly vented their anger at Kahn for telling the truth about the unprecedented reality rather than at the situation itself. Although Kahn insists that he wrote the book "primarily for military and civilian professionals," it sold surprisingly well, nearly forty thousand hardback copies; and so dispassionately did Kahn describe the new world that probably as many doves as hawks were "persuaded" by his prose. Some critics have classified, if not dismissed, *On Thermonuclear War* as a physicist's book or a logician's analysis in which S.U. and U.S. were substituted for *p* and *q*; however, while the quality of Kahn's intelligence does indeed reveal his scientific training, he is nonetheless knowledgeable in several more disciplines. From the study of physics he learned, he thinks, "that theories can seem plausible and yet still be wrong"; yet *On Thermonuclear War*, he continues, raising his pencil from a doodle in a sweeping motion, "does not pretend to be a scientific study, because the issues are not susceptible to scientific treatments. However, there are scientific subtreatments, such as relatively systematic references to the relevant available data or the creation of hypotheses than can be immediately verified." Kahn prefers to classify the book as "policy research," a generalist's interdiscipline partly of his own invention. Seven years after its publication, Kahn characterizes *On Thermonuclear War* as "a left-wing book addressed to a right-wing audience," for one of his major themes holds that if American military men previously learned to wield their strongest weapons aggressively, now both they and their primary antagonist possessed weapons which were so many times more terrible that their power forbade unrestrained aggressive use. In that respect, the book refuted the extreme strategy John Foster Dulles christened "massive retaliation," where every button would be pressed, every weapon used. On the other hand, Kahn also scorned the piety that regarded the new weapons as so horrendous that neither side should expect the other to use them.

Instead, he came out for arms control that would reduce possible damage without jeopardizing a nation's security—a left position at the time (that has since ironically passed to militaristic advocates of "safe limited war")—as well as for the principle he christened Counter-Force as Insurance, which is to say that in time of war both sides should concentrate their attack upon the enemy's armaments rather than his populace. More important, Kahn espoused the maintenance of a complete spectrum of second-strike preparations, capable of meeting every challenge from a small-scale conflict with submaximal armaments to central war that would probably include an exchange of maximal weaponry. Kahn, in short, advocated that the United States pause to consider its enemy's attack and then offer a "controlled and flexible response that need not be larger than the situation requires"—that would repulse, or retaliate, and yet not raise the level of conflict. In 1962, he unpersuasively advocated, in a letter to the Pentagon, that the U.S. unilaterally declare "no first use" of nuclear weapons—a doctrine that he now thinks the government has all but accepted. Its specifics hold that, as he puts it, "the U.S. should be willing to adopt the concept that the only purpose of nuclear weapons is to negate nuclear weapons, and make it national policy not to use nuclear weapons first, but only in retaliation for use by some other nation." In sum, to the American tradition of war as something to be apocalyptically won or lost Kahn brought the traditionally European idea of the threat of war, or even a modest action, as an inevitable extension of diplomacy.

An implicit purpose of *On Thermonuclear War* is the rationalization of deterrence—knowing so profoundly what your enemy's ultimate weapons could do that you would be dissuaded from unwarranted use of your own. "A thermonuclear balance of terror," he coldly judged, "is equivalent to the signing of a non-aggression treaty which states that neither the Soviets nor the Americans will initiate an all-out attack, no matter how provoking the other side may become." Correctly prophesying that superweapons would make small wars more likely than large ones, Kahn wanted to make the strategy of deterrence more sophisticated and systematic, primarily by offering guidelines not only for various degrees of "limited war" but also for mutual diplomacy after war has broken out. That is, a language of mutually understood signals, particularly if announced in advance, would in times of emergency enable one side instantly to communicate with the other; and the "hot line" subsequently lent substance to this tendency. "Now, anybody who walks through a scenario understands that it is quite likely that if war is fought, most of the weapons will probably go unfired; most of the cities will probably be unhit." He peered intently up through his glasses, his language as scrupulously conditional as before. "Furthermore, if a small number of weapons should explode over a country like the U.S., the President is more likely to ask questions over the 'hot line' than to press every button." Although *On Thermonuclear War* seemed radically unconventional, if not farfetched, upon its original publication, its ideas so effectively shaped policy, as well as predicted the future, that by now its text all but effuses that musty quality characteristic of the conventional wisdom.

Not only were Kahn's ideas partly responsible for cooling off the military establishment—even the Vietnamese conflict, one should never forget, is fought at considerably *less* than optimal capability—he also contributed to that chorus of warnings about accidentally initiated war. So many checks and double-checks were subsequently instigated in the early sixties that Kahn has since joked, "Sometimes I seriously doubt if the whole system could ever go at all." The implications of deterrence have so effectively informed both Soviet and American policy that he now judges, "We just haven't been able to write a plausible scenario for a major nuclear war, which means that it is not impossible but, hopefully, just unlikely." In a more recent essay, "Nuclear War," contributed to the new edition of the *International Encyclopedia of the Social Sciences*, Kahn has written, "Nuclear war has but a brief history, involving the use in 1945 of two low-yield weapons against Japanese cities. . . . Nuclear deterrence has had a richer history," much of which has been shaped by Kahn's thought and its influence upon policy planners. Precisely because he clarified the new reality, measured the possible risks, and outlined appropriate policy and procedure, Kahn himself helped make our world a more rational, which is to say safer, place to live—a paradoxical achievement that may one day merit him the Nobel Peace Prize.

The point is that all through the fifties thermonuclear weapons could have been fired impulsively, or stupidly, simply because neither the United States nor the Soviet Union had developed a coherent and responsible policy regarding their possible use or even their most effective deployment. Indeed, so innocent was our government's attitude to the new technology that at one point in the early fifties, Kahn remembers with amusement, all American bombs were stored in only one place, and then two places, where they were vulnerable to unanimous detonation or total sabotage, if not kidnaping. Right now, Kahn holds that, despite small wars here and there, the world is very much at peace—he trusts Russian leaders to be at least as cautious as the American; but his biggest current fear is that further proliferation of nuclear weaponry will upset current stabilities.

Whenever he heard the cliché fashionable some years back,

"Nuclear war is unthinkable," Kahn would earnestly reply, "Well, I thought about it recently." Appropriately enough, *Thinking About the Unthinkable* became the title of his second book, a collection of essays published in 1962. If the incredible objectivity of the first book deceived some readers and critics into a mistaken image of Kahn the man, here he was more manifestly concerned with reducing the likelihood of thermonuclear conflict. "To act intelligently we must learn as much as we can about the risks. We may thereby be able better to avoid nuclear war," he wrote, adding, "Even if [the probability of war] were as low as one in fifty a year, the annual risk would be too high—an even chance that there would be a war before the year 2000." This second book bestowed a more benign and optimistic persona upon Herman Kahn; it also remains to this day the best introduction to his thermonuclear thought.

His third book, *On Escalation* (1965), was a more narrowly conceived detailed exposition of sophisticated signaling, not only so that one country would implicitly but continually announce messages about its actual intentions but also so it would revise its military capabilities in response to an enemy's moves. Its most influential passages contained a metaphoric escalation-ladder of forty-four rungs, a succession of milestones for measuring degrees of involvement in less than "spasm or insensate" conflict. Moreover, the Ballistics Missile Defense systems he outlines here rather closely resembles the program the United States eventually adopted. Like everything else in strategic thinking that Kahn has done, *On Escalation* offers more general concepts than specific strategies—even his scenarios serve more as metaphoric models of how things might happen than programs for how they actually will; and for this reason, military professionals still regard Kahn as more an "intellectual" than a strategist—more an "advisor" than a tactician.

Like Thorstein Veblen and H. L. Mencken before him, as well as Marshall McLuhan and Leslie A. Fiedler today, Herman Kahn is often an incorrigibly American ironist, who not only pushes his thought to extreme, unconventional conclusions and sometimes emphasizes a particularly striking aspect at the expense of a balanced view of the whole, but who also sometimes expresses his most serious insights in such an exaggerated form that he forces each of his listeners to work out a more definitive truth on their own. Kahn particularly uses irony to shock his audience into recognitions that might otherwise pass them by; "You'll never get people to understand what's confusing," he says, "unless you make it stark." Take nothing he says *too* literally, one should warn; yet everything always stems from a real concern and refers to deadly serious problems. "These issues are fun to study," Kahn once remarked with considerable irony. "There are qualities of paradox and absurdity that appeal to (strategic) analysts and other non-serious people."

As the first of the great "megadeath intellectuals," Kahn became the object of controversy, as well as satire. Philip Green, in perhaps the most extensive and considered critique, *Deadly Logic* (1966), charges that Kahn's calculations are factually arbitrary, that much of his evidence is insufficiently supported, that his examples are too random and/or too inconclusive, that his pragmatism is operationally glib, and that the strategist should have devoted more attention to possible American recuperation from Soviet victory. "What Kahn has produced," Green concludes, "is not scientific analysis but prophetic science fiction; unless it strikes our literary imagination it has neither more nor less merit than any other of its kind." (The critic also complains that his subject has a disconcerting knack for anticipating in print the most serious objections to his work.) Erich Fromm argued in *May Man Prevail?* (1961) that thinking so vividly about nuclear war made its occurrence more likely; to this, Kahn replied that not-thinking did not make either the U.S.-S.U. conflict, the weapons or even their potential use disappear. Even so, Kahn actually did conjecture how certain developments, most of them either horrifying or unlikely, might realize world peace. The cutting paradox, an absurd irony worthy of Joseph Heller's *Catch-22*, is that thinking about peace is likely to have little influence upon people responsible for war, while thinking profoundly about war in our time actually contributes to keeping the peace.

The inspiration for the title figure of Stanley Kubrick's film *Doctor Strangelove* (1964) Kahn characterizes as "part Henry Kissinger, part myself, with a touch of [Wernher] von Braun. Kubrick gave us a special advance showing; I liked the movie, while Jane didn't. Since Stanley lifted lines from *On Thermonuclear War*, without change but out of context, I asked him, 'Doesn't that entitle me to a royalty?' He pretended at first not to hear me; but when I asked him again, Stanley replied, in the firmest tone I've ever heard him use, 'It doesn't work that way.' " Thinly veiled portraits of Kahn supposedly appear in a sketch in *Beyond the Fringe*, the novel and film *Fail-Safe*, and the recent British flick *War Games*, while few of his antagonists can resist a satirical reference to Genghis of the same name (but of a different spelling, Khan) who led the Mongol hordes. Generally benign toward his critics, always appreciative of their humor, Kahn regrets only that *Scientific American* would not publish his reply to James R. Newman's *ad hominem* attack.

One of Kahn's major intellectual contributions to the strategic thought is the writing of "scenarios," a technique for stretching the imagination to contemplate extensions of current tendencies and potentialities perhaps for gauging in advance otherwise unexpected possibilities. "The scenario," he writes, "is particularly suited to dealing with events taken together—integrating several aspects of a situation more or less simultaneously. By the use of a relatively extensive scenario, the analyst may be able to get a feeling for events and the branching points dependent upon critical choices." Regarding the scenarios as more of a medium than a message, Kahn will conjecture several possible versions out of the basic fictional crisis and/or even write systematic and detailed plans for developments he thinks unlikely, simply to create a sense of how complex changes might occur and how real leaders might respond. The method is particularly, but not exclusively, useful in strategic thinking, where, says Kahn, "you want to have in mind a picture of a war that is fought through to the very last step." Some scenarios are so tentative that Kahn is liable to conclude by saying, "I don't know it I believe all this, but I think I do."

Since Kahn's mind so successfully fuses empiricism with speculation—complementing an encyclopedic factual knowledge and scores of analytic tools with the capacity to imagine the dimensions and processes of possible but unprecedented occurrences—it was only inevitable that the writing of scenarios would lead into more systematic and comprehensive thinking about the future itself, the subject of the broadly conceived yet heavily detailed book *The Year 2000* (1967), which he recently co-authored with Anthony J. Wiener, a colleague at the Hudson Institute. Perhaps the most thorough of the current crop of futuristic books, if not the fattest, *The Year 2000* contains, among other things, a plethora of charts full of curves, stunningly abundant lists of technological and scientific developments, speculations on the changing pattern of world politics, and horrifying images of future weaponry, all enwrapped in a cautious optimism that sees not catastrophes or revolutions but boundless extensions of major current tendencies; the alleviation, if not solution, of many of mankind's oldest scourges; and, more ominously, whole batteries of unprecedented problems.

To quote their own summary, Kahn and Wiener regard the continuance of such "long-term multifold trends" as "increasingly Sensate (empirical, this-worldly, secular, humanistic, pragmatic, utilitarian, contractual, epicurean or hedonistic, and the like) cultures; accumulation of scientific and technical knowledge; institutionalization of change, especially research, development, innovation, and diffusion; increasing affluence and (recently) leisure; urbanization and (soon) the growth of megalopolises [jocularly christened 'Boswash,' or Boston-to-Washington; 'Chipitts' or Chicago-Pittsburgh; and 'Sansan,' or Santa Barbara-San Diego]; decreasing importance of primary and (recently) secondary occupations; and [increasing] literacy and education."

Beyond that, Kahn and Wiener write both pessimistic and optimistic scenarios for alternative world futures, sometimes questioning whether " 'progress' is the proper model or just a myth" or whether the affluent welfare state is a vital or degenerative social form; and certain of the most controversial pages in *The Year 2000* argue that in the decades ahead Japan will be far more of a power in the world, let alone in Asia, than China. Nonetheless, those who admire Kahn's willingness to cope with revolutionary possibilities might find the book a trifle disappointing; for if he previously took the intellectual leaps that the unprecedented shape of a situation demanded, now he seems less eccentric and less outlandish—indeed, more conservative—than before, particularly in estimating the pace of scientific invention (his justly famous itemization of one hundred technological developments, he privately admits, is more appropriate for 1980 than 2000), as well as in gauging the secondary impact of technical change. Still, one should add, Kahn and Wiener think far ahead of nearly all other futurologists.

One basic Kahn principle holds that "the pace at which various technological, social, political and economic changes are taking place has reduced the relevance of experience as a guide to many public-policy judgments." To put it differently, since the present is considerably different from the past, and the future will be radically unlike the present, then a truly illuminating analysis must concentrate upon those dimensions of the present that know no precedent, in addition to recognizing the likely continuities. Since thermonuclear weapons have capabilities several levels beyond previous conventional armaments, then not only can they not be used as earlier weapons were, but strategic thinkers cannot rely on either historical analogies (experience!) or even the earlier analytic language in talking about them.

For these reasons, Kahn's major philosophical interest is epistemology, and his books and essays can be regarded as a succession of attempts to create concepts and coin words and phrases—indeed, an entire critical language—appropriate to historically unprecedented situations. "Changes occur so rapidly," he once wrote, "that we must make a conscious and vigorous effort to keep our conceptual, doctrinal and linguistic framework up to the needs of the moment." Thus, to old-fashioned minds, his prose often seems as unfamiliar and unconventional as his thought, while the "stylistic barbarisms" that literary critics decry are actually a by-product of a style that is highly idiosyncratic and yet distinctly American, oral yet literate, uneven and exaggerated, freewheeling and energetic, full of stunning phrases that could sometimes be aphoristic if Kahn only exerted some artful pruning care.

Nothing more decisively distinguishes Herman Kahn from Kubrick's character than Strangelove's German accent; for Kahn himself is as thoroughly American as his intellectual style. Born in Bayonne, New Jersey, early in 1922, he spent his earliest years in the Bronx. When he was very young, Kahn's father, an ex-clothing manufacturer, divorced his family; so his Yiddish-speaking mother supported her three sons on the fringe of destitution, twice going on relief. Turning to books quite early and possessing an eidetic memory (that he has since outgrown), Kahn read extensively and precociously, ranging from, he boasts, "every fairy tale in the neighborhood public library by the time I was ten," to adult classics in economics and politics; as an old-time library borrower, to this day he resists the temptation to put pencil marks in books, even those he owns. Like many Jewish-Americans of his age and background, Kahn is acutely aware of everyone's ethnic identity and enthusiastic about Israel's success; to his wife and closest friends, most of whom are also Jewish, he all but epitomizes the ideal of a *mensch*. (His voice changed its tone when he told me, late one night, "I don't believe in cyclical theories of history but don't you think that in America perhaps we've assimilated too much?")

In 1935, the Kahns moved to Los Angeles, where, always short of money, Herman as a teen-ager worked on various occasions as a dishwasher, a machinist, an encyclopedia salesman, a summertime seaman, and clerk-manager of a small grocery store his aunt owned. ("As the stuff was unmarked, I had to keep a thousand prices in my head, including the daily specials.") Although his teachers knew he was exceptionally gifted, Kahn was not pushed beyond his peers, graduating from Los Angeles's Fairfax High School at the normal American age of eighteen. Despite such theoretically scarring disadvantages as an impoverished youth, a fatherless upbringing, and urban public school education, Kahn seems a more or less "adjusted" genius, who judges of himself and his world, "I don't feel alienated at all."

He attended the intellectually prosaic University of Southern California for a year; and upon entering the Army, he scored an unusually high mark on his GCT examination. Since his weak eyesight disqualified him from officer candidacy, he registered at a U.S. Army engineering school. Twice refusing some mysterious "ordnance assignment at Oak Ridge, Tennessee," because of moral objections to Southern mores, he served in Burma as a Signal Corps Technical Sargent, a wire-chief in charge of the country's telephone communications system. As a Bronx-born liberal, he particularly made sure that his wires did not discriminate against Negro troops. "You didn't like having people in charge of you," he now muses, "but I had the time of my life.'" He returned to study at U.C.L.A., where he picked up his B.S. in physics in 1945 and then embarked on graduate studies in applied mathematics and physics at California Institute of Technology.

Again short of funds, he went to work part time for Douglas Aircraft and then Northrop Aviation, first as a human computer (a profession since obsolete) and then as a research physicist. In 1948, the same year that he earned his M.S., Kahn applied for a part-time job at the recently formed RAND Corporation. Since RAND's activities were then classified, Kahn was not exactly sure what his work would entail; but his high school friend, Samuel T. Cohen, already a RAND physicist, eased Kahn's apprehensions by remarking, "It's near the beach in Santa Monica." To his surprise and good fortune, he discovered, "They were doing what I always wanted—

making integrated studies of important questions and pontificating on a range of issues."

As a young "computer" and then a physicist on the RAND staff, Kahn worked first in mathematical theory, making several minor contributions to the field of statistics; but until 1950, he had no clear idea of what he wanted to do, having merely drifted through situations where he picked up knowledge and skills. He several times considered going into some sort of business, even acquiring a California real estate licence to participate in a deal that never came off. Several lectures he gave that year on the much-studied but baffling Monte Carlo theory earned him some professional recognition and a sense of "career," as well as some independent consulting contracts. As a RAND scientist, Kahn worked on particle diffusion, detection physics, shielding design, experimental nuclear physics, radiation hydrodynamics, the mechanics of deformable media—basic research connected with the development of the nuclear-powered airplane, the hydrogen bomb, and protective construction. While at RAND, Kahn also collaborated with the late mathematician John von Neumann, whom Kahn regards as the most brilliant mind he has ever met—"the smart man's smart man."

Around 1952, he finished a research project on Monte Carlo theories that the eminent physicist Richard Feynman would have accepted for a doctorate at Cal Tech, had not the university had an established rule against the submission of commercially sponsored scholarly work. Kahn thought about submitting it elsewhere, even getting promises of its acceptability in advance; but he decided that a year of residency and some course work was too great a price for the academic union card. In 1949, a young New York girl fresh out of a University of South Carolina physics degree took a job at RAND as a "computer" assigned to Kahn; and although she found him so imposing and incomprehensible that three days later she asked to work for someone less difficult, four years later they wed, confirming RAND's reputation as "the greatest marriage broker."

By the middle fifties, Kahn's interests had shifted to politics and economics, fields in which he always did plenty of reading but never took any formal study (let alone a degree!); and his lack of academic training in his subsequently chosen fields may explain the unfettered originality of his thought—how a lack of intellectual inhibitions enables him to illuminate what remain hidden to others. Like other radically original American minds, Kahn received all of his formal education here, partially at less-than-great universities. In both his speech and writing, he conspicuously eschews both the foreign words and anglicisms that once passed as roadsigns to intellect; and although he claims to pick up a reading knowledge of foreign languages rather quickly (and yet, curiously, suffers a tin ear), he forgets them even more rapidly, retaining only the Yiddish he learned as a child.

In his years at RAND, Kahn moved from his base in the physics division to become an unofficial consultant in several "house" projects spread across various fields; and by 1956–7, he had established sufficient reputation to do almost anything he wanted. Although both the RAND administration and the U.S. Air Force (which largely supports RAND) were then opposed to civil defense studies, Kahn won his way, becoming the "project leader" and later the author of RAND Report R-322-RC, "A Study of Non-Military Defense" (1958). This work, as well as his co-directorship of the strategic Air Power Project, produced the ideas that Kahn later poured into *On Thermonuclear War*, which he set to print in 1959 while a Research Associate at Princeton University's Center of International Studies. (Incidentally, though he is motivated by a vain desire for intellectual celebrity, Kahn turned down a commercial publisher's attractive offer for the prestigious Princeton University Press imprint.)

Perhaps because thermonuclear war has become too threatening to be left to the generals, who invariably prepare to fight a war like the previous one, civilian intellectuals have in the past decade displaced military professionals and alumni as the Defense Department's major advisors on general strategy; and so immense has been their behind-the-scenes power that more than one historical critic has compared the new master strategists to the Jesuits in post-Reformation Catholic courts. Before the late 1950's, Kahn remarked, his hands peripatetic, "Military men were suspicious of a guy with long hair, wild eyes, and stains on his tie; but we convinced them those were his credentials." Whenever an officer would put Kahn down as an inexperienced non-combatant, Kahn would look his antagonist straight in the eye and ask, "How many thermonuclear wars have *you* fought recently?"

In the summer of 1961, Kahn resigned from RAND, partially because of a personal disagreement with its president, as well as because, as one friend judged, "he was becoming more important than RAND." After considering several professorships in International Relations at major universities, Kahn joined several fellow intellectuals (and only $10,000 capital) in forming the Hudson Institute, a high-powered, privately controlled, non-profit "think tank" now located in the hills of Croton-on-Hudson, New York. Patterned in parts upon the example of RAND, Hudson is devoted to well-supported, interdisciplinary generalized research into major problems—in Kahn's words, "the important issues, not just the urgent ones." Currently its director, Kahn is so surrounded by conflicting personalities, as well as their disagreements of principle and policy, that he characterizes himself as the "resident objectivist. I'm the only guy here who can communicate with every man at the Institute." Very politic in interpersonal situations, as well as even-tempered and tolerantly permissive, "Herman," says his wife, "never takes anything personally. His detachment is marvelous in a research analyst and an administrator, but sometimes awful in a husband."

One colleague at Hudson estimated, "Herman's mind moves several times faster than mine, while his body works at least twice as hard. That's how he does the work of several people." His presence is so multifarious that the journalist Frances FitzGerald conjectured, "Instead of one Herman Kahn, there seem to be at least six—six thin men in one vast body, six sources of intelligence." A man who contains and apportions his energy well, Kahn labors steadily, yet not compulsively, from morning to night of an eighteen-hour day, arriving at the Hudson office (full of books, papers, records, a luscious hi-fi set, and his Barka lounger) soon after sunrise and occasionally falling asleep over his desk at home or, if necessary, forcing himself to stay up all night. Although he will forsake his daily regime to do some intensive reading, he has not taken a real poop-out vacation in years; and his doctor is continually amazed that a man of his size and drive should keep in such good health. Kahn rarely finishes as much work as he should; for since he is hardly a contemplative recluse, a good conversation that moves within earshot usually persuades him to put everything else aside. "I'm not an organized guy," he admits, "but I think that some people overstate the degree of my disorganization."

Kahn's work as director divides into three major categories: (1) Supervising the Hudson house, which includes arranging seminars, than starring in all home shows, assigning and overseeing research tasks, editing and rewriting the reports that are usually the end products of a Hudson contract, knocking heads together and pushing them apart; and on behalf of the common efforts, Kahn is very generous with himself. (2) Hustling to where the director should be, not only to garner contracts, move information needing his *imprimatur*, greet visiting dignitaries, and give after-dinner lectures, but also to do on-the-spot research in Colombia, Southeast Asia, Japan, and elsewhere; a traveling man and regular commuter on the New York-Saigon line, Kahn estimates that he spends less than two hundred nights of the year at home. (3) Thinking, or rather talking, as well as editing transcripts of his talks; and even though his "writing" is just an auxiliary task, Kahn produces a huge amount of published prose each year. He commits himself so diffusely that even important reports generally get rushed out in a last-minute flurry; yet although Kahn's intelligence often functions at merely its third or fourth level below effectiveness—even his method of thinking with his tongue hardly seems conducive to *maximum* profundity—he is still more brilliant than most everyone else in optimal shape.

Not only does he find it hard to fire someone, who usually gets several months to find another position; but though Kahn's employees stand in awe, sometimes jealous awe, of his intelligence, some eagerly identifying flaws that, by converse implication, aggrandize their own particular competencies, his closest associates have been loyal to him for years, even when, early in its life, the Hudson Institute frequently stood on the verge of bankruptcy. Were Kahn to leave tomorrow, the organization might disintegrate; so one goal of its current fund-raising drive would diversify the administrative burden and provide Hudson's own self-contained interdisciplinary sub-think tank with more free time to devote a greater percentage of his abundant energies to his primary vocation—thinking about the previously unthinkable.

Nowadays, the Hudson Institute does free-lance consultation for institutions both public and private, at the stiff rate of about $42,000 per staff thinker per year; and though contracts are easier to get if Kahn agrees to work on them, among the resident intellectual stars are the noted political analysts Edmund Stillman (who moved to Johns Hopkins, early in 1968) and William Pfaff, the engineer Robert Panero, the mathematician and arms-control strategist Donald G. Brennan, the military analyst Frank E. Armbruster, and two young men with law degrees who double as administrators—Hudson's president, Max Singer, and Anthony J. Wiener, chairman of its Research Management Council. An outer skin of the Hudson onion includes such non-resident consultants as the sociologists Daniel Bell and Raymond Aron, the economist Carl Kaysen, and the novelist Ralph Ellison.

Although most contracts relate to the American national interest, Hudson is also advising the government of Colombia on the construction of an interoceanic canal and creating a master plan for New York City's Welfare Island. Kahn himself would prefer to see only fifty percent of Tudson's thinking time devoted to defense contracts; and he eagerly ferrets out other kinds of commissions, such as the Report on the Year 2000 done for the Corning Glass Foundation and the American Academy of Arts and Sciences. Hudson, he insists, could get greater private beneficence if it went either militarist or pacifist; but its middling position cuts it off from the money that flows readily to the extremes. Contrary to frequent rumor, Kahn does not give partisan political advice, although certain politicians, particularly candidates whose assistants have attended Hudson seminars, refer familiarly to his expertise.

Kahn states that a Hudson report which merely mollifies existing practices and prejudices has not done its job. "It simply isn't worth, say, $150,000 of anybody's money to find out they are doing everything right." As an exponent of the "higher nit-picking," as well as "a position fluctuating between 'loyal opposition' and 'disloyal opposition,' " Kahn says, twinkling enough irony to undercut his smug phrases, "we are very much in the business of telling our contractors things they don't want to hear. If there is any evidence to contradict them, even the Joint Chiefs of Staff, we'll find it. We like to bite the hand that feeds us. When you contract Hudson, you're hiring a group of people who are going to come back with negative reports." Like McLuhan, Kahn compares the critical intellectual to "the snotty kid who proclaimed that the Emperor had no clothes and then persuaded everyone that he was right." To a reporter from *Life*, he revealed some secrets of his unparalleled success: "They take it because they know I'm worried about the country. They take a lot of crap from me which they wouldn't from anyone else. And I'll tell you this: I couldn't happen in any other country."

In contrast to other think tanks, however, Hudson does most of its government-sponsored policy-thinking from the point of view of the three top United States officials. "We play the President, also the Secretary of State, as well as the Secretary of Defense," none of whom, curiously enough, has Kahn himself extensively met. (In fact, various symptoms lead Kahn to believe that both Dean Rusk and Robert McNamara have been less than fond of him.) "In a few years, we hope not to play God but advise Him. We like to take larger views of every issue." As for the content of a Hudson report, he judges, balancing from one foot to the other, "Only rarely do we attempt to persuade; mostly we just deliver a more or less sophisticated analysis." Their function is to criticize existing policies, rather than formulate comprehensive plans or implement existing schemes.

Recently, Kahn and his associates did a two-year-long study of Vietnam for the Advanced Research Projects Agency on what he calls "a hunting license. We could chase after anything we wanted." Much of their findings were publicly published in the book *Can We Win in Vietnam?* (1968), which for detail and general sophistication stands beyond the other discussions of the subject. For the U.S. Air Force, they recently completed "War Termination Studies." "You'd be surprised how little we know about ending a war. How a country gets into war, conducts it, and then terminates it may have as much effect upon a country as the war's ostensible outcome."

In his several visits to Vietnam, Kahn has noticed such remediable deficiencies as inadequate equipment ("Some wasn't as good as what we had in Burma."), the lack of competent native administrative personnel (complicated by excessive United States demands upon the existing administrators), organizational rigidity, such a poor understanding of both politics and tactics that a minor conflict has escalated into an important issue, and an "attrition-pressure-ouch" strategy that, he judges, cannot make the enemy succumb. Regarding the war as a defense less of democracy than of America's reputation with its allies and enemies, Kahn has long viewed many policies, particularly the bombing of the North's industrial areas, as mistaken and ineffective. Negotiations between Israel and the Arabs are, to his mind, more likely to succeed than bargaining with Ho Chi Minh, whom Kahn takes to be "a dedicated Communist who would have a better chance of winning his war if he could drop Communism again, as he did in 1946–52." Always willing to contemplate any alternative proposed, Kahn regards outright United States withdrawal as a feasible possibility that "the U.S. could do two or three times in Asia before it loses credibility. But this is a currency one should spend very carefully, if at all. Also, it would make us incredibly rigid in the next confrontation. Let me tell you another thing. From a cold, amoral point of view, this is a vintage year [1969] for reneging international commitments—no Hitlers, Stalins, or even Maos could take advantage—but from the domestic perspective it would be the worst year in history, escalating enormous internal divisions and strains."

Late in 1968, he thought, first of all, that the United States must posit a persuasive and defendable theory of "victory," which he suggests should be based not only upon "reducing the level of violence in the South to, say, Central Park," but also on territory; so that the point of victory, as well as our proximity to it, can be empirically measured. "Serious negotiations," he remarked anxiously, his sentences leaping from point to point, "are not yet likely, because Ho Chi Minh feels that by holding out he can do better. Twice before—in 1946 and 1954—the North Vietnamese felt that they had lost at the negotiating table what they won on the battlefield. These men are too dedicated and principled to accept an agonizing compromise now, particularly when they are informed by all visitors that the U.S. homefront is collapsing." "As for the short run," Kahn proposes, picking up speed and animatedly pumping his right arm, "the U.S. should advance as generous an offer as it can stand, making clear to both itself and foreigners that it cannot negotiate indefinitely and that, if negotiations fail, it has a serious and plausible strategy for winning the war, probably without escalation." The Hudson Institute, he proudly asserted, leaning back in his chair, "has offered suggestions for such a strategy."

Although Kahn's views so defy conventional categories that such old-fashioned dichotomies as left-right hardly grapple with the complexity and originality of his thinking, Kahn says that he used to consider himself politically liberal (favoring, for instance, benevolent welfare and civil rights) and yet economically conservative (opposing legalized minimum wages, at least in the United States); officially, like most people of his background and education, he is a registered Democrat. However, whereas he could use left-right to characterize the social thought of a decade ago, today, he finds, "We can't use those dichotomous categories for a large range of issues." It would be more correct to classify him as a modernist, rather than a traditionalist; a radical as opposed to a reactionary; a rationalist who believes in necessary change. (Ethically, he regards himself as a "consequential moralist," which is to say, a pragmatist making evaluative judgments on not just the ends but all the intermediate consequences of thoughts and actions. Nonetheless, it is perhaps typical of Kahn that the most moralistic remark I ever heard from him criticized a certain Jewish writer who flagrantly mistreats his wife.)

More important to his own political role is Kahn's presupposition that "our civilization does more things on a consciously 'rationalized' basis than any before in history, rather than succumbing to traditions or explicit emotional desires; but this does not mean that our behavior is always rational." A look of disappointment crossed his face, only to fall away. "It does mean, however, that people in government are willing to listen to arguments based upon rationality. A persuasive position—honed on skeptics, rather than friends and relatives—can be tremendously influential with American bureaucracies. This is particularly true if one goes to the trouble of making his points clear to everyone concerned and then waits for the inevitable crisis that spurs them to action."

The primary deficiencies of Kahn's intelligence are entwined in his virtues. Although he can enumerate and systematically analyze all the obvious forces shaping a situation, he often misses the underlying drift ("hidden music," as they say at Hudson) or general shape and scale; and this partially explains the bloated and disorganized quality of his books. Although he is contemptuous of most superficial thinking, Kahn is nonetheless too much of a generalist to offer an absolutely thorough, definitive exposition of anything he discusses; by emphasizing technological and organizational procedures, he minimizes cultural factors; and though he strives for a complex understanding of a multifaceted problem, he nonetheless simplifies for the sake of a neat analysis, or exaggerates out of a love for scintillating irony. He usually buttresses an argument with abundant statistics and examples; yet too often he facilely establishes a generalization upon merely a striking anecdote as well as arbitrarily using evidence to confirm a point deduced, if not envisioned, in advance. Although he will skeptically question every dimension of American policy, he is too much of a patriot (detached yes, but alienated no) to ask publicly if United States purposes are fundamentally right and just or comfortably conceive of U.S. armies "losing" in Vietnam. Finally, perhaps because his enthusiasm for his own ingenious ideas often deflects his critical sense, he espouses faintly gimmicky solutions at the same time that he decries them in others.

One of his major assets is a thoroughly avant-garde sensibility; for if the experimental artist hesitates to execute works that too closely resemble his earlier successes, so Kahn himself continually forsakes his previous interests to explore uncharted territories. He finds he can no longer think creatively about thermonuclear war, largely because he has so little new to say about it and fears the dull recitation of earlier thoughts. Like all good modernist minds, as well as vanguard artists, Kahn prides himself on being intellectually up-to-date. Not only does he courageously confront the major unthought problems of the moment—thermonuclear war in the late fifties, limited war in the early sixties, the future in the late sixties—but he relishes insights that perceptively measure how the situation today differs from that of six months, a year, or two years ago. He reads new books by the cartload, surveys scores of magazines, accumulates new information and ideas from everyone he meets; by keeping up with the present, he escalates his mind into the future. Before LSD became a popular trip, he volunteered for laboratory experiments, hoping for "a two-bit psychoanalysis but discovering instead that the experience was just fun."

The new book, *The Year 2000,* he considers just the first of several forays into thinking about the future; and in justification for publishing merely, in its subtitle, a "framework for speculation," he explains, "Once you put something into print you make sure that neither you, your associates, nor your consultants will spout those ideas again. It's a way of insuring that we all either dig deeper or move on to something else." He and Wiener are currently doing a sequel tentatively entitled *Faustian Progress,* as well as founding *The International Forum of Future Studies;* and Kahn is directing the compilation of a compendious analytic summary, a cleverly organized encyclopedia of ideas and facts relevant to current policy issues, both domestic and foreign. Rather than ride a thesis, or adopt a position he will espouse to his death, Kahn considers himself a free-ranging intellectual, the possessor of a superb instrument that is loyal first of all to the imaginative and logical processes of rational thought; and so even if his name does not easily associate with any particular idea or sloganeering thesis, the impact of his ideas has been various and enormous.

In his insistence upon the importance of a general perspective, encyclopedic knowledge, original insight, measured judgment, complex thought, coherent analysis, and persuasive argument, Kahn is very much a supreme intellectual, always scornful of idiocy and ignorance, archaic pieties and simple-mindedness; and since his ideas so enormously influence policy, his intellect literally represents a kind of immeasurable national resource. Precisely because mankind's situation today is so unlike the past, to chart our common future we need the substantial and yet imaginative ideas, as well as the singular supermind, of someone like Herman Kahn. More than anything else—more than money, or even munitions—the mind of man is the primary force in contemporary society; for not only does it expose hidden problems and then devise solutions, as well as envision a need and then invent a machine, but minds also function to organize the common resources and available knowledge in the most propitious manner. At the time when "intellectuals" so often bemoan their lack of influence upon public policy or the general thinking, Kahn's work exemplifies how much power the relevant ideas of a great mind can actually exercise over the affairs and thoughts of men; radical jumps in the mind *precede* the revolutions in society.

BIBLIOGRAPHICAL ESSAYS

MILTON BABBITT

The most admired Babbitt pieces are for the Synthesizer; and they should be heard on their stereo recordings, even though two tracks of sound inevitably compromise the original four. Those compositions for Synthesizer which incorporate live performers are *Vision and Prayer* (1961) and *Philomel* (1963), both of which have been recorded but, at last count, not yet released; and those for machine alone are Ensembles for Synthesizer (1961, 1963), Columbia MS 7051, and Composition for Synthesizer (1964), Columbia MS 6566. Nearly all of Babbitt's major early scores have been published by Associated Music, Inc.; but only a few of them are available on record: Composition for Twelve Instruments (1948), Son-Nova, S1; Composition for Four Instruments (1948), CRI 138; Composition for Viola and Piano (1950), CRI 138; *Du* (1951), CRI 138; Partitions for Piano (1957), RCA LM-7042; and *All-Set* (1957), in the disparate "Outstanding Jazz Compositions of the Twentieth Century," Columbia C2S-831. The work he considers to be his richest and most difficult, Composition for Tenor and Six Instruments (1960), has been performed only thrice and never recorded.

Babbitt's essays have appeared sporadically over the years in such miscellaneous places that they should be collected into a single book. Among the more important are "Who Cares If You Listen?" perhaps the most accessible statement of his general position, which was originally in *High Fidelity*, VIII/2 (February, 1958) and since reprinted in both Gilbert Chase, ed., *The American Composer Speaks* (Louisiana State University, 1966) and Elliott Schwartz and Barney Childs, eds., *Contemporary Composers on Contemporary Music* (Holt, Rinehart and Winston, 1967). The definitive formulation of "combinatoriality" appears in "Some Aspects of Twelve-Tone Composition," *The Score*, XII (June, 1955); and later elaborations are "Set Structure as a Compositional Determinant," *Journal of Music Theory* (Spring, 1960); "Twelve-Tone Invariant as Compositional Determinants," *Musical Quarterly* (April, 1960), later reprinted in Paul Henry Lang, ed., *Problems of Modern Music* (Norton, 1962) and several essays published in *Perspectives of New Music* (1962-). The major statement on his inimitable instrument is "An Introduction to the RCA Synthesizer," *Journal of Music Theory* (Winter, 1964). For Babbitt's ideas on musical pedagogy, see "The Structure and Function of Musical Theory: I," *College Music Symposium*, V (Fall, 1965). The chart of Schoenberg's twelve-tone row for *Moses and Aaron* comes from Babbitt's notes to the Columbia Recording (K3L-241), and his one published poem appeared on page 346 of *Politics* (November, 1945). For historical background on electronic music, see Otto Luening, "Some Random Remarks about Electronic Music," *The Journal of Music Theory*, VIII/1 (Spring, 1964), subsequently reprinted in Schwartz and Childs anthology; and Lejaren Hiller, Jr., and Leonard M. Isaacson, *Experimental Music* (McGraw-Hill, 1959). For analysis of the three languages of contemporary music, see my booklet, *Music of Today* (Time, Inc., 1967). Much of the critical writing specifically about Babbitt's music has been inaccurate in detail and mistaken in interpretation—e.g., the remarks in Wilfrid Mellers' *Music in a New Found Land* (Knopf, 1965): for more substantial criticism, see Benjamin Boretz's pamphlet, "Milton Babbitt," published in 1965 by BMI; his essay "New Music and the American Mainstream," *The Nation* (May 4, 1964); and Peter Westergaard, "Some Problems Raised by the Rhythmic Procedures in Milton Babbitt's Composition for Twelve Instruments," *Perspectives of New Music*, IV/1 (Fall–Winter, 1965).

An earlier version of this profile appeared in *Stereo Review* (April, 1969), and this drew in turn upon an essay on both Babbitt and Cage that was published in *The New York Times Magazine* (January 15, 1967) and subsequently translated into Polish, Russian, Czech, Hungarian, Bulgarian, and Rumanian by the USIS. Clare Franco and James Seawright generously helped me over various difficulties, and the epigraph comes from Arnold Schoenberg, *Ausgewahlte Briefe* (B. Schott's Söhme, 1958), as translated into English by Fred Grunfeld.

JOHN CAGE

Nearly all of his prose writings have been collected into two outsized, audaciously produced, and critically sporadic books, *Silence* (Wesleyan University, 1961; M.I.T. paperback, 1966) and *A Year from Monday* (Wesleyan University, 1967). A polemical portion of the last book, *Diary: How to Improve the World (You'll Only Make Matters Worse) Continued Part Three* (1967), appeared as a separate pamphlet (Something Else, 1967), and his anthology of contemporary musical manuscripts is *Notations* (Something Else, 1969). An earlier, more conventional critical work by Cage, coauthored with Kathleen Hoover, appeared as *Virgil Thomson: His Life and Music* (Yoseloff, 1959). For descriptive information about his various pieces and the cost of his scores, as well as a complete bibliography of articles about him to 1962 and an extended interview conducted by the composer Roger Reynolds, see the catalogue *John Cage* (1962), edited by Robert Dunn and issued by Henmar Press, which also publishes most of Cage's compositions; from here I also drew Dore Ashton's remark about Cage's calligraphy. George Kubler's statement is in his *The Shape of Time* (Yale University, 1962). Cage's comments on theater are in Richard Kostelanetz, *The Theatre of Mixed Means* (Dial, 1968), *Tulane Drama Review*, X/2 (Winter, 1965), and *The Arts: Planning for Change* (Associated Councils on the Arts, 1966). The edition of the *The I Ching*, or *Book of Changes* that Cage favors is Cary F. Baynes's rendition into English of the German translation of Richard Wilhelm (Bollingen Foundation, 1950). Critical writing on Cage tends to polarize, much to the detriment of considered discrimination. Typical of the blanket sneers is John Hollander's review of *Silence* in *Perspective of New Music*, I/2 (Spring, 1963), and an example of excess adulation is Peter Yates, "After Modern Music," *Location*, I/1 (Spring, 1963), as well as Yates's pages on Cage in his *Twentieth Century Music* (Pantheon, 1967). My own attempt, a more discriminating comprehensive criticism, is "John Cage: Some Random Remarks," *Denver Quarterly*, III/4 (Winter, 1969).

Regarding his influence on contemporary music, see Wilfrid Mellers, "From Noise to Silence," *Music in a New Found Land* (Knopf, 1965); for his impact on contemporary dance, see Jill Johnston, "Modern Dance," in Richard Kostelanetz, ed., *The New American Arts* (Horizon Press, 1965); on the new theater, see Michael Kirby, *Happenings* (Dutton, 1965), and Dick Higgins, *Postface* (Something Else, 1964): on the new art, see Allan Kaprow, *Assemblage, Environments, Happenings* (Abrams, 1966), Calvin Tomkins, *The Bride and the Bachelors* (Viking, 1965), and Barbara Rose, *American Art Since 1900* (Praeger, 1967).

The most comprehensive library of Cage's music is the three-record collection, *The 25-Year Retrospective Concert of the Music of John Cage*, privately produced by George Avakian and obtainable from him (285 Central Park West, New York, New York 10024). It contains Six Short Inventions for Seven Instruments (1934), Construction in Metal (1937), *Imaginary Landscape No. 1* (1939), *The Wonderful Widow of Eighteen Springs* (1942), *She Is Asleep* (1943), several Sonatas and Interludes for Prepared Piano (1946–8), *Williams Mix* (1952), Music for Carillon (1954), Concerta for Piano and Orchestra (1957–8), as well as a booklet of notes on the various pieces and a few reprints of Cage's scores and short essays. Other Cage compositions available on record include *Amores* for Prepared Piano and Percussion (1943), Time 58000; the complete Sonatas and Interludes for Prepared Piano, CRI 199; *Aria* (1958) with *Fontana Mix* (1958), Time 58003; Cartridge Music (1960), Time 58009; *Fontana Mix* for unaccompanied Magnetic Tape, Turnabout 34046; Variations II (1961), Columbia MS 7051; Variations IV (excerpts) (1963), Everest 6132. A polemical lecture in the form of an aural demonstration is *Indeterminacy* (1959), Folkways FT 3704. The recordings of works composed after 1952 are, one must remember, fixed renditions of pieces which are, by intention, indeterminate in performance and, therefore, lacking any final form.

The epigraph comes from Morris Dickstein, "For Art's Sake," *Partisan Review*, XXXIII/4 (Fall, 1966); Susanna Opper's assistance deserves my gratitude; and some of this material appeared, in considerably different form, in both *The New York Times Magazine* (January 15, 1967), and *Stereo Review* (May, 1969).

ELLIOTT CARTER

His three major recent pieces are available in the following recordings: Piano Concerto (1966), RCA LSC 3001; Double Concerto for Harpsichord and Piano with Two Chamber Orchestras (1961), Col MS 7191; and Second String Quartet (1959), RCA LM-2481. Of the several interpretations of the Piano Sonata (1945), the most satisfactory is Charles Rosen's, Epic BC 1250; and this performance is also available in England, back to back with the Double Concerto, EMI-ASD 601. The sole recording of the First String Quartet (1951) comes from the same Walden Quartet that premiered it, Col ML 5104, while Carter's early Suite from *Pocahontas* (1941) backs the American edition of Rosen's performance of the Piano Sonata. Other recorded Carter pieces include Sonata for Flute, Oboe, Cello and Harpsichord (1952), Col. MS 6176; Woodwind Quintet (1948), RCA LSC 6167; Eight Etudes and a Fantasy (1950), Con-Disc 429 & CRI 118; Sonata for Violincello and Piano (1950), Desto 6419; and Variations for Orchestra (1955), Lou 58–3.

There is no satisfactory critical introduction to Carter's work; but among the more useful essays are Richard Franko Goldman's several treatments in *Musical Quarterly* over the years, Wilfrid Mellers's chapter in *Music in a New Found Land* (Knopf, 1965), and miscellaneous reviews that Benjamin Boretz has published in the *Nation*. The jacket notes to the various albums, particularly those written by Michael Steinberg, Charles Rosen, and Carter himself, are usually perspicacious and informative. The Aaron Copland chronicles to which I refer are collected in *Copland on Music* (Doubleday, 1960). Among Carter's own more important ventures into print are "Expressionism and American Music," *Perspectives of New Music*, IV/1 (Fall–Winter, 1965); "Letter from Europe," *Perspectives of New Music*, I/2 (Spring, 1963); "A Further Step," in Gilbert Chase, ed., *The American Composer Speaks* (Louisiana State University, 1966); and "Shop Talk by an American Composer," in Paul Henry Lang, ed., *Problems of Modern Music* (Norton, 1962) and Elliott Schwartz and Barney Childs, eds., *Contemporary Composers on Contemporary Music* (Holt, Rinehart and Winston, 1967).

This profile originally appeared in *High Fidelity* (May, 1968), Philip Gossett kindly checked it for scholarly errors, and the epigraph comes from Harold Rosenberg, *The Tradition of the New* (Horizon, 1959).

RALPH ELLISON

Ellison's single novel and masterpiece is *Invisible Man* (Random House, 1952), which has been reissued in Signet (U.S.) and Penguin (England) paperback editions. One of the opening sections was published as "The Invisible Man" in *Horizon*, 93–4

(October, 1947), subsequently to appear in *The Magazine of the Year* (1948) and then, in much the same form, as the first chapter of the novel. Ellison has since put in print a long section previously dropped from the book's final version, "Out of the Hospital and Under the Bar," in Herbert Hill, ed., *Soon One Morning* (Knopf, 1963). Perhaps the best and most suggestive of the earliest stories—it was originally written as a section of a novel Ellison never completed—was "Flying Home," in Edwin Seaver, ed., *Cross-Section* (L. B. Fischer, 1944); and this was subsequently reprinted in Langston Hughes, ed., *The Best Short Stories by Negro Writers* (Little, Brown, 1967). Most of Ellison's fugitive essays of the past decade were collected in *Shadow and Act* (Random House, 1964), but an important piece that he neglected to include is "Society, Morality and the Novel," in Granville Hicks, ed., *The Living Novel* (Macmillan, 1957), while one that appeared afterward is "If the Twain Shall Meet," *Book Week* (November 8, 1964). A recent, otherwise uncollected interview with Ellison appeared as "A Very Stern Discipline," *Harper's*, CCXXXIV (March, 1967); and his testimony to Congress, August 30, 1966, was reprinted in *The New Leader*, XLIX/19 (September 26, 1966). Certain remarks were drawn from the unpublished transcript of a conversation I had with him for "New Release," BBC-Television (1965–6). Various sections from the novel-in-progress have appeared in print: "And Hickman Arrives," *Noble Savage*, 1 (Meridian, 1960); "The Roof, the Steeple and the People," *Quarterly Review of Literature*, X/3 (1960); "Juneteenth," *Quarterly Review of Literature*, XIII/3–4 (1965); and "It Always Breaks Out, *Partisan Review*, XXX (Spring, 1963). However, these selections hardly provide a comprehensive sense of the whole.

The most extensive and detailed discussions of *Invisible Man* appeared in Robert E. Bone, *The Negro Novel in America* (Yale University, 1958; revised edition, 1965); Marcus Klein, *After Alienation* (Meridian, 1964); Ihab H. Hassan, *Radical Innocence* (Princeton, 1961); Ellin Horowitz, "The Rebirth of the Artist," in Richard Kostelanetz, ed., *On Contemporary Literature* (Avon, 1964); and my own critical essay, "The Politics of Ellison's Booker: *Invisible Man* as Symbolic History," *Chicago Review*, XIX/2 (1967). Klein's essay is reprinted in Seymour L. Gross and John Edward Hardy, eds., *Images of the Negro in American*

Literature (University of Chicago, 1966). There is a lengthy profile-interview with Ellison in Robert Penn Warren's *Who Speaks for the Negro?* (Vintage, 1966), and three earlier interviews that Ellison gave are reprinted in *Shadow and Act*. Albert Murray's remarks on Ellison's fiction and criticism appear in "Something Different, Something More," in Herbert Hill, ed., *Anger and Beyond* (Harper & Row, 1965), and Stanley Edgar Hyman treats aspects of *Invisible Man* in "American Negro Literature and the Folk Tradition," *The Promised End* (World, 1963), and *Shadow and Act* in his "Ralph Ellison for Our Time," *Standards* (Horizon, 1966). The Irving Howe essay that inspired Ellison's outraged reply is "Black Boys and Native Sons," originally in *Dissent*, X/4 (Autumn, 1963) and since reprinted in *A World More Attractive* (Horizon, 1963). Ellison's relationship with Richard Wright is discussed, in bare outline and from Wright's point of view, in Constance Webb, *Richard Wright* (Putnam, 1968); and Harold Cruse's masterful study of the Negro American literary scene is *The Crisis of the Negro Intellectual* (Morrow, 1968).

This profile originally appeared in *Shenandoah* (Summer 1969); Albert Murray and Harris Dienstfrey both graciously read and criticized an earlier draft; and the epigraph is the opening line of Palinurus (Cyril Connolly), *The Unquiet Grave* (Harper, 1945).

ALLEN GINSBERG

His first book, *Howl and Other Poems* (City Lights, 1956), remains his most famous and most popular; here are most of the best and the best-known pieces. Later compilations include *Empty Mirror: Early Poems* (Totem/Corinth, 1961), *Kaddish and Other Poems* (City Lights, 1961), *Reality Sandwiches* (City Lights, 1963), *Planet News* (City Lights, 1968). *Jukebox All'Idrogeno* (Arnoldo Mondadori, 1965) contains an unusually comprehensive collection of translations, in addition to their English originals and a long introduction by the translator, Fernanda Pivano. Ginsberg's major recent poem, "Wichita Vortex Sutra," was issued as a thin pamphlet (Coyote Books, 1966), while other poems of the early sixties were included in a handsomely printed limited edition, *T. V. Baby Poems* (Grossman, 1968); and all the material in both these books subsequently appeared in *Planet News*. Ginsberg also collaborated with William Burroughs on *The Yage Letters* (City Lights, 1963), as well as contributed several revealing epistles to Timothy Leary, "In the Beginning, etc.," *Esquire*, LXX/1 (July, 1968), which was incorporated into Leary, *High Priest* (World, 1968). Ginsberg has published interviews, introductions, manifestos, prose pieces, and miscellaneous uncollected poems in many magazines, large and small, here and abroad. Extracts from his journals—two long poems, one short poem, one story story—are collected in *Airplane Dreams: Compositions from Journals* (House of Anansi, 1968), and perhaps the most extensive interview is Thomas Clark, "The Art of Poetry VIII: Allen Ginsberg," *Paris Review*, 37 (Spring, 1966). Ginsberg has long been intending to compile his more considered essays into a book; among the more important are "Turning On with LSD and Pot," *The Humanist*, XXVII/5–6 (Fall, 1967); the extract from his journal published in *The Second Coming*, I/2 (July, 1961); "The Great Marijuana Hoax," *Atlantic Monthly* (November, 1966), subsequently reprinted in *The Marijuana Papers* (Bobbs-Merrill, 1966); and "Notes for *Howl* and Other Poems," written for the record jacket of Fantasy 7006 (on which he reads the major poems written prior to 1960) and subsequently reprinted in Donald Allen, ed., *The New American Poetry* (Grove, 1960), which also contains a plentiful selection of poets associated with him during the fifties.

As Ginsberg's early work helped split the world of poetry into two warring camps, his own poems have provided the occasion for partisan critical polemic. Exemplifying the advocates is Kenneth Rexroth, "We Are All Strangers," *New Directions*, 16 (1967), and "Disengagement: The Art of the Beat Generation," *New World Writing*, 11 (1957), reprinted in Gene Feldman and Max Gartenberg, eds., *The Beat Generation and the Angry Young Men* (Citadel, 1958); typical of the detractors is James Dickey, "Allen Ginsberg," *From Babel to Byzantium* (Farrar, Straus, 1968). There has been little analysis in depth of Ginsberg's poetic contribution—at times, the poet himself can be the most illuminating critic of his own work; but among the more extended and discriminating commentaries are M. L. Rosenthal, "Allen Ginsberg," *The New Poets* (Oxford, 1967); Stephen Stepanchev, "Popular Poetry," *American Poetry Since 1945* (Harper & Row, 1965); Paul Carroll, "Allen Ginsberg," *The Poem and Its Skin* (Follett, 1968); and some of the criticism collected in Thomas Parkinson, ed., *A Casebook on the Beat* (Crowell, 1961). Leslie A. Fiedler's remarks come from *Waiting for the End* (Stein & Day, 1964); and the interpretation attributed to Diana Trilling from her monumentally Kinbotean essay, "The Other Night at Columbia," *Partisan Review*, XXVI/2 (Spring, 1959), reprinted in *Claremont Essays* (Harcourt, Brace, 1964). For Ginsberg's place in the larger scene of recent poetry, see Jonathan Cott, "Poetry," in Richard Kostelanetz, ed., *The New American Arts* (Horizon, 1965); Robert Creeley, "Introduction," in Donald Allen and Robert Creeley, eds., *The New Writing in the U.S.A.* (Penguin, 1967); and my own introduction to the anthology of American contemporaries, *Possibilities of Poetry* (Delta, 1969). A fictionalized portrait of young Ginsberg (named "Stofsky") appears in John Clellon Holmes, *Go* (A. A. Wyn, 1952), and Holmes perceptively reconsiders Ginsberg in *Nothing More to Declare* (Dutton, 1967). On Ginsberg's socio-poetic impact, see Elias Wilentz and Fred McDarrah, *The Beat Scene* (Corinth, 1960), and Lawrence Lipton, *The Holy Barbarians* (Messner, 1959). A suggestively revealing photograph of the poet as a beardless young man appears, along with "Howl" and Kenneth Rexroth's prophetic "San Francisco Letter," in *Evergreen Review*, I/2 (1957), while Ginsberg's relations with Hell's Angels are reported in Tom Wolfe, *The Electric Kool-Aid Acid Test* (Farrar, Straus, 1968). On Ginsberg and his father, see Don McNeil, "The Ginsbergs on Stage," *The Village Voice* (January 25, 1968). Among other useful profiles in print are Barry Farrell, "The Guru Comes to Kansas," *Life* (May 26, 1966), and Jane Kramer, "Pater Familias," *The New Yorker* (August 10, 17, 1968), and subsequently expanded as *Allen Ginsberg* (Random House, 1969). Ginsberg also starred in the films *Pull My Daisy* (1959), made by Robert Frank and Alfred Leslie, and *Wholly Communion* (1966), directed by Peter Whitehead; texts of both these movies have been published by Grove Press. The quotation attributed to Irving Layton comes from the foreword to his *Collected Poems* (McClelland and Stewart, 1965).

The profile originally appeared, in considerably different form, in *The New York Times Magazine* (July 11, 1965); Eric Mottram's advice deserves my gratitude; and the epigraph comes from Walt Whitman, *Leaves of Grass* (1857).

PAUL GOODMAN

Perhaps no other important writer of his generation has been as productive as Goodman; none, surely, has dabbled in as many genres and subjects. His output has been uneven and, to a moderate degree, repetitive; for his life has been largely a history of committed engagements in writing. In general, his social criticism has earned more admirers than his imaginative works, and perhaps the most famous and influential book has been *Growing Up Absurd* (Random House, 1960). The key work in his philosophy of anarchist decentralization is *People or Personnel* (Random House, 1965), and an itemized outline of his ideas here appears as "Notes on Decentralization" in Richard Kostelanetz, ed., *Beyond Left and Right* (Morrow, 1968). Other books of social criticism include *Like a Conquered Province* (Random House, 1967); *Drawing the Line* (Random House, 1962), a booklet collecting essays mostly of the forties; and two other compilations of fugitive pieces, *Utopian Essays and Practical Proposals* (Random House, 1962) and *The Society I Live In Is Mine* (Horizon, 1962). The critiques of American education are *The Community of Scholars* (Random House, 1962) and *Compulsory Mis-Education* (Horizon, 1964), both of which have since been collected into a single paperback (Vintage, 1966). The classic in city planning that Goodman coauthored with his brother Percival is *Communitas* (University of Chicago, 1948; revised edition, Vintage, 1960); and the foray into psychology, coauthored with F. S. Perls and Ralph Hefferline, is *Gestalt Therapy* (Julian, 1951; Delta, 1965). The books of literary criticism are *Art and Social Nature* (Vinco, 1946), *Kafka's Prayer* (Vanguard, 1947), and Goodman's doctoral essay, *The Structure of Literature* (University of Chicago, 1954; paperback, 1962). The quotation about the dilemma in affluent societies comes from "Leisure and Work," *Esquire* (July, 1959), reprinted in Morris Philipson, ed., *Automation* (Vintage, 1962).

Goodman has been publishing poems, fiction, and plays since the early thirties; and most, though not all, of it has been collected into books. The poems appear in his section of *Five Young American Poets* (New Directions, 1941), *The Lordly Hudson* (Macmillan, 1962), and *Hawkweed* (Vintage, 1967). Three of his plays—*Jonah* (1945), *The Young Disciple* (1955), and *Faustina* (1961)—were subsequently collected, in their definitive revisions, in *Three Plays* (Random House, 1965); and earlier shorter pieces appeared as *Stop-Light and Other Noh Plays* (5 × 8 Press, 1952). Most of his short stories published in *The Facts of Life* (Vanguard, 1945), *The Break-Up of Our Camp* (New Directions,

1949), and *Our Visit to Niagara* (Horizon, 1960), were subsequently collected, along with other pieces, in *Adam and His Works* (Random House, 1968). His longer fictions include the novels *Parents' Day* (5 × 8 Press, 1951), *Making Do* (Macmillan, 1963), and the tetralogy, *The Empire City* (Bobbs-Merrill, 1959; Macmillan, 1964), which collects *The Grand Piano* (Colt Press, 1942), *The State of Nature* (Vanguard, 1945), *The Dead of Spring* (Libertarian Press, 1950), the *The Holy Terror* (1959). Discussions of his homosexuality run through the memoir entitled *Five Years* (Brussel & Brussel, 1966).

For his position in anarchist thought, see Leonard I. Krimmerman and Lewis Perry, eds., *Patterns of Anarchy* (Doubleday Anchor, 1966), and Goodman's own anthology, *Seeds of Liberation* (Braziller, 1965), as well as his essay, "The Black Flag of Anarchism," *The New York Times Magazine* (July 14, 1968). The Delmore Schwartz story portraying Goodman is "The World Is a Wedding," collected in a book of that title (New Directions, 1948), and the remark about Goodman's reputation at Townshend Harris High School comes from my own father, Boris Kostelanetz, who was also in the class of 1927. For critical discussion of Goodman's social thought, see Stuart Hampshire, "A Plea for Materialism," *The New Statesman* (February 8, 1963), and Harold Rosenberg's remarkable preface to Goodman's *Five Years*. The quotation attributed to Rosenberg comes from his review, "A Hypothetical Tale," *Partisan Review*, XXVI/3 (Summer, 1959), and Harvey Shapiro's was in *The New York Times Book Review* (September 1, 1963).

The epigraph comes from R. Buckminster Fuller's *Education Automation* (Southern Illinois, 1962), and this profile originally appeared, in a considerably different version, as "The Prevalence of Paul Goodman" in *The New York Times Magazine* (April 3, 1966).

GLENN GOULD

From the beginning of his career, Gould has recorded exclusively for Columbia Records, and perhaps the most exemplary of his many performances is the recording of Johann Sebastian Bach's Partita No. 2 (MS 6141), also included in *Glenn Gould Plays Bach* (D3S 754), which contains as well the other Partitas and the Two-Part and Three-Part Inventions. The initial masterwork was his rendition of the *Goldberg* Variations (ML 5060), recently reissued in rechanneled stereo (MS 7096); and of his performances of the *Well-Tempered Clavier*, Columbia has so far released only Book One (D3S 733) and the first portion of Book Two (MS 7099). Gould's dexterity at the organ is apparent in his interpretation of the first half of *The Art of the Fugue* (MS 6338). He has also recorded the first five Mozart Piano Sonatas (MS 7097) and Franz Liszt's transcription of Beethoven's Fifth Symphony (MS 7095), as well as Beethoven Piano Concerti with various conductors: No. 1, with Vladimir Goldschmann (MS 6017); No. 2, with Leonard Bernstein (ML 5211); No. 3, with Bernstein (MS 6096); No. 4, with Bernstein (MS 6262); No. 5 ("Emperor"), with Leopold Stokowski (MS 6888). The complete Schoenberg piano music has been issued alone (MS 7098), as well as part of Vol. IV of the complete Schoenberg (M2S 736); and Gould also contributed to the ensemble performances in Vol. VII (M2S 767). Among the important recordings currently out of print is a spectacular performance of Mozart's Fantasy K. 394 (ML 5274). Of his own compositions, only the String Quartet (1953–4) has been recorded, on a private issue now in the collection of certain libraries and radio stations.

Gould's major essays on the new technologies of musical reproduction are "The Prospects of Recording," *High Fidelity*, XVI/4 (April, 1966); and "An Arugment for Music in the Electronic Age," *Varsity Graduate* (University of Toronto), XI/3 (December, 1964). His extensive lecture on "Arnold Schoenberg: A Perspective" was published solo as a University of Cincinnati Occasional Paper No. 3 (1964); and some of his best prose appears on the dust jackets of his own recordings. Other major essays are "Portrait of Menuhin," *High Fidelity/Musical America*, XVI/13 (December 15, 1967), and "The Search for 'Pet' Clark," *High Fidelity*, XVI/11 (November, 1967), while the quotation about music educators comes from Dr. Herbert von Hochmeister, "L'esprit de Jeunesse, et de corps, et d'art," *High Fidelity*, XV/12 (December, 1965). There also exists a disc of Gould in conversation with the Columbia recording executive John McClure, *Glenn Gould: Concert Dropout* (Col. BS 15), various unpublished scripts for radio and television, and both aural and video tapes of these programs. An earlier profile of Gould by Joseph Roddy, who emphasized his hypochondria and other eccentricities, appeared in *The New Yorker* (May 14, 1960), and the passage attributed to Robert P. Morgan came from a review in *High Fidelity*, XVIII/7 (July, 1968).

The epigraph comes from William Faulkner's *Paris Review* interview, reprinted in Malcolm Cowley, ed., *Writers at Work* (Viking, 1958). Christopher Sager kindly offered some musical advice; and the profile originally appeared in *Esquire* (November, 1967).

RICHARD HOFSTADTER

The keystones in the Hofstadter canon are *The American Political Tradition* (Knopf, 1948), *The Age of Reform* (Knopf, 1955), *Anti-Intellectualism in America Life* (Knopf, 1963), *The Paranoid Style in American Politics* (Knopf, 1965), and *The Progressive Historians: Turner, Beard, Parrington* (Knopf, 1968). The doctorate he rewrote into his first book is *Social Darwinism in American Thought* (University of Pennsylvania, 1944; revised edition, Beacon Press, 1955); and the coauthored forays into academic history are, with DeWitt Hardy, *The Development and Scope of Higher Education in the United States* (Columbia University, 1952), and, with Walter P. Metzger, *The Development of Academic Freedom in the United States* (Columbia University, 1955). Hofstadter's contribution to the latter volume has since been released as a solo paperback, *Academic Freedom in the Age of the College* (Columbia University, 1961). The anthologies he compiled are two volumes entitled *Great Issues in American History* (Knopf, 1958), two volumes coedited with Wilson Smith and entitled *American Higher Education: A Documentary History* (University of Chicago, 1961), and *The Progressive Movement, 1900–1915* (Prentice-Hall, 1963). His important studies of the fifties reactionaries is "The Pseudo-Conservative Revolt," in Daniel Bell, ed., *The New American Right* (Criterion, 1955), revised and reprinted as *The Radical Right* (Doubleday, 1963). The essays on Goldwaterism are "Goldwater and His Party" *Encounter*, XXIII/4 (October, 1964), and "A Long View: Goldwater in History," *New York Review of Books* (October 9, 1964); the article on historical precedents for American disengagement is "Uncle Sam Has Cried 'Uncle!' Before," *The New York Times Magazine* (May 19, 1968). The popular textbooks are Hofstadter, William Miller, and Daniel Aaron, *The United*

States (Prentice-Hall, 1957; second edition, 1967) and Hofstadter, Miller, and Aaron's two volumes, *The American Republic* (Prentice-Hall, 1959).

Hofstadter discusses his own scholarly purposes in "History and the Social Sciences," included in Fritz Stern, ed., *Varieties of History* (Meridian, 1956); in an "Interview," published in *History 3* (Meridian, 1960); and in three lectures delivered over the University of Texas television station, Austin, Texas, in 1963. Transcripts were never taken of these tapes, although videotapes are available from the producer. The interpretations of American history attributed to Louis Hartz and Daniel Boorstin come, respectively, from the former's *The Liberal Tradition in America* (Harcourt, Brace, 1955) and the latter's *The Americans: The Colonial Experience* (Random House, 1958) and *The Americans: The National Experience* (Random House, 1965). A useful survey of recent American historical scholarship is John Higham, ed., *The Reconstruction of American History* (Harper & Row, 1962); and Hofstadter's place in the larger perspective of American historiography is treated in Higham, et al., *History* (Prentice-Hall, 1965) and Andrew S. Berky and James P. Shenton, eds., *The Historians' History of the United States* (Putnam, 1966). For criticism of dimensions of Hofstadter's work, see C. Vann Woodward's *The Burden of Southern History* (Vintage, 1961) and the numerous attacks that Norman Pollack has published in the professional journals over the years.

The epigraph comes from Brian O'Doherty's *Object and Idea* (Simon and Schuster, 1967); David Burner and Otis Graham both gave useful advice; and this profile appears here for the first time.

HERMAN KAHN

His first major book, *On Thermonuclear War* (Princeton University, 1960; second edition, 1961), is the definitive version of the three-day lectures Kahn gave in the late fifties; and subsequent works that pursue his interest in strategy include *Thinking About the Unthinkable* (Horizon, 1962), which is a collection of essays, and *On Escalation* (Praeger, 1965). The RAND publication mentioned in the text, "Report on a Study of Non-Military Defense," is classified as R-322-RC, and his observations on the Vietnamese situation are developed in Herman Kahn, et al., *Can*

We Win in Vietnam? (Praeger, 1968), and Herman Kahn, "If Negotiations Fail," *Foreign Affairs,* XXXXVI/4 (July, 1968). His most recent thoughts on thermonuclear problems are his essays "Nuclear War," in the *International Encyclopedia in the Social Sciences* (Macmillan, 1967), and "Nuclear Proliferation and the Rules of Retaliation," originally published in the *Yale Law Journal* (November, 1966) and subsequently reprinted in Richard Kostelanetz, ed., *Beyond Left and Right* (Morrow, 1968). The first of Kahn's extensive forays into futurology is *The Year 2000: A Framework for Speculation* (Macmillan, 1967), coauthored with Anthony J. Wiener; and this book grew out of several earlier papers originally published by the Hudson Institute, particularly Kahn's "On Alternative World Futures," which was subsequently reprinted in Morton A. Kaplan, ed., *New Approaches to International Relations* (St. Martin's, 1968), in addition to drawing upon the material Kahn and Wiener contributed to Daniel Bell, ed., *Toward the Year 2000: Work in Progress* (Houghton Mifflin, 1968).

The quotation by James R. Newman comes from his review in *Scientific American,* CCIV/3 (March, 1961), which he later reprinted in *The Rule of Folly* (Simon and Schuster, 1962). The critical ideas attributed to Philip Green are in *Deadly Logic* (Schocken, 1968); those by Erich Fromm in *May Man Prevail?* (Doubleday, 1961) and his essay "The Case Against Shelters," written with Michael Maccoby, was published in Melman, ed., *No Place to Hide* (Grove, 1962), which also contains Kahn's "The Case for Shelters." A more extended and hysterical, though less substantial, criticism is Anatol Rapoport, *Strategy and Conscience* (Harper & Row, 1964), while an appreciation from the peacenik left is among the essays in H. Stuart Hughes, *An Approach to Peace* (Atheneum, 1962). Frances FitzGerald's remark comes from her "Metaphors and Scenarios," *New York Magazine* (June, 1965), a Kahn quotation from William A. McWhirter's report, *Life* (Dec. 5, 1968), and an earlier profile of Kahn and the Hudson Institute is in Arthur Herzog, *The War-Peace Establishment* (Harper & Row, 1965). Useful essays in intellectual history are Maj. John W. Chapman, "American Strategic Thinking," *Air University Review,* XVIII/2 (January–February, 1967), and Raymond Aron, *The Great Debate* (Doubleday, 1965). For another kind of intellectual background to

Kahn's contribution, see Robert Gilpin, *American Scientists and Nuclear Weapons Policy* (Princeton University, 1965); and for comparisons within the intellectual trade of strategic thinking, see Henry Kissinger, *Nuclear Weapons and Foreign Policy* (Harper & Bros., 1957); Thomas Schelling, *The Strategy of Conflict* (Harvard University, 1960); and Bernard Brodie, *Strategy in the Missile Age* (Princeton University, 1959).

The epigraph comes from Arthur L. Samuel, "Consequences of Automation—A Refutation," *Science* (September 16, 1960), reprinted in Morris Philipson, ed., *Automation: Implications for the Future* (Vintage, 1962). The help of Donald Cohen and Anthony J. Wiener was indispensable, and this profile appeared, in considerably abridged form, in *The New York Times Magazine* (December 1, 1968).

MARSHALL McLUHAN

He published his first essay in 1935, and since then his pieces have appeared in scores of magazines, both here and abroad. In these shorter works are many of the fertile ideas that were later expanded into his major books, all of which got into print several years after he first wrote them. McLuhan has long been promising to collect his fugitive work; but until then, let me recommend such concise expositions as "American Advertising," *Horizon*, 93–4 (October, 1947), and "Sight, Sound and Fury," *Commonweal*, LX (1954), both of which are reprinted in Bernard Rosenberg and David Manning White, eds., *Mass Culture* (Free Press, 1957); "The Psychopathology of *Time* and *Life*," *Neurotica*, 5 (1949), reprinted in *The Compleat Neurotica* (Hacker Art Books, 1963); "The Electronic Revolution in North America," *International Literary Annual*, 1 (John Calder, 1958); "The Agenbite of Outwit," *Location*, I/1 (Spring, 1963); "The Relation of Environment to Anti-Environment," *University of Windsor Review*, XI/1 (Autumn, 1966), reprinted in Bernard Bergonzi, ed., *Innovations* (Macmillan [London], 1968). The three major McLuhan books are *The Mechanical Bride* (Vanguard, 1951; Beacon, 1967), *The Gutenberg Galaxy* (University of Toronto, 1962), and *Understanding Media* (McGraw-Hill, 1964). His output since 1964 tends to be slighter and glibber—*The Medium Is the Massage* (Bantam, 1967) and *War and Peace in the Global Village* (Bantam, 1968), both of which are illuminated volumes composed in collaboration with Quentin Fiore; and *Through the Vanishing Point* (Harper & Row, 1968), coauthored with Harley Parker. *Counterblast,* published privately and anonymously in 1954, was reissued, in an expanded form, by McClelland and Stewart in 1969. The magazine McLuhan cofounded was *Explorations,* 1–8 (Toronto, 1953–9); and not only did he coedit, with Edmund S. Carpenter, a selection from its pages, *Explorations in Communication* (Beacon, 1960), but the entire eighth issue, which contains twenty-four short essays by McLuhan, has also been reprinted as a book, *Verbi-Voco-Visual Explorations* (Something Else, 1967). McLuhan's remarks on Sigfried Giedion's "anonymous history," as well as Father Walter Ong's on McLuhan, come from Walter J. Ong, S.J., ed., *Knowledge and the Future of Man* (Holt, Rinehart and Winston, 1968). The famous essay on Gerard Manley Hopkins appeared in "The Kenyon Critics," *Gerard Manley Hopkins* (New Directions, 1945), and the Tennyson criticism introduces *Tennyson: Selected Poetry* (Rinehart, 1956). McLuhan reads passages from his work on *The Medium Is the Massage* (Col. CL 2701), which obscures more than it illuminates; and in 1968, the oracle embarked upon issuing his own monthly newsletter, *The McLuhan DEW-Line.*

The major essays on McLuhan's work were collected in Raymond Rosenthal, ed., *McLuhan Pro and Con* (Funk & Wagnalls, 1968); Harry H. Crosby and George R. Bond, eds., *The McLuhan Explosion* (American Book, 1968), and G. E. Stearn, ed., *McLuhan: Hot and Cool* (Dial, 1967). The last volume also collects several of McLuhan's better fugitive essays and contains the editor's extended interview with him. My own lengthy critical discussion of his work is "Marshall McLuhan," *Commonweal,* LXXV/15 (January 20, 1967), which was subsequently reprinted in Rosenthal and Crosby-Bond, as well as Bergonzi's *Innovations;* and I reviewed *Massage* as "McLuhan's Own Trot," *The Reporter,* XXXVI/8 (April 20, 1967). The remarks attributed to Gerald Taaffe appear in "McLuhan—Electronic Medievalist," *Parallel,* I/3 (July–August, 1966). Other books emerging from McLuhan's pool of conversations and concern include Edmund S. Carpenter, *Eskimo* (University of Toronto, 1960), and Dorothy Lee, *Freedom and Culture* (Prentice-Hall, 1959). Harley Parker presents his ideas on museum display in the journal of the Royal Ontario Museum, *Meeting Place,* I/1 (Summer, 1964); and the impact of his paleontology exhibition was reported by John M. Lee on page 32 of *The New York Times* (February 24, 1967). Glenn Gould's McLuhanisms are discussed elsewhere in this book; and USCO's indebtedness is outlined in Richard Kostelanetz, *The Theatre of Mixed Means* (Dial, 1968).

This profile, much of which originally appeared in *The New York Times Magazine* (January 29, 1968), has been extensively expanded and revised, incorporating material subsequently contributed to *Dialogue*, I (1968), and the *Book of the Year* (Encyclopaedia Britannica, 1968). Ralph Baldwin and Harris Dienstfrey both helped me with this essay; and the epigraph comes from Herman Kahn, *On Thermonuclear War* (Princeton University, 1960).

BERNARD MULLER-THYM

As a predominantly verbal intellectual, Bernard Muller-Thym has committed less to print than any other figure studied in this book. Of the essays that have appeared, among the more important are "The Real Meaning of Automation," *Management Review* (June, 1963), and "The Management of Business," *The Environment of Change* (privately published by Time, Inc., 1964), both of which were reprinted in Richard Kostelanetz, ed., *Beyond Left and Right* (Morrow, 1968). Other major Muller-Thym essays are "Restructuring the Supervisory Job," *Personnel* (March, 1954); "Cultural and Social Changes," in Hoke Simpson, ed., *The Changing American Population* (New York: Institute of Life Insurance, 1962); "New Directions for Organizational Practice," in *Ten Years Progress in Management, 1950–1960* (New York: American Society of Mechanical Engineers, 1961). A more complete record of Muller-Thym's thinking exists in tapes and transcripts in various private and corporate hands.

Evidences of his earlier career as a medieval scholar include *The Establishment of the University of Being in Meister Eckhart of Ockham* (Sheed & Ward, 1939), and Étienne Gilson's preface to that volume testifies to Muller-Thym's prowess as a critic. There are also his articles "The Common Sense, Perfection of the Order of Pure Sensibility," *The Thomist*, II/2 (July, 1940), "Recapturing Natural Wisdom," *The Modern Schoolman*, XVIII/4 (May, 1941), and "Dr. Adler's *Problem of Species*," *The Modern Schoolman*, XVIII/1 (November, 1940). There is in print no previous record of Muller-Thym's achievement, as well as practically no citations of his ideas in the literature of management. The quotation attributed to Father Ong comes from his "Knowledge in Time," in Walter J. Ong, S.J., ed., *Knowledge and the Future of Man* (Holt, Rinehart and Winston, 1968).

The epigraph to this profile comes from Marshall McLuhan, *Explorations*, 8 (1958), reprinted in *Verbi-Voco-Visual Explorations* (Something Else, 1967); and the help of both Ralph Baldwin and Colin Park deserves my gratitude. This profile appears here for the first time.

REINHOLD NIEBUHR

The oldest of the figures discussed in this book, he is also the most prolific—dozens of books and hundreds of essays and articles. The most important political works are *Moral Man and Immoral Society* (Scribner, 1932), *The Children of Light and the Children of Darkness* (Scribner, 1944), *The Irony of American History* (Scribner, 1953), *Pious and Secular America* (Scribner, 1958), and *The Structure of Nations and Empires* (Scribner, 1959). Innumerable statements on politics are woven into an expository anthology entitled *Reinhold Niebuhr on Politics* (Scribner, 1960), edited by Harry R. Davis and Robert C. Good. Niebuhr's crucial contributions to theological discussion are *An Interpretation of Christian Ethics* (Harper, 1935), *Beyond Tragedy* (Scribner, 1937), the two-volume *The Nature and Destiny of Man: A Christian Interpretation* (Scribner, 1941, 1943), and *The Self and the Dramas of History* (Scribner, 1955). *Leaves from the Notebook of a Tamed Cynic* (Willett, Clark & Colby, 1929; reprinted, Meridian, 1957) collects passages from his personal journal, and a memoir has been deposited with the Columbia University Oral History Project. Two useful anthologies of shorter pieces, both edited by D. B. Robertson, are *Love and Justice* (Westminster, 1957; Meridian, 1967) and *Essays in Applied Christianity* (Meridian, 1959); another collection, edited by Ronald H. Stone, is *Faith and Politics* (Braziller, 1968); and Professor Robertson compiled *Reinhold Niebuhr's Works: A Bibliography* (Berea College Press, 1954), which, as a professor at Syracuse University, he continues to keep up to date. Certain statements of recent vintage were drawn from interviews by John Cogley in *McCall's* (February, 1966) and Patrick Granfield,

O.S.B., in *Commonweal* (December 16, 1966). For recent views on the Vietnam conflict, see Niebuhr's conversation with Hans Morgenthau, "The Ethics of War and Peace in the Nuclear Age," *War-Peace Report*, VII/2 (February, 1967), and Niebuhr, "Fighting an Intractable Dwarf," *The New Leader*, LI/15 (August 5, 1968).

Of the several works entirely on Niebuhr's ideas, Nathan A. Scott's pamphlet *Reinhold Niebuhr* (University of Minnesota, 1963) is more useful than Gordon Harland, *The Thought of Reinhold Niebuhr* (Oxford, 1960), or Edward J. Carnell, *The Theology of Reinhold Niebuhr* (Eerdmans, 1951). June Bingham's *Courage to Change* (Scribner, 1961) is a factually invaluable but ineptly organized biography. For laudatory discussions of Niebuhr by Paul Tillich, John C. Bennett, and Morgenthau, see Harold R. Landon, ed., *Reinhold Niebuhr* (Seabury, 1962), while *Reinhold Niebuhr: His Religious, Social and Political Thought* (Macmillan, 1956) contains numerous fine essays by Arthur Schlesinger, Kenneth Thompson, Paul Ramsay, Emil Brunner, and many others, as well as their subject's own autobiographical memoir, which is frequently quoted. For background in intellectual history, see Donald M. Meyer, *The Protestant Search for Political Realism* (University of California, 1960), and *The Positive Thinkers* (Doubleday, 1965); Ralph Henry Gabriel, "The Social Gospel and the Salvation of Society," *The Course of American Democratic Thought* (Ronald, 1956); Arthur M. Schlesinger, Jr., *The Vital Center* (Houghton Mifflin, 1949) and *The Politics of Hope* (Houghton Mifflin, 1962); regarding Niebuhr's criticisms of Billy Graham, see William G. McLoughlin, *Modern Revivalism* (Ronald, 1959). More critical scrutinies of Niebuhr's thought and activity are incorporated into Christopher Lasch, *The New Radicalism in America* (Knopf 1953), Charles Frankel, *The Case for Modern Man* (Harper & Bros., 1954), and Morton White, *Social Thought in America* (Beacon, 1957); a classic criticism from a contemporary still loyal to the Social Gospel tradition is A. J. Muste, "Theology of Despair," in Nat Hentoff, ed., *The Essays of A. J. Muste* (Bobbs-Merrill, 1967). The famous *Time* cover story appeared in the 25th Anniversary issue (March 9, 1948).

This profile, originally written for Niebuhr's seventy-fifth birthday, did not appear in the magazine that commissioned it; so it is published here for the first time. The cooperation of Ursula

Niebuhr, Elisabeth Sifton, and William G. McLoughlin deserves my gratitude; and the epigraph comes from Arthur M. Schlesinger, Jr., "The Intellectual vs. Politics," in Marquis Childs and James Reston, eds., *Walter Lippmann and His Times* (Harcourt, Brace, 1959).

JOHN R. PIERCE

He has been a prolific contributor of articles to both scientific and more popular journals, and some of the best of these, as well as an important autobiographical memoir, are collected in *Science, Art and Communication* (Clarkson Potter, 1968). Among the more important fugitive essays not collected here are "Communications Technology and the Future," in Frank E. Manuel, ed., *Utopias and Utopian Thought* (Beacon, 1967), "Communications," *Science Journal* (October, 1967). "The Transmission of Computer Data," in Scientific American, ed., *Information* (W. H. Freeman, 1966), "What Computers Should Be Doing," in Martin Greenberger, ed., *Computers and the World of the Future* (M.I.T., 1962), and "Computers, Communication and Control," in John R. Whinnery, ed., *The World of Engineering* (McGraw-Hill, 1965). Pierce discusses preparations for Echo in "Systems Research and Management," in Fremont E. Kast and James E. Rosenzweig, eds., *Science, Technology and Management* (McGraw-Hill, 1963), and an early appraisal of the art of communications satellites is his essay on "Satellite Relays," in Carl F. J. Overhage, ed., *The Age of Electronics* (McGraw-Hill, 1962).

Pierce's two major professional treatises are *Theory and Design of Electron Beams* (Van Nostrand, 1949: second edition, 1954) and *Traveling-Wave Tubes* (Van Nostrand, 1950). His popular introductory text was *Electrons, Waves and Messages* (Doubleday, 1956), which has since been superseded by three paperback volumes: *Electrons and Waves* (Doubleday, 1954), *Quantum Electronics* (Doubleday, 1966), and *Waves and Messages* (Doubleday, 1967). In collaboration with Edward E. David, Jr., a colleague at Bell Labs, Pierce wrote *Man's World of Sound* (Doubleday, 1958); and with Dr. David, as well as Willem A. van Bergeijk, he did *Waves and the Ear* (Doubleday, 1960). Pierce's concise and suggestive study of information theory is *Symbols, Signals and Noise* (Harper & Row, 1961), which in turn draws upon the path-breaking book coauthored by his Bell colleague, Claude E. Shannon, *The Mathematical Theory of Communication* (University of Illinois, 1949). The launching of Echo is dramatically rendered in Calvin Tomkins, "Woomera Has It," *The New Yorker* (September 21, 1963), and a useful and unbiased history of the several stages in communications satellite development is Donald R. MacQuivey, "Joint Venture Approach to Practical Space Utilization," in Lawrence L. Kavanau, ed., *Practical Space Applications* (American Astronautical Society, 1967). Regarding Edison's social invention, see Matthew Josephson, *Edison* (McGraw-Hill, 1959).

Some of Pierce's early music for computer is available on "Music from Mathematics" (Decca DL 79103), while the poem inspired by Arthur Waley's translations was "Notes on a T'ang Poet," *Coronet*, II (June, 1937). The poems quoted here were drawn from a later batch which appeared in the IRE Student *Quarterly*, IV (December, 1957). Early in 1968, two of Pierce's paintings were hanging in the Mathematics Commons Room of Bell Laboratories, Murray Hill, New Jersey. He has yet to collect his science fiction into a book; but some of his better stories appear in such anthologies as Groff Conklin, ed., *Great Science Fiction by Scientists* (Collier, 1962), and J. W. Campbell, Jr., ed., *The Astounding Science Fiction Anthology* (Berkeley, 1964).

The epigraph comes from Sir Robert Watson-Watt, "Technology in the Modern World," in Carl F. Stover, ed., *The Technological Order* (Wayne State University, 1963). Donald Cohen generously provided background knowledge and checked the text, and this profile appears here for the first time.

ROBERT RAUSCHENBERG

The most useful guide to his work, even though it is slightly dated and most of the reproductions are in black and white, is Alan Solomon's' catalogue, *Robert Rauschenberg* (New York: The Jewish Museum, 1964), which also contains the most extensive of Solomon's several essays on the artist's work. Other gatherings of first-rate reproductions are in the catalogues that various dealers and museums have issued for Rauschenberg's one-man shows, as well as miscellaneous issues of *Time*, *Life*, and the art journals. Photographs of the artist at work fill one section of Ugo Mulas and Alan Solomon, *New York: The New Art Scene* (Holt, Rinehart and Winston, 1967), and the Dante drawings, some of which are reprinted in *Life* (December 17, 1965), are collected in the extravagantly priced *Illustrations for "Dante's Inferno" by Robert Rauschenberg* (Abrams, 1963). The English critic Andrew Forge is currently completing a heavily illustrated monograph on Rauschenberg, who also designed the book, that Abrams promises to publish in 1969 or 1970; portions of Forge's text have appeared in various magazines, as well as the catalogue to the Rauschenberg retrospective at the Stedelijk Museum Amsterdam (February 23–April 7, 1968), which also contains very fine reproductions and a thorough chronology, mostly in Dutch, alas, of the artist's activities.

The quotations attributed to interviews are taken primarily from Richard Kostelanetz, "A Conversation with Robert Rauschenberg," *Partisan Review*, XXXV/1 (Winter, 1968); another, earlier interview is Dorothy Gess Seckler, "The Artist Speaks: Robert Rauschenberg," *Art in America*, LIV (Mary–June, 1966). Rauschenberg's most-quoted aphorisms come largely from his half-page statement included in Dorothy C. Miller, ed., *Sixteen Americans* (Museum of Modern Art, 1959), subsequently reprinted in Barbara Rose, ed., *Readings in American Art Since 1900* (Praeger, 1968). An early foray at art criticism is B. H. Friedman, "Robert Rauschenberg," in David Meyers, ed., *School of New York: Some Younger Artists* (Grove, 1959); while John Cage's suggestive essay is "On Robert Rauschenberg, Artist, and His Work," *Silence* (Wesleyan University, 1961). For Rauschenberg's place in the larger history of recent art, see William C. Seitz, *The Art of Assemblage* (Museum of Modern Art, 1961); Henry Geldzahler, *American Painting in the Twentieth Century* (New York Graphic Society, 1965); Lucy R. Lippard, et al., *Pop Art* (Praeger, 1967); Allan Kaprow, "Experimental Art," *Art News*, LXV/1 (March, 1966) and *Assemblage, Envornments & Happenings* (Abrams, 1966); and two anthologies edited by Gregory Battcock, *The* Richard Kostelanetz. *The Theatre of Mixed Means* (Dial, 1968), Most severe, yet less than persuasive, remarks fill the essays and reviews that Hilton Kramer has published in various magazines over the years. Regarding Rauschenberg's theater pieces, see Richard Kostelanetz, *The Theatre of Mixed Means* (Dial, 1968), where the chapter on his work incorporates but some of the material in the *Partisan Review* conversation, in addition to Jill Johnston, "Three Theatre Events," *Village Voice* (December 23, 1965), Brian O'Doherty, "The Armory Show," *Object and Idea* (Simon and Schuster, 1967), and Billy Klüver, et al., "Nine

Evenings of Theatre and Engineering," *Artforum*, V/6 (February, 1967). Harris Dienstfrey's comments are drawn from an unpublished essay on Pop Art; E. H. Gombrich's from "Visual Discovery Through Art," *Arts*, XL/1 (November, 1965); Dean Swanson's from *Robert Rauschenberg: Paintings 1953–1964* (Walker Art Center, 1965); and Robert Whitman's from the chapter on his work in *The Theatre of Mixed Means*. An earlier extensive profile of Rauschenberg appears in Calvin Tomkins, *The Bride and the Bachelors* (Viking, 1965); a shorter one is Lawrence Alloway, "Rauschenberg," *Vogue* (October, 1965); and Tomkins also wrote on Rauschenberg's winning the 1964 Venice Bienale prize for painting, "The Big Show in Venice," *Harper's* (April, 1966).

This profile originally appeared, in considerably different form, as "The Artist as Playwright and Engineer," *The New York Times Magazine* (October 9, 1966); the help of Susanna Opper deserves my gratitude; and the epigraph comes from Clement Greenberg, *Art and Culture* (Beacon, 1961).

INDEX